THE MAKING OF
IRANIAN MODERNITY

THE MAKING OF IRANIAN MODERNITY

ESSAYS IN HONOR OF HOUCHANG E. CHEHABI

EDITED BY

Roham Alvandi
Afshin Marashi
David Motadel

Ilex Project
Boston, Massachusetts

Distributed by Harvard University Press
Cambridge, Massachusetts and London, England

The Making of Iranian Modernity: Essays in Honor of Houchang E. Chehabi
edited by Roham Alvandi, Afshin Marashi, and David Motadel

Published by Ilex Project, an imprint of New Alexandria Foundation,
84 Revere Street, Boston, MA 02114.
cd@ilexfoundation.org

Distributed by Harvard University Press, Cambridge, MA and London

Printed by Gasch Printing, 1780 Crossroads Drive, Odenton, MD 21113.
info@gaschprinting.com

EU GPSR Authorized Representative: LOGOS EUROPE,
9 rue Nicolas Poussin, 17000, La Rochelle, France.
Contact@logoseurope.eu

Production editor: Christopher Dadian
Cover design: Joni Godlove
Printed in the United States of America

Cover image: Sepah Square, Tehran, 1946, unknown photographer. Wikimedia Commons, ©AP.

Library of Congress Cataloging-in-Publication data is available from the Library of Congress at
https://lccn.loc.gov/

ISBN: 9780674301771

Contents

The Scholar As Dandy

Roham Alvandi and David Motadel

Among Houchang E. Chehabi's most iconic articles are those that thematize the figure of the dandy, whom he defines as follows:

> The most basic characteristic of the dandy is that he is both a conformist and a rebel, in the sense that dandyism, while respecting conventionalities, "plays" with these modes of living, and "[w]hile admitting their power, it suffers from and revenges itself upon them, and pleads them as an excuse against themselves." The dandy is thus a liminal figure in Victor Turner's sense of an entity that is "neither here nor there" and "betwixt and between the positions assigned and arrayed by law, custom, convention, and ceremonial."[1]

This description of the "dandy" as a liminal figure in Houchang's article on Musa Sadr, the vanished imam of the Lebanese Shi'a, can help us understand the author and his four decades of work. Houchang's body of work reflects a profound cosmopolitanism and deep curiosity for the world beyond Iran that is a challenge to the nationalism that imbues the very choice to dedicate oneself to the study of one's own country. This is hardly surprising, given the circumstances of his birth. "One common feature of dandies," Houchang observed, "is their indeterminate social and/or national origin. They lack deep roots in the social scene upon which they burst and which they dazzle. Moreover, they play on this indeterminacy to add to their mystique."[2]

Born to a German mother and an Iranian father in Tehran in 1954, he was raised in a German-speaking home where his father, a professor of German, spoke to him only in German until the age of eight to ensure that he spoke German properly. His inner world, within the intimacy of his home was German, while the external world was Persian. Houchang's liminal existence, between Iran and Europe, made him not only a bilingual child but a congenital cosmopolitan. He attended the Ravesh-e Now elementary school in Tehran, until his father was appointed the Councillor of Iranian Students in Germany in 1962, prompting the family to move to Cologne. There the young Houchang was pri-

---

1. Chehabi 2018a, 149.
2. Chehabi 1996a, 27.

vately tutored at home in the entire Iranian school curriculum, for fear that he would lose his Iranian identity. Now his inner world at home became Iranian, where his father now spoke to him in Persian, while the external world became German. In Cologne he was now also taught English.

The family would return to Iran in June 1967, just after the tumultuous visit of Mohammad Reza Shah Pahlavi to West Germany. The very Iranian students that Houchang's father was supervising clashed with pro-Shah *jubelperser* in West Berlin, bussed in by the Iranian authorities to cheer the shah. Returning to Iran, Houchang enrolled in the elite Alborz High School, where he started learning French, which he continued at the Institut Franco-Iranien in Tehran. The polyglot young Houchang, reveled in the cultural atmosphere of Tehran in the late 1960s and early 1970s, dividing time between the cultural institutes and concert halls of the capital; he also attended the Shiraz Festival of Art.[3]

Iranian students were banned from going to Germany after the anti-shah protests there, so Houchang continued his studies in France at the Université de Caen in Normandy, where there would be few Iranian students making it easier to immerse himself in French culture. There he obtained a *licence* (BA) in Geography in 1975 with a minor in History, while also studying Russian (at his father's urging given his belief – or fear – that the Russians would win the Cold War) and Spanish, which was prescient given the extraordinary transformation that Spain was undergoing following the death of Francisco Franco. Houchang then entered the Institut d'Études Politiques (Sciences Po) in Paris, where he obtained a *diplôme* (BA) in International Relations in 1977, graduating first in his cohort. Finally, in September 1977, he entered Yale University to study for an MA in International Relations, with plans to join to the Iranian diplomatic service.[4] Throughout his studies, most of the courses he took were in history. Growing up between the German and Persian worlds, his academic education brought him to the French and Anglo-Saxon worlds.

The wave of democratization in Spain and Portugal, followed by the fall of the shah in Iran in 1979, set the backdrop for Houchang's encounter with the teacher who would have the most profound effect on his intellectual journey: the great sociologist and political scientist Juan J. Linz, whose work examined the typology of regime types and the transition from one form of regime to another. The Iranian Revolution had put an end to his ambitions to join Iran's diplomatic service and he seemed destined for an academic career. Houchang had little interest in Iranian Studies. He had written a paper on Sri Lanka for Linz's class on "Religion and Politics" and proposed to write a PhD dissertation

---

3. Chehabi 1999a; and Chehabi 2018a, look at these cultural institutions.
4. Chehabi 2014, 28.

on regionalisms in western Europe, looking at the Azores and the Canary Islands. Linz convinced him to make use of his then rare Persian-language skills and instead work on the transition that was then underway in Iran from the Pahlavi monarchy to the Islamic Republic, which Houchang did with the help of a second adviser, Ervand Abrahamian.

While writing his dissertation, he was at times so bored with his narrow focus on Iran that he started auditing courses in comparative literature, a field for which Yale was famous. Among the seminars he attended were "Dandies and Dandyism" and "Readings in Basic Decadence," both taught by George C. Schoolfield.

After completing his PhD at Yale, in 1986, he became assistant and then associate professor in the Departments of Government and Social Studies at Harvard. Leaving Harvard in 1994, Houchang held a series of visiting appointments at St Antony's College, Oxford, and then UCLA, until he settled as professor of international relations and history at Boston University in 1998. He retired twenty-four years later, in 2022.

Houchang once joked, reflecting on Isaiah Berlin's famous separation of the scholarly world into two types of academic – the hedgehogs, specialists interested in one big thing (like Plato, Pascal, or Braudel), and the foxes, generalists interested in many things (like Aristotle, Erasmus, or Goethe) – that he was more like a butterfly. This is a half-truth. Houchang is one of those rare scholars who is both a hedgehog, a leading figure in the field of modern Iranian history, who has produced groundbreaking specialist works, and at the same time a fox, who has ventured out into subjects such as international relations, international law, international history, geography, and island studies. Although it is impossible to give a complete account of his academic oeuvre here, we shall mention some of his key contributions as both a hedgehog and a fox.

As a hedgehog, Houchang has made his most important contributions as a scholar to the of modern Iranian history. His first major works, influenced by his experiences of (and trauma inflicted by) the excesses of the Islamic Revolution, explored the intersection of religion and politics in post-war Iran. Drawing on a dazzling amount of primary material, his first monograph, *Iranian Politics and Religious Modernism* (1990), which resulted from his doctoral dissertation at Yale, looked at Mehdi Bazargan's religious-nationalist Liberation Movement of Iran, the country's second-oldest political organization after the Tudeh Party.[5] Houchang took the Liberation Movement of Iran, which Khomeini charged with leading the provisional government of the Islamic Republic, to be the Iranian equivalent of Europe's Christian Democrats. He hoped that they might

5. Chehabi 1990.

oversee the transition to democracy following the fall of the shah. While Iran did not follow the democratizing path of Spain and Portugal, Houchang's book demonstrated in painstaking detail how Islamism superseded secular politics in post-war Iran, reshaping our understanding of the origins of the Islamic revolutionary movement under Mohammed Reza Shah. One reviewer later noted about the work:

> His tone in assessing the philosophy and contributions of Bazargan and other members of the Liberation Movement of Iran is admirably neutral. He neither approves nor disapproves but presents the facts as they seem best evidenced in the historical record. The result is a book that will be much appreciated by supporters of the former monarchy, by supporters of the new regime, and by those who support neither. Those who are familiar with the volatile world of Iranian politics know how hard a task this has been.[6]

Since then, Houchang has published widely on the politics of religion in Iran, with studies ranging from the ideas and mechanisms of theocracy to the country's religious minorities.[7] His more recent writing on the subject is his work on the myth of Moses and Pharaoh in Iranian revolutionary thought.[8]

His work on contemporary Iranian politics explained the institutionalization of Khomeini's revolution and the ways in which the Islamic Republic resolved the contradictions within an Islamic state that was a republic born of a popular revolution. Houchang was able to show how the Islamic Republic was both religious authoritarian and yet responsive to the demands of its citizenry and the realities of governing a state in the modern world.[9] One of the most amusing articles is his account of how the Islamic Republic protected Iran's lucrative caviar industry by decreeing that the sturgeon fish was *halal*.[10] A primary concern in much of Houchang's work on contemporary Iranian politics is the fate of moderates in times of political transition or change.[11] This reflects not only the influence of Juan Linz, but Houchang's own dandiacal sensibilities. He wrote:

> The dandy mocks the social order but is no rebel, as his originality could not manifest itself without the existence of conventions he can

---

6. Beeman 1992, 227.

7. Chehabi 1985a; Chehabi 1991; Chehabi 1993a; Chehabi 1996b; Chehabi 1997b; Chehabi 2001a; Chehabi 2001b; and Chehabi 2007a.

8. Chehabi 2010.

9. Chehabi 1991; Chehabi 1996b; Chehabi 1997a; and Chehabi 2001a.

10. Chehabi 2007b.

11. Chehabi 1995a; and Chehabi 2013.

mock. Neither the uncultured proletarian nor the philistine bourgeois is likely to appreciate his innate superiority, which makes the dandy, too, "an unreliable ally of either left or right."[12]

His own apparent political neutrality, born of his liminal identity as an insider-outsider to Iran and Iranianness, informs his attraction to political actors who advocate for moderation, pluralism, tolerance, and reconciliation, as distinct from the militancy, populism, and fundamentalism of much of the Iranian political spectrum.

A visit to Iran in 1990 caused a change in the direction of Houchang's work on modern Iran. One aspect of dandyism that Houchang personifies is "'the joy of astonishing others, and the proud satisfaction of never oneself being astonished. The dandy constantly produces the unexpected, that which could not logically be anticipated by those accustomed to the yoke of rules'."[13] Fascinated by the ways in which Iranians were navigating the cultural policies of the Islamic Republic and no longer tethered to a political science department after 1994, Houchang astonishingly transformed himself into the preeminent cultural historian of modern Iran.[14]

When Houchang began his academic career in the 1980s, the field of Iranian history, in contrast to today, was rather small, and dominated by works of political history. It was, generally speaking, untouched by the "cultural turn" that had been transforming the broader field of historical studies since the 1970s, with the work of Emmanuel Le Roy Ladurie, Natalie Zemon Davis, Robert Darnton, and Lynn Hunt in French history, of Carlo Ginzburg, Anthony Grafton, and Peter Burke in Italian history, of E. P. Thompson and Keith Thomas in British history, of Alf Lüdtke and Wolfgang Reinhard in German history, and so on. Houchang almost single-handedly pioneered the "cultural turn" in modern Iranian history, producing pathbreaking works on subjects such as Persian clothing and dress codes, from hat laws to veil rules; culinary culture; music, including women singers; sport, from the *zurkhāneh* to polo to football; and the making of the Persian middle classes.[15] Combined – and one day as a book – they form the definitive study of modern Iranian cultural history. At the same time, they have fundamentally reshaped our understanding of nation-building in modern Iran. His most recent monograph, *Onomastic Reforms* (2020), explores the introduction of surnames as part of twentieth-century bureaucrati-

---

12. Chehabi 1996a.
13. Chehabi 2018b.
14. Chehabi 2014.
15. Chehabi 1993b; Chehabi 2004; Chehabi 2000; Chehabi 2003a; Chehabi 2003b: Chehabi 1999b; Chehabi 1995b; Chehabi 2001c; Chehabi 2002a; Chehabi 2002b; and, for an updated version, Chehabi 2006; and Chehabi and Guttmann 2002; and Chehabi 2019.

zation and state-building in Iran.[16] James C. Scott praised it as a "luminous volume" that offers "a perfect lens for understanding modern state making: Deeply researched, bristling with thought-provoking aperçus, humor, and international comparisons, it enlarges our intellectual horizon."

The various threads of Houchang's work on the cultural and social history of modern Iran come together in his concept of Iran as a "dual society." Houchang observes that the most important fault-line in Iranian society for much of the late nineteenth and the twentieth century was the adoption of European culture and civilization.

> The gradual adoption of European manners, ideas, social norms,
> and consumption patterns by growing numbers of Iranians led to a
> cultural bifurcation in society that, if it did not cause the revolution
> of 1979, at least conditioned its outcome.[17]

While other scholars have indeed highlighted this bifurcation in Iranian society and its connection to the Iranian Revolution, not least the narrative of *Westoxification*, Houchang's work locates the origins of Iran's "culture wars" in the late nineteenth century, when Iranian elites sought to convince Europeans that Iran was a "civilized" country and therefore worthy of treatment as a fully sovereign country in international society.

The cultural clash between cosmopolitanism and nativism in Iranian society is, as his works have demonstrated, also a product of Iran's struggle for full sovereignty in international society. What this means is that the history of Iran's modern politics and international relations should now be read through the daily lives of Iranians, just as the cultural history of modern Iran should be read through the diplomatic and transnational history of Iran's encounter with the world. In a sense, Houchang's research challenged historians of modern Iran to be more cosmopolitan. A Chehabi-esque approach to the study of modern Iranian history is global and comparative. To understand the fault lines of Iranian society, he has shown, one must consider international political fault lines. The divisions between classes in Iran were cultural, more so than economic.[18] Iran's modern history, like other unconquered states in Asia, is the product of that encounter not only with European culture but with the notion of "civilization" that was the basis of the European society of states.

Houchang's works on modern Iran all reflect their author's sharp eye for detail, love of stories, and conceptual brilliance. Empirically rich, they are ana-

16. Chehabi 2020.
17. Chehabi 2018c, 17.
18. Chehabi 2019.

lytically focused, never antiquarian. Yet, unlike many of his contemporaries who ventured into the field of cultural history, he has remained critical of the intellectual acrobatics of post-modernism. He was never mesmerized by a Hayden White, a Michel Foucault, and least of all by an Edward Said. In many ways, through the pages of Houchang's oeuvre shines the certainty of a scholar shaped by the Enlightenment ideals of modernity. He is, in many ways, a disciple of Max Weber, a scholar who influenced him perhaps more than any other.

Ever the dandy, Houchang's work on cultural history contains an irreverence and humor that is lacking in much academic work in the age of post-colonialism. In a chapter on dress codes for men in Turkey and Iran, Houchang includes an endnote reference to a work by a G. LaForge entitled *Visors: Their Uses and Abuses*, published by the SFA (that is, Star Fleet Academy) Press in San Francisco.[19] Afficionados of *Star Trek: The Next Generation* will appreciate that Houchang left out the date of the publication to dissimulate the joke. This mischief is not just whimsy. It is central to understanding Houchang's approach to the dandiacal study of history. His sense of irreverence and mischief frees him from having to wave ideological flags. For Houchang, the writing of history is decidedly not political. Instead, he adopts the role of the

> *flâneur*, a "man of leisure who went into the street in search of some satisfaction of his overdeveloped sensibilities," a social type to whom Baudelaire ascribes a cosmopolitan susceptivity: 'For the perfect *flâneur*, for the passionate spectator, it is an immense joy to … be away from home and yet to feel oneself everywhere at home.' To 'feel everywhere at home' is of course the mark of a cosmopolitan.[20]

Finally, in contrast to most other experts of cultural and social history working on Europe or other parts of the world, Houchang has also always retained a more general interest in political, diplomatic, and international history. Testament to this are also his substantial contributions to our understanding of Iran's global political entanglements. The most important works here are his *Distant Relations* (2006), exploring Iranian-Lebanese connections over the centuries, and, co-edited with Grace Neville, *Erin and Iran* (2015), looking into Iranian-Irish encounters.[21] His studies in the field are extensive, ranging from the history of Iranian-Iraqi relations, to Reza Shah's exile in Mauritius, to Iran's twentieth-century relations with South Africa.[22] Many of these works on Iran's

---

19. Chehabi 2004, 234, note 55.
20. Chehabi 2018b.
21. Chehabi 2006; and Chehabi and Neville 2015.
22. Chehabi 2012; Chehabi 2016; and Chehabi forthcoming.

relations with the outside world go beyond mere political and diplomatic histories, exploring the history of entanglements between societies in general, something Houchang called the history of "intersocietal relations." His volume *Iran's Constitutional Revolution* (2010), co-edited with Vanessa Martin, enquired not only into the nature of popular politics in Iran but also, from a comparative and connective perspective, into Iran's place in the revolutionary world in the aftermath of the Russo-Japanese War of 1904–1905.[23]

As a fox, Houchang has ventured far beyond the subject of modern Iranian history, producing works to the highest standards on the most diverse subjects. That he has been able to do so is the result partly of his broad education in various subjects – studying geography in Caen, international relations at Science Po in Paris, and international relations and, afterwards, political science at Yale – partly of his linguistic skills, and partly of his curiosity in the world.

He has shown much interest in global comparative political history and global comparative political studies more generally. His volume *Sultanistic Regimes* (1998), which he co-edited with his doctoral advisor, the great Juan Linz, now a classic, explored authoritarian regimes based on personal power and favor, looking at contemporary regimes in countries such as the Dominican Republic, Cuba, Haiti, Iran, and the Philippines.[24] Among his many works on comparative politics is the volume *Politics, Society, and Democracy: Comparative Studies* (1995), co-edited with Alfred Stepan.[25] More recently, *Unconquered States* (2024), co-edited together with David Motadel, examined the struggles for sovereignty of the few nominally independent non-Western states in the imperial age, exploring the ways in which countries such as China, Ethiopia, Japan, the Ottoman Empire, Persia, and Siam managed to keep European imperialism at bay, whereas others, such as Hawaii, Korea, Madagascar, Morocco, and Tonga, long struggled, but ultimately failed, to maintain their sovereignty.[26] Looking at armed conflict and military reform, unequal treaties, and capitulations, diplomatic encounters, and royal diplomacy, the book provided the first comprehensive global history of the engagement of the independent non-European states with the European empires. This latest book reflected in many ways the influence of global history on Houchang's work. Kenneth Pomeranz called it an "excellent collection" on "an important set of states, which deserve to be considered together;" Sebastian Conrad praised its "original" view on the world; Paul Kennedy lauded it as "an ingenious collection" and a "really fine

23. Chehabi and Martin 2010.
24. Chehabi and Linz 1998; and, for the Persian translation, Chehabi and Linz 1380/2001.
25. Chehabi and Stepan 1995.
26. Chehabi and Motadel 2024. Chehabi 1992 also mentioned the states.

revisionist history"; and Martti Koskenniemi described it as "global history at its kaleidoscopic best."

Finally no appraisal of Houchang's oeuvre would be complete without mentioning his contributions to the field of island studies. His interest in the subject dates back to his undergraduate days as a geography student. A keen traveler to islands, he has over the years written numerous articles on subjects ranging from the absence of consociationalism in Sri Lanka (his first scholarly publication, in 1980) to the Falklands conflict.[27] It was also Houchang who wrote the "Small Island States" entry in Seymour Martin Lipset's *Encyclopedia of Democracy* (1996).[28] His work in this field was crowned by his *International Bibliography of Islands* (2022), which is the first bibliography ever produced on the subject, a lifelong project which he started as a student in Caen. Houchang's body of work, it is fair to say, surpasses in its breadth that of most other scholars of his generation.[29]

Throughout his life, he has translated many works of scholarship. He is, in fact, one of the few scholars who has translated works from five languages (Persian, German, French, Spanish, and Portuguese) into English.

Houchang is a true intellectual, not just an academic, with an insatiable curiosity in the world, someone who, as anyone who has ever met him will agree, can hold conversations on the most diverse subjects and who will still always surprise you with some wonderful new insight or some quirky, obscure anecdote. (This is one of the reasons why conversations with him are so much fun.) He has been (and will long be) a presence at scholarly conferences around the world. He has been generous to students and colleagues, particularly junior scholars, throughout his career.[30] It is therefore not surprising that though never having built his own empire of doctoral students (something that would have benefitted the field of Iranian studies immensely but was impossible given the institutional constraints of his university), he has influenced enough scholars that a festschrift of this kind is feasible. In fact, if we had not been constrained by the length of a book, we could have easily doubled the number of contributions. This volume, in short, is a testimony to the impact Houchang has had over the last half century. The authors are connected by their friendship with and the mentorship they have received from Houchang Chehabi, a dandy in the world of scholarship.

27. Chehabi 1980; Chehabi 1982; and Chehabi 1985b.
28. Chehabi 1996c.
29. Chehabi 2022.
30. Chehabi received the inaugural Mentorship Award of the Association of Iranian Studies in 2022.

Works Cited

Beeman, William O. 1992. "Review of H. E. Chehabi, *Iranian Politics and Religious Modernism: The Liberation Movement of Iran under the Shah and Khomeini*." *Annals of the American Academy of Political and Social Science* 523:226–27.

Chehabi, H. E. 1980. "The Absence of Consociationalism in Sri Lanka." *Plural Societies* 11: 55–65.

———. 1982. "Die Falkland-Affäre: Ein Einzelfall?" *Aus Politik und Zeitgeschichte* B46/82:33–36.

———. 1985a. "Society and State in Islamic Liberalism." *State, Culture, and Society* 1:85–101.

———. 1985b. "Self-Determination, Territorial Integrity, and the Falkland Islands." *Political Science Quarterly* 100:215–25.

———. 1990. *Iranian Politics and Religious Modernism: The Liberation Movement of Iran under the Shah and Khomeini.* Ithaca, NY: Cornell University Press.

———. 1991. "Religion and Politics in Iran: How Theocratic is the Islamic Republic?" *Daedalus* 120:69–91.

———. 1993a. "Klerus und Staat in der Islamischen Republik Iran." *Aus Politik und Zeitgeschichte* B33/93:17–23.

———. 1993b. "Staging the Emperor's New Clothes: Dress Codes and Nation-Building under Reza Shah." *Iranian Studies* 26:209–29.

———. 1995a. "The Provisional Government and the Transition from Monarchy to Islamic Republic in Iran." In *Between States: Interim Governments and Democratic Transitions*, edited by , 127–43 and 278–81. Cambridge: Cambridge University Press, 127–143 and 278–281.

———. 1995b. "Sport and Politics in Iran: The Legend of Gholamreza Takhti." *International Journal of the History of Sport* 12:48–60.

———. 1996a. "The Imam as Dandy: The Case of Musa Sadr." *Harvard Middle Eastern and Islamic Review* 3 (1–2): 20–42.

——— 1996b. "The Impossible Republic: Contradictions of the Islamic State in Iran." *Contention* 5:135–54.

———. 1996c. "Small Island States." *The Encyclopedia of Democracy*, vol. 4. Washington, D.C., Congressional Quarterly Inc., 1134–37.

———. 1997a. "Ardabil Becomes a Province: Center-Periphery Relations in the Islamic Republic of Iran." *International Journal of Middle East Studies* 29 (2): 235–53.

———. 1997b. "Das politische Regime der Islamischen Republik Iran." *Welt-Trends* 15:124–41.

———. 1999a. "Goethe Institute." In *Encyclopaedia Iranica*, volume 11. New York: Bibliotheca Persica Press: 43–44.

———. 1999b. "From Revolutionary *tasnif* to Patriotic *surād*. Music and Nation-Building in Early Twentieth-Century Iran," *Iran* 37:143–54.

———. 2000. "Voices Unveiled: Women Singers in Modern Iran." In *Iran and Beyond: Essays in Middle Eastern History in Honor of Nikki R. Keddie*, edited by Rudi Matthee and Beth Baron. Costa Mesa, CA: Mazda, 151–66.

———. 2001a. "The Political Regime of the Islamic Republic in Comparative Perspective." *Government and Opposition* 36 (1): 48–70.

———. 2001b. "Jews and Sport in Modern Iran." In *The History of Contemporary Iranian Jews*, edited by Homa Sarshar and Houman Sarshar, 3–24. Beverly Hills: Center for Iranian Jewish Oral History.

———. 2001c. "US-Iranian Sports Diplomacy." *Diplomacy and Statecraft* 12 (1): 89–106.

———. 2002a. "The Juggernaut of Globalization: Sport and Modernization in Iran." *International Journal of the History of Sport* 19 (2–3): 275–94.

———. 2002b. "A Political History of Football in Iran." In Special Issue on Sports and Games of *Iranian Studies* 35 (4): 371–402.

———. 2003a. "The Banning of the Veil and its consequences." In *The Making of Modern Iran: State and Society under Riza Shah, 1921–1941*, edited by Stephanie Cronin. London: Routledge, 193–210.

———. 2003b. "The Westernization of Iranian Culinary Culture." *Iranian Studies* 36 (1): 43–61.

———. 2004. "Dress Codes for Men in Turkey and Iran." In *Men of Order: Authoritarian Modernization under Atatürk and Reza Shah*, edited by Touraj Atabaki and Erik Zürcher, 209–37. London: I.B. Tauris, 209–37.

———. 2006. "The Politics of Football in Iran," *Soccer and Society* 7, 2–3: 233–261.

———, ed. 2006. *Distant Relations: Iran and Lebanon in the Last 500 Years*. London: I.B. Tauris.

———. 2007a. "Anatomy of Prejudice: Reflections on Secular Anti-Baha'ism in Iran." In *Anatomy of Prejudice: Reflection on Secular Anti-Baha'ism in Iran*, edited by Dominic Brookshaw and Seena Fazel, 184–99. London: Routledge.

———. 2007b. "How Caviar Turned Out to Be *Halal*." *Gastronomica* 7 (2): 17–23.

———. 2010. "Li Kulli Fir'awn Musa: The Myth of Moses and Pharaoh in the Iranian Revolution in Comparative Perspective," Crown Paper 4 (November).

———. 2012. "Iran and Iraq: Intersocietal Linkages and Secular Nationalisms." In *Iran Facing Others: Identity Boundaries in a Historical Perspective*, Abbas Amanat and Farzin Vejdani 191–216. New York: Palgrave Macmillan.

———. 2013. "The Shah's Two Liberalizations: Re-Equilibration and Breakdown." In *Iran and the Challenges of the 21st Century: Essays in Honour of Mohammad-Reza Djalili*, edited by H. E. Chehabi, Farhad Khosrokhavar, and Clément Therme, 24–49. Costa Mesa: Mazda.

———. 2014: "Beyond 'The Case of Spain.'" In *Juan J. Linz: Scholar, Teacher, Friend*, edited by H. E. Chehabi, 28–34. Cambridge: Ty Aur Press.

———. 2016. "South Africa and Iran in the Apartheid Era." *Journal of Southern African Studies* 42 (4): 687–709.

———. 2018a. "The Shiraz Festival and its Place in Iran's Revolutionary Mythology." In *The Age of Aryamehr: Late Pahlavi Iran and Its Global Entanglements*, edited by Roham Alvandi, 168–201. London: The Gingko Library.

———. 2018b. "A Cosmopolitan Dandy: Amir Abbas Hoveyda." In *The Age of Aryamehr: Late Pahlavi Iran and Its Global Entanglements*, edited by Roham Alvandi, 147–67. London: The Gingko Library.

———. 2018c. "Culture Wars and Dual Society in Iran." Farman-Farmaian Research Project (SFFRP) 2 (Amsterdam: International Institute of Social History).

———. 2019. "The Rise of the Middle Class in Iran before the Second World War." In *The Global Bourgeoisie: The Rise of the Middle Class in the Age of Empire*, edited by Christoph Dejung, David Motadel, and Jürgen Osterhammel, 43–63. Princeton: Princeton University Press.

———. 2020. *Onomastic Reforms: Family Names and State-Building in Iran*. Boston: Ilex Foundation.

———. 2022. *International Bibliography of Islands*. Cambridge, MA: Tŷ Aur Press.

———. Forthcoming. "Royal Exile in the Indian Ocean: Reza Shah's Sojourn in Mauritius." In *Iran and Persianate Culture in the Indian Ocean World*, edited by A. C. S. Peacock, London: I.B. Tauris/Bloomsbury.

Chehabi, H. E., and Allen Guttmann. 2002. "From Iran to All of Asia: The Origin and Diffusion of Polo." *International Journal of the History of Sport* 19 (2–3): 384–400.

Chehabi, H. E., and Juan J. Linz, eds. 1998. *Sultanistic Regimes*. Baltimore: Johns Hopkins University Press.

Chehabi, H. E., and Juan J. Linz, eds. 1380/2001. *Nezamha-ye soltani*. Tehran: Nashr-e Shirazeh.

Chehabi, H. E., and David Motadel, eds. 2024. *Unconquered States*. Oxford: Oxford University Press.

Chehabi, H. E., and Grace Neville, eds. 2015. *Erin and Iran: Cultural Encounters between the Irish and the Iranians*. Boston: Ilex Foundation.

Chehabi, H. E., and Alfred Stepan, eds. 1995. *Politics, Society, and Democracy: Comparative Studies*. Boulder, CO: Westview.

Holly Honors Houchang:
A Brief Note on Iranian-centered Poetics of Royalty as a Glorification of European-centered Globalism

Olga M. Davidson

IN HONORING MY FRIEND HOUCHANG CHEHABI, I offer here a briefest of notes highlighting a curious fact that has preoccupied me in my research, over a long stretch of time that is coextensive with my long-standing academic links with Houchang, more recently as colleagues at Boston University but also even earlier, as members of the Harvard community of scholars at Currier House, where Houchang was tutor and where I, together with Greg (Nagy), were "House Masters" (both of us are now renamed in a rather disarming way, ex-post-facto. as "faculty deans"). The fact, which I just described as "curious," has to do with the *Shahnameh* of Ferdowsi. What is so curious, to my mind, about this masterpiece of classical Persian verbal art can be formulated as a question: why did this shining example of literature from the "East," glorifying a long-dead Zoroastrian empire in the historical context of the later Islamic world that superseded it, hold such appeal, once it became known, in the so-called "West"? Such a question, which can be answered in many ways by many different experts, will I know appeal in its own right to my friend Houchang, who can be described, charismatic personality that he is, as a perfect blend of "Eastern" and "Western" sensibilities. Even if he and I may not fully agree on my own formulation of a tentative answer to my rather stark question, I sense that Houchang will feel at least engaged, in his customarily playful way, with what I am trying to express.

I start by putting on record that I have always marveled at the adaptability of the *Shahnameh* of Ferdowsi, dating from the late tenth and early eleventh century CE, to a broad range of Muslim sensibilities throughout the history of Islamicized Iran. Although the patronage systems in East Iran during the life and times of Ferdowsi were predominantly Sunni, as exemplified especially by Mahmud of Ghazna, the royal potentate who was the main patron of Ferdowsi during the poet's lifetime, the subsequent reception of this poet's *Shahnameh* as a pre-eminent form of court poetry in later centuries, dominated by later dynasties, tended to be Shi'ite. A striking example of the latter kind of patronage was a lavish new "recension" of the *Shahnameh* that was commissioned in 1426 CE and "published" in 1430 under the aegis of a prince named Bāysonghor. The preface for that "recension," which was likewise commissioned by the prince, tells the story of the poet and of his poetry (I offer an analysis in part 1 of my book *Poet and Hero in the Persian Book of Kings*).[1] Such a story can be mined by literary historians as a source for reconstructing the reception of the *Shahnameh* – not only in the era of Ferdowsi but also in later times, culminating in the era of Bāysonghor. From the standpoint of the preface, I have argued in my own work, the reception of the *Shahnameh* can be described in modern literary critical terms as a model of globalism.[2]

But the globalism of the *Shahnameh*, in the court of a prince like Bāysonghor in the fifteenth century CE, was still to be seen in terms of empire – an Iranian empire that glorified itself by way of a *Book of Kings* that recorded a form of court poetry that transcended regionalism but was global only in terms of addressing the political and cultural diversity of an imperial – and thus royal – project.

So, how did this royal project evolve into a truly world-wide thing, into a global project? Such an evolution is still rooted in the realia of royalty, but the royalism eventually faded in the light of the exceptional merits of the poetry itself, even in translation. It started with the publication, sponsored by a French government that had reverted to royalism in the French post-Revolution, of the *Shahnameh* in a new edition, together with a most accomplished French translation on the part of the editor, Jules Mohl, who was a learned expert in the Persian poetic language of Ferdowsi. This edition by Mohl, in seven volumes (1838–1878), is a key to the reception of the *Shahnameh* as world literature. Later editions are listed in my bibliography, under the names of the editors, who are, in reverse chronological order: Khaleghi-Motlagh, Bertels, Nafisi/Vullers, Vullers. But the earlier edition, by Mohl, deserves pride of place as the trend-setter for "Western" reception.

Much has been written about this reception, but my aim here is not to account for all the research that has been done. Instead, I single out here just one example of such research, by Reza Taher-Kermani, because I think that this work is a most helpful general introduction to the study of the *Shahnameh* as world literature.[3]

As a shortcut for those who do not know about the "Western" reception of Ferdowsi, I also recommend, after a reading of the helpful article by Taher-Kermani, a careful reading of a poem by Matthew Arnold,[4] "Sohrab and Rustum," 892 lines long, which was inspired by a paraphrase, by Charles Augus-

1. Davidson 2013a.
2. Davidson 2021; Davidson 2016.
3. Taher-Kermani 2015.
4. Arnold 1853.

tin Sainte-Beuve,[5] of the most celebrated episode of the *Shahnameh*, recounting a tragic duel to the death between the hero Rostam and his unrecognized son, Sohrab. Thirdly, I recommend a reading of the original version of this episode – as most deftly translated from the Persian text into English by Dick Davis.[6]

The article by Taher-Kermani provides a helpful tracking of the relevant portions of this translation by Davis, placed side by side with the corresponding paraphrases of Sainte-Beuve, translated from the original French into English. As for analyzing the lament of Tahmina, mother of Sohrab, over the death of her son fathered by Rostam, I take this opportunity to recommend my own translation and analysis, where I argue that the poetry here is a shining example of an oft-neglected genre of Iranian song culture, women's lament.[7]

I note, in closing, that the learned correspondence between Arnold and Sainte-Beuve, which led to Arnold's epic-style composition of "Sohrab and Rustum," can be analyzed in the light of essays by these two literary figures on Classicism as a point of comparison in appreciating the universal appeal of the *Shahnameh* as epic poetry.

5. Sainte-Beuve 1850.
6. Davis 2006.
7. Davidson 2013b, Essay 7: "Women's Lamentations as Protest in the [*Shahnameh*] of Ferdowsi."

WORKS CITED

Arnold, Matthew. 1853. "Sohrab and Rustum."
  https://www.poetryfoundation.org/poems/43604/sohrab-and-rustum.
  https://www.gutenberg.org/files/13364/13364-h/13364-h.htm.
  https://librivox.org/sohrab-and-rustum-by-matthew-arnold/.
———. 1861. *On Translating Homer*. London: Routledge.
  https://web.archive.org/web/20151208135658/.
  http://www.victorianprose.org/texts/Arnold/Works/on_translating
  _homer.pdf.
Bertels, Y. E. [Evgenii Eduardovich], et al., eds. 1960–1971. Ferdowsi: *Shāhnā-ma* I–IX. Moscow. For details about supplementary volumes, see Yarshater 1988, ix.
Davidson, Olga M. 2013a. *Poet and Hero in the Persian Book of Kings*. 3rd ed. Ilex Foundation Series 11. Cambridge, MA (2nd ed. 2006, Costa Mesa, CA; 1st ed. 1994, Ithaca, NY). https://ilexfoundation.org/book/poet-and-hero-in-the-persian-book-of-kings/.
———. 2013b. *Comparative Literature and Classical Persian Poetics*. 2nd ed. Ilex Foundation Series 12. Cambridge, MA (1st ed. 2000, Costa Mesa, CA). https://ilexfoundation.org/book/comparative-literature-and-classical-persian-poetics/.

———. 2016. "The Written Text as a Metaphor for the Integrity of Oral Composition in Classical Persian Traditions and Beyond." In *Singers and Tales in the 21st Century: The Legacies of Milman Parry and Albert Lord*, edited by David F. Elmer and Peter McMurray. Classics@ Issue 14. http://nrs.harvard.edu/urn-3:hlnc
.essay:DavidsonO.The_Written_Text_as_a_Metaphor.2016.

———. 2020 (March 2; rewritten June 1, 2020). "Ecumenism and Globalism in the Reception of Ferdowsi and his Book of Kings: Evidence from the Bāysonghori Preface." *Classical Inquiries*. https://classical-inquiries.chs.harvard.edu/ecumenism-and-globalism-in-the-reception-of-ferdowsi-and-his-book-of-kings-evidence-from-the-baysonghori-preface/. Preprint version of Davidson 2021.

———. 2021. "Ecumenism and Globalism in the Reception of Ferdowsi and his Book of Kings: Evidence from the Bāysonghori Preface." *Persian Literature and world Literature* , ed. Mostafa Abedinifard, Omid Azadibougar, Amirhossein Vafa, 123–36. New York, London, and Dublin, 2021.

Davis, Dick. 1992. *Epic and Sedition: The Case of Ferdowsi's Shāhnāmeh*. Fayetteville, Ark.

Davis, Dick, trans. 2006. *Shahnameh: The Persian Book of Kings*. New York.

Khaleghi-Motlagh, Djalal, ed. 1988–. *Shahnameh / Book of Kings* I-. Costa Mesa and New York.

Mohl, Jules, ed. 1838–1878. *Le livre des rois* I–VII. Paris.

Nafisi, Said, and Johann August Vullers, eds. 1934–1936. *Shāhnāma*. 10 vols. Tehran.

Sainte-Beuve, Charles Augustin. 1850. "Le Livre des Rois, par le poëte persan Firdousi, publié et traduit par M. Jules Mohl." In *Causeries du Lundi*, vol. 1:332–50. Paris: Garnier Frères.

———. 1890. 'What is a Classic?' In *Essays by Sainte-Beuve* translated by Elizabeth Lee, 1–12. London: Walter Scott. Via 1850, "Qu'est-ce qu-un *classique*," in vol. 3:38–55 of the *Causeries*.

Shahbazi, A. Shapur. 1991. *Ferdowsī: A Critical Biography*. Costa Mesa, CA.

Taher-Kermani, Reza. 2015. "Persia by Way of Paris: On Arnold's 'Sohrab and Rustum.'" *Middle Eastern Literatures* 18:22–40. To link to this article: https://doi.org/10.1080/1475262X.2015.1067015.

Vullers, Johann August, ed. 1877–1884. *Shāhnāma*. 3 vols. Leiden.

Warner, Arthur George, and Edmond Warner, trans. 1905–1925. *The Shahnama of Firdausī* I–X. London.

Yarshater, Ehsan. 1988. Introduction to Khaleghi-Motlagh 1988:v–xi.

De Paris à Tehran:
The Qajar Translation of a French Bestseller

Sunil Sharma

THE GLOBAL NINETEENTH CENTURY witnessed the beginning of a serious and sustained attention to literary translation. While Europeans at a high point of colonialism were occupied with translating mostly classical works of eastern literature, in the Middle East and South Asia there was more attention to translating contemporary works from European languages into various languages. In the case of Persian in Iran, at the official level the newly established Bureau of Translation (Dār al-Tarjomeh), was an active sponsor of this intellectual activity. Farzin Vejdani explains the connection between politics and power: "translators selected histories with the dual purpose of legitimizing the Qajar dynasty and providing individual rulers with exemplary models for top-down modernization in the form of biographies of European autocrats."[1] The Bureau of Translation was headed by the eminent statesman, E'temād al-Saltaneh, who either singlehandedly or with a team produced scores of translations. One of these was a somewhat unusual choice: Félix Maynard's French work, *De Delhi à Cawnpore: Journal d'une dame anglaise* (1858), a dramatic narrative of the Indian rebellion of 1857 narrated by a female survivor. The Persian translation was published in 1887 as *Ketāb-e sargozasht-e Mestres Hortestet, khānom-e englisi dar Hendustān*. The multiple contexts of both the original French work and its obscure author, as well as the Persian translation and its renowned translator, plus the afterlife of the translation, provide a fascinating case study in the annals of the history of the Persian book.

Statesman and polymath Mohammad Hasan Khan (1843–96), known as "E'temād al-Saltaneh," is remembered for his various services to the government and the Qajar monarch, Nāser al-Din Shāh (r. 1848–96). One of the first students to be trained at the newly established polytechnic institution (Dār al-Fonun), his study of French facilitated his role as a translator. Making an illustrious career at the Qajar court, in 1871 E'temād al-Saltaneh became the head of the government Bureau of Printing (Dār al-Entebā'āt) and the Bureau of Translation, and in 1883 he rose to be the minister for publications. He was a member

---

1. Vejdani 2014, 18.

of the Geographical Society of Paris, as well as of the Asiatic Societies in France, Britain, and Russia.[2] He authored or translated around three dozen books, many of which were on the topics of history and travel. He undertook translations and adaptations of various news reports, as well as historical and literary works, from Arabic, English, French, Russian, and Turkish into Persian. He also seems to have had a particular interest in the history of women's lives. The *Khayrāt al-hesān* (1888) was a biographical dictionary of famous Muslim women, including members of the prophet's family, royalty and poets, based on an Ottoman Turkish original, *Meşahir ün-nisa,* by Sayyed Moḥammad Zehni Efendi. In addition, he produced *Manteq al-vahsh* (1888), an adaptation of *Mémoires d'un āne* by Sophie Rostopchine, Comtesse de Ségur (Paris, 1860) and *Sargozasht-e Madmoʾāzel du Monpānsiyeh* (1894) based on the *Mémoires* of Anne Marie Louise d'Orléans, Duchess de Montpensier, "La Grande Mademoiselle" (London, 1746). Although Eʿtemād al-Saltaneh "clearly leaned in the direction of absolute monarchy,"[3] some of the translations which were, apparently, "veiled criticisms of despotic rule, corruption of the court, and the threat of popular revolt, stirred some dismay in the minds of the shah and his conservative courtiers."[4] In choosing works with foreign settings, Eʿtemād al-Saltaneh "attempted to reduce the hazards of his enterprise by the use of screens, cues, and ambiguity. He employed such tools despite his closeness to and support for the shah, because Iranian print culture in the 1890s was still characterized by intolerance of straightforward criticism of government officials."[5] It is no surprise, then, that Eʿtemād al-Saltaneh was drawn to a French work about the Indian rebellion against the British, a momentous historical event that occurred during his lifetime.

The French author Félix Maynard (1813–1858) is largely unknown today, although some of his works enjoyed long spells as bestselling books.[6] Having

2. For detailed biographical information, see Amanat 1998, 662–66; also, Clark 2016, x–xi. Clark discusses the various debates around the question of the authenticity of attributing the Qajar statesman as author or translator of many of the works that were published in his name (xii–xv); Amanat mentions the Orientalist E. G. Browne's negative view on this topic: "However, the accusation that he was a 'charlatan and a scoundrel, ignorant, illiterate and pretentious' who 'could not even spell decently' and published in his own name the work of 'men of learning acting under compulsion and prompted by fear of his malice' ... is unjustifiably harsh. Eʿtemād-al-Salṭana was certainly instrumental in the selection, execution, and final presentation of works produced by his team. Yet as the general editor who laid claim to the compilation (*taʾlif*) and editing (*tasnif*) of these works, he did fail to give due credit to his aides and subordinates."

3. Clark 2016, xv.

4. Amanat 1998: apparently, "aides in the Ministry of Publication also translated allegorical tales and historical works by Fénélon, Voltaire, and other European writers critical of royal autocracy."

5. Cole 1996, 35–56.

6. The few biographical details about him can be found in Mortelier 2005, 47. Surprisingly, there

trained as a doctor, Maynard traveled around the world as a surgeon on ships in the Atlantic and Pacific oceans and later as a medical officer in the Mediterranean Sea during the Crimean War. He gained attention when the literary giant Alexandre Dumas helped him organize his journal notes for publication and contributed a preface to his *Les Baleiniers, voyage aux terres antipodiques* (1858), translated into English as *The Whalers: A Vivid and Exciting Story of Adventure and Exploration in New Zealand Waters from 1837 to 1846.*[7] According to Christiane Mortelier, his works were "colourful and slightly digressive, but show a keen eye for picturesque details and dramatic incidents."[8] Maynard's *De Delhi à Cawnpore: Journal d'une dame anglaise* was serialized as a "roman-feuilleton" in *La Presse* in 1857, immediately after the occurrence of the events described in the narrative, and then as a book in 1858 (Figure 1), the same year as his death.[9] Translations of this work appeared in Portuguese, German, Danish, and Swedish in the same year, and later in other languages: Spanish (1864), Persian (1887), Arabic (1900), Italian (1910), and Urdu (1935). There was only an ephemeral English translation, most likely done from the Persian, published in Calcutta in 1909,[10] but already in 1858, a synopsis of the story appeared in a popular London magazine, and was immediately reprinted in an American one.[11] The original French work was also reprinted several times under slightly varying titles,[12] as was the Persian translation, both in Iran and India in the twentieth century.[13]

---

is almost no information on Maynard on the internet, including no Wikidpedia entry in English or French as of this date.

7. Dumas was sometimes credited with having written this work; see Mortelier 2005, 47. More details on Dumas' interaction with Maynard are described in the preface to the English translation by F. W. Reed (Maynard 1937, 17–24). Maynard's other books were *Notice sur les eaux salines thermales et les eaux ferrugineuses froides d'Alet près Limoux (Aude)* (1854), *Souvenirs d'un zouave devant Sébastopol* (1855), *Voyage et aventures au Chili* (1858) and *Un drame dans les Mers Boréales* (1859).

8. Mortelier 2005, 47.

9. Maynard 1858; more detailed publication information can be found in Frith 2014; for a long list of historical and fictional works produced in French on this topic, see Frith 2014, 24; for the impact of the work on Italian literature, see Nicora 2011, 177.

10. Maynard n.d. [Translated by a Muhammad Kazim and published by J. N. Mazumdar as *Literal English translation of The narrative of Mrs. Hortestet; or, Khanum-i-Inglisi dar balwa-i-Hind.*] The only copy of this in online databases is a microfilm held by the New York Public Library.

11. *Bentley's Miscellany* 43 (1858): 642–650. This account was reprinted in an American journal, *Eclectic Magazine of Foreign Literature, Science, and Art* 44 (1858): 505–11.

12. The various French editions are: *L'insurrection de l'Inde: journal d'une dame anglaise* (Paris: Michel Lévy Frères, 1863); then as *De Delhi à Cawnpore: les drames de l'Inde* in the series "Bibliotheque de voyages, de chasses et d'aventures" (Paris: Gautier, 1888); and later as *L'Inde en feu, 1857* (Paris: Impr. de Montsouris, 1944); it was reissued by Elibron Classics (2005) and the Bibliothèque nationale (2016).

13. The alternate Persian titles were *Ketāb-e sargozasht-e Mestres Hortestet, khānom-e englisi dar*

Figure 1.   First French edition

The title page of the first Persian lithographed edition of Maynard's work, *Ketāb-e sargozasht-e Mestres Hortestet, khānom-e englisi dar Hendustān*, identifies Eʿtemād al-Saltaneh as the translator and the press and place of publication as Dār al-Tebāʿeh-ye Khāsseh-ye Dowlati, Dār al-Khelāfeh Tehrān (Figure 2). The colophon indicates that the calligraphy was completed on 22 Rabiʿ al-sāni 1304 AH [17 January 1887] at the royal hunting ground in Jajrud, near Tehran, by the calligrapher, Hājji Mohammad Rezā "Safā" Soltān al-Kottāb, son of the late Hājji Mirzā Habibollāh Khāqāni, who is known to have copied other texts.[14] This royal edition included twelve illustrations that are not found in most sub-

shuresh o balvā-ye Hendustān (Bambaʾi: Matbaʿeh-ye Mozaffari, 1325/1907), and recently as *Sargo-zasht-e khānom-e englisi dar hendustān, beh-ehtemām-e Mohammad Rezā Afshāri* (Tehran: Shaqāyeq, 1363/1984 or 5) (Figure 4).

14. His name appears in at least seven works of classical Persian literature as listed in Marzolph 2001, 281.

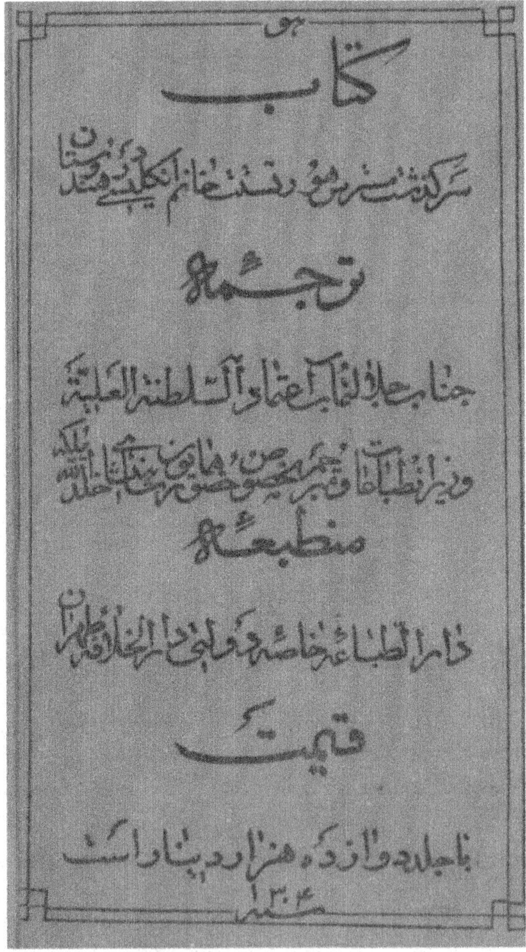

Figure 2. E'temād al-Saltaneh's Persian translation published in Tehran, 1304/1887.

sequent reprints. Since the first French edition did not include any illustrations, the provenance of the European-style drawings remains somewhat of a bibliographical mystery (Figure 3).

The translation of Maynard's book is framed by a preface by the translator that provides a historical context for the narrative. The Indian or "Sepoy Mutiny," now invoked by historians of South Asia as the "First War of Independence," was an uprising of Indian troops employed by the British East India Company that lasted a few months in 1857. The outcome of the momentous events was

Figure 3.   Mrs. Hornsteet with a group of Catholic nuns and a priest confronting Indian soldiers.

both the exile of the last Mughal emperor, Bahadur Shah II (r. 1837–58) from the capital Delhi to Burma, marking the end of more than three centuries of Timurid rule in India, and consolidation of British colonial power. In E'temād al-Saltaneh's words, this was "the biggest event that occurred on earth" that year.[15] The historical background of the event is too complex to narrate here, and although E'temād al-Saltaneh provides a brief outline of the causes, for him it was comparable to other recent historical moments involving the imperial ambitions of the British:

> It was a cause for alarm and fear, and led to a great upheaval for the British government, as well as huge outlay and the loss of many lives. This mutiny was just as it happened in the Battle of Sevastopol, as well as the period of strife between Iran and British governments [First Anglo-Afghan War, 1842], and there was a possibility that British power would cease in India. Investigation has established, and British politicians themselves have admitted, that the causes of this rebellion arose from the stirring up of people's minds and was due to the bad government, lack of attention and resolve, and the excessive greed of Lord Dalhousie, governor-general of India.[16]

He declares that he found the narrative he was presenting in translation a source

---

15. *Sargozasht-e khānom-e englisi dar hendustān*, 31.
16. *Sargozasht-e khānom-e englisi dar hendustān*, 31–32.

of wonder and warning (mowjeb-e hayrat va māyeh-ye 'ebrat) that would be beneficial to his readers.

There is yet another frame in the narrative: it begins with the author, Félix Maynard, meeting up with a female survivor of the rebellion in India who has been traumatized by her experiences:

> Accident brought it about that I recently resided in an hotel, where I met with a poor English lady, Mrs. Hornstreet,[17] a victim to the mutiny of Bengal. She was one of that procession of widows and orphans brought by the Calcutta steamer every fortnight to Suez. She had landed at Southampton and come to France to find a refuge with her husband's family, who had for a long period resided in Touraine. On her passage through Paris she was taken ill, and I was called in to her. We physicians are, as a general rule, somewhat curious.[18]

This opening frame then allows the author to give the semblance of objectivity: "Maynard thus operates as the extradiegetic narrator, who remains external to the main story, listening, evaluating, recording, and transcribing Hornsteet's journey"[19] He goes on to write, "I inquired of the lady as to the cause of her illness, and she told me in consequence all her sufferings in India, for the cause of her illness was misery, exhaustion, and grief – incurable maladies." This English translation from the London magazine is a fairly close translation of the French text. In the Persian version, the translator provides a more subjective interpretation for the benefit of his readers, "I realized that the chief cause of this lady's bad condition was mental (*ruhi*), and a large part of her illness arose from sorrow and grief, having become destitute and unsettled; there was less of a connection between her physiological condition and her mental illness."[20]

Maynard goes on to express his horrified reaction to the violent tale he hears from the lady and which he records:

> I shuddered with horror at the narrative of her long martyrdom. The lady had been rich, and lived happily with her husband, daughter,

---

17. In French, she is called Mistress Hornsteet, but in the English précis of the book that appeared in *Bentley's Miscellany* she is called Mrs. Hornstreet. Hortestet is clearly due to a misreading of the vowels in the name.

18. A bit later in the narrative Mrs. Hornsteet offers more information to the author about her French origins: "Je ne suis pas anglaise de naissance, je ne le suis devenue que par mariage, aussi aurais-je sacrifié volontiers tous les drapeaux et toutes les gloires de ma patrie adoptive, toutes les provinces, toutes les armées, tous les arsenaux, tous les trésors de la compagnie des Indes, pour sauver la vie de mon mari et celle de mes enfants," *De Delhi à Cawnpore*, 35–36.

19. Frith 2014, 78.

20. *Sargozasht-e khānom-e englisi dar hendustān*, 36.

> and son. These are all dead; fortune and happiness are lost: the son, a
> boy of two years of age, was crucified to a wall in his mother's pres-
> ence; the daughter, a maiden of eighteen, is mouldering in the well
> of Cawnpore, after being exposed to the most fearful brutalities from
> the Sepoys. The father was least unhappy, for he died first, by a bullet
> through his heart. His widow buried him with her own hands, lest his
> body should become the prey of the vulture. I asked Mrs. Hornstreet's
> permission to publish this lamentable narrative of her sufferings.
> Many prejudices had to be removed, many doubts settled; at last I
> succeeded in gaining her consent, and so I now give the story just as I
> received it from her lips.[21]

Maynard negotiates the boundaries of historical truth and fiction by using this
device of acting as an amanuensis for another person's narrative.

E'temād al-Saltaneh's translation is generally close to the original without
being slavish to the source text. It conveys fully the dramatic tone of the narrative and, given the cultural differences, he makes adjustments to make the story
more accessible for his readers. But in a few instances he does comment on the
original work without the knowledge of his Persian reader. An example from
the second half of the book will illustrate the sorts of interventions the translator makes in his version. In this scene (Figure 3), Mrs. Hornsteet has joined
a group of Catholic sisters and a priest, after which the group is ambushed by
some rebel soldiers.

> A bandit rushed towards Father Paul, took him by the collar of his
> cassock, shook him roughly, placed the pistol on his forehead, and
> said to him in Bengali, "You are going to die, villain!"
> The nuns cried out, "In the name of God, mercy! Mercy!" as one
> of them seized the soldier's arm with both hands and tried to pull him
> off.
> "Show me your God," said the soldier not budging at all.
> "Worship him, and he will forgive you," the priest responded,
> pulling the crucifix from his bosom and showing it to the sepoy.
> The sepoy looked at the crucifix and recoiled in amazement; then
> without saying a word or making any threats, he rejoined his compan-
> ions who were still at the threshold. A sergeant had just joined the
> group of our attackers and addressed them; they seemed to listen with
> great impatience. During this time, our anxiety and terror increased,

21. Only selected sections, including the frame, from the book were translated verbatim in the
précis, which is in the third person, in *Bentley's Miscellany*.

and it must have been the same in the adjoining rooms. The soldiers finally seemed to consent to what the sergeant asked of them, and the latter, turning to us said in English: "We have orders to kill you, but we prefer your money to your blood; so, pay a ransom, give us all that you have and you will not be harmed."[22]

This same scene is rendered into Persian with some striking differences:

> The outlaw soldiers ran towards him with drawn swords and grabbed him by the collar. They wanted to cut off his head. The nuns (*zanān-e rāhebeh*) fell at the feet of the savages, one of the bolder ones of whom said to the priest in Urdu, "Show me your God." The priest took off the crucifix from around his neck and showing it to him said, "We co-religionists do not blame this prophet for being killed; our meekness is the source of our strength and the probity of our faith." He spoke in this way, for if all the heads of religions and nations were not meek and didn't bravely put their lives in the service of religion, then by no means would their words have an effect in upholding divine law (*shari'at*). Then the soldiers said, "We won't kill you on the condition that you surrender everything you have to us by way of ransom."[23]

Describing the language of the soldiers as Urdu rather than Bengali may be puzzling, but it is most likely because the former would be more familiar to Persian(ate) readers. Furthermore, instead of the priest's proselytizing response, he assumes a moralizing tone that is then picked up by the narrator. In the Persian text, the sepoys also do not react to seeing the crucifix. Whereas in this scene, the narrative was shortened slightly, in another place E'temād al-Saltaneh makes a more substantial intervention in the story, when for a whole page he includes a discourse against tyrannical rule, comparing the British to the Mongols and Tatars, and the impossible dream of keeping Indians in an oppressed state. To drive his point home, he cites two verses from the classical Persian ethical text, *Golestān* by Sa'di: "A swarm of mosquitos can bite an elephant, despite all its strength and firmness. / When ants band together, they can remove the hide of a fierce lion."[24] The translator is explicating the text here and speaking directly to his audience. After this interruption of the narrative, he resumes translating the text.

22. *De Delhi à Cawnpore*, 238–39.

23. *Sargozasht-e khānom-e englisi dar hendustān*, 206–7.

24. *Sargozasht-e khānom-e englisi dar hendustān*, 201. The verse is from Chapter 3 ("On the Virtues of Contentment"), story 28: pasheh chu par shod be-zanad pil rā / bā hameh tondi o salābat keh ust // murchegān rā chu bovad ettefāq / shir-e zheyān rā be-darānand pust.

Figure 4.　Cover of the modern reprint (Tehran, 1363/1984 or 85).

At the end of the book, we hear Maynard's voice again in the closing frame, when he informs his readers of Mrs. Hornsteet's fate: "She is now living in the Touraine, with her husband's family. As, however, he was not in the Company's service, she does not yet know whether the Court of Directors will award her any compensation or pension for her terrible losses."[25] This part was not translated into Persian; instead, she herself speaks to the reader, echoing the same sentiments expressed by the translator on the moral of her story:

> This was the story of my difficult days and misfortune, which I told as
> a lesson to others. Especially those who are drowned in seas of riches
> and enjoy affluence and happiness for which they should not cease
> to be grateful. They should know that hand of fate, in an instant, can
> bring down the wealthy from the apex of honor to the lowest depths,

25. *Bentley's Miscellany*, 650.

and place the fortunate from riches to rags. *Honor those you wish to and bring down those you will with your benevolent hand, for you are powerful in all things.*[26]

Maynard evinces a typically fatalistic, even Sufi, view of the vicissitudes of fortune and the relentless cycle of time that runs through so much of premodern Persian literature. The story of a European woman who underwent a horrifying experience in a foreign land would obviously elicit sympathy from many readers; in fact, the violence against women and children in Lucknow and Kanpur (Cawnpore) had truly been particularly gruesome. Did readers of this book believe that Mrs. Hornsteet really existed, or did they think they were reading a work of historical fiction? The immense popularity of fictional and non-fictional writings about the 1857 events, especially female-centered episodes such as in the Bibighar Massacre during the siege of Kanpur, would go on to become a popular theme in European literature,[27] and French works "have repeatedly revived the ghosts of Cawnpore with female captives that live to tell the tale."[28] In fact, when the English précis of Maynard's work appeared in *Bentley's Miscellany,* the brief introduction suggested that the more popular character Highland Jessie, heroine of a ballad set in the siege of Lucknow during the rebellion, was inspired by Mrs. Hornsteet.[29] But was there sufficient human interest in it for someone such as E'temād al-Saltaneh to deem it worthy of translation?

Viewed in the context of the intertwined politics and history of various empires and nations in the nineteenth century, Hornsteet's story functioned as "a genuine corrective to the hysterical Anglo-centric representations of the massacre ... Thus, Hornsteet, as literary creation, is a highly provocative character – despite and because of being a "Cawnpore victim," she is a powerful figure through which to challenge the official versions of Nana Sahib."[30] In one of his works, *Khābnāmeh,* E'temād al-Saltaneh explains the insidious way that British commercial and political power was extended over different parts of the globe: "the policy of the nation and government of the English in all parts of the world,

26. *Sargozasht-e khānom-e englisi dar hendustān,* 222.

27. This topic is explored in Chemmachery 2019, 1–14; Frith 2010.

28. Frith 2014, 127.

29. The text of the ballad can be viewed here: https://digital.nls.uk/broadsides/view/?id=15105); there was also a painting about this episode attributed to the English artist Frederick Goodall: https:// artu.org/discover/artworks/highland-jessie-182687.

30. Frith 2014, 79. The Maratha Nana Saheb Peshwa II (d. 1859) was a central figure in the events of 1857, who gave the order for the massacre of women and children taking refuge in the Bibighar; he was portrayed negatively in British sources. Incidentally, Jules Verne's novel, *La maison à vapeur* (1880) was translated into English as *The End of Nana Saheb: The Steam House.*

and especially in Asia and our country, is that they combine commercial problems with political matters, [and] they introduce their influence inside oriental
countries by means of commerce." He goes on to warn his readers: "Knowledgeable people know that those people have repeatedly done those kinds of things.
Did they not just conquer India by means of its own popularizing merchandise? They came to own most parts of Africa by that same method."[31] This is in
keeping with the strong views that he expressed on the tyrannical nature of the
British in the middle of Mrs. Hornsteet's story.

The Persian translation of Maynard's book had a fascinating afterlife in India, where it continued to be read for several decades. Although it was not translated into English by a London publisher, the government of India seemed to
have had no such qualms in promoting the Persian version. It was announced in
an official publication that the Home Department was replacing some classical
prose works (Sa'di's *Bustān* and Kāshefi's *Anvār-e Sohayli*) in the curriculum for
the higher standard examination in Persian with modern texts; the official announcement stated: "Experience has shown that the present system of examination is not calculated to ensure such a knowledge of the spoken language as it is
essential that officers should have in dealing with Persian-speaking people. The
Governor General in Council attributes the failure of the present system in this
respect largely to the fact that most of the existing text-books are antiquated and
do not introduce candidates to modern and colloquial Persian." The three modern texts added were: "1. A selection from the "Tarikh-e-Sassaniyan"; 2. A selection from the "Safar-Nama-i-Shah-i-Iran"; and 3. "Narrative of Mrs. Hortestet"
translated by Itimad-us-Sultana."[32] In 1905, and again in 1910 (Figure 5), these
texts were published together in one volume with the title, *Hadiqeh-ye fasāhat*,[33]
for use by students and candidates for the Indian Civil Service (ICS) examination. The "Tarikh-e Sasaniyan" was based on Mohammad Hosayn Khān Zokā'
al-Molk Forughi's *Tārikh-e salātin-e Sāsāni, tabaqeh-e chahārom az moluk-e Fors*
(published in Iran in 1895).[34] The second text was Nāser al-Din Shāh's 1873
travelogue, popularized in James Redhouse's English translation as *Diary of H.*

31. E'temād al-Saltaneh 2016, 128.

32. The announcement appeared as: "Reform of the Examinations in the Persian Language," *Government Gazette: The United Provinces of Agra and Oudh* (August 13, 1904): 227–228.

33. In the edition published in Calcutta (1910), the order of the three texts is different, with the
Tārikh-e Sāsāniyān being last.

34. It seems that Zokā' al-Molk's *Tārikh-e Sāsāniyān* and E'temad al-Saltaneh's *Tārikh-e Bani
Ashkān* "were seminal texts in the modern Persian historiography of the ancient period. They were
both largely derivative of [George] Rawlinson's texts but were not strict translations," Marashi 2008,
156–57.

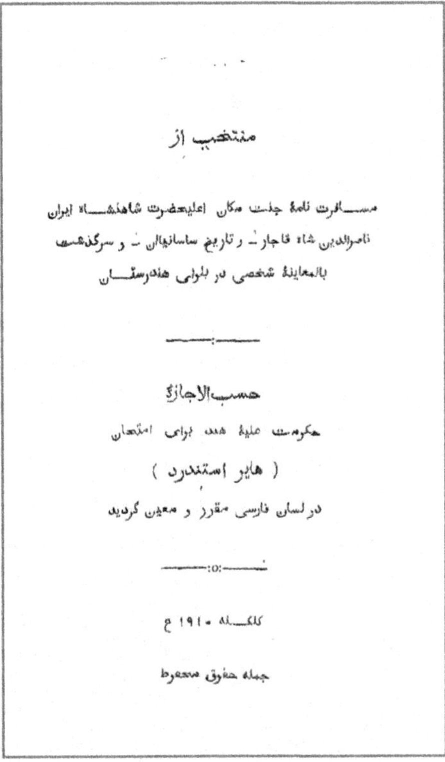

Figure 5. *Hadiqeh-ye fasāhat*, selections from three texts (Calcutta, 1910).

M. the Shah of Persia during his tour through Europe in A.D. 1873.[35] For more than one reason it is surprising to find the *Sargozasht-e khānom-e englisi* as the third text in this triad, but by this time, the 1857 rebellion was in the distant past, and the subject matter may have been thought to have some appeal for Indian students of Persian.[36]

From a different context altogether, but nonetheless quite fascinating in the mapping of the travels of Maynard's book, is this statement in an entry on Muslim ethical conduct in an early twentieth-century British encyclopedia: "An Englishwoman, Mrs. Hortestet, who has written a very interesting account of her adventures at the time of the Sepoy rebellion, praises the integrity of the Mussalmans of India, and relates how her elephant-driver, although himself a

35. Aspects of the Shah's travelogues are analyzed in Sohrabi 2012, chapter 4; Motadel 2011, 563–79.

36. Two articles on the broader aspects of this topic are: Rahman 1999, 49–62; Bruce 2022, 719–40.

Mussalman, hid her so that she might escape the rebels."[37] Here too there is an assumption that the narrator was a historical character and her story was real.

The French original and Persian translation of Félix Maynard's *De Delhi à Cawnpore* cannot be said to be completely forgotten since there have been recent reprints produced in Paris and Tehran. It was certainly one of the author's lesser-known works, but sadly he and his writings have not found any notable mention in the histories of French literature. Whereas, E'temād al-Saltaneh's Persian version of the text illustrates a vibrant phenomenon of transcultural translation and readership in the late nineteenth and early twentieth centuries. In addition to the political theme of the book, which would surely have interested the Qajar government with its uneasiness about British imperialism, its popularity as a riveting story illustrates the eclectic reading tastes of educated people in Iran, and in the larger sphere of the circulation of books in the Persianate world its unique place in British India as a textbook. In this regard, attention has been paid mostly to the reception of and printing of classical Persian texts in India, and although the Persian curriculum there in the colonial period was heavily premodern, nevertheless there is clear evidence that modern books lithographed in Qajar Iran had found readers. Moreover, such bibliographical instances of translation and printing ought to be included in the history of the development of modern Persian fiction writing.[38] In this paper I have refrained from calling Maynard's book a novel, although it certainly reads like one, and in all likelihood, it is a fictionalized account of a story that he may have heard from a female survivor of the 1857 rebellion in India. Whether she was Mistress Hornsteet or Mrs. Hornstreet, or in her Persianate avatar as Khānom-e Hortestet, her narrative as told by Félix Maynard and then E'temād al-Saltaneh is most certainly a compelling one and deserves to be read in the original and in Persian.

37. "Righteousness (Muhammadan)," *Encyclopaedia of Religion and Ethics,* edited by James Hastings, with the Assistance of John A. Selbie, and Louis M. Gray (New York: Charles Scribner's Sons, 1919), v. 10, 811.

38. E'temād al-Saltaneh's contribution to literary culture is mentioned by Balaÿ 1998, 68.

Works Cited

Amanat, Abbas. 1998. "E'temād-al-Saltanah, Mohammad-Hasan Khan Moqaddam Marāǧa'i." *EIr* 8, 662–66.

Balaÿ, Christophe. 1998. *La genèse du roman persan modern.* Téhéran: Institut français de recherche en Iran.

Bruce, Gregory Maxwell. 2022. "Persian Studies in India and the Colonial Universities, 1857–1947." *Iranian Studies* 55:719–40.

Chemmachery, Jaine. 2019. "Fiction to Historical Metafiction and neo-Victorianism." *Commonwealth Essays and Studies* 42:1–14.

Clark, James D. 2016. "Introduction." In Eʿtemād os-Saltaneh 2016, i-lvii.

Cole, Juan R. I. 1996. "Marking Boundaries, Marking Time: The Iranian Past and the Construction of the Self by Qajar Thinkers." *Iranian Studies* 29:35–56.

Eʿtemād os-Saltaneh, Mirza Mohammad Hasan Khan. 2016. *The Rapture, or The Book of Sleep.* Translated from the Persian with an introduction and annotations by James D. Clark. Costa Mesa: Mazda.

Frith, Nicola. 2010. "Rebel or Revolutionary? Representing Nana Sahib and the Bibighar Massacre in English- and French-Language Texts and Images." *interventions* 12:368–82.

———. 2014. *The French Colonial Imagination: Writing the Indian Uprisings, 1857–1858, from Second Empire to Third Republic.* Lanham: Lexington Books.

Marashi, Afshin. 2008. *Nationalizing Iran: Culture, Power, and the State, 1870–1940.* Seattle: University of Washington Press.

Marzolph, Ulrich. 2001. *Narrative Illustration in Persian Lithographed Books.* Leiden: Brill.

Mortelier, Christiane. 2005. "French Whalers in New Zealand." In *The French and the Pacific Worlds, 17th-19th Centuries: Explorations, Migrations and Cultural Exchanges,* edited by Annick Foucrier, 43–54. London: Routledge.

Motadel, David. 2011. "The German Other: Nasir al-Din Shah's Perceptions of Difference and Gender during His Visits to Germany, 1873–89." *Iranian Studies* 44:563–79.

Nicora, Flaminia. 2011. "The Stirring Story of the 'Cipays': Italian Narrative Responses." In *Insurgent Sepoys: Europe Views the Revolt of 1857,* edited by Shaswati Mazumdar, 171–88. New Delhi: Routledge.

Rahmān, T. 1999. "Decline of Persian in British India." *South Asia: Journal of South Asian Studies* 22:49–62.

Sohrabi, Naghmeh. 2012. *Taken for Wonder: Nineteenth-Century Travel Accounts from Iran to Europe.* New York: Oxford University Press.

Vejdani, Farzin. 2014. *Making History in Iran: Education, Nationalism, and Print Culture.* Stanford: Stanford University Press.

A Domestic Affair:
Prostitution, Temporary Marriage,
and the Sale of Wives in Qajar Iran

Farzin Vejdani

IN HIS PROVOCATIVE ARTICLE, E. P. Thompson describes a curious English phenomenon that appears to have emerged in the seventeenth century: husbands selling their wives to the highest bidder in a highly ritualized and symbolic parade. This ritual was a convenient solution to unhappy marriages in a legal context which made divorce nearly impossible.[1] By contrast, in nineteenth-century Iran, husbands sold their wives in a more literal sense; historical sources refer to husbands as pimping out their wives, not as a way of divorcing them but in order to profit from their sex work. In Shi'i Iran, divorce was relatively easy; furthermore, men could take women as temporary wives (*sigheh*), a peculiarity of Shi'i Muslim societies. And while some viewed these temporary marriage contracts as a lawful solution to the "problem" of prostitution, domestic arrangements involving prostitution continually blurred the lines between licit and illicit.[2] In order to more fully explore the pimping of wives, and the familial dimensions of prostitution and procurement more broadly, this essay examines a host of sources, ranging from lexicons, satirical sexual treatises, reformist texts, and government reports. At its core, it asks why there were so many instances of prostitution in nineteenth-century Qajar sources of families being involved in prostitution, procurement, and pimping? Typically, prostitution is thought of as the domain of unmarried, unanchored and transient migrant women, who were therefore considered morally suspect. Certainly, this was broadly true of nineteenth-century Iran as well, but there were also many cases of husbands pimping out their wives, fathers and mothers pimping out their daughters, and husbands and wives or other family members being involved in procurement operations. One of the main reasons for this familial form of sex work appears to be the absence of a widespread institution of public brothels: instead, prostitution and procurement often took place inside the home, a cottage industry rather than the "industrial" prostitution of government-sponsored brothels

---

1. Thompson 1993, 404–66.
2. For the definitive study of the phenomenon in Iran, see Haeri 2014.

33

found elsewhere in the Middle East, South Asia, or Europe at the time.[3] As a result, individuals could credibly deny the charge of prostitution, pimping, or procurement by portraying themselves as an upstanding member of the community who lived with their family and had no reason to engage in illicit sexual activities. This strategy of deflection allowed families to shield themselves as much as possible from charges of immorality that would otherwise have led to their banishment or corporal punishment.

Single Women, Suspicions of Prostitution, and Temporary Marriage

Scholarship on prostitutes in the Middle East presents them as single women without familial ties. The overall picture of Muslim prostitutes in eighteenth-century Istanbul, for example, is that of rural migrants, single women, homeless women, or women who lived alone in a dwelling.[4] Zarinebaf characterizes the situation in the following terms: "Both organized and unorganized prostitution were on the rise due to the spread of commercial sex and the economic difficulties faced by single, divorced, and widowed women as well as by slaves."[5] Single women, she notes, "had a hard time protecting their reputations in the more crime-ridden quarters of Galata and Kasım Paşa."[6] It is precisely this difficulty in protecting one's reputation as a single woman that made an individual suspect. Given that names were often recorded in official government documents in terms of familial relations (so-and-so the son or daughter of so-and-so), the lack of familial markers of identification rendered an individual, especially a woman, morally suspect. Avner Witznitzer has argued that, in eighteenth-century Istanbul, anonymity was a liability since city dwellers often made allegations for those who hosted "unrelated people" (*ecnebi*) or those of "unknown status" (*mechulu-l ahvāl*).[7] It was through the legal mechanisms of surety or bond (*kefālat*) that someone of unknown (and thus suspect) status was rendered legible within a community.[8]

Neighbors in Qajar cities had a similar set of assumptions about the rootless individual; when it came to women, this suspicion frequently veered into charges of prostitution or procurement. And while the same mechanisms of surety existed in Iran under different terminology (*eltezām* or *zemānat*), a wom-

3. The scholarship on prostitution in all three contexts is vast. For three representative works that make arguments along these lines, see Corbin 1990; Hammad 2016; Tambe 2009.
4. Zarinebaf 2010, 90–92.
5. Zarinebaf 2010, 87.
6. Zarinebaf 2010, 131.
7. Wishnitzer 2014, 517.
8. Başaran 2014, 165; Turna 2008, 170.

an living with her family, especially a household with a mature male figure who would act as a guardian, was more capable of deflecting charges of being morally compromised. Married prostitutes or madams were either in a permanent or temporary marriage; this granted them a claim to legitimate residency in the neighborhood in a way that being a single woman, whether divorced, widowed, or simply unmarried, would not.

The category of temporary marriage (*sigheh* or *mot'eh*) deserves further elaboration since it was a unique feature of Shi'i societies, of which Iran was one in the nineteenth century. *Mot'eh* could alternatively mean giving benefit for a short time, enjoyment and pleasure, or having the "usufruct" of something.[9] The term *sigheh*, on the other hand, referred to a "form or type of contract" but came to be pejoratively used to refer to a woman in a temporary marriage but not to a man.[10] Instead of either term, Shi'i jurists typically refer to this as permanent (*dā'em*) and temporary (*movaqqat*) marriage (*ezdevāj*).[11] According to Shahla Haeri, the four components of a temporary marriage are the form of contract (*sigheh*), limits on interfaith marriage (*mahal*), duration of the marriage (*ajal*) and payment consideration (*ajr*).[12] The duration of the temporary marriage could last anywhere between one hour and ninety-nine years.[13] Classical Shi'i authors referred to the temporary wife as the object of lease (*mosta'jereh*) in much the same way that a property is leased.[14] Women, especially those who were widowed or divorced, had greater autonomy in negotiating such marriage contracts, although there was some legal dispute about whether virgin women could do so.[15] Unlike a permanent marriage, a *mot'eh* marriage did not need to be witnessed.[16] Temporary wives had to typically wait two menstrual cycles and forty-five days after the end of their contract to ensure that she was not pregnant before arranging for a new marriage contract.[17]

In their discussions of Qajar-era sexuality, Willem Floor and Janet Afary have argued that most temporary wives were from lower socio-economic classes.[18] Floor accepts the premise of most European travelers in Iran: the majority of *sigheh*s were, in socio-economic terms, akin to prostitutes unless they married

9. Haeri 2014, 50.
10. Haeri 2014, 50–51.
11. Haeri 2014, 50.
12. Haeri 2014, 51.
13. Haeri 2014, 2.
14. Haeri 2014, 52.
15. Haeri 2014, 54.
16. Haeri 2014, 56.
17. Haeri 2014, 57.
18. Afary 2008, 137.

a wealthy man.[19] Afary has a more complex understanding of the relationship between prostitution and temporary marriage: she argues, "prostitutes often passed as temporary wives to avoid social ostracism."[20] It is this final statement which bears keeping in mind: temporary marriage still conferred a level of respectability for prostitutes, who otherwise would be seen as outside the acceptable socio-legal order, much like permanent marriage or integration into a family unit (especially a father or mother) did.

THE PIMP, THE CUCKOLD, AND THE PROSTITUTE/TEMPORARY WIFE

While temporary marriage was a licit way for two people to enter into a sexual relationship involving the exchange of money, prostitution and pimping were prohibited by ethico-legal standards. The category of prostitute is strikingly missing in Islamic jurisprudence, although the activities of the pimp (Arabic, *qawwād*; Persian, *qavvād*), in the sense of someone who facilitates adultery (*zenā*), are prohibited. However, the pimp is not condemned for profiting from prostitution but for the facilitation of the illicit sex act itself.[21] The lines between legal marriage and prostitution became blurred in scenarios where doubt could be used to deflect charges of adultery. While *hodud* crimes, including *zenā*, held notoriously heavy penalties – 100 lashes for the unmarried and capital punishment for the married – the evidentiary bar was significantly quite high: the individuals involved had to either confess or four consistent male witness testimonies to the penetrative sex act had to be produced at the shari'ah court.[22] Further dissuading conviction was what Intisar Rabb has called the doubt canon: the shari'ah judge had to avoid carrying out *hodud* punishments if there was the slightest doubt that the act had been carried out.[23]

In illicit sexual situations, this element of doubt provided clients and prostitutes with an argument for plausible deniability within Islamic law. They could theoretically claim that they believed the money being exchanged was a bride price rather than a prostitution fee, therefore nullifying the necessity to carry out the fixed mandatory punishment.[24] Discussing the Ottoman context, James Baldwin notes that Ottoman jurists excluded prostitutes and their clients from *hodud* punishments because of the principle of ambiguity (*shobheh*): on the surface, prostitution was too close to lawful intercourse between a husband and

19. Floor 2008, 146.
20. Afary 2008, 66.
21. Majlesi 198[?], 24.
22. Peters 2005, 59–62.
23. Rabb 2010, 63–125.
24. El-Rouayheb 2005, 123.

wife or master and slave, both of which included an exchange of money (a dower and a purchase price, respectively).[25] The study of the practice of prostitution through domestic arrangements suggests an even more intriguing legal phenomenon: husbands and parents treated their spouses and children as property from which they could obtain rent. Even in cases of temporary marriage, which could be thought of as a fixed form of rental of sexual services to begin with, the husband could "rent" his temporary wife to a client.

Like prostitution, situations in which husbands pimped out their wives or parents pimped out their children were not explicitly addressed in Islamic jurisprudence. And yet, there is evidence of this phenomenon in Persian expressions, reformist texts and draft codes, and even a satirical account of a court official's sexual escapades. Husbands who pimped out their wives could be seen as cuckolds who allowed their wives to have sexual relations with other men. The English term cuckold, however, does not suggest the exchange of money, nor in fact do all Persian terms. But some Persian terms do in fact suggest a financial transaction in this form of pimping. For example, *zan beh mozd,* literally "woman for money," was a term used to describe a husband who pimped out his wife for money, or simply a cuckold.[26] This brings us to "meat eating" metaphors for cuckolds. The Persian suffix *khwār* not only means "to eat" but also "to profit" or "to benefit from."[27] Thus, profiting from the flesh became a telling metaphor for pimping or being a cuckold in terms like meatball eater (*kofteh khwār*), pounded meat eater (*khuzi khwār*), and dressed meat eater (*qaliyeh khwār*).[28] Intriguingly, the first of these metaphors is used in an early modern Ottoman law code, in which husbands who failed to divorce their adulterous wives paid a "cuckold" (*koftehorluk*) tax.[29] Not only did the failure to divorce dishonor the man, but it also suggested culpability and collusion in his wife's illicit sexual activities (in other words, pimping).

In light of these expressions, one might consider this form of cuckoldry to be a mere metaphor to shame a dishonorable man who did not have the requisite honor (*ghayrat*) to block his wife from sexual liaisons with unrelated men.

25. Baldwin 2012, 125.

26. S.v. "zan beh mozd," in Dehkhodā 1947. Both the common term *kasb,* meaning trade, and *kasbi-bāzi,* connoted prostitution. S.v. "kasb" and "kasbi-bāzi" in Steingass 1975. Similarly, the son of a prostitute or pimp was referred to derisively as "born of property wealth" (*mālzādeh*). S.v. "māl-zāda," in Steingass 1975.

27. See for example the term *moft-khwār,* meaning parasite, i.e. someone who eats for free. S.v. "muft-khwār," in Steingass 1975.

28. S.v. "kofta-khwār," "khuzi-khwār," and "qalya-khwār," in Dehkhodā 1947; Steingass 1975. Persian has several other terms that refer to a man who pimps out his wife: *gharcheh, qartabān, qurnās,* or *fughāk* s.v. "gharacha," "qartabān," "qurnās," and "fughāk" in Steingass 1975.

29. Peirce 2010, 112.

Historical sources from nineteenth-century Iran, however, paint a more complex picture. A Qajar-era reformist text which drew heavily from the language
of Islamic jurisprudence, advice literature, and draft codes, the *Qānun-e Qazvini*, did draw an explicit connection between cuckoldry and pimping. Its author,
Mohammad Shafi' Qazvini, describes a category of people who deserved the
death sentence as married men who "gave" their wives to clients (*harif*), which
he considered to be commonplace (*ma'mul shodeh*) in Tehran.[30] In a Persian
draft penal code based directly on the Ottoman Penal Code called the *Qānun-e
Jazā*, crimes related to prostitution were to receive set punishments. Those who
misguided youth to engage in lewd acts or obscenities (*fahshiyyāt*) were to be
imprisoned for between one month and a year. If a father and/or a mother did
this to their child in their status as a guardian, then the punishment was increased to six to eighteen months in prison.[31]

Resāleh-e Fojuriyeh, a satirical account by a Qajar statesman of his sexual
escapades, also provides some clues as to the thin lines between prostitution
and temporary marriage. Composed in 1872/3 (1289 H.) by Vali ben Sohrāb
Gorjestāni for Nāser al-Din Shāh's benefit, much of the text is a list of various women and young men the author had sex with.[32] Even if the exact details
should be taken with a grain of salt, especially those detailing adulterous affairs
with women of higher status, the text still has valuable insights into the common fees charged by prostitutes (which are consistent with available reports).
Of the fifteen prostitutes he includes in his list, a list which he readily admits
is not exhaustive, six were described as temporary wives (*sigheh*) and one as the
wife of local men in Tehran.[33] Two of these were the temporary wives of the
same person, Mehdi Khān, who was protective of them and was upset when he
found out about Gorjestāni's rendezvous with one of them (he fined his temporary wife one tuman and Gorjestāni two tumans for the moral injury).[34] In
the other cases, the husbands' reaction are unknown, so it is unclear if they were
involved in pimping, unaware of their wives' profession, or merely lacking "hon-
or." The fact that he categorized a fair number of these women (almost half) as
being somehow married and also prostitutes indicates that marriage provided a
certain cover for their activities by lending them a degree of social respectability.

Although Gorjestāni was at pains to distinguish between common prostitutes, on the one hand, and women married temporarily or permanently to

30. Qazvini 1991, 120.
31. Article 201, "Qānun-e Jazā" 1884.
32. For a brief discussion of this text in the context of sex with beardless youths (*amrads*), see Najmabadi 2005, 23.
33. Gorjestāni 2017, 192–94.
34. Gorjestāni 2017, 192.

notables or princes, on the other, some of the descriptions of the women in the second category seem to suggest that they were prostitutes as well. One example of this is the fact that he paid them for their services. For instance, he paid the hefty sum of ten tumans to supposedly have sex with Fātemeh Soltān, the wife of Mirzā Hasan ʿAli Quz.[35] He also described another woman, Sakineh ʿAraqchin Duz, as an old woman but a great dancer. He paid her five tumans for two nights.[36] Another temporary wife of a notable, Khānum Namāzi, appears to have also been a prostitute. She was almost caught by the head attendant, Hājji Mohammad Hasan Khān Farrāshbāshi, when he was informed that she was at the house of a client, Mehdi Khān. He ordered his men to catch her when she left the house. Mehdi Khān learned of this, so in order to circumvent the accusation, he took Khānum Namāzi as a temporary wife for one month. Gorjestāni's comment at the end of this story is indicative of why she was a prostitute: "After one month, she came out [of his house]; the poor woman, for fear of her life, gave free pussy (*kos-e moft*) to Mehdi Khān, that bear [of a man]."[37] In other words, the terms of her temporary marriage contract involved much less money than she would have made under normal circumstances.

POLICE AND GOVERNMENT REPORTS ON FAMILIAL PROSTITUTION AND PROCUREMENT

According to government and police reports, prostitution was often a family affair that could involve the father, mother, sisters, brothers, sons and daughters, aunts and nephews, and so on.

This provided the family an aura of respectability and more legitimate cover for their activities than if they were a single person. When thinking about family involvement in prostitution and pimping, one should not automatically assume that nineteenth-century Iran was an outlier in comparison to other Muslim societies. Comparisons with other Muslim societies provide clues as to parallel underlying logics for why domestic arrangements rooted in private neighborhood dwellings were common in nineteenth-century Iran. In medieval Mamluk domains, a Damascene female pimp (*qawwādah*) was involved in providing women with a safe spot to meet "comely" young men for sexual pleasure. After this, her husband would take over as pimp. This operation also included a female slave who eventually informed the city governor (*wāli*) who had the female pimp tortured to confess to her crimes.[38] In the Egyptian context, ear-

---

35. Gorjestāni 2017, 192.
36. Gorjestāni 2017, 191.
37. Gorjestāni 2017, 191–92.
38. Petry 2016, 151.

ly nineteenth-century travelers described a class of female singers (*ghawāzi*) as being sold to the highest bidder in marriage by their fathers and continuing their trade as prostitutes even after marriage, with their husbands acting as their pimps.[39] And while Karin van Nieuwkerk is rightly suspicious of some of the sensationalist dimensions of these accounts, it is worth considering that prostitutes were not always outside of familial relations in the Middle East. Zarinebaf, who otherwise finds overwhelming evidence of eighteenth-century prostitutes in Istanbul being single women, notes that "a whole family was sometimes involved in commercial sex," such as in a case of a father and daughter operation that led to the two individuals' exile to Cyprus.[40] The spatial context of prostitution and procurement by families is also of paramount importance. Marinos Sariyannis's study of early modern Istanbul prostitution suggests that some prostitutes were married women working from home, either because their husbands were usually absent or because the husbands were consenting to having customers come to their home.[41] Drawing on archival court documents, Elyse Semerdjian observes that "several of the cases that appeared before the court involved procuring by couples or family members."[42] The reason for this closely parallels what we will see was also true of nineteenth-century Iran: such cases involved prostitution occurring in "private homes as spaces of business," since this afforded greater privacy.[43] By contrast, single women living alone would receive much more scrutiny from neighbors, which weakened the otherwise accepted privacy of the domicile.[44]

In a series of nineteenth-century Tehran government reports, husbands and wives were regularly involved in prostitution, procurement, and pimping operations. Ahmad Khān Qajar and his wife, who was a prostitute turned pimp, were involved in one such operation. In 1870/1 (1287 H.), we learn that Ahmad Khān Qajar's wife, who lived close to the Gate of Sepāh Big in the Chāl-maydān Neighborhood, had once been a prostitute but was now engaged in pimping (*jākeshi*). Potential clients who wanted an "immoral woman" (*zan-e harzeh*), meaning a prostitute, would notify the woman of their intention and she, "without saying a word," would bring such a woman to them.[45] Similarly,

---

39. Nieuwkerk 2021, 27.
40. Zarinebaf 2010, 91.
41. Sariyannis 2008, 53–54.
42. Semerdjian 2008, 118.
43. Semerdjian 2008, 118.
44. Semerdjian 2008, 122; Zarinebaf 2010, 91.
45. "Gozāresh-e kambud-e nān talaf shodan-e mardom az gorosnegi va zarb va shatm-e nān-vāyān nā amni serqat bi ābi va fahshā va Maygusāri dar Mahallāt-e Tehrān," dated 1870/1 (1287 H.), Sāzmān-e Asnād va Ketābkhāneh-e Melli [Herafter, SAKM], no. 295/2465, ff. 3. Her name was never

in the Bāzār Neighborhood of Tehran, Ja'far and his wife, a prostitute, were involved in transporting prostitutes around the area, which the police described as causing disorder. They were therefore detained and brought to the station, where appropriate punishments (*mojāzāt*) could be determined.[46] In other cases, it was the house of Ahmad Khān Qajar that was the locale of prostitution parties. In Chālmaydān, three men – Hasan Sābun Paz, Hosayn Khān Qajar, and Fath 'Ali – were at the house of the aforementioned Ahmad Khān Qajar, where they drank and engaged in debauchery (*harzegi*).[47] On another night, there were sounds of music and singing at Ahmad Khān Qajar's wife's house. Mohammad Hasan, the son of Mashhadi 'Ali Zargar, a neighbor, was drunk and wanted to enter the party, but he was barred from doing so by the owners of the house.[48] What these cases reveal is that pimping operations could include bringing women to clients or having them over for parties at the Ahmad Khān Qajar home.

Other reports provide insights into the procurement process. Generally, procurement was described as a form of trickery, one in which a woman, sometimes married or otherwise labeled as respectable, was duped into prostitution by a predatory madam. In 1871/2 (1288 H.) in the 'Udlājān Neighborhood, a female pimp named Naneh 'Ali was involved in "duping a woman" (*za'ifeh'i farib dādeh*) by offering to take her to the personal hammam in the house of Ahmad Khān Qajar. The wife of Ahmad Khān, a fellow pimp, was in on the ploy. From the residence, they took the unsuspecting woman to a son of 'Emād al-Dowleh, where she was kept in hiding for three days and nights, implying she had been groomed for prostitution. The woman's family searched for their missing family member in vain until they found Naneh 'Ali, beat her up, and took the woman back from her.[49] Similarly, in the Bazar Neighborhood, close to the hammam of Nowruz Khān, a woman named Shāh Bāji, who was herself presumably a madam, would "mislead married women (*zanhā-ye showhardār*

---

mentioned in any of the reports that I could locate. Gorjestāni mentions how in the house of Mehdi Khān Qajar, the wife of a certain Ahmad Khān (possibly Qajar?) named Khorshid, whom he describes as a procurer (*dallāl*), set him up with a prostitute. Since this text was written around the same time as the reports mentioning the wife of Ahmad Khān Qajar, it is possible that this was in fact the same woman. Gorjestāni 2017, 189.

46. Shaykh Rezā'i and Āzari, 1999, 683.

47. "Khabarnāmeh-e Serri: Ruznāmeh-e Makhfi-ye Tehrān," dated 1871/2 (1288 H.), SAKM, no. 295/244.

48. "Khabarnāmeh-e Mahramāneh: Ruznāmeh-e Makhfi-ye Tehrān dar Mowred-e Fasād," dated 1872/3 (1288 H), SAKM 295/271.

49. "Khabarnāmeh-e Serri: Ruznāmeh-e Makhfi-ye Tehrān," dated 1871/2 (1288 H.), SAKM, no. 295/244.

rāhzani minamāyand)" into drinking alcohol, performing entertainment music (*tarab*), and engaging in debauchery (*harzegi*)."[50]

In a number of cases, husbands pimped out their wives and/or daughters to clients, or at least tried to do so. In one instance from the Dowlat Neighborhood in Tehran, Akbar had taken a temporary wife and decided to invite clients over to his house so that he could profit from her. He brought a man by the name of Asghar Haddad for this purpose, but the woman started screaming by the end of the night, possibly because she had not consented to this arrangement. Neighbors complained about the noise to the deputy of the neighborhood (*nā'eb-e mahalleh*). Since Akbar was connected to the Russian Embassy, the Russian Embassy became involved in the investigations. Akbar was released with a warning and made to pledge (*moltazem*) not to engage in such actions again before being entrusted to members of the Russian Embassy.[51] An even more striking case involved Ostād 'Ali Akbar Sabbāgh, who for four months had been secretly pimping his wife and daughter out for sex (*dar khāneh-e u manzel dārad makhfiyan dokhtar va zanash ra beh ertekāb-e 'amal-e shani' bāzdāshteh*). Two Jewish clients came to his house to have sex with the women, but the police detained them all. The Jewish suspects maintained their innocence, claiming they had come to see Ostād 'Ali Abkar to receive repayment of their loan. In the meantime, Ostād 'Ali was kept in custody until the truth could come to light.[52] In 'Udlājān, Sayyed Abu al-Qāsem, who had a home in Sarchonbak, had unrelated men visit his house for illicit sex (*harakāt-e shani'eh*) with his wife and sister. This led to the three being investigated and detained.[53] An executioner (*mir ghazab*) named Qāsem pimped out his wife, who was described as "sexually immoral" (*harzeh*), indirectly through a madam named Nuri. The wife would earn 4,000 dinars for her work (*kārgari*). When Qāsem went to collect the money that she had earned, Nuri responded that his wife consumed ten *shāhi*s worth of bread and the expenses of her children (*'ayyāl*) cost another ten *shāhi*s. Of the remaining 3,000, Nuri's pimping fee (*haqq-e jākeshi*) was thirty *shāhi*s leaving thirty *shāhi*s for the husband. Qāsem and Nuri started fighting over this issue, which led the Dahbāshi of 'Udlājān to arrive on the scene and bring about a reconciliation between the two.[54]

50. "Khabarnāmeh-e Mahramāneh: moztamen-e akhbār-e serri-ye mahallāt-e Tehrān," dated 1871/2 (1288 H.), SAKM, no. 295/278.
51. Shaykh Rezā'i and Āzari 1999, 380. See also Floor 2008, 140.
52. Shaykh Rezā'i and Āzari 1999, 646.
53. Shaykh Rezā'i and Āzari 1999, 73.
54. "Gozāresh beh Shāh Kasrat-e Fahshā dar Dār al-Khelāfeh nā rezāyati-ye Firuz Mirzā az Shāh 'Amal-e Qabih-e Vazir Mokhtār-e Englis Mirzā 'Isā Vazir va Digarān," dated 1870/1 (1287 H.), SAKM, no. 295/2523, ff. 7.

In a remarkable testimonial document (*esteshhādiyeh*) dated April/May 1853 (Rajab 1269 H.), a group of respected *'ulamā*, jurists, and sayyids along with other members of a community in Tehran complained about a man named Hashem, the son (*khalf*) of Mullah Qāsem Langarāni, who, along with his mother and aunt, were involved in "tricking the wives of people" (*beh farib dādan-e zanān-e mardom*) and causing them to "stray from the [straight] path" (*az rāh dar mizanand*) by having them carry out "ugly acts" (*a'māl-e qabiheh*), a euphemism for prostitution. The document's authors claimed to have refrained from "hiding testimony" (*kitmān-i shahadat*) in narrating the family's crimes and "ornamented [the document] with their noble seals" to grant it legal weight. They decried the family's operations in the "stronghold of Islam" (*bayża-yi Islām*), meaning the neighborhood in which the religious signatories resided.

Some of the signatories were particularly distraught by what they called the "bride affair" (*amr-e arus*): Hashim took the wife (*zowjeh*) of his brother, Āqā Taqi, as his bride (*'arus*) to make himself appear as a married man, but everyone in the neighborhood knew it to be a ruse. Another signatory mentioned that the aforementioned men and women were repeatedly captured (*gereftār*) by the city's police (*dārugheh*), proving they were repeat offenders. Sayyed Mirzā provided an even more detailed look into one of the accused's past punishments. He stated:

> For several years, the children of the deceased Hājji Hosayn have been
> employed in pimping (*jākeshi*), especially Nabāt, who is the other daughter
> which I, this servant of God, removed from that [immoral] path and even
> had beaten up quite a bit (*chub-e besyāri zadeh*) in the Qaysariyeh during
> the time of Mohammad Hāshem. She repented [and swore] that she would
> no longer act as a pimp. She was released from the hands of Hāshem but she
> is still employed in this work. This bride affair has recently become public
> (*shoyu'*).

As this passage indicates, Nabāt blamed her relative Hāshem for her involvement in pimping and procurement, by implying she had been coerced into such activities. This claim along with repentance became the basis of her release.[55]

Husbands pimped out beardless young men (*amrad*s) in two cases from Tehran, while wives pimped out women, allowing both to navigate homosocial spaces. This arrangement appears to have allowed both parties to have a measure of social respectability and to find a dwelling within a broader neighborhood without having to self-segregate. A female madam was married to a male pimp

---

55. "Esteshhādiyeh'i dar Khosus-e 'Amal-e Mānafi-ye 'Effat," dated April/May 1853 (Rajab 1269 H.), SAKM, no. 999/31793.

who employed female and male prostitutes respectively. E'temād al-Saltaneh knew Galin since his youth as both a pimp (*qavvādi mikard*) and a prostitute who "would provide benefits herself" (*az khodash ham ābi garm mishod*). She employed four or five female prostitutes, aged fourteen–fifteen years old, whom she dressed up in scantily-clad and ornamental clothing (*lebāshā-ye 'āriyeh zinat*). Her main client was the shāh's son, 'Aziz al-Soltān, who would host them in a private garden named 'Aziziyeh. Meanwhile, her husband, who was previously employed as a carriage driver (*kāleskehchi*) of Sādeq al-Dowleh, had trained some *amrad* children and brought them to the same garden for parties.[56] While Galin and her husband catered to upscale clients, namely royalty, lower-status male and female prostitutes similarly paired up. In a case dealing primarily with theft, we learn about Samad Khān, an *amrad* youth who "engaged in debauchery," taking a female prostitute as a temporary wife. They both resided in a house owned by Amirzādeh Khān in the 'Arabhā Neighborhood, which presumably served as both their dwelling and their base of commerce.[57]

Another familial pattern of prostitution involved mothers and daughters. In the Sangalāj Neighborhood, a Shirazi divorcee summoned her daughter from Shiraz. From the mother's home, both engaged in prostitution. One night, the women had four or five men over for a party, who became drunk and started yelling and screaming, leading the neighbors to complain to the head of the neighborhood (*ra'is-e mahalleh*) and to Kāmrān Mirzā Nā'eb al-Saltaneh, the shāh's son, who was also involved in policing. A police investigation ensued.[58] A member of the Cossack Brigades in Tehran, Ghaffār Āqā'i, sought to break off his engagement with Karbalā'i Khānum in the Dowlat Neighborhood. The reason was that he suspected that his fiancé and her mother were in fact engaged in prostitution. One day, he saw a man crossing the roof of a neighbor and showing three fingers to the woman's mother. She responded by showing four; Ghaffār Āqā'i took these gestures to be gestural bargaining: three and four corresponding to the number of tumans for the sexual transaction. The Cossack concluded that the mother and daughter "were engaging in misdeeds" (*bad 'amal hastand*) of a sexual nature.[59] A less common all-female prostitution arrangement was a group of sisters. Four sisters, who were all prostitutes, rented a house of Hosayn 'Ali Kāleskehchi and entertained Yusof, the brother of Eskandar Mostowfi al-Mamālek, with drinking and debauchery.[60]

In contrast to this familial patter of prostitution and procurement, several

56. E'temād al-Saltaneh 2000, 947.
57. Shaykh Rezā'i and Āzari 1999, 114–15.
58. Shaykh Rezā'i and Āzari 1999, 600.
59. Shaykh Rezā'i and Āzari 1999, 64.
60. "Khabarnāmeh-e Serri: Ruznāmeh-e Makhfi-ye Tehrān," dated 1871/2 (1288 H.), SAKM, no. 295/244.

have noted the similarity between the practice of temporary marriage and prostitution, despite the theoretical and legal nuances involved. Russian travelers, for instance, typically considered temporary marriage to be "legalized profligacy" and avoided making distinctions between it and prostitution.[61] In Kerman, parents were selling their daughters into prostitution, according to both European and Iranian observers. A Russian recounted, for instance, that parents there would sell their daughters into temporary marriage for five–ten tumans.[62] The account of one contemporary critical observer, Hājj Sayyāh Mahallāti, described parents in Kerman who gave their daughters, as young as nine years old, to clients in temporary marriage. He described this by using three different terms: farming out their revenues (*moqate'eh*), renting (*ejāreh*) them out, and selling them. This was typically done not directly but through seminarians in the Madrasah-e Namadmālān and in other madrasahs who would pair women with men in temporary marriage (*sigheh*) so that money could be obtained for the woman or her family (*kasān*). He described the women's earnings as rent income (*vajh-e ejāreh*).[63] In this model, *ākhund*s were responsible for setting the prices and drawing up the contracts for the women. Hājj Sayyāh described Kerman as unique; while in other cities, such as Karbala or other major Iranian cities, temporary marriages were common, it was giving these temporary wives to others and renting them out (*beh digarān dādan va ojrat gereftan*) that was unusual. In other words, it was the renting out of already rented property to a third party for further profit that constituted a unique twist not commonly found elsewhere.[64]

Conclusion

In conclusion, this article has examined the intersection of the spatial and kinship dimensions of prostitution and procurement. The two were often intertwined: living with family made one's dwelling less morally suspect, at least in theory. This particular arrangement occurred within a context in which brothels were not widespread. As a result, most prostitution, whether by individuals who were single or otherwise living with family, took place in residential areas. The figures of the prostitute and the pimp/madam described here are a far cry from the stereotypical image of the rootless woman, single, cut off from her family (possibly disowned), and automatically suspected for her lack of filial connections. Based on the evidence presented here, we have a much more complete picture of those prostitutes and madams who had husbands (temporary or

61. Andreeva 2010, 162.
62. Andreeva 2010, 162.
63. Mahallāti 1980, 164.
64. Mahallāti 1980, 165.

permanent), nephews, mothers, daughters, and sisters who not only approved
of but actively participated in their profession. The question of why requires a
more nuanced understanding of Qajar society. Since public brothels, especially
state-run brothels seen elsewhere in the Middle East, Europe, and South Asia,
were not particularly common, most prostitutes and pimps resided in ordinary
neighborhoods rather than red-light districts. As such, they often sought ways
to deflect the moral scrutiny of nosey neighbors, police, and others who might
have had cause to request that they be banished or otherwise punished. At least
in theory, being married or otherwise residing with family provided a level of
social respectability through which those involved in prostitution could deny
any wrongdoing when confronted by their critics. The role of the female family
member involved in prostitution, procurement, and pimping, and the question
of agency, is somewhat more difficult to resolve. Were these women being coerced, or "tricked" into prostitution operations, as was sometimes suggested by
the evidence presented here? Were they single prostitutes who later married for
greater protection, or were they entering a marriage and then pimped out by
their husbands against their will? Rather than suggest a definitive answer either
way, it is likely that there was a spectrum of arrangements, which further research into the topic will hopefully uncover.

Works Cited

Afary, Janet. 2009. *Sexual Politics in Modern Iran.* New York, NY: Cambridge
     University Press.
Andreeva, Elena. 2010. *Russia and Iran in the Great Game: Travelogues and
     Orientalism.* London: Routledge.
Baldwin, James E. 2012. "Prostitution, Islamic Law and Ottoman Societies."
     Journal of the Economic and Social History of the Orient 55:117–52.
Başaran, Betül. 2014. *Selim III, Social Control and Policing in Istanbul at the
     End of the Eighteenth Century: Between Crisis and Order.* Leiden: Brill.
Corbin, Alain. 1990. *Women for Hire: Prostitution and Sexuality in France
     After 1850.* Cambridge, MA: Harvard University Press.
Dehkhodā, ʿAli Akbar. 1947. *Loghatnāmeh.* Tehran: Majles.
El-Rouayheb, Khaled. 2005. *Before Homosexuality in the Arab-Islamic World,
     1500–1800.* Chicago, IL: University of Chicago Press.
Eʿtemād al-Saltaneh, Mohammad Hasan Khān. 2000. *Ruznāmeh-e Khāterāt-e
     Eʿtemād al-Saltaneh.* Edited by Iraj Afshār. Tehrān: Amir Kabir.
Floor, Willem M. 2008. *A Social History of Sexual Relations in Iran.* Washing-
     ton, DC: Mage Publishers.

Gorjestāni, Vali Khān ebn Sohrāb. 2017. "Resāleh-e Fojuriyeh." In *Haft Resāleh-e Fokāhiyeh*, edited by Qāsem Baykzādeh. Los Angeles, CA: Ketāb va Enteshārāt-e Pars.

Haeri, Shahla. 2014. *Law of Desire: Temporary Marriage in Shiʿi Iran*. Syracuse, NY: Syracuse University Press.

Hammad, Hanan. 2016. *Industrial Sexuality: Gender, Urbanization, and Social Transformation in Egypt*. Austin, TX: University of Texas Press, 2016.

Mahallāti, Mohammad ʿAli Sayyāh. 1980. *Khāterāt-e Hājj Sayyāh, ya, Dowreh-e khowf va vahshat*. Edited by Hamid Sayyāh and Sayf Allāh Gulkār. Tehrān: Amir Kabir.

Majlesi, Mohammad Bāqer. 198[?]. *Hodud va Qesas va Diyat*. Edited by ʿAli Fāzel. Qom: Nashr-e Āsār-e Eslāmi.

Najmabadi, Afsaneh. 2005. *Women with Mustaches and Men Without Beards: Gender and Sexual Anxieties of Iranian Modernity*. Berkeley: University of California Press.

Nieuwkerk, Karin van. 2021. *"A Trade like Any Other": Female Singers and Dancers in Egypt*. Austin, TX: University of Texas Press.

Peirce, Leslie. 2010. "Domesticating Sexuality: Harem Culture in Ottoman Imperial Law." In *Harem Histories: Envisioning Places and Living Spaces*, edited by Marilyn Booth, 104–135. Durham, NC: Duke University Press.

Peters, Rudolph. 2005. *Crime and Punishment in Islamic Law: Theory and Practice from the Sixteenth to the Twenty-First Century*. Cambridge: Cambridge University.

Petry, Carl F. 2016. *The Criminal Underworld in a Medieval Islamic Society: Narratives from Cairo and Damascus under the Mamluks*. Chicago, IL: Middle East Documentation Center.

"Qānun-e Jazā." 1884. Mss. 10–32094. Majlis Library. Tehran, Iran.

Qazvini, Mohammad Shafiʿ. 1991. *Qānun-e Qazvini: Enteqād-e Owzāʿ-e Ejtemāʾi-ye Irān-e Dowreh-e Nāseri*. Edited by Iraj Afshār. Tehran: Talāyeh.

Rabb, Intisar. 2010. "Islamic Legal Maxims as Substantive Canons of Construction: Hudūd-Avoidance in Cases of Doubt." *Islamic Law and Society* 17: 63–125.

Sariyannis, Marinos. 2008. "Prostitution in Ottoman Istanbul, Late Sixteenth-Early Eighteenth Century." *Turcica* 40: 37–65.

Sāzmān-e Asnād va Ketābkhāneh-e Melli [SAKM]. Multiple Documents.

Semerdjian, Elyse. 2008. *"Off the Straight Path": Illicit Sex, Law, and Community in Ottoman Aleppo*. Syracuse, NY: Syracuse University Press.

Shaykh Rezā'i, Aniseh and Shahlā Āzari, eds. 1999. *Gozāreshhā-ye Nazmiyeh az Mahallāt-e Tehrān: Rāpurt-e Vaqāye'-e Mokhtalefeh-e Mahallāt-e Dār al-Khelāfeh [1303–1305 Hejri Qamari]* (Tehrān: Sāzmān-e Asnād-e Melli-ye Irān.
Steingass, Francis. 1975. *A Comprehensive Persian-English Dictionary*. Beirut: Librairie du Liban.
Tambe, Ashwini. 2009. *Codes of Misconduct Regulating Prostitution in Late Colonial Bombay*. Minneapolis, MN: University of Minnesota Press.
Thompson, E.P. 1993. *Customs In Common: Studies In Traditional Popular Culture*. New York, NY: The New Press.
Turna, Nalan. 2008. "Pandemonium and Order: Suretyship, Surveillance, and Taxation in Early Nineteenth-Century İstanbul." *New Perspectives on Turkey* 39: 167–89.
Wishnitzer, Avner. 2014. "Into the Dark: Power, Light, and Nocturnal Life in 18th-Century Istanbul." *International Journal of Middle East Studies* 46: 513–31.
Zarinebaf, Fariba. 2010. *Crime and Punishment in Istanbul: 1700–1800*. Berkeley, CA: University of California Press.

Language Purism in Early Nineteenth-Century Iran: The Case of Yaghmā-ye Jandaqi

Roxane Haag-Higuchi

During the consolidation period of the Iranian nation-state in the early Pahlavi period, the political agenda included not only military, administrative, and infrastructural measures, but also linguistic reform and language planning activities aimed at establishing Persian as a national language and adapting it to contemporary requirements. Representing an important part of Iranian culture, Persian language was supposed to play an essential role as an integrative communication tool in the multilingual state of Iran. Moreover, it was the ideal means of affirming national identity both domestically and abroad. Against this background, it is only a small step from language "reform" to purist linguistic intervention, and linguistic homogenization is consequently a widespread phenomenon in the formative period of nation-states. In Iran, language planning concepts were institutionalized with the establishment of the Farhangestān-e Zabān-e Irān (Language Academy of Iran, 1935), whose main task was to coin and disseminate Persian words in order to serve as alternatives for words of non-Persian origin and as denominations for new realities.[1]

Language purism associated with ideological and political agendas dates back to the late nineteenth and early twentieth centuries in Iran. The Qajar poet Yaghmā-ye Jandaqi (1196–1276/1782–1859), who is the focus of this essay, is sometimes referred to as an early reference point of modern language purism.[2] The way he engaged with the phenomenon, however, reveals contexts, motivations, and ideas that differ from the positions of later advocates of "pure Persian." I will explore the specific framework of language purism in which Yaghmā operated and discuss how he negotiated his own position within that framework. The extent to which the components of a language defined as foreign are eliminated, the significance of language use that has evolved over time, and techniques of word formation or word invention are central issues in the discourse of purism.[3] Moreover, specific questions like the scale of language-"purifying" measures, the particular trigger of purist activities, their purpose, and

1. Jazayeri 1999; Paul 2010.
2. Jazayeri 1983, 254.
3. Schiewe 1998, 154–75; Sauter 2000, 167–200.

their social and political implications must be addressed. Was Yaghmā acting against an ideological – patriotic, anti-clerical – background? Or was he just a haphazard precursor who happened to trigger later, ideologically motivated purist positions? In other words, are purist activities necessarily to be located within a secular, religiously dissident, or anti-clerical setting, or can language purism also occur without ideological or political implications? Discussing these issues will help locate a language professional like Yaghmā more precisely within the discourse of purism.

Yaghmā left an extensive collection of letters, which occasionally comment on the question of pure Persian. His approach to language purism emerges even more clearly when juxtaposed with the texts of his younger contemporaries Jalāl al-Din Mirzā and Farhād Mirzā.

Rahim Abu l-Hasan Yaghmā-ye Jandaqi

Poets of the early Qajar period are not part of the literary canon in Iran today. Only a few are generally known by name, including the prominent court poet Habibollāh Qā'āni (1223–1270/1808–1854), and Yaghmā.[4] His name is associated with seemingly contradictory genres such as obscene invective poetry on the one hand and religious elegies sung at Moharram processions and *taʿziyeh* (Shiite passion play) performances on the other. Moreover, as mentioned before, the name Yaghmā often comes up in the context of early purist activities, that is, writing in "pure Persian" (today generally referred to as *fārsi-ye/pārsi-ye sareh*).

Yaghmā was born as Rahim in Khur on the western fringes of the Dasht-e Kavir in the Jandaq-Biābānak district. According to his great-grandson, the literary figure, scholar, and journalist Habib Yaghmā'i, he stood out in his childhood for his refined use of language.[5] Coming from a non-intellectual background, he nevertheless trained as a secretary, a profession that was often passed down through the generations in established families, but also, as in Yaghmā's case, provided an opportunity for social advancement. Like other secretaries, Yaghmā excelled in poetry. The high standards of general education, literary learning, and language mastery that were required to compose official correspondence closely conjoined the two professional fields in pre-modern times.[6] Initially using Majnun as nom de plume, he changed it into Yaghmā ("pillage") after having been sentenced to the bastinado, expropriated, and stripped of

---

4. Āryanpur 1357/1978, 1:109–27; Khātami 1373/1994, 2:342–48; Rypka 1968, 328–34.
5. Yaghmā'i 1924, 486.
6. Hanaway 2012.

all offices as a result of an intrigue against him. In contemporary anthologies, Yaghmā is described as an independent nonconformist with Sufi inclinations.[7]

His professional life took Yaghmā to Kashan, Tehran, Qom, and Isfahan. However, he kept his landed property in Khur, to which he returned at the end of his life. From the first two of his three marriages Yaghmā left three daughters and four sons, who formed the nucleus for further generations of literati and intellectuals. Widely known is the aforementioned Habib Yaghmā'i, who referred to his famous ancestor with the foundation of the journal *Yaghmā*.[8]

Persian Language Purism

According to a broad definition, language purism is understood as "the opening and closure of sources for enrichment. [...] Purism is the opening of the native sources and closure of the non-native sources."[9] Language purism operates primarily in the lexicon with the main objective being to remove components defined as foreign from a language. Such endeavors have occurred worldwide in various socio-political constellations. They receive particular impetus in periods of crisis and transition and serve to delimit, constitute and consolidate cultural and political identity.[10]

The discourse on language "purification" in Iran that arose in the context of the social upheaval and political unrest resulting from the confrontation with the European powers also fits into this framework. More widespread, however, was the demand for a generally comprehensible language as opposed to the ornate language that dominated parts of written prose. A new secular elite in the 19th century strove to create a "new amalgam" of European and native cultures that would form the basis for a viable, "stable self-definition" of society.[11] Along with the historical focus on pre-Islamic grandeur and the "Aryan myth" which extended theories of language into a racial construct,[12] the ideal of a plain and comprehensible written idiom played a significant role in shaping this self-definition:

7. Qājār 1346/1968, 1:264–67; Divān-Begi Shirāzi 1364–1366/1985–1987, 3:2121–27; Hedāyat 1336–1340/1957–1961, 6:1204–9.

8. He was the son of the daughter of Yaghmā's eldest son, Esmaʿil Honar, and his wife Montakhab al-Sādāt Āl-e Dā'ud. With thirty volumes (1327–1357/1948–1978), *Yaghmā* was a long-lived scholarly journal by Iranian standards.

9. Annamalai 1979, 36, cited in Jernudd 1989, 4. For a general overview, see Jernudd and Shapiro 1989; for language purism in Iran (focusing on the 20th century), see Karimi-Hakkak 1989; Kia 1998; Jazayery 1983; Banani 1981. On the purism debate in the Ottoman Empire, see Foy 1998.

10. Jernudd 1989, 3.

11. Karimi-Hakkak 1989, 84.

12. Schwartz 2020, 9; for a detailed study on the making of the "Aryan myth" see Motadel 2014.

> [...] the secular intellectuals endeavored to move toward a notion of
> language "reform" as the pursuit of simplicity, direct expression, and
> naturalness which, they argued, characterized both the speech of the
> man in the street as well as that of the great poets and prose-stylists of
> a glorious past.[13]

The pursuit of simplicity had also characterized the classicist poetic movement
of "literary return" (*bāz-gasht*) beginning in the mid-eighteenth century, which
drew on classical poetry of the tenth–fifteenth centuries as stylistic models and
later expanded to prose writing.[14]

In the late nineteenth and early twentieth centuries, the call for simplification of the written language that even the proverbial "man in the street"
should understand also resonated with a purist tone, for incomprehensibility
was blamed on the excessive use of Arabic elements in Persian. In his study
Sabk-shenasi (Stylistics), Mohammad Taqi Bahār (1886–1951) bases his evolutionary concept of Persian prose literature on the statistical increase in the adopted Arabic lexicon through history.[15] Ahmad Karimi-Hakkak considers the
establishment of the Shia and the immigration of Arab theologians to Iran in
the Safavid period as responsible for an increasingly Arabicized language as the
Shiite confession became an Iranian identity marker as distinct from the neighboring empires and the Arabic language represented both authenticity and the
exclusivity of theological learning.[16]

The argument merges Arabicized Persian, religion, ornate style, and linguistic complexity into a conglomerate whose antithesis – secularization, "purification" of Persian from Arabic elements, plain and straightforward language
– contains essential factors of the nation-building program. As plausible as this
line of reasoning may seem, it is nevertheless necessary to isolate its individual
components in order to examine whether similar phenomena or simultaneities
also substantiate causal relations.

Language purist approaches in the nineteenth century predominantly
turned against Arabic vocabulary in Persian: "[...] the highly Arabicized literary
dialects [...] became the bête noire of the purists."[17] Adoptions from European
languages only became relevant in the twentieth century. But the postulated
antagonism of "plain Persian" and "complicated Arabic" is a construction that
does not do justice to the manifold functional domains of languages. Yaghmā's

13. Karimi-Hakkak 1989, 87; see also Parsinejad 2021, 490–493.
14. Hanaway 1989.
15. Bahār 1349/1970, 1:283–89 (*goftār-e* 9–1).
16. For the entire argumentation see Karimi-Hakkak 1989, 83–87.
17. Perry 1985, 296.

use of pure Persian proves that Persification of lexicon and clarity of expression do not necessarily go hand in hand.

In his pure Persian writings and the avoidance of Arabic vocabulary, Yaghmā did not merely target "overarabicized diction"[18] with long Arabic quotations, but also eliminated common Persian words of Arabic origin. He did not reform an incomprehensible Arabicized style for the sake of greater intelligibility and with the intention to simplify communication, but rather substituted established Arabic words with Persian expressions that were not in common use in his time with no net increase in simplicity.[19]

Yaghmā's Proficiency in Arabic

Yaghmā wrote numerous letters in pure Persian and occasionally reflected on this experiment in language and style. His letters, however, do not reveal what might have prompted him to engage in this kind of linguistic creativity. Some scholars attribute Yaghmā's interest in Persian purism to his often-attested deficiencies in Arabic. A contemporary secondary source that comments on this subject is Divan-Begi Shirāzi's *tazkereh Hadiqat al-sho'arā*. The entry on Yaghmā mentions his competence in "ancient Persian" and his incompetence in Arabic side by side, but without explicitly connecting the two:

خلاصه در قواعد و رسوم شاعری و وضع و وزن انواع شعر خیلی با خبر و از لغات قدیمه و غیر مِصطلحهٔ فرس بی‌نهایت مستحضر. چنانچه رسایل و مکاتیب چند که ملتزماً به فارسی باستانی نوشته و هیچ کلمهٔ خارج از آن زبان در آن نیاورده در دیوانش مسطور است. عربیتش قدری کم، اما قوتَ طبعش در سراییدن اشعار لطیف زیاد بود.[20]

He is knowledgeable in prosody and immensely versed in ancient, unfamiliar Persian words. He has composed writings and correspondence in ancient Persian without using any foreign word. His knowledge of Arabic was poor but he had a great talent for composing fine poetry.

Literary histories written in the twentieth century even claim that he had a strong dislike for the Arabic language. For example, Rypka states that:

18. Karimi-Hakkak 1989, 85.

19. The edition of Yaghmā's works includes an 18-page glossary of uncommon words at the end of the second volume: Yaghmā-ye Jandaqi 1362/1983, 2:385–403. According to the editor's note, the glossary "explains words from the Jandaq-Biyābānak dialect, some difficult idioms, and rare pure Persian expressions" (384).

20. Divān-Begi Shirāzi 1364–1366/1985–1987, 3:2121.

[i]t was probably due to his mediocre education that Yaghmā, unlike
other important poets, was not well acquainted with Arabic. He
even showed a distinct aversion to this language and maintained that
Persian could very well manage without it.[21]

In Āryanpur's literary history we find the same argument in a combination of
incompetence and dislike:

یغما از زبان عربی بیزار بوده [...] شاید علت این امر آن باشد که وی
تحصیلات عمیق نکرده و به رموز دستور زبان و ادبیات عرب به حد کمال آشنا
نبوده است.[22]

Yaghmā detested Arabic [...] Perhaps the reason is that he had not received a profound education and was not fully versed in the complexities of Arabic grammar and literature.

This assessment is further shared by Eqbāl Yaghmā'i and Nasrollāh Nuh in their
biographical essays on Yaghmā dating from 1977.[23] Khātami also takes up this
point: "It seems that Yaghmā disliked Arabic" yet he differs from other literary
historians in terms of Arabic language competence:

اگرچه بعضی گفته اند این حالت به خاطر مسلط نبودن یغما به زبان عربی بوده
است، اما این مطلب با توجه به منشأتی که با نام «مکاتیب مرکب» شهرت یافته و
یغما در آنها از کلمات و اصطلاحات عربی استفاده کرده است، نقض می شود،
زیرا شیوهٔ کار او در مکاتیب مرکب حکایت از تبحر او در زبان عربی دارد.[24]

Although some [people] have argued that [the eradication of Arabic
words in his writings] was due to Yaghmā's lack of proficiency in
Arabic, the letters known as composite writings in which he employs
Arabic words and phrases, prove otherwise. For the way he works in
these writings reveals his proficiency in Arabic.

In Yaghmā's correspondence itself, there are a few statements about his sparse
knowledge of Arabic. "Alas, I do not know Arabic" (*darighā keh ʿarabi na-
dānam*),[25] he states in one letter, and to his friend Hājji Mohammad Esmāʿil
Tehrāni he addresses an orthographic problem in a marginal note: "I do not
know whether I spelled *salavāt Allāh ʿalayhumā* correctly or not, salvation from

21. Rypka 1968, 334.
22. Āryanpur 1357/1978, 1:114.
23. Yaghmā'i 1356/1977, 397; Nuh 1356/1977, 692.
24. Khātami 1373/1994, 2:345.
25. Yaghmā-ye Jandaqi 1362/1983, 2:126.

ignorance (*amān az bi-savādi*)!"[26] Yaghmā generally settles for vocabulary of
Arabic origin widely used in Persian. Longer Arabic phrases do not occur, and
the only Arabic sentence in the correspondence is a hadith quotation:

انت المولا و انا العبد و هل يرحم العبد الا المولا[27]

> You are the master and I am the slave, and [who] forgives the slave but
> the master?

In practice, Yaghmā is not guided by stylistic preferences or dislikes, but by professional requirements. The linguistic register he chooses is often adapted to the
addressee. For example, a letter to a cleric begins with increased frequency of
Arabic vocabulary including religious connotations:

جناب قبله حاجات و کعبه مناجات راکه به فر سیادت و فضل کفایت محمود
دولت و دین است و مرجع سبحه و نگین زحمت میدهم.[28]

> I cause inconvenience to you, Excellency, *qibla* of wishes and Kaaba
> of prayers, who is praised for his glorious magnificence [*siyādat*, or
> relationship to the Prophet] and outstanding abilities by both state
> and religion, and who is the reference point of prayer beads and seal.

Eventually, it is pointless to speculate about Yaghmā's knowledge of Arabic,
since any shortcomings in this field do not explain the intellectual effort he put
into substituting Persian for Arabic words.

Pure Persian in Yaghmā's Prose

That Yaghmā was interested in language history and engaged in lexicological
research is evident from the fact that he copied the Persian dictionary *Borhān-e
qāte'*, the influential reference work of Indo-Persian lexicography from the
seventeenth century, and supplemented it with his own entries. Furthermore,
under his guidance and with his support his son Ahmad Safā'i worked on a dictionary that contained only genuine Persian vocabulary.[29] In addition to letters,
other pure Persian prose pieces are included in the modern edition of Yaghmā's
collected works: the transposition of two stories from the *Zinat al-majāles* into
pure Persian, a long dream account, reflections on munificence, a story admon-

---

26. Yaghmā-ye Jandaqi 1362/1983, 2:192.

27. Yaghmā-ye Jandaqi 1362/1983, 2:280. For the Imamite hadith, see Majlesi 1983, 91:110.

28. Yaghmā-ye Jandaqi 1362/1983, 2:237. Another letter with a high frequency of Arabic words is
cited in Oskuee 1393/2014, 140–41.

29. Āl-e Dā'ud 1367/1988, 50. A specimen of this hitherto unedited dictionary is kept in Khur.

ishing people to avoid disputes, and a story about local childbirth customs in Biyābānak.[30] Yaghmā uses various terms to refer to the persified style. At times he calls it "Pārsi," "Pahlavi," or "Dari": *nāmeh-ye pahlavi pardākht bar farhang-e pārsi, neveshtehhā-ye pārsi-negār, farhang-e dari, negāreshhā-ye pahlavi.*[31]

But how did Yaghmā employ pure Persian in his professional and private practice? In the first edition of his works, the lithograph *Kolliyāt-e Yaghmā-ye Jandaqi* from 1283/1866–67, the writings without Arabic vocabulary amount to over seventy percent (137 out of 190 pieces).[32] The modern edition of Yaghmā's correspondence (*Majmu'eh-ye Āsār*, vol. 2) also includes writings from other manuscripts (part 2) and previously unpublished autographs (part 3). In these texts the ratio of pure Persian to non-purist "composite" texts is only 22:88 and 19:53 respectively.

The lithograph edition is based on a collection of works (poetry and prose) assembled by a friend, the above-mentioned bookseller Hājji Mohammad Esmā'il Tehrāni. At times, Yaghmā deplored his friend's uncontrollable passion for collecting his texts. He complained that Tehrāni was amassing all sorts of writings bearing Yaghmā's name, "stealing them by means of money, lamentation, and force (*bā zar-o zāri-o zur*), and without testifying to their authenticity." But he also admits that his friend is acting "out of kindness and sympathy, not impudence and malevolence (*az sar-e mehrbāni-o del-suzi na pardeh-dari va kin-tuzi*)."[33] In a letter to Tehrāni himself, however, Yaghmā explicitly instructs him to collect his correspondence:

[...] از من تا گور دمی دو بیش نمانده. خواهشمندم از این پس هر گونه نامه مرا خواه پارسی پیکر و شیوا، خواه بر هنجار دیگر و نازیبا بی‌کاست و فزود بدان نگارش های پهلوی گوهر در فزائی.[34]

[...] I am only two breaths from my grave. From now on, please collect
all my letters, whether written in pure Persian and eloquent or in
another style and unattractive and add them to the essential Persian
writings without any modification.

Tehrāni's son was the court physician Mirzā 'Abd al-Bāqi Tabib,[35] who, as a

---

30. *Zinat al-majāles* is a historical work by the Safavid author Majd al-Din Mohammad al-Hoseyni al-Hā'eri "Majdi", see Yaghmā-ye Jandaqi 1362/1983, 2:376. Yaghmā-ye Jandaqi 1362/1983, vol. 2, nos. 104 and 195 (stories); no. 171 (dream account); no. 201 (munificence); no. 276 (admontion); no. 284 (local customs).

31. Yaghmā-ye Jandaqi 1362/1983, 2:42, 51, 74, 206.

32. Yaghmā-ye Jandaqi 1283/1866.

33. Yaghmā-ye Jandaqi 1362/1983, 2:117.

34. Yaghmā-ye Jandaqi 1362/1983, 2:206.

35. Bāmdād 1371/1992, 2:235–36.

member of the learned establishment, promoted the printing of Yaghmā's works that his father had compiled. The official editor of the lithographed *Kolliyāt* was the minister of science ʿAliqoli Mirzā Eʿtezād al-Saltaneh (d. 1298/1880), an uncle of Nāser al-Din Shah who, with his broad range of functions, served as a sort of ministerial jack-of-all-trades in the field of new technologies and media. He was responsible, among other things, for the supervision of printing houses in Tehran and the provinces,[36] and hence also for the selection of works to be published. Given the high ratio of pure Persian writings in the lithograph, one can imagine – and perhaps deduce from Yaghmā's words to his collector – that Tehrāni aimed primarily at collecting the novel, Persianized writings, and this focus may also have played a role in the selection of the volume for print. Looking at the modern edition, however, the pure Persian pieces account for only slightly more than half of the prose writings (178 out of 338 writings). Hence, based on the assumption that the modern edition contains a larger or representative part of Yaghmā's oeuvre the ratio of pure Persian and composite writings is fairly balanced, which proves that he drew on various linguistic registers as required.

Writing in "Pure Persian" as a Trained Skill

Scattered comments in the correspondence betray Yaghmā's undeniable interest in an experimental and innovative approach to Persian. For example, he refers to a letter sent to him for evaluation by a certain Mirzā Hasan as a "trial in the know-how of Dari writing (*āzmun bar farhang-e dari-negār*)."[37] Moreover, he was not isolated or marginal in his linguistic ventures, but rather an active member of a broader intellectual movement. "A large group of writers in Qazvin, Reyy, and Isfahan have firmly established themselves in this style of writing," he writes to his son Ahmad Safāʾi and continues: "I think in your third and fourth letters you should also follow the movement of the friends and wordsmiths writing in pure Persian."[38] The trend of purist writing had obviously spread in literary circles.

Yaghmā instructed several disciples in employing the new style, particularly his sons: "My son Dastān is composing Persian writings, and every morning he asks me for recommendations on a dexterous (*sabok-dast*) style."[39] Yaghmā seems to have considered his eldest son Esmaʿil Honar the most gifted of his offspring since he treats him as his equal in matters of language. For instance, he

36. Bāmdād 1371/1992, 2:442–48; Amanat 1998.
37. Yaghmā-ye Jandaqi 1362/1983, 2:100.
38. Yaghmā-ye Jandaqi 1362/1983, 2:85.
39. Yaghmā-ye Jandaqi 1362/1983, 2:51. Ebrāhim Dastān was Yaghmā's third son.

asks Esmaʿil to revise his letters, and in doing so he discloses some of his stylistic principles.

اسمعیل خود دانی از دراز درائی گریزانم [...] در این سه نگاشته آن فزایش گفتار از دلتنگی و جنبش خشم خاست، پهنهٔ بیغاره فراخی گرفت و خامهٔ بی خواسته من ساز گستاخی انگیخت. اگرت دست و دلی هست در هر سه از در دید نگاهی کن و هر مایه که دانی و توانی کوتاه نمای تا آنان از خواندن خسته نیفتند و زبان نکوهش گران نیز بر من بسته ماند.[40]

Esmaʿil, you know that I flee from verbosity [...] These three writings have grown too lengthy out of grievance and anger, insults have spread and my pen, which is devoid of will power, behaved impudently. If possible, check all three and shorten them wherever you can, so that they [the addressees] will not tire of reading and I will not be overwhelmed with reproaches.

The focus here is not on discussing isolated lexical units; persification is rather presented in a larger communicative context. Yaghmā's rejection of verbosity echoes the classicist approach of the *bāz-gasht* poets, but his advocacy for short writing should not be mistaken for the intention to achieve general comprehensibility. Yaghmā's focuses on the aesthetics of language and their particular effects, and not on barrier-free communication. The text must meet rhetorical standards and satisfy the reader. Writing to an unnamed disciple, he states:

بازگشت و نگاهی سرسری در این نگارش پارسی گزارش کردم، چندان ناهموار و پیچیده و سبکسار و نسنجیده نیست. زنهار هنگام نگارندگی پاس هوش‌آور و سراپا چشم و گوش زی، تا آنجا که پیوسته سزاست گسسته نیفتد و جائی که گسسته روا پیوسته نگردد. دیده خوانندگان بیشتر بدین تازه روش نودیدار است [...][41]

I have skimmed this pure Persian piece, and it is not clumsy or complicated, nor is it lightweight or unreasonable. Careful! When you are writing, let your mind be alert and keep your eyes and ears open, so that wherever a connection is appropriate, let it not be separate, and wherever things should be kept separate, they are not connected. To the eye of most readers this new method is unfamiliar [...]

In the letters dealing with pure Persian, Yaghmā appears as an authority and reference point for a group of secretaries and poets who discussed the new lexical

40. Yaghmā-ye Jandaqi 1362/1983, 2:19–20.
41. Yaghmā-ye Jandaqi 1362/1983, 2:74.

and stylistic concept and practiced its implementation at a professional level.[42] The question remains, however, whether in their case the linguistic phenomenon arose already from the ideological foundation that was later to forge a close connection with language purism.

"Pure Persian" as Ideology and Entertainment: Jalāl al-Din Mirzā and Farhād Mirzā

In the case of Yaghmā's younger contemporary, the Qajar prince Jalāl al-Din Mirzā (1242–1289/1826–1872), language purism fits into an overall conception of history. His chronicle *Nāmeh-ye Khosravān* ("Book of Kings"), written in pure Persian, presents a coherent narrative of Iranian history from its mythical beginnings to the fall of the Zand dynasty and identifies the Arab conquest and Turkish and Mongol rule as the main forces behind Iran's decline.[43] Inspired by European concepts, he is an early pioneer of a dichotomous view of Iranian history divided into pre-Islamic periods of political and cultural self-determination and Islamic periods under foreign rule,[44] which informs the nationalist reconstruction of the past. By employing pure Persian and at the same time aiming at general comprehensibility, he emphasizes his historical message along with a didactic approach.

Jalāl al-Din Mirzā expressed his ideas in the correspondence with the Azerbaijani playwright Mirzā Fath 'Ali Ākhundzādeh (1812–1878), a kindred spirit to whom he sent his work for review.

چون بنده به اندیشهٔ این افتادم که زبان نیاگان ما که چون دیگر دانشهامان به تاراج تازیان رفته و اکنون جز نامی ازو نمانده، به زبانی [ساده] بگویم و به روش چیز نویسی فرنگیان که اکنون دانایان روی زمینند نامهٔ بنگارم که شاید مردمان زاد و بوم‌را سودی بخشد، سزاوارتر از داستان پادشاهان پارسی که با همه بزرگواری نامشان از دست‌درازی تازیان از میان رفته، ندیدم.[45]

Since it occurred to me that the language of our ancestors, as well as all other knowledge of ours, was stolen by the Arabs, and that in the meantime nothing but its name has remained, I wish to speak in

---

42. For more examples of Yaghmā's didactic approach and his role in the pure Persian movement of his time see Oskuee 1393/2014, 138–39. I became aware of this article only after completing this paper. Taking a different approach, with a focus on a detailed analysis of linguistic and stylistic procedures in Yaghmā's pure Persian letters, Oskuee comes to similar conclusions.

43. Amanat 1999; Bāmdād 1371/1992, 1:254–55; Khātami 1373/1994, 2:345; Kia 1998, 11–12.

44. Kia 1998, 10.

45. Letter to Mirzā Fath 'Ali Ākhundzādeh, see Ākhundzādeh 1963, 373 and Amanat 1999, 14–15 (*sādeh* added by Amanat).

simple language, and in the manner of the Europeans, who are now
the most knowledgeable on earth, and to write a book which may be
useful to the people of our native land. And to this end I find nothing
more appropriate than telling the story of the Persian kings whose
names, despite their glory and magnificence, have been obliterated
due to the Arab incursions.

The correspondence with Ākhundzādeh also addresses the history of the Zo-
roastrians, who were considered the preservers of an original and genuine Iranian civilization by the pioneers of national awakening.[46] Abbas Amanat assumes that Jalāl al-Din Mirzā had Zoroastrian proclivities and was influenced
by the writings of the neo-Zoroastrian movement headed by Āzar Keyvān (d.
between 1609 and 1618), especially the prophetic *Dasātir*, the most important
reference work of this movement from the time of the Mughal ruler Akbar (r.
1556–1605).[47] Written in an artificial language using Sanskrit, Hindi, Avestan,
Persian, and Arabic components, *Dasātir* includes a commentary in an invented
"pure Persian" devoid of Arabic words. This source fed later Persian dictionaries,
most of which were produced in India in the seventeenth century, including
the well-known *Borhān-e qāte'* copied and extended by Yaghmā. Iranian critics voiced their indignation with regard to the transmission of fabricated vocabulary with dubious etymologies.[48] Yaghmā, however, although he worked
extensively with the dictionary, used but little fake or archaic vocabulary in his
writings.[49]

Yaghmā knew the young prince Jalāl al-Din Mirzā, whose name is mentioned in his correspondence,[50] but not with regard to the topic of pure Persian.
It was probably too early – when Yaghmā died in 1859, the prince was only
thirty-two years old. The *Nāmeh-ye Khosravān* was published a decade later
between 1868/9 and 1871/2 (in three volumes) while the prince's correspondence with Ākhundzādeh dates from 1870/1. Among other sources, Yaghmā
may have provided linguistic inspiration for Jalāl al-Din Mirzā's work. The two
authors, however, apply pure Persian in completely different ways: as we have
seen, Yaghmā uses persified diction while exerting his entire administrative pro-

---

46. Algar 1969, 116–30; Algar 1984.
47. Amanat 1999, 36; Amanat and Vejdani 2008.
48. Borhān-e Tabrizi 1330–1342/1951–1963, introduction with an article by Ebrāhim Pur-e
Dā'ud, "Dasātir," 1:52–59; Bahār 1349/1970, 3:291; Corbin 1987, with a critical addendum regarding
Dasātir by the editors of the *Encyclopaedia Iranica*; Mojtaba'i 1994. On *Borhān-e qāte'* and its use by
poets and language purists in the 19th century see Tavakoli-Targhi 2001, 106.
49. Oskuee 1393/2014, 141.
50. Yaghmā-ye Jandaqi 1362/1983, 2:193 and 212.

fessionalism. He promotes concise expression but general comprehensibility is not on his agenda. Jalāl al-Din Mirzā, on the other hand, uses language with reference to the European model as an uncomplicated means of communication in order to spread his ideas, although with questionable success. The Azerbaijani educator and writer Mirzā ʿAbd al-Rahim Talebof (ca. 1834–1911) already objected that in a country like Iran with a high illiteracy rate, language purification was pointless and absurd.[51] In our context, however, the underlying purpose for practicing the persified style is more interesting than the actual effect.

Farhād Mirzā Moʿtamad al-Dowleh (1233–1305/1818–1888), a younger brother to Mohammad Shah, was yet another contemporary who left behind a volume of correspondence.[52] The forty-eight letters included in the published volume mainly date from the decade 1863–73 and feature mostly prominent addressees. Farhād Mirzā's name does not occur in the Yaghmā correspondence but the prince included an anecdote about Yaghmā in his anthology *Ketāb-e Zanbil*.[53] In the introduction to his collection of letters Farhād Mirzā outlines a cheerful, convivial background for his writing in pure Persian.

در آن میان یکی از سخن‌سرایان، که در سخن پایهٔ بلند و مایهٔ ارجمند داشت، بر زبان آورد که در پارسی نامه نوشتن که سخنان تازی آلوده نباشد بسی دشوار و فزون از اندازه دشوار است، چه بیشتر سخنان هنگام نوشتن و گفتار به تازی آمیخته و مُشک به لادن بیخته شده است.

چون این سخنان را از آن یار آموزگار [...] شنیدم، به خود نپسندیدم که آن یار دمساز از این آرزو باز ماند [...][54]

[In a meeting among friends] an eloquent person who was highly respected for his quality of speech, said: "Writing letters in Persian that are not polluted with Arabic words is difficult beyond measure. After all, the words in written and spoken language are mixed with Arabic, just as musk is interspersed with ladanum." When I heard these words from the erudite [...] friend [...], I did not like to see him deprived of the fulfilment of his heart's desire [...]

Although Arabic here is given a derogatory comment, only the first letter of the collection meets the standards of pure Persian. In the remaining letters, Arabic vocabulary is not avoided; in fact, there are pieces that abound in Arabic quotations and phrases (for example, nos. 3–5, 7). In Farhād Mirzā's case, the

---

51. Kia 1998, 15.
52. Eslami 1999.
53. Āl-e Dāʾud 1367/1988, 60.
54. Farhād Mirzā 1369/1990, 10.

impression prevails that persification was an intellectual entertainment rather than a political agenda, a feat in the same vein as the second piece in the collection: a letter to Nāser al-Din Shah presenting three stories, each one without using the letters *alef*, *be*, and *te* respectively.[55] In other words, language purism appears here on the level of a witty parlor game to prove the author's subtlety and linguistic proficiency.

YAGHMĀ IN THE DISCOURSE OF PERSIAN LANGUAGE PURISM

Jalāl al-Din Mirzā's *Nāmeh-ye Khosravān* and his related correspondence with Ākhundzādeh show the integration of purism, simplification of language for the sake of general comprehensibility, and emancipatory ideology. It can be understood as the starting point of an continuous discourse that brought forth a language reformer like Ahmad Kasravi (1890–1946), and the language planning measures of the Pahlavi era.[56] Immediate reactions to the *Nāmeh-ye Khosravān* among protagonists of literary modernization ranged from wholehearted approval (Ākhundzādeh), to support of its cultural-historical but not linguistic concept (Mirzā Āqā Khān Kermāni, 1851–1896), to outright rejection ('Abd al-Rahim Talebof, 1838–1909).[57] Bahār also considered the fabrication of pure Persian rather a nuisance for the reader.[58]

Yaghmā is often referred to as an early representative of the purification movement and "forerunner" of the later purists. Jan Rypka's *History of Iranian Literature*, for example, states:

> But what is more important is that he [Yaghmā] avoided Arabic
> expressions even when writing in normal language, being thus a
> predecessor of the purists who later on, borne by a powerful wave of
> nationalism, attempted to effect a too radical purging of the Persian
> language [...][59]

Mehrdad Kia refers to a group of precursors at the time of Mohammad Shah who attempted to create a de-Arabicized form of Persian and continues: "Poets such as the anti-Islamic and anti-clerical poet Yaghmā [...] tried to write in a simplified Persian free from borrowed Arabic words." Jalāl al-Din Mirzā, it is said here, continued this tradition.[60] This comment places Yaghmā not only

---

55. Farhād Mirzā 1369/1990, 33–37.
56. Amanat 1999; Kia 1998; Banani 1981. Contrary to Kasravi, Jalāl al-Din Mirzā did not engage in coining neologisms: Amanat and Vejdani 2008.
57. Kia 1998, 11–15.
58. Bahār 1349/1970, 3:292.
59. Rypka 1968, 334.
60. Kia 1998, 31, n. 8.

linguistically but also ideologically at the beginning of a direct line of tradition leading to the later purists. By linking a specific linguistic style to the attributes "anti-Islamic" and "anti-clerical," it is assumed that Yaghmā shared Jalāl al-Din Mirzā's dichotomous conception of history.

Yaghmā's correspondence, however, proves neither an anti-Islamic nor a generally anti-clerical attitude. The letters identify several addressees as clerics of varying ranks, from the local mullahs of his native region (specified, for example, as Khuri, Ardakāni, or Biyābānaki)[61] to distinguished religious scholars. They document a broad range of contacts – friendly ties and strained relationships, discussions of family problems as well as everyday issues and business transactions. Particularly close was his connection to the prominent cleric Mollā Ahmad Narāqi (d. 1245/1829–30). Yaghmā was a secretary at Mollā Ahmad's *fatwā* court in Kashan, married a relative of his, and named his son Ahmad Safā'i after him.[62] Several anecdotes bear witness to their friendship and Mollā Ahmad saved Yaghmā from being punished after the Emām Jom'eh of Kashan had accused him of alcohol consumption.[63]

As already mentioned, Yaghmā also makes no effort to use simple language.[64] To give an example, I quote the opening passage from a letter in pure Persian "To a notable," which employs rhetoric devices typical of Yaghmā's letters to distinguished figures. With the following words, he deplores the fact that he did not find the addressee at home when he passed by his house for a visit:

روز گذشته پرسش روزگار گرامی را بدان فرخ کاخ و فرخنده کوی فرا رفتم.
چه کوی و کدام کاخ، دور از دیدار همایون، لانه درد و شکنج و کاشانه تیمار
و رنج، چرخ بی خورشید و کاخ بی نگار، تخت بی جمشید و شاخ بی بهار،
دادم از دل بر خاست و دود از سر، آبم از دیده ریخت و خون از جگر، دل تپیدن
گرفت و رنگ پریدن، خرد شیوائی انگیخت و شکیب رسوائی، ناله چرخ پیما
گشت و اشک زمین فرسا، لب خوشیدن آورد و خون جوشیدن، چندان نماند که
تن بدرود جان آرد و روان از پیکر بر کران پوید [...] [65]

Yesterday, in order to inquire about your worthy condition, I went
to your joyous palace, to that blessed quarter. But what quarter, what
palace? Far from the auspicious meeting, a nest of pain and anguish,
a home of sorrow and grief, a heavenly sphere without sun, a palace

61. Yaghmā-ye Jandaqi 1362/1983, 2, letters nos. 20, 62, 239.

62. Yaghmā's son named after Mollā Ahmad: Āl-e Dā'ud 1367/1988, 66. On Mollā Ahmad Narāqi see Dabashi 1989, and Arjomand 2005.

63. Āl-e Dā'ud 1367/1988, 29 and 62; Yaghmā'i 1344/1965, 614–615; Divān-Begi Shirāzi 1364–1366/1985–1987,2122.

64. Amanat refers to the difference between Yaghmā and Jalāl al-Din Mirzā, see Amanat 1999, 37.

65. Yaghmā-ye Jandaqi, 1362/1983, 2:144.

without a beloved, a throne without Jamshid, a branch without
spring. A cry for help rose from my heart and smoke from my head
[that is, I was out of my mind RHH], water poured from my eyes and
blood from my liver, my heart began to pound and my face turned
pale, my mind let insanity rise and patience caused disgrace, my
laments traversed the heavenly spheres. My tears eroded the earth,
my lips began to parch and my blood started to boil; and it did not
take much for the body to separate from the soul and for the spirit to
hurriedly depart from the body.

The passage is written in plain syntax, but it is a metaphor-laden, hyperbolic piece in which even a cursory examination brings to light a whole range of
rhetorical figures, such as alliteration and internal rhyme, antitheses (*tazādd*),
parallelisms, multiple types of paronomasia (*tajnis*); rhetorical revocation and
self-correction (*rojuʿ*) as well as the use of terms from the same sphere (*morāʿāt
al-nazir*). The rhetoric remains conventional, only Yaghmā works with different
lexis and thus creates his individual style. Stylistic innovation is particularly evident in composites formed with rhyme, alliteration, and meter.[66] In the dupli-
cation of terms which traditionally combine a Persian and an Arabic term (for
example, *bakht-o dowlat* "happiness")[67] he employs two words of Persian origin,
such as "*lāneh-ye dard-o shekanj va kāshāneh-ye timār-o ranj*," in the citation
above. According to Narges Oskuee, the rhymed prose (*nasr-e mosajjaʿ*) resulting from such stylistic creativity in pure Persian makes Yaghmā's texts difficult
tounderstand.[68]

Yaghmā employs his professional tools of various linguistic registers to en-
code his relation to the respective addressees. Needless to say, the letters to his
sons cannot be compared with the one quoted above. Here, Yaghmā indeed
maintains a direct style, which, however, should not be confused with a basic
tendency of simplification in order to appeal to a wide audience.

The constituents of language purism can be perceived as multiple facets
of a single phenomenon, but these facets are embedded in diverse cultural and
political contexts. To argue for a closed complex consisting of language purism, simplification, general intelligibility, religious dissidence or anti-clericalism, and modernization is, to say the least, an anachronistic misunderstanding
that considers the phenomenon as congruent with the nationalist discourse of

66. For a detailed linguistic analysis see Oskuee 1393/2014, 141–43.
67. Fragner 1999, 31.
68. Oskuee 1393/2014, 143.

the activists involved ("Purism was mostly taken to be what the purists and an-ti-purists themselves thought and claimed it to be"[69]).

Jalāl al-Din Mirzā's linguistic practice in the *Nāmeh-ye Khosravān*, his theo-retical as well as historical and political reflections, form an integral composite, termed "ideological purism" by the Czech linguist Jiří Neustupný.[70] Following Neustupný's dictum, Arabic elements in Persian can be called symbols of "un-desirable" historical relations and social realities,[71] and against this backdrop be-come ideologically charged. By implication, therefore, their elimination would change social realities and create new political conditions. In contrast, the ideo-logical connotation remains weak in the case of Farhād Mirzā, who practiced language purism only in the laboratory of one isolated letter.

In Yaghmā's writings we look in vain for patriotic retrospection or for the enlightened impetus to general comprehensibility. Since Divān-Begi Shirāzi's *Hadiqat al-sho'arā*, the story of Yaghmā's disapproval of Arabic has been hand-ed down, but while Yaghmā himself comments in general terms on his lack of Arabic education, he does not discuss the role of Arabic elements in Persian, nor is there any explicit criticism of the prevailing stylistic norms except for the rejection of prolixity. Yaghmā, as a secretary, was committed to a professional ethos that accorded utmost importance to the use of language, and his com-ments on language echo this spirit. Although he wanted to spread pure Per-sian through teaching, his stylistic and linguistic innovations remain within the scope of his professional skills. Anchored in poetic and secretarial circles, his practice of pure Persian appears to be an intellectual innovation independent of ideological agenda.

Even if Yaghmā gives the impression of a nonconformist who shuns prox-imity to power, he nevertheless skilfully employs refined language, tradition-ally used as an instrument of power. He handles the medium of language with unquestioned exclusivity (as opposed to inclusive common parlance), and a professional awareness of quality resonates in Yaghmā's variant of pure Persian. Juxtaposing him with Jalāl al-Din Mirzā and his *Nāmeh-ye Khosravān*, the short period of just over a decade between Yaghmā's death and the publication of Jalāl al-Din Mirzā's history may perhaps account for the different ways of working with *fārsi-ye sareh*. In my view, the gap between Yaghmā's rhetorical approach and Jalāl al-Din Mirzā's embedding language in political concepts reflects not

---

69. Neustupný 1989, 220.

70. "Ideological purism [is] defined by the political aims of the idiom and the discourse correction processes involved [...]" Neustupný 1989, 212.

71. On foreign elements as "symbols of undesirable relations" see Neustupný 1989, 217–18.

so much the difference between a "traditional" and a "modern" or "secular" intellectual but a changing awareness of crisis among Iranian educated elites. The period in which Iran saw itself as an equal player on the political stage ended with the second Herat crisis. Until then, Iran's military ventures – the Russo-Iranian wars (1804–13 and 1826–28) and the Herat campaigns (1837/38 and 1856/57) – suggest that Iran considered itself on a par with the European powers. Only after Yaghmā's lifetime did the awareness of political, military, and economic inferiority and the perception of cultural backwardness spread among the people. Yaghmā himself belongs to a generation of learned civil servants who remained attached to an endemic perspective and barely realized the new realities on the global level.

Works Cited

Ākhundzādeh, Fath-ʿAli. 1963. *Alefbā-ye jadid va maktubāt.* Edited by Hamid Mohammadzāda and Hamid Arasli. Baku: Azerbajdzhan SSR Elmler Akademijasy.

Āl-e Dāʾud, Seyyed ʿAli. 1988/1367. "Moqaddameh." In Yaghmā-ye Jandaqi 1362/1983 and 1367/1988, 1:23–80. Tehran: Tus.

Algar, Hamid. 1969. "Malkum Khān, Ākhūndzāda and the Proposed Reform of the Arabic Alphabet." *Middle Eastern Studies* 5:116–130.

Algar, Hamid. 1984. "Āḵūndzāda." In *EIr* I, 735–40.

Amanat, Abbas. 1998. "Eʿteżād-al-Salṭāna, *Alīqolī Mīrzā.*" In *EIr* VIII, 669–72.

———. 1999. "Pur-e khāqān va andisheh-ye bāz-yābi-ye tārikh-e melli-ye Irān: Jalāl al-Din Mirzā va *Nāmeh-ye Khosravān.*" *Iran Nameh* 17:5–54.

Amanat, Abbas and Farzin Vejdani. 2008. "*Jalāl-al-Din* Mirzā." *EIr* XIV, 405–410.

Annamalai, Elay. 1979. "Movement for Linguistic Purism: The Case of Tamil." In *Language Movements in India*, edited by E. Annamalai, 35–59. Mysore: Central Institute of Indian Languages.

Arjomand, Said Amir. 2005. "Political Ethic and Public Law in the Early Qajar Period." In *Religion and Society in Qajar Iran*, edited by Robert Gleave, 21–40. London: RoutledgeCurzon.

Āryanpur, Yahyā. 1978/1357. *Az Sabā tā Nimā: Tārikh-e 150 sāl-e adab-e fārsi.* 2 vols. 5th ed. Tehran: Ketābhā-ye Jibi.

Bahār, Mohammad Taqi. 1349/1970. *Sabk-shenāsi yā Tārikh-e tatavvor-e nasr-e fārsi.* 3 vols., 3rd ed. Tehran: Ketābhā-ye Parastu.

Bāmdād, Mahdi. 1371/1992. *Sharh-e hāl-e rejāl-e Irān, qarnhā-ye 12 va 13 va 14h.* 6 vols. 4th ed. Tehran: Zavvār.

Banani, Amin. 1981. "Ahmad Kasravi and the 'Purification' of Persian: A Study in Nationalist Motivation." In *Nation and Ideology: Essays in Honour of Wayne S. Vucinich*, edited by Ivo Banac, 463–479. New York: Columbia University Press.

Borhān-e Tabrizi, Mohammad Hoseyn b. Khalaf. 1330–1342/1951–1963. *Borhān-e qāteʿ.* 5 vols. Tehran: Zavvār.

Corbin, Henry. 1987. "Āẕar Kayvān." *EIr* III, 183–87.

Dabashi, Hamid. 1989. "Mulla Ahmad Naraqi and the Question of the Guardianship of the Jurisconsult (*Wilayat-i Faqih*)." In *Expectation of the Millennium. Shiʿism in History*, edited by Seyyed Hossein Nasr, Hamid Dabashi, and Seyyed Vali Reza Nasr, 287–300. Albany: State University of New York Press.

Divān-Begi Shirāzi, Ahmad. 1364–1366/1985–1987. *Hadiqat al-shoʿarā,* edited by ʿAbd al-Hoseyn Navāʾi. 3 vols. Tehran: Enteshārāt-e Zarrin.

Eslami, Kambiz. 1999. "Farhād Mīrzā Moʿtamad-al-Dawla." *EIr IX,* 260–64.

Farhād Mirzā, Moʿtamad al-Dowleh. 1369/1990. *Monshaʾāt-e Farhād Mirzā.* Edited by Gholāmrezā Tabātabāʾi Majd. Tehran: ʿElmi.

Foy, Karl. 1998. "Der Purismus bei den Osmanen." *Mitteilungen des Seminars für Orienatlische Sprachen an der Königlichen Friedrich Wilhelms-Universität*, 1:20–55.

Fragner, Bert G. 1999. *Die 'Persophonie': Regionalität, Identität und Sprachpolitik in der Geschichte Asiens.* Berlin: Das Arabische Buch.

Hanaway, William L. 1989. "Bāzgašt-e adabī." In *EIr* IV, 58–60.

———. 2012. "Secretaries, Poets, and the Literary Language." In *Literacy in the Persianate World: Writing and the Social Order*, edited by Brian Spooner and William L. Hanaway, 95–142. Philadelphia: University of Pennsylvania Museum of Archaeology and Anthropology.

Hedāyat, Rezā Qoli Khān. 1336–1340/1957–1961. *Majmaʿ al-fosahā*, edited by Mozāher Mosaffā. 6 vols. Tehran: Amir Kabir.

Jazayeri, Mohammad Ali. 1983. "The Modernization of the Persian Vocabulary and Language Reform in Iran." In *Language Reform. History and Future*, edited by István Fodor and Claude Hagège, 2:241–67. 6 vols. Hamburg: Buske.

———. 1999. "Farhangestān." In *EIr* IX, 273–79.

Jernudd, Björn H. 1989. "The Texture of Language Purism: An Introduction." In Jernudd and Shapiro 1989, 1–20.

Jernudd, Björn H., and Michael J. Shapiro, eds. 1989. *The Politics of Language Purism.* Berlin: De Gruyter.

Karimi-Hakkak, Ahmad. 1989. "Language Reform Movement and its Language: The Case of Persian." In Jernudd and Shapiro 1989, 81–104.

Khātami, Ahmad. 1373/1994. *Tārikh-e adabiyāt-e Irān dar dowreh-ye bāz-gasht-e adabi. Az soqut-e Safaviyeh tā esteqrār-e mashruteh.* 2 vols. Tehran: Mo'assaseh-ye Farhangi va Enteshārāti-ye Pāyā.

Kia, Mehrdad. 1998. "Persian Nationalism and the Campaign for Language Purification." *Middle Eastern Studies* 34:9–36.

Majlesi, Mohammad Bāqer b. Mohammad Taqi. 1983. *Biḥār al-anwār al-jāmiʿa li-durar akhbār al-aʾimma al-aṭhār.* Edited by Jawād al-ʿAlawī. 111 vols. Beyrut: Dār Iḥyā at-Turāth al-ʿArabī.

Mojtabaʾī, Fatḥ-Allāh. 1994. "Dasātīr." *EIr VII*, 84.

Motadel, David. 2014. "Iran and the Aryan Myth," in *Perceptions of Iran. History, Myths and Nationalism from Medieval Persia to the Islamic Republic,* edited by Ali Ansari, 119–145. London: I.B. Tauris.

Neustupný, Jiří V. 1989. "Language Purism as a Type of Language Correction." In Jernudd and Shapiro 1989, 211–24. Berlin: de Gruyter.

Nuh, Nosratollāh. 1356/1977. "Yaghmā-ye Jandaqi. "Obeydi digar dar dowreh-ye Qājār." *Yaghmā* 30:685–92 and 731–37.

Oskuee, Narges. 1393/2014. "Yaghmā-ye Jandaqi, sokhan-sāz-e rasteh-ye pārsi-negārān." *Pazhūheshhā-ye adabī va balāghī* 2,3:135–48.

Parsinejad, Iraj. 2021. "The Development of Modern Persian Prose: From the Nineteenth to the Early Twentieth Century." In *A History of Persian Literature. Volume V Persian Prose,* edited by Bo Utas, 481–520. London: I.B. Tauris.

Paul, Ludwig. 2010. "Iranian Language Reform in the Twentieth Century: Did the First Farhangestān (1935–40) Succeed?" *Journal of Persianate Studies* 3:78–103.

Perry, John R. 1985. "Language Reform in Turkey and Iran." *International Journal of Middle East Studies* 17:295–311.

Qājār, Mahmud Mirzā. 1346/1968. *Safinat al-Mahmud,* edited by ʿAbd al-Rasul Khayyāmpur. 2 vols. Tabriz: Dāneshgāh-e Adabiyāt-e Tabriz.

Rypka, Jan. 1968. *History of Iranian Literature.* Edited by Karl Jahn. Dordrecht: Reidel.

Sauter, Anke. 2000. *Eduard Engel: Literaturhistoriker, Stillehrer, Sprachreiniger. Ein Beitrag zur Geschichte des Purismus in Deutschland.* Bamberg: Collibri.

Schiewe, Jürgen. 1998. *Die Macht der Sprache: Eine Geschichte der Sprachkritik von der Antike bis zur Gegenwart.* München: Beck.

Schwartz, Kevin. 2020. *Remapping Persian Literary History, 1700–1900.* Edinburgh: Edinburgh University Press.

Tavakoli-Targhi, Mohamad. 2001. *Refashioning Iran: Orientalism, Occidentalism and Historiography.* Basingstoke: Palgrave.

Yaghmā'i, Eqbāl. 1356/1977. "Mirzā Abu l-Hasan Yaghmā. Shā'eri bozorg va
   āzādi-andish." In *Yādgārnāmeh-ye Habib Yaghmā'i*, edited by Gholām-
   Hoseyn Yusofi *et al.*, 383–412. Tehran: Tus.
Yaghmā'i, Esma'il Honar. 1344/1965. "Khānedān-e Yaghmā," *Yaghmā*
   18:497–500, 614–16, and 660–64.
Yaghmā'i, Habib. 1924. "Sharh-e hāl-e Yaghmā [Joghrāfyā-ye Jandaq va
   Biyābānak va sharh-e hāl-e Yaghmā, bā moqaddameh-ye 'Abbās Eqbāl
   Āshtyāni]." *Armaghān* 5:402–418, 481–501, and 636–42.
Yaghmā-ye Jandaqi, Rahim Abu l-Hasan. 1283/1866. *Kolliyāt-e Yaghmā-ye
   Jandaqi*. Edited under the auspices of 'Ali-Qoli Mirzā E'tezād al-Saltaneh.
   Tehran.
———. 1362/1983 and 1367/1988. *Majmu'eh-ye Āthār-e Yaghmā-ye Jandaqi*,
   edited by Seyyed 'Ali Āl-e Dā'ud. 2 vols. Tehran: Tus. Vol. 1 *Ghazali-
   yāt, masnavihā, marāthi, Sardāriya*, 2nd, revised ed. 1367/1988. Vol. 2
   Makātib va munsha'āt, 1362/1983.

From Dis-enchantment to Re-enchantment:
Renan's *Vie de Jésus* between Historicism and *Homo Religiosus*

Monica Ringer

"J'ai tout critiqué, et, quoi qu'on dise, j'ai tout maintenu."[1]
— *Renan*

ERNEST RENAN (1823–1892), the famous nineteenth-century French philologist and Orientalist, was, in his day, considered one of France's most commanding intellectuals alongside Baudelaire, Flaubert, and Stendhal.[2] His renown stretched from academic circles into political and popular circles due to the controversies surrounding him, as well as his widely read, and equally widely criticized, *Vie de Jésus* (Life of Jesus), first published in 1863. *Vie de Jésus'* "remarkable capacity to be read in conflicting directions" propelled its controversy.[3] "It was precisely the hybridity of *Vie de Jésus*," Priest aptly notes, "the fact that it gathered together so many diverse strands in contemporary culture, which underpinned its prominence and success across such a broad range of audiences."[4] Indeed *Vie de Jésus* became "one of the cultural landmarks of the Second Empire era."[5]

This article explores Renan's historical methodology in *Vie de Jésus* and argues that his commitment to historicism serves as a tool for identifying and retrieving religious essence from historical context – the freeing of religion from history. Historicism, long recognized for its inherent disenchantment with the mythologies of tradition, was also harnessed to affect a modern 're-enchantment' – a renewed commitment to the place of religion in modern man, the eternal *homo religiosus*. *Vie de Jésus* embodied Renan's twin commitments to history as scientific method and to religion as faith.

Renan was deeply influenced by the German tradition of philosophical and biblical criticism. Certain limitations and possibilities inherent in the project

---

1. "I have criticized everything, and, whatever one might say, I have maintained everything." Renan n.d., "Le prêtre de Nemi," in *Oeuvres Complètes* 3:529.
2. Lee 1996, 1.
3. Priest 2015, 108.
4. Priest 2015, 69.
5. Hazareesingh 2001, 108.

of reexamining Christian tradition and texts had become accepted by the nineteenth century. On the one hand, biblical criticism foreclosed the possibility of arriving at any empirically verifiable knowledge of Jesus – either through a reconciliation of the texts themselves, or through a reconstruction of the historical context. Yet even as this forced the separation of Jesus from a historicized Christianity, with all the attendant stresses on the Christian doctrine, it also opened up new possibilities for the reinterpretation of Christianity. As scholars historicized Christian doctrine, the quest for the *historical Jesus* gave way to the quest for the *essence of Jesus.* The identification of essence opened up any number of possible interpretations. It did, as Max Weber famously noted, require the embrace, not the rejection, of perpetual uncertainty, but in so doing freed Jesus from the confines of history and enabled a revivification of Christian belief, thought and faith.

It is here that Renan made his seminal contribution – historicizing Christianity, yet at the same time constructing a spiritualized, fulfilling, personal and deeply aesthetic Christianity that allowed individual Catholics to re-embrace their faith. The book was not primarily a scholarly work, but a creative venture of re-enchantment. This, arguably, was Renan's greatest achievement, and the one nearest his heart. This was his objective in his (in)famous *Vie de Jésus,* the work that most fully embodied his religious project and which he considered his greatest achievement, calling it, "my life's greatest work."[6]

Vie de Jésus self-consciously hails from the German Protestant tradition of biblical criticism. Yet as the first Catholic Life of Jesus, Renan parted ways with the objectives of the long list of lives of Jesus penned by German Protestant biblical critics in the quest for the historical Jesus. For him it was not about textual criticism, nor about rejecting or defending Catholic dogma, nor yet about historicizing the Bible. Renan abandoned all pretenses of working within the paradigms of either Catholic doctrine or biblical criticism. Instead, he wrote what was, intentionally, a creative interpretation of Jesus, with all the spiritual intimacy and aesthetic beauty that he believed were necessary components of a more evolved, rational religious sensibility that could propel, rather than impede, the ongoing evolution of human consciousness, science, and ultimately, progress. It is precisely for these reasons that *Vie de Jésus* drew the ire of Catholic critics and Protestant biblical exegetes alike. Renan's success in this endeavor, however, is evidenced by *Vie de Jésus'* enormous popular reception. *Vie de Jésus* went through eight editions in three months. Eighteen months after its publi-

---

6. Renan attested to this in a letter to his wife dated Aug 14, 1861. Psichari 1937, 222. All translations from the French are my own, unless otherwise noted.

cation, it had sold 168,000 copies.[7] Reardon described it as "one of the events of the century."[8]

Historicism and Historical Empathy: Renan's Exegetical Hermeneutics

Renan was deeply concerned with resolving tensions between science and religion, between rationalism and historicism on the one hand, and the place of faith on the other. Yet the competition between science and religion was not simply a destructive dichotomy, but equally a dialectic that made possible the emergence of new ways of envisioning religion's place in the future modern. The subjection of religious texts and traditions to historical criticism certainly led to a religious crisis, but the crisis created multiple, contradictory possibilities. Deliverance from dogma and freedom to reinterpret religion thus went hand in hand.[9] Renan's genius was his departure from the model of reconciliation of science and religion and his proposal instead of integration.

Historicism was the keystone of Renan's methodology. As he himself explained, "the great progress of criticism has been to substitute the category of becoming for the category of being, the conception of the relative for the conception of the absolute, movement towards immobility.... [N]ow everything is considered as existing in a state of becoming."[10] This process of 'becoming' and the associated rejection of absolutes were corollaries in the triumph of historicism – defined as the recognition of the perpetual existence of humankind in historical context.

Renan argued that the embrace of historicism was liberating and equated it with intellectual freedom of mind. He insisted that the recognition of context was the necessary means to the retrieval of essence. He spent his life trying to make the point, often lost on his detractors, that historical context allowed for the identification of that which was not contextual, nor subject to historical change, that is, essence; in his case, the essence of Christianity. Renan went further, seeking to free this essence from history itself – if indeed one admitted to historicism, then one must admit the consequence that all consciousness of truth is contextually contingent and that therefore humanity was engaged in a continual process of becoming, a process of spiritual enlightenment. Renan embraced the permanence of context and the continual need to revise, rewrite, and re-imagine religious truth. Religious history in his view was the story of human-

----

7. Priest 2015, 110.
8. Reardon 2010, 296.
9. Charlton 1963, vii.
10. Renan 1861, vi-vii.

ity's religious grasping of the infinite, of greater and lesser degrees of consciousness and spirituality, not, as the Catholic Church insisted, the preservation and perpetuation of truth as Tradition. Religion thus must be embraced as a shared human phenomenon, as human experience, a perpetual becoming – not as a set of discreet doctrines. Renan proposed historicism as a resolution of reason versus revelation, empiricism and the empirically unverifiable; he embraced historicism and its inevitable destruction of certainty, even as he reaffirmed the certainty of faith in truth itself.

Historicism permitted the identification of context and the primordial, unchanging essence of a given society. The essence was not always visible in contemporary time but could be archaeologically retrieved by going back to the linguistic or, alternatively, religious, origin. The notion that origins embodied primordial essence was deeply, even self-consciously, embedded in Christian notions of the origins of mankind, and of origins as manifesting the essence of difference between societies and civilizations.[11] Renan, as a historian, philologist and religious studies scholar, was deeply imbued with the premises of these disciplines and deployed them masterfully to argue for a new definition of the 'essence of Christianity.' Renan embraced the loss of enchantment as the inevitable consequence of historicism, yet insisted that historicism, because it enabled the harmonization of religion with the human sciences and the identification and retrieval of a-historical essence, opened up the possibility of re-enchantment – the renewal of spiritual possibility:

> Without a doubt, this enchanted world where humanity lived before arriving at a life of considered thought, this world conceived of as moral, as passionate, as full of life and emotion, had an inexpressible charm. It is possible that, despite our having created rationalism in the face of this severe and inflexible nature, some of us have begun to miss the miracle and to criticize the experience of having banished it from the universe. But this can only be the result of an incomplete view of the results of science. Since the true world that science has revealed to us is far superior to the imaginary world created in the imagination.... One day science will rediscover a reality a thousand times more beautiful and in so doing, criticism will have been but the first step towards adopting beliefs more consoling than those that they seemed to have destroyed.[12]

Renan longed for "the enchanted world," not in the sense of a Romantic nos-

11. Olender 2008, 44.
12. Renan 1890, 803–5.

talgia for a former enchantment, but for a newly enchanted world that retained the power of emotion and truth as beauty, even in the embrace of criticism. Re-enchantment entailed the rescue and embrace of the power of the essence of Christianity, not its subjugation and imprisonment in tradition and dogma. The essence, truth, and beauty of Christianity, while imprisoned in history, could be released through history's dissolvent – historicism. The disenchantment of history was thus a means to re-enchantment:

> Science, in complete freedom, without any other chains than that of reason, without any fixed symbols, without temples, without priests, will flourish in what we call the profane world. This is the form of beliefs that alone, henceforth, will produce humanity…. Priests will be philosophers, sages, artists, poets – that is to say men who have taken the ideal as their portion of human heritage and who have renounced their earthly share. Thus will the poetic priesthood of the earliest civilizations return.[13]

Historicism permitted the destruction of accepted truths, even as it enabled the retrieval of the enduring essence of truth, "the reconstitution of the sacred in the very act of its destruction."[14] As Renan argued, "criticism knows no respect: It judges gods and men. As far as it is concerned, there is neither standing nor mystery; it destroys all magic, disturbs every veil. It is the sole authority without bridle, for it is but reason itself."[15] Renan thus shared a desire to lay bare the falsity and constructedness of Catholic traditions and dogmas with the Rationalists, yet for him this was not an end in-and-of itself, but a necessary means of resuscitating the essence that lay behind the accretions of tradition and distortions of dogma. For him, there was an essence of Christianity, and this distinguished him from both his Rationalist and Catholic reformist contemporaries, who either rejected a definable essence or insisted that the Catholic Church had access to it, respectively.

Renan also used what might be termed historical empathy in order to ascertain historical context and identify the eternal essence of Christianity. The attempt to put oneself in the place of another, or in another time by means of intellectual empathy, was a common tool in the historian's belt in the nineteenth

---

13. Renan 1890, 812.

14. Lee 1996, 106.

15. Renan, opening lines of "Les historiens critiques de Jesus" (March 1849), 365 cited in Lee 1996, 98. Mott notes that these lines did not appear in the original essay, published eight years earlier. See Mott 1921, 78.

century. Whereas historicism might fruitfully be understood as the deployment of critical distance, 'historical empathy' is the deployment of emotional proximity. Historicism was premised on distance between the historian and their subject of inquiry; distance was equated with impartiality, rationalism and critical, scientific scrutiny. Historical empathy tapped into the ability of the historian to emotionally identify with, experience, and thus effectively inhabit a different context.

Historical empathy was valued as it permitted proximity. It enabled the historian to become a virtual eyewitness to an event or context, to experience it for themselves. Emotion and visual experience were both thought to have connective effects that enabled a certain intrinsic connection of the historian with their object of study. Vision and experience created the capacity for empathy, and empathy of understanding – the immersion of Self in a context permitted consciousness of the Other's essence.

Emotion and visual experience were also understood as transportative – physically and temporally. The historian, through empathy, could be transported to a different context and a different time via methodological rabbit holes. The historian moved virtually into a different space and time but retained the critical distance that derived from their native context. The historian benefitted from virtual sight, but this sight was not equivalent to immersion. Immersion implied a loss of self, loss of distance, and thus loss of critical capacity. Historical empathy enabled the historian to retain the benefits of the distance implicit in hindsight.

The nature of historical empathy involved a difficult balancing between a desired immersion in the past, and the danger that such an immersion might lead to the loss of critical distance. Paradoxically, the transportative imperative of historical empathy depended on a recognition of – a consciousness of – difference of context over time – of the impossibility of recovery and thus its romantic mythologization. The desire to empathize with, to immerse oneself in, the historical past was thus inextricably bound to a longing for the irretrievably distant, and the desire to overcome this distance was inextricably bound with the recognition of the limitations of its possibility.

In *Vie de Jésus* Renan masterfully deployed the twin methods of historicism and historical empathy to suggest novel solutions to some of the thorny questions of biblical exegesis. His project was simultaneously the quest of the historical Jesus and the resurrection of Jesus as the enduring and eternal essence of Christianity. In other words, the retrieval of Jesus from history was a prerequisite for the re-enchantment of Christianity.

Historicizing the Gospels

Renan's approach to the hermeneutics of the Gospels was innovative and, above all, creative. He treated the Gospels as profane sources, rejecting the Catholic imperative of their divine inspiration. Yet he also resisted the impulse of some of his German Protestant forerunners toward what Renan might term an over-emphasis on the literal text. He side-stepped the conventions of the quest of the historical Jesus genre of exegesis and made no attempt to reconcile their divergent accounts into a harmonious narrative, believing that this objective was not only impossible but ultimately inconsequential.

Renan insisted that the Gospels were merely a collection of contingent historical sources that could only fruitfully be read for their authors' experience of Jesus – as a man, and as a personality. The Gospels could and should not be read to assemble specific facts, as their inconsistencies and corruptions simply could not be reconciled, but the Gospels did, collectively, contain truths – truths of the experience that disciples had of Jesus. There were truths to be gleaned, but truths suggestive of the essence of Jesus, not factual truths. A critical reading of the Gospels thus should not attempt any reconciliation of the disparate facts concerning Jesus but must be read between the lines for the effect Jesus had on his disciples – the subconscious or unconscious effects of being in his presence. Renan likened this approach to interviewing witnesses under the presumption that each witness would have a mixture of perspectives, facts and also misunderstandings, which simply could not be mutually reconciled. The value of the witnesses was not the possible extraction of fact but the teasing out of their experience, however subjective, however imperfect.[16]

In seeking to resolve the questions surrounding the historical Jesus and his relationship to Christianity, Renan deployed the twin concepts of context and essence. This permitted him to simultaneously historicize Jesus as Jewish, and essentialize him as Christian. Jesus was both of, and not of, his context. Renan took great pains to create the historical Jesus, but at the same time, subtly suggested reasons why ultimately, Jesus transcended the limitations of his Jewish context.

Jesus and the 'Essence of Christianity'

From the outset, Renan hinted at the possibility of Jesus' historical transcendence. Jesus, while influenced by and at some level a product of his context, was nevertheless not completely bound by it. Jesus, already described as a pos-

---

16. Renan 1863, xliv-xlv.

sible exception to the natural and racial determinism inherent in the Palestinian landscape, moves from being a reformer of Judaism, to rejecting Judaism as irreconcilable with his religious ideas. Renan portrayed Jesus as an outsider – he was a Jew, but distinctly outside of Jewish scholastic, legal and theological traditions. Jesus began as a Jew but as his religious consciousness developed and expanded, he rejected Judaism entirely, thereby transcending historical context by virtue of his incomparable religious 'essence': "In other words, Jesus was no longer a Jew. He was a revolutionary of the highest order; he called all men to a religion founded solely on their being children of God."[17] At the very moment of Jesus' rejection of and separation from Judaism, he is transformed into the origin of Christianity. As such, he embodied the 'essence' of Christianity – the universal religion of mankind par excellence. Renan insisted on Jesus' rejection of the particular (Judaism) and embrace of the universal: "He proclaimed the rights of man, not the rights of Jews; the religion of man, not the religion of Jews; the deliverance of man, not the deliverance of Jews."[18]

Jesus embodied the religious ideal for all mankind for all of time. Christianity was claimed as the universal religion of mankind, and definitively severed from Jesus' own origins in the Jewish context. "Jesus was more than a reformer of an old religion, he was the creator of the eternal religion of humanity."[19]

As with every great event in history, the legend of Jesus distorted the man. Jesus was fundamentally misunderstood by those around him, not least of which, his disciples. Unable, unlike Jesus, to transcend the limitations of their historical context, the disciples were profoundly affected by Jesus, but were nevertheless incapable of comprehending his message. They were bounded by their limited imaginations, limited consciousness, and as a result, interpreted his words literally.

The spiritual limitations of Jesus' disciples also meant that Jesus' Christianity miscarried after his death. There were no religious practices to be found in Jesus' time, only simple prayer, no formalized rituals or performances, no religious hierarchy, in other words, no church. Jesus' religion was "a pure religion, one without priests and without external observances, resting entirely on the feelings of the heart, on the imitation of God, on the direct relation of the conscience with the heavenly Father,"[20] a religion that proclaimed "the moral judgment of the world, entrusted to the conscience of the just man and to the arms of the people; God, conceived simply as Father – this was the entirety of Jesus'

17. Renan 1863, 223.
18. Renan 1863, 223.
19. Renan 1863, 332.
20. Renan 1863, 85–86.

theology."[21] Rituals, hierarchies and institutions crept in and distorted the pure, simple teachings of Jesus himself. Christianity developed apart from, if not in contravention of, Jesus' teachings.

As a result, the Gospels must be read for the inspiration that lay behind them. According to Renan, the essence of Christianity resided in the purely spiritual: "Jesus only wanted the religion of the Heart; that of the Pharisees consisted almost entirely in observances."[22] He thus differentiated God from the texts of the Gospels, separating God from Jesus; Jesus was the most perfect example of a man who exhibited an extraordinary capacity for the consciousness of God. God was discernable through elevated levels of consciousness, but no longer via the authors of the Gospels themselves. The Gospels thus moved into the realm of the secular text, albeit with sacred inspiration. Only God was divine.

By making the distinction between the Christianity of historical time and Jesus' Christianity, Renan redefined Christianity and called for its purification – the return to origins, the reclaiming of its essence through historicization and the shedding of historical detritus. Renan's most profound criticism of the church was that it sought to preserve dogma as truth, thus preventing the liberation of each individual soul to seek its own spiritual consciousness of God. It was the church's role as intermediary between man and God, and the inhibition of individual spirituality that inevitably resulted, that Renan sought to overcome. In claiming that "the true kingdom of God that everyone carries in their Heart" was the essence of Christianity, Renan sought to liberate Christianity from the Catholic Church.[23] Renan explicitly contrasted Jesus' Christianity with the Christianity of his time, remarking that "the breath of God was free amongst them; with us, it is chained by the iron bonds of an impoverished society and condemned to an unmitigated mediocrity."[24]

Renan issued a powerful call to his readers to embrace the essence of Christianity – one which Jesus' disciples were not sufficiently evolved to understand, but one which Europeans of the nineteenth century were finally prepared to comprehend. After the passage of eighteen centuries of history, the retrieval of true Christianity was finally possible. Renan cast the essence of Christianity and its retrieval from history as entailing the final embrace of Jesus by his readers. Renan invoked Jesus' own words, reciting the Gospel of John: "the time is coming," Jesus called out, "when you will worship the Father neither on this mountain, nor in Jerusalem.... But the time approaches, indeed it is already here, when

21. Renan 1863, 76, 284–85.
22. Renan 1863, 329.
23. Renan 1863, 78.
24. Renan 1863, 449.

those who are real worshippers will worship the Father in spirit and in truth."[25]
Renan then provided his own biblical exegesis:

> The day that [Jesus] uttered this saying he was truly the son of God.
> For the first time, he said the words upon which the edifice of eternal
> religion will forever rest. He established a pure religion, for all time,
> for all peoples, one which all elevated souls will practice until the
> end of time. Not only on this day did his religion become the true
> religion of humanity, it became religion itself; and, if other planets
> have inhabitants endowed with reason and morality, their religion
> cannot be different from the one that Jesus proclaimed near the well
> of Jacob. Man has not been able adhere to it; for ideals are realized but
> for a fleeting moment. Jesus' words were light in a dark night; it has
> required eighteen hundred years for the eyes of mankind (what am I
> saying! for an infinitely small portion of mankind) to become accus-
> tomed to it. But the light will become full day, and, after having run
> through all the cycles of error, mankind will return to these words, as
> the immortal expression of its faith and hopes.[26]

On 'Becoming': Jesus in The Mind's Eye

Vie de Jésus clearly does not belong to the genre of exegetical or historical scholarship on the Bible and was heatedly denounced at the time for being a novel.
Yet I would argue that Renan fully recognized the possibilities of the novel as
a vehicle to enable his readers to see what he saw, to be transported alongside
himself to Jesus' time. Renan chose the novel as the vehicle for the construction
of a new Christian idiom – the retrieval of the essence of Christianity through
Jesus. The invitation to accept a rationalized, internalized, spiritualized and thus
revivified Christianity of Jesus was conveyed in a form that facilitated the active
agency of the reader. It offered the possibility of the "subjectivity of becoming"
– not obedience, but the embrace of the permanent state of spiritual development. As Lee notes, the novel as a participatory genre "invites entry through
imagination's gate."[27] It is precisely this accessibility – of the novel, and via the
novel, to Jesus – that lies at the heart of the work and its ultimate objective of
the re-enchantment of Christianity. *Vie de Jésus* was "unashamedly accessible"
and deliberately so.[28]

25. Renan 1863, 234. Renan, quoting the Gospel of John (IV: 21–23).
26. Renan 1863, 234–235.
27. Lee 1996, 39.
28. On the subjectivity of Renan's readers, see Priest 2015, 23.

The novel as a form is particularly well suited to the creation of image, of familiarity, of access, of empathy, of imagination. Renan deployed a variety of strategies for creating and sharing his image of Jesus, including historical empathy and the construction of familiarity. The bringing alive or painting the scene of Jesus's context, life and thoughts for his readers was a deliberate strategy for creating in his readers an empathetic capacity to journey with him, to see what he saw, and ultimately, to join him in the embrace of Jesus as the ideal manifestation of true Christianity. The creative capacity for imagination that Renan generated in *Vie de Jésus*, permitted his readers to move from passive recipients of the image of Jesus to active participants; readers were summoned to share Renan's image of Jesus and, as such, were invited to become Jesus' disciples. *Vie de Jésus* was thus an invitation to his readers to accompany him back in time, to embrace Jesus, and to bring Jesus back with them to late nineteenth-century France. It was a rescue operation, and one on which mankind's progress and civilization depended.

The practice of reading itself, embracing both the passive receipt of image and the active imagining made possible by this image, enabled readers to empathize with and embrace Jesus as a contemporary. The novel offered a means to move the concept of religion into the spiritual and beyond the domain of a utilitarian cause/effect, beyond the notion of the individual relating to God as a petitioner – of requests for interference, aid, and sustenance. There should be no intermediaries, Renan argued, no prescribed ritual, only the capacity of each individual to commune with God. *Vie de Jésus* offered the possibility of a rationalized, internalized, and deeply individualized spirituality where each reader could recognize themselves as being the son of God – retracing, as it were, the spiritual footsteps of Jesus himself.

Vie de Jésus was written largely from detailed notes and drafts Renan made in situ, which Renan believed provided him with a prerogative for empathy, understanding, and, ultimately, insight. This insight depended on claims of physical and historical proximity. Renan believed that being in the same physical location as Jesus (walking in his footsteps) produced invaluable insight. But he also firmly believed that the benefits of physical proximity were enhanced by his own capacity as a scholar and a man of faith. He was convinced that his profound Christian sympathies enabled him to identify and thus extract the essence of Christianity in ways that most scholars and theologians could not. He claimed to marry scholarly methodology with an understanding of faith:

> If love of a subject can aid in one's understanding of it, one must
> also recognize, I hope, that I am not lacking in this condition. To

write the history of a religion it is necessary, first of all, to have believed in it (without which, one cannot understand how it has charmed and satisfied the human conscience); and second, to no longer believe in it absolutely, because absolute faith is incompatible with sincere history. But love persists without faith.[29]

Renan claimed a combination of authorities here: the historicism and critical distance of the scholar, the capacity to understand faith, and the capacity to engender the historical empathy occasioned by visual proximity. Renan thus was both the recipient of imagination, as well as its producer – he channeled his insight into re-creating it for his audience. He reproduced his visual experience, blended with his empathetic historical imagination, to paint Jesus in his context for his readers. In so doing, Renan creatively blended the advantages of distance with proximity, rational historical method with intuition, emotion and spirituality. The deployment of physical proximity and scholarly critical distance enabled him to transport himself back in time and see what Jesus and his contemporaries saw.

Historical empathy as an umbrella term for enabling proximity between subject and object was generated by using visual imagery and time travel. Each of these techniques created proximity between Jesus and Renan's readers, proximity that, in turn, led to empathy as the sensation of commonality, of familiarity, of sameness. This powerful sense of commonality enabled Renan's readers to understand Jesus' message. Renan did not render Jesus understandable to readers through explaining or decoding difference, he made Jesus recognizable to readers as familiar. Their empathy with him depended on proximity, but proximity as familiarity, the erasure of difference – a recognition of the self. Jesus was recognizable to the readers. His proximity was not so much created as revealed. Jesus was not an Oriental Other but a European Self. Renan painstakingly painted Jesus in stark dichotomy to other Jews, in ways deliberately engineered to create familiarity with his readers, enabling his readers to imagine, or re-imagine, Jesus as European. Readers recognized themselves in him.

Renan's granddaughter, commenting on his journals from this period, noted the essential role that Renan's physical experience played in his belief that he could imagine and thus see Jesus' context: "One must thus attribute one sole objective to the voyage in Palestine of 1860–1861: the pursuit of the ambiance, breathing of the same air, the plunge into the past with the desire of seizing hold those things which never change, scents, lakes, the shape of the mountains, the

---

29. Renan 1863, lviii-lix.

changing of seasons."[30] Direct experience of the physical and social environment of Palestine produced the imaginative capacity to go back in time and experience Jesus' context. "Eighteen centuries collapsed," Henriette noted, "thanks to direct personal contact with nature and the climate. As far as individuals were concerned, Renan willfully assumed that they were identical to those of the past." Renan provided "an absolutely direct sensation of who Jesus was,"[31] he "wanted to discern the traces of the comings and goings of Jesus, he entered into a perpetual state of existing in a past life."[32]

Through visual imagery, Renan painted Jesus' context for his readers as a familiar one, and deliberately so. *Vie de Jésus* is replete with images designed to resonate with his readership. These images reinforce the hint of the dichotomy between Europe and the Orient, allowing the French reader to identify with Jesus and thus to extract him from his context.

Renan's strategy of familiarizing his readers with Jesus as a person, his experiences, the landscape surrounding him, was multidirectional. Jesus' context was imagined and conveyed to the reader, at the same time as the reader's own particular European/French context was superimposed on Jesus. Jesus was Europeanized, his landscape was Europeanized. Even his spirituality was Europeanized by Renan's confirmation that the prayer known to all of Renan's readers was a valid point of access to Jesus' spirituality.

The creative and spiritual possibilities for self-realization inherent in Jesus' relocation in time and space are manifest in Renan's portrayal of him as the 'incomparable man.' Renan unapologetically depicts Jesus as human. Jesus' feelings and inner thoughts, his psychology, his relationships and interactions with other people, are all divulged and described, providing the reader an unprecedented level of intimacy with Jesus. Renan "sought a third way between Jesus the God and Jesus the charlatan," Priest observes, "Jesus the 'psychological fact.'"[33] Yet Jesus' humanity is not simply an alternative to the two available options of Catholic theology or rationalist critique. Jesus is immediate, emotional, and, as such, accessible. Renan repeatedly insisted that Jesus' greatness lay not in his divinity, but in his consciousness of God. This enables Jesus to be *both* historicized, *and* essentialized as the embodiment of the most perfect consciousness. The historical Jesus exists simultaneously alongside the essential, a-historical Jesus. Renan historicized Jesus but liberated him from history – Jesus was revivified as an ideal. This essentialization of Jesus allows Renan to achieve the true genius of his work – to retrieve Jesus and transplant him to contemporary France.

30. Psichari 1937, 195.
31. Psichari 1937, 201.
32. Psichari 1937, 206.
33. Priest 2015, 24.

Renan strategically ignited the imagination of the reader, and transported them, via his own historical empathy, to Jesus' time. Renan invited the reader to move from being passive recipients of this image, to active participants in time travel. In recreating Jesus' life, Renan claimed to achieve what he declared no follower of Jesus ever could – to fully understand Jesus. Indeed, it was Renan's firm foothold in post-revolutionary France, his critical distance, that allowed him the scholarly and intellectual capacity to understand Jesus in ways that the writers of the Gospels could not – limited as they were by their context. Renan thus positioned himself as the first true disciple of Jesus. In so doing, he challenged his readers to similarly embrace Jesus and to become Jesus' new disciples.

Jesus becomes at once a man in history, and, at the same time, an essence that could transcend history and become an abstract embodiment of spiritual consciousness. Readers were invited to participate in sharing the consciousness of truth that Jesus attained. Renan's readers were the agents of revolution and, ultimately, the progress of mankind. Each reader was called upon to be Jesus' disciple, to embrace the essence of Christianity. The permanent state of spiritual becoming writ large was manifest in the method of historicism itself; the insistence on context was also the acceptance of the permanence of change, the unending process of becoming, of human evolution, and with it, greater capacity for consciousness of God. "We are the true Christians," Renan insisted, "Christian tradition has little claim on the truth that was Jesus. In this sense, we are Christians, even when we diverge on nearly all points from the Christian tradition that preceded us. If Jesus were to return among us, he would recognize as disciples, not those who claim to encompass him entirely with a few phrases of the catechism, but those who labor to carry on [his work]."[34]

By insisting that true religion had been derailed since the time of Jesus but was nevertheless ultimately achievable in the Europe of his day, Renan fundamentally redefined the essence of Christianity and its potential future universalization. The readers of *Vie de Jésus* are an essential part of the success of the re-enchantment of Christianity. They enable Renan's Jesus to become a shared imaginary. Renan depended on his reader's embrace of Jesus, their re-enchantment, to actualize the last revolution of mankind. The emphasis is on the individual reader, their capacity for agency, for creation through recognition of Jesus, and, ultimately, their donning the robes of Jesus' disciples.

There is a profound ambivalence between Renan's attempts to claim the essence of Christianity as Jesus, and his reliance on the context of his readers for its retrieval.[35] *Vie de Jésus* depends for its creation on the empathetic capacity of

34. Renan 1863, 447.
35. Foucault 1969.

the author, on his authorial imagination. Jesus, as the essence of Christianity, cannot exist outside of or apart from Renan himself. Renan claims that Jesus is the essence – an a-historical truth that is not contingent on context. Yet he is dependent on context to do so – his own context as an author who claimed unique authority in his creation, and the readers' context as their own imaginative capacity. Without both his and his readers' capacity for imagination – a capacity that depended on their shared nineteenth-century context and enabled them to empathize with Jesus, to 'recognize' him as familiar – Jesus could not exist.

In *Vie de Jésus*, Renan attempts to replace Tradition (historically contingent) with Truth (historically independent). He destroys Tradition's claim to be un-authored, un-constructed. Yet even as he deploys historicism to insist that Christian is constructed and thus context-dependent, he fails to accept the implications of this embrace of context. Despite his claims to retrieve essence from context, the inescapable consequence of the existence of context is the impossibility of any essential truth. Any claim to essence is, by definition, bound within its own context. Renan claims universal truth, independent of his authorship, but cannot escape his own methodology: that Jesus is retrievable via his own context and recognizable due to his audience's context.

Despite his claims to essence, to Truth and to universalism, Renan is unable to escape the consequences of historicism, and his imagined Jesus remains dependent on both him and his readers for its existence. Far from being essentialized and universalized, Renan's Jesus remains deeply embedded in the historical context of his creators. Renan attempted to free Jesus from history, but the Jesus of *Vie de Jésus* remained firmly tethered to Renan's own historical moment.

Homo Religiosus

Renan's revivification of religion centered on his conception of *homo religiosus*. He attempted to integrate science with the religious nature of man – *homo religiosus* – and the product of these efforts, *Vie de Jésus,* clearly manifests this attempt. For Renan then, religion was not Catholic dogma, nor the Church, but the eternal spiritual core of man. Renan viewed the integration of religion and science as an imperative, arguing that "our rationalism … is the recognition of human nature, consecrated in all its forms, it is the simultaneous and harmonious use of all the faculties, it is the exclusion of all exceptions."[36]

On the one hand, Renan concurred that tradition, orthodoxy and even theology were indefensible when subjected to rational scrutiny:

36. Renan 1890, 780.

> The modern spirit is well-considered intellect. Belief in revelation, in
> a supernatural order, is the antithesis of criticism, it is the remnant of
> the old anthropomorphic conception of the world, formed in an era
> when man had not yet arrived at a clear understanding of the laws of
> nature.[37]

On the other hand, rationalism tout court failed to accommodate the necessity and utility of religion beyond instrumentalist arguments concerning social function. Rather than repeating the well-trodden paths of subjecting religion to scientific methods of rationalism and historicism, or aligning science with religious truth and social function, Renan proposed instead to integrate religion and science – methodologically and conceptually. He argued for a rationalization of religion, and the criticism of biblical texts and traditions according to scientific method.

Yet on the other hand, Renan insisted that religious truth did exist, and that it could not be reduced to anthropomorphisms, social functionality, or the inherent veracity of Catholic tradition. He argued for religion's centrality to man's nature. Man, as *homo religiosus,* could not dispense with religion; he required it for inspiration, creativity, and spirituality, which ultimately contributed to the progress of humankind. Renan sought to revive religion by subjecting it to scientific criticism, convinced that the true essence could be identified and delivered from the inaccuracies of history.

The concept of beauty was thus an essential component of Renan's understanding of both religion and *homo religiosus.* It was integral to his methodology and to the project of re-enchantment. Yet the scholarship on Renan either ignores it entirely, or else dismisses it as Romantic 'sentimentality.'[38] The clue to Renan's understanding of the nature and importance of beauty can be found in a comment where he describes himself as neither Catholic nor Protestant but torn irreconcilably between the two. Apparently, when asked why, having rejected the Catholic Church and having aligned himself so firmly with Protestant scholarship (and even marrying into a Protestant family), he did not convert to Protestantism, Renan explained: "Protestantism appeals to me as a schol-

---

37. Renan 1890, 764.

38. Schweitzer described the book as imbued with a specifically French sentimentality typified by Renan's description of Jesus riding "a long-eye lashed gentle mule." Schweitzer 1926, 162. Schweitzer derided the book, asserting that "there is scarcely any other work on the subject which so abounds in lapses of taste – and those of the most distressing kind – as Renan's *Vie de Jésus.*" Schweitzer 1926, 159. The description of Jesus' mule ride may have been indebted to Renan's own mule-riding experience, which he described in a letter to his sister dated December 15, 1860. See Psichari 1937, 200.

ar and a thinker, but as an actual religion among the people it is impoverished (*mesquin*): no church-bells, no cathedral, moral coldness."[39]

This schizophrenia, between an intellectual predilection for unreserved criticism and an aesthetic appreciation of religious space and ritual, led to Renan's distinct sensation of homelessness in either Protestantism or Catholicism and to his quest to integrate what he considered to be the essential components of each. Renan was clearly expressing the view of many other Catholics who were disenchanted with the institution of the Catholic Church – with its power, authority, dogma, and illiberalism – but who desired an alternative to either its complete destruction or its wholesale preservation. Perhaps it is no coincidence that Chateaubriand defended Catholicism partly on grounds of the beauty of its practices. Chateaubriand first published his famous defense of Christianity, entitled *Le génie du christianisme* in 1802, amidst what he described as "the wreckage of our temples." In the introduction, he pleaded for "those who want to love Christianity," to remember "the beauty of its worship, the genius of its orators, the science of its doctors, the virtues of its apostles and of its disciples."[40] His plea may have been intellectually unsatisfying for those committed to rationalism, yet clearly indicates that 'beauty' was one of the elements of Catholicism held most dear to defenders and opponents alike, including one of its most ardent critics, Renan, who likewise imagined a Christ that embodied humanity's need for esthetics, "a Christ who represented not only the pinnacle of morality, but also the esthetic and scientific facets of humanity."[41]

Renan's view of the place of beauty is elegantly conveyed via a metaphor in *Vie de Jésus*. It was undeniably true, Renan stated, that diamonds were composed of carbon. But acceptance of this scientific truth did not negate the additional truth of its beauty – a beauty that could not be expressed via the chemical formula alone. Renan passionately argued that these two components were mutually consistent, just different facets of the same truth. One cannot reduce beauty to science. In other words, religion *could and must be* subject to rational critique and historicism. Yet there was another aspect of religion that was not reducible through scientific and historical method – its beauty– and a beauty no less true and no less essential for the future of mankind than science. Renan reasoned that "the chemist knows that the diamond is nothing but carbon; he knows the paths through which nature induces her profound transformations. Is he thereby obliged to refrain from speaking like everyone else and to see only a simple piece of carbon in the most beautiful of jewels?"[42]

39. Psichari 1937, 272.
40. Chateaubriand 1828, 7. Emphasis added.
41. Renan 1890, 738.
42. Renan 1863, 9.

This new definition of Christianity – the essence identified and resuscitated – and this new way of being Christian – as an ongoing spiritual process of enlightenment, a perpetual becoming – justified a break with the dogma and traditions of the Catholic Church and enabled the re-enchantment of Christianity. Renan painted a powerful and compelling alternative to the rejection of Catholicism or the embrace of deist rationalism. It was a third way, a pious possibility in an era seeking just such an alternative.

THE LIMITS OF RENAN'S EPISTEMOLOGICAL METHODOLOGY

Renan's *Vie de Jésus* inhabits neither a fully scholarly place, nor one acceptable to Catholic theological tradition. This was a deliberate choice on Renan's part, and a strategy necessitated by his ultimate goal of re-enchanting his readers. *Vie de Jésus* was not intended as a work of exegetical scholarship, nor as a 'reconciliation' of critical scholarship and rationalism with contemporary Catholicism. It was intentionally and self-consciously creative, both in form and content, and, despite Renan's own claims to the contrary, depended not on his impartiality as a historian, but on his convictions as a man of faith. *Vie de Jésus* was a creative historical possibility, one that depended on its revolutionary message conveyed in its revolutionary form, and a readership willing and able to share in Renan's empathetic historical imagination. *Vie de Jésus* provided readers for the first time with the creative possibilities of re-enchantment, a re-enchantment not with dogmatism, scholasticism, tradition or ritual, but a re-enchantment with the essence of Christianity: a re-imagined Jesus. Indeed, it was precisely this hybrid form, the historical novel, which led to its enormous popularity, not with Protestant scholars or defenders of Catholicism, but precisely with the general public left dissatisfied with either of these reigning options.

Renan's objective ran parallel to his insistence on the integration of *homo religiosus* into the social sciences, and parallel to his deployment of historicism in order to identify and retrieve a non-contingent essence from the contextually (historically) contingent. *Vie de Jésus* was a product of the integration of his religious and scholarly commitments, which neither Protestant scholarship nor the Catholic Church believed were fully reconcilable, but which Renan nevertheless insisted must be, and that his readers enthusiastically concurred.

The principal achievement of *Vie de Jésus,* and the source of its enormous popularity, was that it created a possible alternative to Catholicism, not for those who remained deeply committed to the Church or those for whom religion was irretrievably irrational, but for those who remained profoundly ambivalent. As Priest noted, *Vie de Jésus* "enraged and entranced generations of French men and women because it presented a new Jesus for the nineteenth century."[43] *Vie de Jésus* permitted the deliverance *from* dogma, *from* Tradition as unchanging precedent and canonical, definitive Truth; freedom *to* reimagine religion, *to* move it squarely out of institutional authority into the realm of the individual conscious agent. *Vie de Jésus* replaced the performance of ritual obedience with spiritual 'becoming' as an alternate pious sensibility. *Vie de Jésus* offered an imaginative possible Christianity, enabling the re-enchantment with religion through its definitive severing from history – this was a rationalized, individualized, spiritualized Christianity firmly divorced from Catholic history and tradition. Renan's 'essence' of Christianity, its beauty, its rejection of definition, existed only in the spiritual consciousness of the readers. It opened up individual agency; it made possible the redefinition of Christianity as faith and as practice. It was deeply embedded in the tradition of Enlightenment humanism and Rationalist anti-clericalism, and clearly struck a chord with the spiritual needs of the nineteenth-century French public.

Yet the very success of its appeal, its triumph as a creative, imaginative possibility, necessitated its departure from historical method. Ultimately, Renan's insistence on integrating *homo religiosus* into the historical and social sciences failed in practice. By definition, this imaginative possibility could not be tethered to historical methodology – its fundamental dependence on proximity, empathy, and imagination precluded Renan from retaining critical distance. The success of *Vie de Jésus* depended on its imaginative qualities, on Renan's ability to share his historical empathy with his readers. It was Renan's aesthetics, his concept of the indefinable yet critical element of beauty, that lay at the center of this project of re-enchantment.

Historicism was a useful tool in demolishing claims to definitive Truth and claims to Tradition as unerring precedent. But, premised on context itself, it was a clumsy tool in identifying and retrieving an a-contextual, a-historical essence. Historicism's utility was located solely in its destructive capacity; it problematized certainty, it could not recreate it. Renan's claim to identify the 'essence of Christianity' was, in the end, a conceit that he was unable to substantiate.

One could argue that Renan embraced the lack of certitude historicism entailed and merely constructed a Jesus who 'might' have existed. Yet this humility is belied by his hubris in claiming to re-discover the true Jesus, the 'essence of Christianity.' As Zachuber notes, "religion was and remained a paradigmatic case of a tradition that had lost its unquestioned validity" and no amount of imagination could alter this.[44] *Vie de Jésus* was first and foremost Renan's at-

43. Priest 2015, 3.
44. Zachhuber 2017, 15.

tempt to rectify what he deemed to be the religious needs of the spirit.[45] Renan's claims to historical criticism and obedience to the obligations of scholarship may have been genuine convictions, but he was ultimately faithful to his religious commitments, commitments that necessitated the transgression of scientific method. Renan failed to reconcile his commitment to science with his commitment to re-enchant his readers with the beauty of Christianity. He wrote: "criticism knows no respect. It judges Gods and men. It destroys all magic, disturbs every value."[46] Yet it was not simply the magic of superstition that criticism destroyed – criticism destroyed all certainty; all claims to truth, leaving only a variety of possible truths. "Renan both attempts an authoritative 'modern' interpretation of Jesus," explains Wright, "and signals the impossibility of the attempt," or what Lee would call, "the reconstitution of the sacred in the very act of its destruction."[47] It was precisely Renan's claim to have discovered truth, the truth of Jesus, of Christianity, that sentenced *Vie de Jésus* to scholarly condemnation.

When Renan explained his use of Gospels to discover an elusive truth, not in their textual or factual reconciliation, he claimed that: "These details are not true to the letter, but they express a superior truth; they are more true than naked truth, in the sense that they are the truth rendered expressive and communicative, raised to the level of an idea."[48] It was this 'superior truth' that led Renan to prioritize faith over scholarship, a priority that seduced him from the "absolute coldness of the historian, who takes as his unique objective to see the smallest and most precise nuance of truth."[49] Historicism gave way to the imperative of the imagined.

Renan's powerful mastery of image is apparent despite these criticisms. Colani described the sensation of reading *Vie de Jésus*, where "fine and poetic thoughts in which you might say he embalmed his book, like an oriental perfume that is at once soft yet penetrating ... plunges you into delicious dreams, even if they are sometimes somewhat unhealthy."[50] More telling is Colani's use of color to describe the effect of the book:

> This portrait [of Jesus] is, in my opinion, of dubious resemblance, and moreover, it is not living. The is not the Christ of history, the Christ

<hr>

45. Lee 1996, 221 (IV, 470)
46. Renan, "Les historiens critiques de Jesus," (1849), quoted in Lee, 1996, 365.
47. Wright 1994, 58; Lee 1996, 106.
48. Renan 1863, xlviii.
49. Renan 1863, 7–8.
50. Colani 1864, 73.

of the synoptics; it is the Christ of the Fourth Gospel, but deprived
of his metaphysical aura and retouched by a (paint) brush where
are found a strange mixture of a melancholy blue of modern poetry,
pink of the utopia (*idylle*) of the eighteenth century, and some sort of
greyish moral philosophy borrowed, one might say, from Larochefou-
cauld.[51]

Renan's own words in his historical drama written some twenty years later in
1885, "Le prêtre de Nemi," perhaps explain the psychology of both his triumph
and his failure: ""I have criticized everything, and, whatever one might say, I
have maintained everything."[52]

51. Colani 1864, 73. François de La Rochefoucauld (1613–1680) was famous for his moralistic
maxims.

52. "J'ai tout critiqué, et, quoi qu'on dise, j'ai tout maintenu." Renan, "Le prêtre de Nemi"(The
Priest of Nemi), in Psichari 1937, 3:529. The title is an overt reference to the "primitive" religious practices of the priest of Nemi described in Scottish anthropologist James George Frazier's (1854–1941)
foundational work on comparative religion, *The Golden Bough: A Study of Magic and Religion* (1890).
Frazier gave a speech at the centenary of Renan's birth at the Sorbonne on February 28, 1923. See Frazer
1923.

Works Cited

Charlton, D. G. 1963. *Secular Religions in France 1815–1870*. Oxford: Oxford
    University Press.

Chateaubriand, François-René de. 1828. *Le génie du Christianisme*, Paris:
    Garnier Frères.

Colani, Timothée. 1864. "Examen de La *Vie de Jésus* de M. Renan." In *Revue
    de Théologie et de philosophie Chrétienne*. N.p.

Foucault, Michel. 1969. "What is an Author?", Lecture at the Collège de
    France. https://www.open.edu/openlearn/pluginfile.php/624849/mod_
    resource/content/1/a840_1_michel_foucault.pdf

Frazer, James George. 1923. *Sur Ernest Renan: précédé d'un buste de l'auteur
    par Antoine Bourdelle*. Paris: Claude Aveline.

Hazareesingh, Sudhir. 2001. *Intellectual Founders of the Republic*. Oxford:
    Oxford University Press.

Lee, David C. J. 1996. *In the Shadow of Faith*. London: Duckworth.

Mott, Lewis Freeman. *Ernest Renan*. New York & London: D. Appleton and
    Co.

Olender, Maurice. 2008. *The Languages of Paradise: Race, Religion and Philolo-
    gy in the Nineteenth Century*, translated by Arthur Goldhammer. Cam-
    bridge, MA.: Harvard University Press.

Priest, Robert D. 2015. *The Gospel According to Renan: Reading, Writing and Religion in Nineteenth-Century France.* Oxford: Oxford University Press.

Psichari, Henriette. 1937. *Renan d'après lui-même.* Paris: Librairie Plon.

Reardon, Bernard. 2010. *Liberalism and Tradition: Aspects of Catholic Thought in Nineteenth-Century France.* Cambridge: Cambridge University Press.

Renan, Ernest. N.d. *Oeuvres Complètes de Ernest Renan*, edited by Henriette Psichari. Paris: Calmann-Lévy.

———. 1861. *Averroès et l'averroïsm: essai historique*, 2nd edition. Paris: Michel Lévy.

———. 1863. *Vie de Jésus.* Paris: Michel Lévy Frères.

———. 1890. *L'avenir de la science: pensées de 1848.* Paris : Calmann Lévy.

———. 1898. *Vie de Jésus, édition populaire*, 65th edition. Paris: Calmann Lévy.

Schweitzer, Albert. 1926. *The Quest for the Historical Jesus: A Critical Study of its Progress from Reimarus to Wrede*, Second English edition. London: A. C. Black.

Wright, Terence R. 1994. "The Letter and the Spirit: Deconstructing Renan's *Life of Jesus* and the Assumptions of Modernity." *Religion & Literature* 26:55–71.

Zachhuber, Johannes. 2017. "The Historical Turn." In *The Oxford Handbook of Nineteenth Century Christian Thought*, edited by Joel Rasmussen, Judith Wolfe, and Johannes Zachhuber, 53–71. Oxford: Oxford University Press.

Britain and the Great Famine of 1917–19:
A Case Study in Paranoid Historiography[1]

Ali M. Ansari

IN HIS INFLUENTIAL ARTICLE on the "Paranoid Style in Iranian Historiography" Houchang Chehabi discusses the various ways in which the Iranian historiographical tradition has been infected with a tendency towards conspiracy theories and paranoia.[2] As he notes, such historical expressions are far from unique to Iran but are perhaps developed and established to a far greater extent than in other countries where such views, as a rule, are on the margins of historical writing. In Iran on the other hand, as Chehabi notes, such views have become endorsed and promoted by the political establishment as part of a wider tendency to challenge and disrupt narratives that are produced in the Western world.[3] While conspiratorial views predated the advent of the Islamic Republic in 1979, 'paranoid historiography' has since become very much part of the ideological armory of the revolutionary state; a political tool to be energetically cultivated. For the authorities of the Islamic Republic, 'History', is regarded less as a discipline for the discernment of 'truths', but as a political means to validate a larger 'Truth.'[4]

It has been argued that paranoid historiography reflects a certain secularization of the mind with supernatural unknowns replaced by natural unknowns, providing relatively simple explanatory frameworks paradoxically validated by the absence of evidence.[5] This absence of evidence simply confirms the conspiracy in what amounts to an unvirtuous circle. At the same time the most effective examples will build on accepted truths to reinforce a wider narrative towards a Truth which ultimately makes little sense. If scholarship exists to make sense out

1. I am grateful to both Paul Luft and Sam Taylor for reading and commenting on this piece and to Sam Taylor in particular for providing a basic mathematical framework on which I could model the various estimates and projections for demographic change that are used in this article.

2. Chehabi 2009, 155–76. Chehabi draws from Richard Hofstadter's seminal essay, "The Paranoid Style in American Politics" First delivered as a lecture at Oxford University in 1963 the essay was reissued in a revised and expanded edition (Hofstadter 2008).

3. President Ahmadinejad excelled in this sort of behavior, most notoriously in his attack on the history of the Holocaust.

4. For the sake of clarity "History" with a capital H, will refer in this essay to ideological and official histories. Truth here refers to larger moral Truths as distinct from the truth of particular events.

5. Chehabi 2009, 156.

of 'non-sense,' paranoid historiography does the opposite and will combine facts to produce non-sense. Information is not analyzed to produce knowledge but to serve ideological preconceptions.

There are clear echoes of Soviet historiography in the Islamic Republic's approach to History, including a belief that while the future is clear and pre-destined, it is the past which remains contested, and which must be fought for. Paranoid historiography has long been a feature of what we might term 'popular' or 'demotic' history, where myths, memory and folklore sit side by side with historical scholarship, (a reality which has been reinforced by the acceleration and exponential increase of information during the internet age). These are relatively easy to discern and can often be consigned to the category of propaganda. More interesting is the historical writing at the margin, where mythologies – narratives of meaning – are accorded a scholarly apparatus (references) in order to enhance their legitimacy. There are paranoid constructions which seek historical validation, and there are historical studies that are conversely forced to conform to the wider ideology. At this end of the spectrum the line between sound scholarship and speculation can often be blurred. This can be most often witnessed in the fanciful numbers – normally associated with military history – articulated by historians with little appreciation of the practical realities.[6]

Dramatic statistics are of course an important element of the revelatory nature of paranoid historiography, and just as the absence of evidence can rein-force the paranoia, so too the sudden discovery of a particular source, normally in isolation, will likewise serve to enhance the narrative. Devoid of either con-text or further supporting evidence a particular source is fetishized, extrapo-lated, and emphasized, often without critical analysis, as the hitherto hidden source now revealed to support a position. Ironically, and in contrast to the general suspicion of authorized, or government sources that permeates much of the ideological narrative, particular government sources – revealed for the first time – which support the narrative are treated as sacrosanct. That said, the ideological imperative often means that even these sources are used selectively and out of context to their wider narratives.

A further important dynamic relates to the ahistorical readings of national-ist narratives, which tend to read the present reality back into the historical re-cord without any realistic appreciation of the nature of historical development or progression. In simple terms this often relates to the back projection of an eternal and unchanging national identity – projected equally to that 'nation's' enemies – as well as an ahistorical understanding of the nature of the state.

---

6. It was not uncommon for example to hear scholars express the idea that Xerxes marched one million men across the Hellespont into Greece, without any appreciation of the logistics this would involve.

Perfidious Albion

Chehabi details two forms of historical narratives 'informed by conspiracy paradigms': particularistic and universalistic.[7] The former he ascribes to particular powers that have influenced Iran be they in Great Britain, the United States, and occasionally the Russian Empire/Soviet Union, while the latter refers to more abstract global forces, including but not limited to Zionism, Bahaism, and Freemasonry. It goes without saying that these two forms frequently overlap and the more damning the conspiracy the more elements are included.

Britain enjoys a special status insofar as its particular influence is frequently combined with its ability to manipulate universal trends, notably the three global forces noted above. Britain in this sense is the mastermind, and as the pioneer of the industrial revolution and the seedbed of industrial capitalism, the key driver behind the modern world system so disliked – even detested – by many on the left of the political spectrum. As such Britain exceeds the United States in culpability but more than that continues to be seen as the real force behind a range of malignant actions directed towards Iran.[8] Britain's imperial reach, far in excess of its formal empire, and its critical role in the formation of the modern world system have made it a natural target of nationalist critiques, with many national states having emerged from and defined against the British Empire. As an imperial project renowned for its indirect means of control it is natural that post-colonial critiques will lean towards non-coercive – hegemonic – means of control, one of which has been the weaponization of famine as a means of dominating societies. These approaches have been energized by the work of Mike Davis, whose study of climate and imperial policy in the late nineteenth century argued that the British imperial system effectively created the environment for widespread famines in what is now the Third World.[9] The two famines most clearly associated with the failure of British policy are the Irish potato famine in the 1840s and the Bengal famine of 1943, both of which have generated considerable literature in terms of causality and responsibility. More sober assessments have eschewed nationalist narratives, which lay the blame squarely at the feet of the British, and while critical of the initial government response see the causes of the famines elsewhere.[10] Amartya Sen's seminal study of the famine in Bengal

7. Chehabi 2009, 157.

8. Hojjat-ol Islam Aliasghar Rahmani-Khalili, quoted in the ISNA website, 2 February 2002, BBC SWB Mon MEPol. It is worth noting here that in Persian, the term "englis" and "englisi" is used as a synonym for Britain.

9. Davis 2001. As one reviewer noted, "Climate history meets Marxist political economy in this structural analysis of hunger at the close of the British imperium," Carney 2002, 173. .

10. "It seems clear enough that the British government neither caused the Famine nor acted with genocidal intent during it." English 2006, 163.

meanwhile has refocussed attention poor local administration and hoarding, arguing that famines are rarely caused by shortages of food, rather they result from hoarding and poor administration.[11]

The Iranian suspicion of Britain is naturally founded on the experience of British interference in Iranian political affairs not least the coup against Dr Mohammad Mosaddeq in 1953, but the myth of Perfidious Albion, has been developed to an extraordinary degree in Iran,[12] (though recent developments suggest that Russia may be running Iran a close second in this regard). Not that the anxieties about Perfidious Albion were uniform in the years leading to 1979. But after 1979 the narrative was both more emphatic and consequential, though far from limited to the revolutionaries. The animosity towards Britain became a staple of revolutionary ideology despite the contradiction manifest in personal preferences among many in the elite. One might even conjecture that the strength of the ideological animosity served to disguise this paradox.

Empowered by the tools of the modern mass media and the resources available to it, the post-revolutionary state has seen the greatest energy and effort placed in producing knowledge to this effect. The anniversary of the Coup in 1953 is witness to an annual review of the wickedness of Perfidious Albion ranging far and wide beyond the coup itself to review malign activities throughout the nineteenth century, often to the exclusion of other parties, most obviously Russia. Strikingly, depending on the political mood, the United States is frequently relegated to a minor and subservient role to Britain in 1953, with the role of the Great Satan, occupying a lower rung on the ladder to the 'evil state' of Britain, the eternal and constant enemy to the eternal and constant nation.

The 'wily fox' acts in mysterious ways that only a particularly penetrating analysis can discern, though that discernment will sooner or later reveal the British hand behind most egregious events that have affected Iran.[13] The former British Foreign Secretary, Jack Straw, was helpfully handed a list of grievances by protesting Basijis on a visit to Iran which ranged from the separation of Afghanistan from Iran (in the Treaty of Paris 1857), passing through the Constitutional Revolution of 1906 and the coup of 1953, to more recent interventions in the "Sedition of 88" (the Green Movement of 2009).[14] Iranian

11. Sen 1977, 33–59. On the debate over Sen's thesis see, O'Grada 2010, 36–39.

12. For further details of this process, see my "The Myth of Perfidious Albion" (2013), and "Britain, Iran and the Idea of Reform" (2019).

13. An especially good depiction of the wily fox can be seen here: https://www.historytoday.com /archive/feature/iran-and-'old-enemy'(accessed January 16, 2023).

14. These are reproduced in his book, see Straw 2019, 367–72, in both Persian and an English translation. The list, interestingly, omits any reference to the famine of 1917–19.

television meanwhile has produced a forty-five minute documentary charting the malign influence of Britain from the reign of Edward I.[15]

Such popular accounts are reinforced by attempts at scholarly conferences, which draw together politicians and academics in an attempt to validate the narrative through scholarly scrutiny. One such conference – "Iran and British Colonialism" – held in the spring of 1388 (2009) was illuminating in terms of both attendance and coverage, with the selective reading of sources, omission of inconvenient truths, absence of context, and in the case of the academics present, an earnest attempt to make the sources fit the ideological imperative.

The conference was convened with two keynotes from former President Hashemi Rafsanjani and the former speaker of the parliament, Gholamali Hadad Adel, receiving the imprimatur of the establishment.[16] The papers that followed covered much of the usual ground from the interventions of the nineteenth century to the murder of Amir Kabir, the economic concessions, not least oil, the Anglo-Persian Agreement of 1919 and the rise of the Pahlavis, along with the development of freemasonry and the connections between Savak and the British intelligence service. In his introduction, Rafsanjani noted that while the British did support the Constitutional Revolution, it was a revolution divested of the religious input the people had wanted, and consequently twisted to their own needs.[17] Hadad Adel's speech, recognizing that Rafsanjani has already covered the 'history', proceeded on a more thematic model, taking the long view (including the Crusades) to show how and why British imperialism succeeded.

What was striking about both submissions was the relative absence of any criticism of Russia with Rafsanjani arguing that Britain was the greatest beneficiary of the second Perso-Russian War (1826–28) and the subsequent Treaty of Turkmenchai (1828). Hadad Adel went further and suggested that it was the only the advent of the Soviet Union that prevented Britain from taking advantage of Iranian weakness after the Great War.[18] He went on to mention the Allied occupation in the Second World War but says nothing about the Azerbaijan Crisis of 1946.[19] This whitewashing of Russian imperialism and the transfer of blame to Britain is a reflection of the political priorities of post-revolutionary Iran, for which friendship with Russia was gaining in importance.

The weight of this political imperative can be seen in a subsequent paper

15. The first part of this documentary, from the Roman invasion to the nineteenth century has been downloaded and is in the author's possession.

16. *Irān va estemār englisi*, 735.

17. Rafsanjani 2009, 18.

18. Adel 2009, 26.

19. Adel 2009, 29.

by an academic contributor on the occupation of Azerbaijan, which does not ignore anxieties over Russian ambitions – not least over the separatist movement in Azerbaijani – but seeks nonetheless to place the blame for this on the British who were driven by a desire to protect their oil concession in the south.[20] The author, in passing, makes the important point, of relevance to the ongoing historiographical discussion, that Russian documents are, as yet, not available to confirm various suppositions and it is notable that the authors in this symposium rely almost exclusively on British documentary sources for their assessments.[21]

But for our purposes perhaps the most striking aspect of this collection of thirty-one papers, is the absence of any specific investigation into the Great Famine of 1917–19, and Britain's culpability for it. Indeed, despite the ubiquity of the famine narrative today, especially in the utterances of the supreme leader Ali Khamenei, Britain's culpability for the famine at the end of the Great War is a relative latecomer to the list of grievances cited by Iranians – it did not for example make the list submitted by the Basijis to Jack Straw.

Britain and The Great Famine

The notion of a great famine at the end of the Great War, and Britain's culpability for it has been a grievance that has gained in popularity over the last decade, with the supreme leader, Ali Khamenei, being a keen advocate.[22] As such it has entered the mainstream of popular discourse, with the more extreme versions of the narrative seeking to conjoin both the particularistic and universalistic tropes by suggesting that Britain was persuaded to cause a famine through the intrigues of global Zionism, marrying, simplifying, and reinforcing conspiratorial tropes into a single narrative.[23] These oversimplified, vulgar narratives, nonetheless serve to highlight some of the characteristics of paranoid historiography noted above: secrecy, revelation (usually from a single un-contextualized source), selective reading of sources combined in ways to fit the ideology, along with an ahistorical if not wholly fanciful reading of the past. Setting aside the absurd reading of British policy making, a major flaw in assessments, especially as it relates to famine, is to see Qajar Iran as a coherent political economy, fully func-

20. Lalavi 2009, 556.

21. Lalavi 2009, 552.

22. "8–10 million Iranians died over Great Famine caused by the British in late 1910s, documents reveal," https://web.archive.org/web/20151116004256/http://english.khamenei.ir/news/2197/8 -10-million-Iranians-died-over-Great-Famine-caused-by-the-British (accessed January 14, 2023).

23. See https://www.youtube.com/watch?v=ibtLnWwrgx4 (accessed January 14, 2023). In this clip, a grateful Rothschild, following the Balfour Declaration, suggests famine as a means of political control to George V.

tional and integrated. This nationalist projection of modern Iran backwards has major implications for any understanding of the causes and consequences of famines in pre-modern Iran.

A good example of this reading back into the historical record, norms, attitudes and approaches of the present, is the use of the term "genocide" in relation to the famine at the end of the Great War. The term was introduced in relation to the famine and Britain's apparent culpability, by Mohammad Gholi Majd in his short study entitled, *The Great Famine and Genocide in Persia 1917–19,*[24] a text which has informed much of the debate in official circles in Iran and is reported to be a favourite of the supreme leader, Ali Khamenei. The use of the "genocide" – a term which entered the international legal lexicon after the Second World War[25] – Majd clearly intended to excite attention, encourage an emotive reaction, and suggest a legal remedy in the form of reparations, a possibility which at least one president, Mahmoud Ahmadinejad, raised.[26]

Majd's book, which was published in 2003, does not refer to Mike Davis's study, which was published a year earlier – too late perhaps to inform it – but Majd pays due deference to this study in a subsequent book, which refers to the earlier famine in 1870–71 and whose title is clearly a homage to Davis' study.[27] This book is intended to be the second in a triptych of studies on famines in Iran – with a third volume planned to look at famine during the Allied occupation in the Second World War. The central thesis of the books is the demographic calamity inflicted by imperial powers, principally Britain (indirectly or directly) over a period of seventy years and three famines, from 1870–1944.

The figures deployed are stark. According to Majd the famine of 1917–19 was one of the greatest calamities to have affected Iran resulting in the deaths of some forty percent of the population. He elaborates on this figure in his subsequent study of the Great Famine of 1870–71, to claim more specifically that between 1869–1944 "Iran suffered three famines which claimed twenty-five million lives." He argues that the first famine "carried off some twelve million Iranians, or two thirds of the population'. (The implication of these figures, though he does not specify it, is that another thirty percent, at least four million were lost in World War II). The result was that while the global population doubled in the same period Iran's population effectively remained static from the eleven million recorded in 1841 through to the end of the Second World War.

Majd is not alone in claiming striking figures for the famine of 1870–71.

24. Majd 2003.

25. For details see Sands 2017.

26. "Iran's President Demands World War Reparations," Radio Free Europe, January 12,2010, https://www.rferl.org/a/Iran_President_Demands_World_War_Reparations/1927565.html (accessed January 15, 2023). On Khamenei's defence of Majd see footnote 22 above.

27. Majd 2018.

Indeed, contrary to his claim that there has been scant attention paid to the famine of 1870, this is the one famine that has received scholarly attention. John Gurney concludes in his own translation of an account of the famine in Qom that is it entirely possible a third of the population – up to three million – died.[28] Another study by Okazaki, draws attention to Gilbar's assessment that twenty to twenty-five percent of the population died, some one and a half million from an estimated population of six to seven million.[29] Gurney adds for good measure, as Majd does, that the reason it has not imprinted itself emphatically on the popular imagination was because the catastrophe, which included episodes of cannibalism, was simply too traumatic (and shameful), and resulted in "collective amnesia." Comparisons are also drawn to the Irish Potato Famine (1845–52) reflecting on the fact as Majd himself does, that the Irish case has regrettably received a good deal more scholarly attention despite the fact that the fatality rate in Iran may have been worse.

Such arguments clearly touch a nerve, in part because they feed into a broader narrative about the evils of British imperialism, which is felt in some circles to have escaped the criticism it deserves. The scale and revelatory nature of the findings also feed a deeper anxiety among a populace that feels that matters are regularly hidden, by the powers that be, from their gaze and scrutiny. Above all, in reinforcing a narrative, that is generally if not specifically known, it builds on truths to develop and promote a larger and more significant Truth. We know that Iran did suffer at least two devastating famines, around 1870 and again at the end of the Great War, and if Britain was far from culpable for the first, it was certainly present on the ground during the second.[30] The revelatory nature of the arguments pushed by Majd and others is nonetheless somewhat dampened by the fact that the main accounts of the famine – used extensively by Majd himself – come from foreign observers, not least the British themselves, whose accounts are far from sanitized.

Indeed, the one group that make less of the famines than they might, are the Iranians. It is not that they are suffering collective amnesia. Both famines are certainly acknowledged, along with Gurney's translation of an obviously Persian account of the famine in Qom in 1870. But it is true that they don't appear to have quite the social impact that such a calamity would normally induce, and there is none of the psychological scarring that we witness with the Irish experience. The famine at the end of the Great War is, for example, mentioned in the claims formally presented to the Paris Peace Conference by the Iranian delegation, but it forms part of a wider list of grievances and, much to Majd's

28. Amanat 2013. 1013. This is a review of D. J. Gurney and M. Sefatgol 2008.
29. Okazaki 1986, 185.
30. On administrative failures in 1870 see Okazaki 1986, 192.

rage, directs its criticisms against the Russians and the Ottomans – a sensible tactic one would think when the British were being approached for support as one of the victors[31]. The document is far from a shrinking violet as far as Iran's claims were concerned – the scale of the territorial restitution was so large as to illicit mockery[32] – and Britain's culpability for Iran's ills is not ignored in the document.

But the focus of the anger is the 1907 convention with Russia, which was widely regarded (including by a number of British officials) as a betrayal of the Constitutional Revolution. Interestingly this is echoed in a Persian newspaper editorial from 1923 (the subject of some protestation by the British embassy) which noted that until, "Sir Edward Grey canceled the former policy of England [*sic*], and agreed with Russia upon the convention of 1907," Britain had been quite popular in Iran. The ire is then turned towards Curzon and the ill-fated Anglo-Persian Agreement, along with the coup of 1921 and British attempts to turn Mesopotamia into a colony.[33] At no stage in the lengthy diatribe is the famine mentioned.

Majd, frustrated by the fact that the Iranian government did not press its claims in Paris, dismisses the document as a deliberate whitewash clearly prepared by a prime minister (Vosuq) beholden to the British: "By mixing a heavy dose of mendacity and falsification with the demands and grievances of Persia, the intention was to discredit Persia and weaken her case."[34] Unsurprisingly his tendency to dismiss evidence that does not fit the narrative he wishes to pursue has resulted in a good deal of criticism from historians who consider Majd's argument self-indulgent, selective, and excessive.[35] Certainly, Majd's figures far outstrip those of other historians in the level of the demographic decimation inflicted upon Iran in this period and the absence of social, economic, and psychological scarring is remarkable. One possible reason, not widely considered, is that the rate of fatalities was either not as dramatic, or not as extraordinary, as later historians had imagined, and for contemporary Iranians at least, were regarded as the routine experience of an unforgiving existence.

But the figures demand greater scrutiny because even the figures claimed by Gurney, Gilbar, and others in relation to the famine of 1870 and the consequences of Great War are dramatic. Taking any of these figures at face value, we

31. "Claims of Persia before the Conference of the Preliminaries of Peace at Paris," Paris, March 1919.

32. Sykes 2004 (1915), 519.

33. Leading article in the Tehran newspaper *Shafaq Sorkh* dated May 4, 1923, reprinted in Burrell 1997, 6:499–501.

34. Majd 2003, 138.

35. Abrahamian 2015, 27. See also Willem Floor's review, Floor 2005.

are looking at a population loss of anything between twenty-five and sixty percent of the population – Gurney suggests thirty percent in 1870, Gilbar twenty to twenty-five percent; Majd meanwhile assesses forty percent in 1917–19 and sixty percent for 1870. To put this in comparative perspective, the Irish Potato Famine resulted in one million fatalities from a population of eight million, with another one to two million lost through emigration, mainly to the United States. Ireland, which had hitherto matched England in terms of its population, never recovered from this catastrophe, which left it socially scarred. The fatalities amount to about twelve percent of the population, far short of what was supposed to have been experienced at regular intervals by Iran. The Bengal Famine meanwhile experienced a fatality rate of around five percent, if one accepts Amartya Sen's larger figure of around three million from a total of sixty million. Despite incurring fatalities at least twice as large as those endured by Ireland, the memory of this experience, we are told, was suppressed.[36]

Even if this were the case, the historian might reasonably expect to see some striking social and economic consequences from such a reduction in population, be it in economic production or indeed wage costs for a much-depleted labor force. A comparable experience would have been that of the Black Death in fourteenth-century Europe, which is estimated to have reduced the European population by some fifty percent. The economic repercussions of this were profound and long term. Such a situation does not appear to have been replicated in Iran, which suggests that figures have been exaggerated as a result of a false extrapolation, ascribing the devastating consequences of famine in one town or region to the wider country. But Iran at least until the modernization of the twentieth century was an integrated economy as we understand today. There was limited connectivity and transport infrastructure, resulting in a tapestry of often isolated local markets. This meant that when famine hit a particular region or town, the absence of wider communication both exacerbated the consequences (it was difficult to bring food in) but also contained it. Observers might rightly be horrified at the effects of famine in their particular locale, but it would be a mistake to automatically assume that the local extended nationally.

Other ways in which we might transpose "modernism" erroneously to the past is in the understanding of population growth. It is worth reminding ourselves that one of the key problems in assessing the population data for this period, is that the data simply does not exist. This allows for a wide range of what

36. For further comparison, the Ukrainian famine of 1933, the "Holodomor" caused an estimated 10% loss to the population, see in this regard Oleh Wolowyna, "Understanding Holodomor Loss numbers," *Ukrainian Weekly*, June 29 2018, https://www.ukrweekly.com/uwwp/understanding-holodomor-loss-numbers/ (accessed January 15, 2023).

we might best describe as conjecture. To quote Afkhami, "the scarcity in both quantity and quality of data on the prevalence of death, deprivation, and disease in Iran during this period has been the principal driver of interpretive divergence, distortions, and conspiratorial constructs in the scholarship."[37]

Iran's first formal decennial census was conducted in 1956, and while there were some local censuses conducted in towns including Tehran in the nineteenth century – one notable one being for Tehran in 1868[38] – these are best viewed as guides rather than reliable indicators of the population, even if they do serve the useful purposes of curtailing more wayward suggestions of population size. The consequence is that population estimates are calculated backwards from the data produced in 1956 with the most reliable and frequently used assessment being that calculated by Julian Bharier.[39]

Bharier's analysis, starting with the figure of 27.07 million in 1966, and back through to 20.38 million in 1956, while recognizing the difficulties with data collection even in this period, and factoring in issues of infant mortality, population growth, and famine, assesses the population to have been just under 10 million in 1900, 10.89 million in 1914, and 11.29 million in 1919. He assesses a growth figure of 0.75% – not unusual for pre-modern societies without the benefits of modern healthcare – rising to around 1.5% in the interwar period and rising further to above 2% in the post Second World War period. These would be indications of demographic transition, the imposition of modern healthcare programs including vaccination, with the resultant reduction in mortality rates, especially infant mortality.

On a purely mathematical basis it would be conceivable for Iran to have suffered a thirty percent loss in population in the Great Famine of 1870 and with a one percent annual growth in population, replenish its population to the figures assessed by Bharier for 1900. It would not however be possible to achieve this on the lower estimate of six to seven million (Gilbar's assessment) without a higher rate of growth. Both growth rates are higher than that considered reasonable by Bharier for this period and are considerably higher than the global average. But even if mathematically feasible, for the reasons noted above, they must be considered historical implausible, not least when compared to the impact upon Ireland with a fatality rate far less than that of Iran.

Matters become more problematic if we apply Majd's figures, which assume a loss of 25 million over three famines, two of which reduce the population by forty and sixty percent respectively. Mathematically this assessment only

37. Afkhami 2020, 202.
38. Tawfiq 1990.
39. Bharier 1968, 273–79.

works if we assume a population of 18 million in 1868 with a consistent growth in population of two percent thereafter. This would allow the population to recoup its losses and achieve the totals surveyed in 1956. But again, taken in comparative perspective this requires the expectation that far from reeling from the demographic shock of systematic losses of nearly half the population, the remaining population, without much afterthought, continued reproducing at rates far higher than the global average at the time and comparable only with advanced and modernizing societies.

One further factor for consideration in terms of population loss in the aftermath of the Great War is the onset of Spanish flu, which according to Sykes, affected southern Iran badly.[40] Estimates of fatalities vary ranging from twenty-five to fifty million globally, with around one percent of the European population to around five percent of the population of India, though Afkhami estimates that Iran may have suffered an even greater loss at around 8%-21.7% of the population on account of the weakened resistance resulting from other accumulating factors, including the ongoing famine. Afkhami reaches this figure by projecting a higher mortality rate for rural over urban areas, though what data we do have available, largely from British sources, relates to urban centers and indicates a mortality rate of 0.8% for Tehran, reaching the outlier of 46.2% for Bam.[41] What is interesting here is that Sykes, clearly shocked by the impact of the Spanish flu, considers that 10,000 people died in Shiraz from a total of population of 50,000, some twenty percent of the total, while the records submitted to the Foreign Office by Sir Percy Cox in 1920 suggest a death rate of four percent for Shiraz.[42] Assuming Afkhami's estimates are correct, and for the reasons noted, this author is skeptical of the larger figures, then the highest share of the fatalities in this period were a consequence of the Spanish flu, not famine, even if one could argue that the latter enabled the former.[43]

But the figures here, as debatable as they are, continue to also highlight the problems posed by contemporary sources, especially those witnesses to the mass deaths that clearly elicited shock. Sykes, who is far from an unreliable witness, is still inclined to report a death rate in Shiraz five times higher than the official statistics compiled a year later. It is a salutary reminder to treat sources relating traumatic events with caution, that figures cited reflect less a statistical inquiry and more the sense of the individual reporting. Much of the assessment of

40. Sykes 2004 (1915), 515.

41. Afkhami 2003, 391.

42. Quoted in Amir Afkhami 2003, 384.

43. Abrahamian is certainly of the view that chief culprits were Spanish flu, typhus, and cholera; see Abrahamian 2015, 27.

the fatality rates are garnered from reports, mainly of US diplomats witnessing the horrors of particular towns and villages and then extrapolating for the entire country.[44] Majd draws on these select accounts to help paint the picture he wishes to draw and adds for good measure the graphic accounts of the famine in western Iran, especially around Hamedan, provided by Lionel Dunsterville and Martin Donohoe.

As noted above, Majd is accepting of those sources that serve his narrative and dismissive of those which might contradict it. But in his use of Dunsterville and Donohoe he also highlights some of the problems inherent in trying to ensure that sources conform to a particular argument, which is that the British both caused and exacerbated the famine by wilfully hoarding and shipping grain abroad. The evidence that exists in these texts reveals at worst a military establishment wedded to methods of famine relief that reflected an outdated Christian ethic – that is as Dunsterville notes in his efforts towards famine relief in Hamedan, that the best way to alleviate famine was to put people to work. But there is no indication from these sources that the British were engaged in hoarding or the deliberate manipulation of the markets. By exaggerating his arguments Majd undeniably undermines whatever case he might have.

Take for example a passage quoted by Majd of Dunsterville that recounts his need for supplies.:

> In the midst of the terrible famine that was now at its height I did not wish to draw supplies from the country that would still further reduce the stock available for the starving people. But we soon had accurate intelligence on the supply question and found that there was suffi-cient grain and fodder for all, although no abundance, and it was only being held up to secure higher prices. Unfortunately, however, the result of our small purchases was to send prices even higher, and each fractional rise meant the death of many individuals.[45]

Majd ignores the obvious fact that the local Iranians traders were hoarding foodstuffs to suggest that this proves British callousness in purchasing much needed grain. He omits the continuation of the passage in Dunsterville's account that reads, '

> Only a properly regulated wheat control system could meet the case, and we were not at present strong enough to enforce our views on

---

44. Majd of course assumes that these American diplomats are reliable witnesses; but many came with baggage of their own. See in this regard, Louis 1985, 395–420.
45. Dunsterville quoted in Majd 2003, 74.

this subject, but we were able to undertake the necessary measures when Brigadier General Byron came up to Hamedan as my second in command. General Byron remained for a long time in Hamedan and was able to deal with the famine and wheat control in a businesslike way which did much to enhance our popularity.[46]

Further on Majd quotes a single line from a letter Dunsterville wrote that shows his satisfaction at having secured supplies despite the continuing difficulties. He completely omits to include the wider context of the letter, which reads in part,

> Meantime, though wheat and barley are short, they do exist. I could collect by force enough to feed the troops and stop the famine, but I have no force to employ. I know where the wheat is, but have difficulty in getting it. Firstly, the owner holds on in the hope of higher prices; secondly, the villagers resent it being taken from a village while they starve; thirdly, brigands attack grain convoys on the road; fourthly, the extreme democrats threaten to kill anyone who supplies the British; and fifthly, the governor shows me an order he has received from the Government in Teheran to the effect that he is to see it I get no supplies.

He adds, "The country is naturally rich in grain, fruit and sheep, and there will be no supply difficulty as soon as the new crop is in."[47] When recounting the supply of rice from Glan to Baku, where Dunsterville's men were then stationed, Majd omits to point out that his supplier was none other than Kuchek Khan, the leader of the Jangalis, with whom he had been negotiating.[48]

All in all, Majd account is focused on reading the worst intentions into the actions of the British. At one stage he describes Donohoe's burning of the local stores so that they would not be used by an advancing Ottoman army as, "a war crime and genocide."[49] Those sources that conform to the argument are endorsed enthusiastically, those that do not are dismissed and quoted out of context. None are approached with a critical eye. The British sources, especially those that are autobiographical, are likely to paint a sympathetic portrayal of the author and there can be little doubt that the need to supply troops would affect the market and access to crops. But it is not at all clear that the British were decisive in this respect, not least because their presence, in relative terms, remained

---

46. Dunsterville 2007 (1920), 62.
47. Dunsterville 2007 (1920), 124.
48. Majd 2003, 87. The relevant passage is in Dunsterville 2007 (1920), 255.
49. Majd 2003, 77.

small even at the end of the war when they became, by default the dominant foreign power in Iran. As a consequence, what purchases of foodstuffs that took place was by and large done with the cooperation – some might say complicity – of the Iranian authorities, at local and national level.

When Dunsterville was instructed to lead a force into Iran towards the Caucasus in an effort to contain the fallout from the Russian Revolution, the force he took with him was a small volunteer force, which at the outset numbered little more than 100 men. The original idea was to dispatch a force of some 400 with a view to recruiting local soldiers, as well as the White Russians available in the Cossack Brigade, which had remained intact. In the event, with the pressure of time and the need to secure control of those areas the Russians had effectively vacated, with a view to obstructing the Ottoman advance, Dunsterville proceeded with a total of twelve officers, two clerks, forty-one chauffeurs, one armored car and thirty troops.[50] As he noted, the Iranians he encountered never failed to exaggerate the forces he had with him, a consequence perhaps of the fact that few could believe the British Empire would "invade" Iran with such a force. The incredulity has arguably lasted to this day.[51] But this was above all a reconnaissance force of specialist troops (the chauffeurs might be better understood as mechanics and engineers), well-funded and motivated. But it is difficult to see this force as placing significant pressure on the country's resources.

Dunsterville's account portrays a country in administrative chaos, with a central government that had lost whatever authority it might have enjoyed as the Constitutional Revolution ground to a halt. Fought over by Ottoman and Russian troops, which never reached the size of the armies that marauded across the Caucasus (still less the main European battlefields) due to the logistical difficulties presented by Iran, these armies nonetheless caused huge disruption and damage to the local economies, compounding the earlier problems of the absence of government. By far the worst perpetrators were the Ottomans, followed by the depredations of the Russians following their revolution and the departure of most of their officers.[52] When drought affected the crop, it was unsurprising that local officials and merchants would take advantage. Added to this mixture were the nationalist Democrats, whose vigorous anti-British agitation has continued to inform assessments, despite the fact that the views of the Germans towards them – "Persian patriotism has become an industry which

50. Dunsterville 2007 (1920), 85.
51. Safavi and Ghofori 1396/2017:169. Safavi and Ghofori are a lecturer and doctoral student respectively at the Payam-e Nour University.
52. Amanat 2019, 395.

seems to look for its gains to extortion" – were no more complimentary than those of the British.[53]

In this broader context, whatever culpability the British held with respect to the tragedy that befell Iran in this period was some-way down the pecking order of responsibility. This was in fact the conclusion reached by two Iranians scholars who saw the centenary of the famine as an opportune moment for a reassessment. What is striking about the article is that despite the obvious pressures to conform to an official narrative, their conclusions mirror in important ways the assessment made by Dunsterville of the internal situation. They are rightly skeptical of the "ethics" that drove Dunsterville's famine relief operation – though this reflected the sentiments of the time – and clearly struggle to digest the size of Dunsterville's force (the term "chauffeur" clearly suffers in translation both in terms of language and time!), suggesting that Dunsterville underreported the size of the force and hence his responsibility. There is no evidence to indicate that at this stage Dunsterforce – as the mission was dubbed – was larger than Dunsterville reported, and by the end of the war Norperforce, as the military mission in northern Iran was called, along with the South Persia Rifles, (which was largely composed of native troops), amounted to little more than 15,000 soldiers in total.[54]

Their conclusion highlights the activities of the British and the Russians, even if the body of the text gives more weight to the Ottomans. But crucially they do not withhold criticism from the mismatched array of domestic forces, from the failure of the government to the hoarding of local officials and merchants. This is not history viewed through a nationalist lens, in which the perspectives of the present day are transplanted without modification to the past, where Iranians are regarded as uniquely virtuous and their enemies as blandly evil. As more sober historical assessments have concluded, for all the intent of neutrality Iran's governing party (the Democrats) wilfully engaged in politics, actively courting German support and eliciting little sympathy. Above all, they avoid providing numbers. The lack of reliable data they argue precludes any meaningful assessment of the number of deaths. This reflects the fact that contemporary attempts to measure with any exactness the scale of a trauma need to be viewed with especial caution. It is, within the constraints of their political environment, a commendable assessment, and a reminder that even in Iran, there are limits to paranoid historiography.

53. See the assessment of Field Marshal von der Goltz, on the situation in Persia, dated 16 February 1916, included in Moberly 1987 (1929), 472–73.
54. There were of course far more British troops in Mesopotamia, but even Majd (2008, 8) admits that Mesopotamia had ample grain of its own.

Works Cited

Abrahamian, Ervand. 2015. *The Coup: 1953, the CIA and The Roots of Modern US-Iranian Relations.* New York: The New Press.

Adel, Hadad. 2009. "Estemār englisi dar Irān." In *Irān va estemār englisi.* Tehran: Institute for Political Studies and Research.

Afkhami, Amir. 2003. "Compromised Constitutions: the Iranian Experience with the 1918 Influenza Pandemic." *Bulletin of the History of Medicine* 77: 391.

———. 2020. "Mortality Matters: Sources on Population Health and Mortality during the First World War in Iran." *Iranian Studies* 53: 202.

Amanat, Abbas. 2013. "Of Famine and Cannibalism in Qom." *Iranian Studies* 47:1013.

———. 2019. *Iran: A Modern History.* New Haven: Yale University Press.

Ansari, Ali. 2013. "The Myth of Perfidious Albion: Anglo-Iranian Relations in Historical Context." *Journal of Asian Affairs* 44:378–91.

———.2019. "Britain, Iran and the Idea of Reform." In *Iran, Islam & Democracy – The Politics of Managing Change,* edited by Ali Ansari, 543–656. London: Gingko, third expanded edition.

Bharier, Julian. 1968. "A Note on the Population of Iran, 1900–1966." *Population Studies* 22:273–79.

Burrell, R. M. ed. 1997. *Iran: Political Diaries 1881–1965.* Fourteen volumes. Chippenham: Archive Editions, 1997.

Carney, Judith A. 2002. *Annals of the Association of American Geographers* 92:173.

Chehabi, Houchang. 2009. "The Paranoid Style in Iranian Historiography." In *Iran in the 20th Century: Historiography and Political Culture,* edited by Touraj Atabaki, 155–76. London: I.B. Tauris.

Davis, Mike. 2001. *Late Victorian Holocausts: El Niño Famines and the Making of the Third World.* London: Verso.

Dunsterville, Lionel. 2007 (1920). *The Adventures of Dunsterforce.* Ukfield: The Naval and Military Press.

English, Richard. 2006. *Irish Freedom: The History of Nationalism in Ireland.* London: Macmillan.

Floor, Willem. 2005. Review of Ervand Abrahamian's *The Coup. Iranian Studies* 38:192–96.

Gurney D. J., and M. Sefatgol. 2008. *Qom dar qahti-ye bozorg, 1288.* Qom: Mar'ashi Library.

Hofstadter, Richard. 2008. *The Paranoid Style in American Politics.* New York: Vintage.

Lalavi, Mahmood. 2009. "Englis va bohrān-e Azerbaijān" in *Irān va estemār englisi*. Tehran: Institute for Political Studies and Research.

Louis, W. Roger. 1985. "American Anti-colonialism and the Dissolution of the British Empire." *International Affairs* 61:395–420.

Majd, Mohammad Gholi. 2003. *The Great Famine and Genocide in Persia*. Lanham: University Press of America.

———. 2018. *A Victorian Holocaust: Iran in the Great Famine of 1869–1873*. Plymouth: Hamilton Books.

Moberly, F. J. 1987 (1929). *Operations in Persia, 1914–19*. London: Imperial War Museum, 472–73.

O'Grada, Cormac. 2010. "Revisiting the Bengal Famine of 1943–4." *History Ireland* 18:36–39.

Okazaki, Shoko. 1986. "The Great Persian Famine of 1870–71." *Bulletin of the School of Oriental and African Studies*, Special Issue in Honour of Ann K. S. Lambton, 49:185.

Rafsanjani, Hashemi. 2009. "Sokhanrāni-ye eftetāhiye." In *Irān va estemār englisi*. Tehran: Institute for Political Studies and Research.

Safavi, Alireza Ali and Shahram Ghofori. 1396/2017. "Elal va payamadhaye ghahti nashi az jang-e jahāni-e aval dar Hamedān." *Taghighāt-e tārikh-ejtemāi,* 7:169.

Sands, Philippe. 2017. *East West Street*. London: Weidenfeld & Nicolson.

Sen, Amartya. 1977. "Starvation and Exchange Entitlements: A General Approach and Its Application to the Great Bengal Famine," *Cambridge Journal of Economics* 1:33–59.

Straw, Jack. 2019. *The English Job*. London: Biteback.

Sykes, Percy. 2004 (1915). *A History of Persia*. London: Taylor and Francis.

Tawfiq, Firuz. 1990. "Census i. In Iran." *EIr* V, 142.

Railway Masculinity in Early Pahlavi Iran

Mikiya Koyagi

IN THE LAST FEW DECADES, historians have explored the construction of the new hegemonic masculinity advocated and embodied by the emerging modern middle class in the late nineteenth and early twentieth-century Middle East.[1] Characterized by his distinct appearance, education, and sociocultural attitude, the normative modern man was distinguished from the rest of the male population with different outlooks on how to be a man. As Sivan Balslev details, this process in Iran was inseparable from the authoritarian modernization undertaken by the newly established Pahlavi state, which implemented conscription, male and female sartorial reforms, and Western-style education, including physical education, to name a few most relevant projects.[2] Being both the promoters and beneficiaries of these projects, modern middle-class men vilified social institutions that produced and maintained an older ideal of masculinity called *javānmardi*, a crucial behavioral quality possessed by the *luti*.[3] However uneven and incomplete this process may have been in twentieth-century Iran, the making of new masculinities was central to class formation.

The working class is generally absent in Middle Eastern historiographies of masculinity.[4] This is a noticeable lacuna considering the important role of industrial workers in Middle Eastern national political movements, especially during the second half of the twentieth century. As studies of masculinity in other geographical contexts illustrate, workers formulated and reformulated distinct notions of masculinity in response to rapidly changing socioeconomic conditions, coopting or rejecting aspects of hegemonic middle-class values,

1. Ghoussoub and Sinclair-Webb 2000. Jacob 2011; Balslev 2020. For male physical culture, see Yildiz 2015, 192–214.

2. Amin 2002; Atabaki 2007; Cronin 1997; Cronin 2006, 26–27; Cronin 2007; Cronin 2010; Cronin 2003; Marashi 2008; Vejdani 2015; Chehabi 1993.

3. I define the *luti* as an urban "riffraff" who lived on the margins of legality yet could act honorably to protect the weak from the oppressor or act dishonorably in helping the oppressor, depending on one's perspective. For *lutis*, see Balslev 2010, especially chapter one: Ideals and Practices of Masculinity in Qajar Society; Bell 2015; Gölz 2021, 120–47. For a comparative view on the *lutis*, see Sato et al. 1994.

4. For a detailed study of competing masculinities and femininities among workers, see Hammad 2016. Kaveh Ehsani also analyzes gender relations through the spatial structure of company housing in Iran's oil industry. See Ehsani 2003, 361–99.

while differentiating themselves from other industrial workers.[5] Through these formulation and reformulation, individual workers accepted, modified, and re-tooled various ideals of masculinities in specific social contexts and inscribed manliness onto their bodies in numerous ways.[6] Thus, exploring a working-class masculinity unsettles the modern/traditional axis in understanding Middle Eastern masculinities and rectifies the literature that sometimes dichotomizes masculinities between middle-class aspirations and traditional ideals of manliness as their antitheses.

This essay examines the ideals of masculinity among workers in Iran's railway industry. The case of railway workers deserves particular attention. The Trans-Iranian Railway, the country's first long-haul railway, began its full operations only in 1938, considerably after the global railway boom in the nineteenth century. Because the newly-established Pahlavi state implemented the railway project as the pillar of its centralization policies, the Iranian State Railway came to occupy a prominent status as the symbol of technological modernity achieved by the state in the heavily-censored interwar Iranian press. Once the Allied occupation began in 1941, the Iranian State Railway was used to transport American lend-lease materials from the Persian Gulf to the Soviet Union and became the symbol of Iran's sacrifice and contribution to the allied cause in World War II. Having gained the name "Victory Bridge," the Iranian State Railway developed into the largest state sector in Iran, with 36,000 employees by the mid-1940s. As employees of this symbolically significant institution for Iranian nationalism, railway workers occupied a unique status in Iranian society as elite industrial workers.

This essay is based primarily on the official monthly gazette of the Ministry of Roads, called *Nāmeh-ye Rāh*, whose stated objective was to familiarize employees in Iran's transport sector with theoretical and practical knowledge about transport infrastructures.[7] The journal's usefulness rests on two factors. First, as its presumed readership was literate employees in the transport sector, the journal helps us get a glimpse of the elite industrial employees' aspirations to coopt modern middle-class values. Second, as the journal was distributed among employees in the general transport sector, it sometimes reveals the tension among transport workers, conveying how railway workers situated themselves in relation to other transport workers, especially automobile mechanics and drivers.

---

5. Baron 2006, 143–60. Meyer 2016. For interwar Chilean miners' responses to paternalist social welfare policies and nuclearization of family structures, see Klubock 1996, 439–41.

6. For the critique of a unitary subject in the original conceptualization of hegemonic masculinity, Connell and Messerschmidt 2005, 841–42.

7. "Manzur-e Nāmeh-ye Rāh," *Nāmeh-ye Rāh* vol. 1, nos. 5–6 (1940): 2.

Reading this source closely, I argue that many middle- and upper-echelon Iranian railway workers came to embrace "railway masculinity," defined by their unique relationship to technology, by the mid-twentieth century.

I have discussed elsewhere how Iran's railway industry cultivated a sense of belonging among its workers through the establishment of housing, athletic, and recreational facilities for socialization. By the late 1940s, the normative masculine ideals of the railway workforce came to reproduce certain aspects of modern middle-class masculinity, including patriotism, the ability to provide for one's family (including modern education for their children) as the single breadwinner, and the sound use of leisure time.[8]

The process of socialization that contributed to the shaping of railway workers' masculinity started from their training as students of technical schools, established in the late 1930s as part of the Pahlavi state's attempt at indigenizing the skilled transport workforce. The Railway Technical School (Āmuzeshgāh-e Fanni-ye Rāh Āhan) is a prime example of these schools. After its establishment by the Iranian Railway Organization (IRO) in 1937, the school trained over seven hundred locomotive engineers, repair workers, station masters, stokers, and others within four years.[9] Although many railway workers, especially older generations, did not go through the same formal training provided by Iranian state institutions, those who went to the new schools interacted with their peers and fellow workers from the beginning of their training, living in the dormitories on the school premises. For example, the students of the Railway Technical School took a five-day group trip that combined learning and recreation to Mazandaran. While studying how to operate the railway system on site and visiting repair factories, they interacted with railway workers of Mazandaran by playing soccer together, cementing the bond among the geographically scattered railway workforce.[10]

Nāmeh-ye Rāh regularly featured similar school trips and intra-organizational sporting events. It not only celebrated the activities of the IRO's intra-organizational soccer, wrestling, and bicycling teams but also introduced their participation in national sporting events, where railway school students marched in major stadiums along with other teenage school boys and girls.[11] At-

8. Koyagi 2021, especially chapter six.

9. "Dāyereh-ye fanni-ye āmuzesh-e rāh āhan," *Nāmeh-ye Rāh* vol. 1, no. 3 (1940): 32. For another school, see "Āmuzeshgāh-e fanni-ye rāh cheh khedmati anjām dād?" *Nāmeh-ye Rāh* vol. 3, nos. 11–12 (1943): 350.

10. "Mosāferat-e 'elmi-ye dāneshāmuzān-e bongāh," *Nāmeh-ye Rāh* vol. 2, no. 3 (1941): 80–82.

11. For example see "Honarestān-e rāh āhan-e dowlati-ye irān," *Nāmeh-ye Rāh*, vol. 1, no. 10 (1941), 6–7; "Do ruz-e bozorg dar tārikh-e irān," *Nāmeh-ye Rāh* vol. 1, no. 10 (1941): 3–5; and "Ahamiyat-e āmuzeshgāh-e bongāh-e rāh āhan," *Nāmeh-ye Rāh* vol. 2, no. 1 (1941): 5–10.

tendance at these events symbolized railway workers' status as elite industrial workers whose bodies were displayed in public next to those of other modern middle-class teenagers.[12] They were an integral part of the youth athletic culture of early Pahlavi Iran.

The social duty of railway workers also mirrored that of the modern middle class. A 1941 article in *Nāmeh-ye Rāh* enumerated the benefits of transport infrastructure. Aside from the creation of a national economic market, the article stressed the impact of transport infrastructure in transforming the local populations. Labor discipline required in infrastructural projects would transform lazy and lethargic locals into productive workers, who would also make disciplined soldiers during military service. Moreover, along with government officials and engineers, workers from urban centers would bring their families to their countryside. These family members would propagate a modern way of life, which would be manifested in the increased use of glass windows, desks, and chairs among rural populations.[13] The role assigned to transport workers closely resembled that of the modern middle class, who were encouraged to travel across the nation as missionaries to spread civilized (euphemism for European) customs and inculcate national consciousness from urban centers to the countryside.

Reflecting their elite status, railway workers had additional duties that went beyond disseminating new customs and national consciousness, as modern middle-class men were expected to do. As operators of the symbol of the national technological achievement, they were to function as missionaries of technoscientific knowledge to the general population. Another *Nāmeh-ye Rāh* article encapsulated this role when it proclaimed the establishment of railway technical schools. The significance of training a small number of students could not be overstated because they were also members of Iranian society at large. They would interact with their families and friends, elevating the levels of their own lives as well as those of whoever interacts with them, ultimately uplifting the general level of Iranian technoscientific knowledge.[14] Despite the small number of students trained at these technical schools, their impact was to amplify incrementally as they continue to disseminate technoscientific knowledge.

Disseminating technoscientific knowledge was all the more urgent because, according to technocrats, Iranians hopelessly lacked basic exposure to technology since childhood. Unlike Euro-Americans, who grew up with new technologies, Iranian youths lacked such experience, making it hard for them to under-

12. Koyagi 2009, 1668–96.

13. "Rāhha-ye shuseh: pishrafthā-ye keshvar dar bist sāl-e gozashteh," *Nāmeh-ye Rāh* vol. 1, no. 9 (1941): 25–26.

14. "Ahamiyat-e āmuzeshgāh-e bongāh-e rāh āhan," *Nāmeh-ye Rāh* vol. 2, no. 1 (1941): 5–10

stand the meaning of basic things such as the school bells at the beginning and end of class.[15] To make up for this absence of technology in childhood, students at Iranian technical institutes had to be surrounded by all kinds of technologies at the school. A 1941 report on the new facilities of the technical institute illustrates this desire, as it paid meticulous attention to the presence of machines and technological gadgets in the three-story building, noting every detail of technology from hot and cold water pipes and telephones to electronic clocks and school bells.[16]

The curriculum of the technical schools was also designed to produce future missionaries of technoscientific knowledge. During the three-year program students could join after completing middle school, they studied numerous subjects including physics, mechanics, chemistry, accounting, algebra, and French. The curriculum became more specialized during the second year, when students could choose from studying: 1) how relevant tools, machines, and technologies worked, including steam engines and motors; 2) how construction and maintenance worked, including rail building and bridge building; 3) how railway business worked, including duties of station employees, railway regulations, and telegraph.[17] Importantly, students had to acquire comprehensive knowledge of technology, not limited to the mastery of locomotives and steam engines. They needed to have knowledge of adjacent fields such as electricity, welding, water purification, and construction to be the future operators of rail infrastructure.[18] In short, at least in theory, students received intensive training on both practical and theoretical technoscientific knowledge to become familiar with various aspects of the rail infrastructure system, which would prepare them to bring a broad range of expertise to the Iranian provincial life.

This emphasis on theoretical *and* practical mechanical knowledge was a critical aspect that separated railway workers from modern middle-class men. Political cartoons of the early Pahlavi period aptly captured modern middle-class men's relationship to technology. For example, in a cartoon printed in the satirical newspaper *Setāreh-ye Sobh*, a man in westernized clothing sat in the back seat of an automobile driven by a chauffeur, with trains, airplanes, and factories in his background. This image was juxtaposed with another cartoon that showed men in traditional clothing who used donkeys and camels for transport.[19] Another article mocked an old parliamentarian who completely

15. "San'at va āmuzesh," *Mardān-e Ruz*, April 11, 1945.
16. "Honarestān-e rāh āhan-e dowlati-ye irān," *Nāmeh-ye Rāh*, vol. 1, no. 10 (1941), 6–7.
17. Malakuti 1948, 202–4.
18. "Ahamiyat-e āmuzeshgāh," *Nāmeh-ye Rāh* vol. 2, no. 1 (1941): 5–6.
19. For this political cartoon, see Koyagi 2021, 77–78.

panicked during his first flight, conflating the wind generated by the airplane with the duel between Rostam and Afrasiyab from the *Shāhnāmeh*, while the journalist remained calm without infusing the technological experience with mythological stories.[20] In contradistinction with his traditional antithesis, who was too ignorant and superstitious to appreciate mechanized modes of transport, the modern man had access to them. He appreciated the transformations brought about by them.

Railway workers had a different relationship to technology. In fact, transport workers in general had a different relationship to technology, as illustrated in a translated series of articles called "The Automobile and Driving" printed in *Nāmeh-ye Rāh*. In a 1941 article, the series introduced an encounter between a mechanic and his customer, who came to the auto repair shop to have his car's engine fixed. It turned out that the customer tried to fix his car's strange noise by following directions from his son, who had made good grades at school, and tampered with the engine. The article's main point is to explain to the reader step by step how to fix engine problems, but the most important part for us comes at the end of the article, when the mechanic finishes fixing the engine. He proclaimed, "the driver was a rich man, but he was no repairer.... Repairing cars is not for everybody. There is a division of labor; each person is knowledgeable in one job."[21] The article reiterated the same point in a separate section: "Do not overhaul your own car. Give several riyals to the repair shop for safety, speed, and time-saving. Repairing should be completed by a knowledgeable person."[22] Each episode in the series provided the reader with a different aspect of practical mechanical knowledge, revolving around an encounter between a wealthy automobile owner who could not repair his car and a knowledgeable mechanic who saved the day.[23] It was the practical mechanical knowledge to repair machines that differentiated transport workers from modern middle-class men, who may have owned technology and benefited from it but did not know how to fix it.

Railway workers' need to differentiate themselves intensified in the context of the Allied occupation, when three crises jeopardized their manhood. First, rapid inflation and the consequent deterioration of economic conditions made it difficult for workers to provide for their families. Some even complained about the shame of receiving financial help from their parents.[24] The elite workers could no longer fulfill the most basic manly duty. Second, the occupation

20. "Vāgunchi negah dār!" *Nāhid*, November 1, 1927.
21. "Otumobil va rānandegi," *Nāmeh-ye Rāh* vol. 2, no. 6 (1941): 226–29.
22. "Otumobil va rānandegi," *Nāmeh-ye Rāh* vol. 2, no. 6 (1941): 226–29.
23. For example, see "Otumobil va rānandegi," *Nāmeh-ye Rāh*, vol. 2, no. 7 (1941): 270, vol. 2, no. 9 (1941): 341, and vol. 3, no. 2 (1943): 64.
24. "Kārgarān-e rāh āhan rā beshnāsid," *Mardān-e Ruz*, February 6, 1946.

relegated Iranian railway workers to a subordinate position to the Allies. As the Allies took control of Iran's transport infrastructure, they placed Iranian workers at stations and factories under constant supervision and surveillance, humiliating the proud workers of the national symbol of technological modernity. Third, the occupation made it clear that railway workers did not have a monopoly over expertise in transport technology. Even before the occupation, road transport took precedence over rail transport in Iran. Once the occupation began, the number of automobile mechanics and truck drivers increased rapidly, as the Allies needed to mobilize everything they could to transport lend-lease materials to the Soviet Union. Due to the high transportation cost of the railway, the competitive edge of road transport over rail transport was becoming clear, especially by the end of the occupation. Confronted by these crises, railway workers had to reformulate the meaning of their masculinity.

In light of this context, it is noteworthy that *Nāmeh-ye Rāh* printed articles that distinguished railway workers from their chief competitors in the transport sector. In 1943, an employee of the Iranian State Railway named Esma'il Nasrollahi wrote a letter to the journal. He shared a recent incident with an automobile repair shop in Tehran when his car had an engine problem. Since the shop seemed chic and modern with a qualified *ostād*, (master) Nasrollahi initially felt comfortable explaining to him the engine problem, especially the thick smoke and the gasoline smell. One hour later, when he returned to pick up his car, he asked the *ostād* if the carburetor of his car had been fixed, to which the *ostād* responded, "I don't speak *farangi* (European/Western)."[25] For Nasrollahi, the *ostād*'s ignorance of the proper term to refer to a basic component of the automobile was indicative of his lack of theoretical mechanical knowledge. Despite the fancy appearance of the repair shop, it was only a façade; it was in fact symbolic of the *ostād*'s superficial mechanical knowledge. After adding that his car was in fact not fixed at all by the repair shop and almost caught fire on his way home, Nasrollah concluded, "there are many automobile mechanics in the streets of Tehran, but it is astonishing that these men call themselves mechanics despite their lack of qualifications."[26] This article reflects a railway employee's desire to fashion a distinct masculine ideal by distinguishing himself and his colleagues from their allegedly inferior competitors.

A letter sent to the journal in response to an episode of "The Automobile and Driving" expressed a similar complaint addressed to automobile drivers and chauffeurs. The letter lamented how illiterate individuals with no basic mechanical knowledge became drivers and chauffeurs through an apprenticeship,

25. "Rāje' beh ta'mirkārān-e otumobil," *Nāmeh-ye Rāh* vol. 3, no. 2 (1943).
26. "Rāje' beh ta'mirkārān-e otumobil," *Nāmeh-ye Rāh* vol. 3, no. 2 (1943).

especially in the absence of a driving school with a standardized curriculum. He concluded, "These people see driving only as a way of going fast. They assume that all they need to move speedily is a chauffeur, never understanding or bothering to understand how a motor works or movement works. They cannot identify motor problems. Nor can they fix them.... These individuals make innocent people victims of their 'stunt' all the time."[27] The letter's assertion that drivers and chauffeurs did not go to a driving school was an implicit comparison with railway workers, many of whom in theory (if not in reality) attended new state-run institutions before joining the workforce to study a wide range of subjects from physics to current railway regulations; his criticism that drivers and chauffeurs put passengers in danger was also a comparison with the presumably higher level of safety of Iran's state railway thanks to employees with superior knowledge.[28]

Another article asserted the superiority of railway workers over drivers and chauffeurs based on the combination of their knowledge as well as physical and mental toughness. It repeatedly noted the physically strenuous nature of the work of Iranian locomotive engineers and stokers, as they were frequently exposed to extremely low and high temperatures near the locomotive furnace. They also worked long shifts to make up for the small number of qualified Iranian workers, especially in the early years of railway operation in Iran. But being physically tough was not enough. They also had to be technologically knowledgeable to operate the train safely because of the autonomy given to locomotive engineers, who had to operate the machinery like his "eyes and ears," and stokers, who had to keep locomotive engineers informed of potential dangers. Thus, "unlike automobile drivers," the railway crew had to be highly trained to maintain a maximum level of attention on the machinery at work. To do so, they were required to have a sound mind (*ruh*) and not to be worn out from fatigue (*khastegi va kuftegi*), which would cause accidents. Furthermore, locomotive engineers and stokers had to be like "dutiful soldiers," who exposed themselves to a high level of danger and showed a willingness to sacrifice themselves.[29] At this juncture, railway workers embodied a distinct masculine ideal that separated them from both modern middle-class men and other transport workers. Railway workers had to possess the technological and mechanical expertise to operate the complex machinery safely, the physical strength to withstand the dreadful working conditions, and the mental strength to stay focused while dealing with the dangerous machinery.

27. "Nāmeh-ye vāredeh," *Nāmeh-ye Rāh* vol. 2, no. 11 (1942): 437.

28. For new state institutions to train the Iranian railway workforce, see Mahbubi-Ardakani 1978, 383–86.

29. "Rānandegān va ātashkārān," *Nāmeh-ye Rāh* vol. 1, nos. 5–6 (1940): 16–17.

It is significant that the article also mentioned railway workers' willingness to sacrifice themselves. Valorization of railway workers' sacrifice intensified especially during the Allied occupation, when rail traffic volume skyrocketed. Along with the traffic volume, railway accidents dramatically increased, reaching a stunning number of 1,119 accidents at the peak of the occupation in the Iranian calendar year of 1322 (March 1943–March 1944). Most casualties and fatalities came from railway workers, prompting the publication of a number of awareness-raising articles for workers in *Mardān-e Ruz*, the official newspaper of the IRO. During the four years of the Allied occupation, 740 were injured, many of whom were permanently disabled, in railway accidents, while 416 lost their lives.[30]

A short story that glorified the self-sacrifice of railway workers appeared in *Nāmeh-ye Rāh* in this context. Adapted from unspecified foreign stories, it revolves around two railway workers, the hardworking family man Simon Andre and Phillip, who has been recently released from prison. The incident takes place when the two workers are assigned the task of maintaining the railway track by tightening loose nuts. Simon Andre witnesses Philip loosening the bolts to steal parts of the railway track and sell them to the black market. Having been seen, Philip strikes Simon Andre in the head, resulting in Simon Andre losing consciousness. When Simon Andre wakes up in the dark, he sees parts of the railway track dug up, creating dangerous holes. Since the red flag to wave to the train to inform the crew of danger is missing, Simon Andre, already in serious pain, cuts his chest with a knife, dyes his shirt red, and keeps running toward the train while waving the red shirt until he no longer had any strength left. As he breathes his last breath, he sees Philip, who has apparently repented and is running toward the train with the red shirt in hand on Simon Andre's behalf. Simon Andre smiles as he knows he has fulfilled his duty of protecting hundreds of innocent lives. The train eventually runs Philip over before stopping completely, ending the story with the deaths of the two railway workers who prevent a disastrous accident.[31]

Not all accidents resulted in the loss of workers' lives. As illustrated by numerous petitions, many railway construction and operation workers survived with varying degrees of permanent disability. A 1937 petition by Hoseyn Naziri, a former head laborer who worked in railway construction, serves as an

30. Koyagi 2021, especially chapter five.
31. "Dar rāh-e vazifeh," *Nāmeh-ye Rāh*, vol. 2, no. 11 (1942), 428–31. A version of this story was later incorporated into Iranian school textbooks. For a film about a schoolboy who presumably prevents a railway accident to repeat the heroic story in the textbook, see Kamran Shirdel, *Un Shab ke Bārun Umad* (1967).

example. In a dynamite accident on a construction site in Mazandaran, he lost his right eye and right arm, leading to his long hospitalization. After his release, however, he was yet to be compensated, leaving him and his family destitute as he could not work anymore. He concluded his letter by asking rhetorically how this treatment was fair "in the era of His Majesty's justice."[32] In petitions like Naziri's, workers' missing limbs functioned as the visual evidence of their utmost sacrifice for the national project in ways that modern middle-class men did not experience; missing limbs placed workers as the noblest patriots who sacrificed their bodies. Petitions juxtaposed this nobleness with the economic reality of destitution. Thus, through missing limbs, disabled workers embodied the masculine ideals of self-sacrifice for the nation and the emasculating reality of being unable to provide for the family simultaneously.

As railway workers came to embody their sacrifices through their missing limbs, in 1944, the popular magazine *Khāndanihā* printed an article about the lives of American amputees who had lost their legs in wars and railway accidents. Translated from an unspecified American journal, it introduced several stories of amputees, including a former worker of the Erie Railway, whose lives had been transformed thanks to prosthetic legs. The point of the stories was clear: amputees should not consider themselves helpless and despair; prosthetic legs would restore normalcy to their lives, from being able to walk to playing sports. But the final anecdote of the article gave a twist to this point. It revolved around a dialogue between a man who had a successful business, was respected in local politics, and had a wife and two children, and another man who despaired after losing his leg. The despaired man refuses to get a prosthetic leg, complaining, "What good is life when no woman would marry me." The other man responds, "If I were a woman, I would not marry somebody so weak in willpower (like you)." When the despairing man retorts that the other man has no right to disparage him because the condition of his leg makes his life so different, the successful man reveals that he has a prosthetic leg, his own having been amputated in his childhood, and had overcome his handicap with his will power. The article concluded by stating that the despairing man later regained hope, got a prosthetic leg, married and had children, and lived happily and successfully.[33] In the context of Iran under the occupation, the story had a powerful implication. The technology of prosthetic legs could potentially transform the lives of many amputees, but the amputees needed to have strong willpower to reclaim their

32. Majles Library (ML)11/19/39/1/3. For similar petitions, see ML10/134/7/1/20 and ML8/10/21/1/10.

33. "Moʻjezāt-e ʻelm: kār kardan va rāh raftan bedun-e dast va pā!" *Khāndanihā* 4: 19 (January 1, 1944), 7–8.

lives. Only when prosthetics and willpower converged, a man could gain respectability through wealth, marriage, and fatherhood. As the amputees in the
story did, if Iranian railway workers had technology and willpower, they would
be able to regain their manliness while embodying their noble self-sacrifice for
the nation through their missing limbs.

Cyrus Schayegh has shown how the modern middle class differentiated themselves from the rest of Iranian society by asserting their roles as the bearers of
modern scientific knowledge.[34] Similarly, Iranian railway workers carved out
a distinct position for themselves in Iranian society by presenting themselves
as the bearers of technological knowledge. As elite industrial workers, railway
workers' masculine ideals accepted many aspects of modern middle-class ideals,
most clearly exemplified by their self-appointed role of becoming the missionaries of civilization to the countryside. At the same time, their relationship to
technology placed them in a distinct position vis-à-vis the rest of society. Railway workers possessed theoretical *and* practical mechanical knowledge as well
as physical *and* mental toughness to operate and fit the complex technological
assemblage of rail infrastructure. Combined with their incomparable self-sacrifice for the nation, these qualities separated railway workers from other men,
particularly modern middle-class men and automobile mechanics and drivers,
their primary competitors in the socioeconomic hierarchy.

The masculinities of the Iranian working class deserve further studies.
While I have relied mostly on official publications of the Ministry of Roads to
study the discourse of masculinities, there is much more to explore when we
shift attention to everyday gender performance at workplaces, as Hanan Hammad has shown in the case of Egyptian industrial workers.[35] Likewise, official
publications do not tell us much about how railway workers' masculine ideals
intersected with the *luti* masculinity, although given their socioeconomic backgrounds, many railway workers were likely to have inhabited the socialization
spaces of both the modern middle class and the *luti*s, depending on social contexts.[36] Studying these issues will enrich our understanding of Iranian masculinities beyond the modern middle class and the *luti*s.

34. Schayegh 2009.
35. Hammad 2016.
36. The prime example is Gholamreza Takhti, the legendary wrestling champion. For Takhti, see
Chehabi 1995, 48–60. In addition, some railway workers mentioned in interviews that they participated in activities of the *zurkhāneh*, a traditional wrestling gymnasium that was frequented by the *luti*s.
The *zurkhāneh* was vilified in the nationalist discourse as unhygienic and unscientific. See "Kārgarān-e
rāh āhan rā beshnāsid," *Mardān-e Ruz*, March 13, 1946 and April 17, 1946.

WORKS CITED:

Amin, Camron Michael. 2002. *The Making of the Modern Iranian Woman: Gender, State Policy, and Popular Culture, 1865–1946.* Gainesville: University Press of Florida.

Atabaki, Touraj, ed. 2007. *The State and the Subaltern: Modernization, Society and the State in Turkey and Iran.* London and New York: I.B. Tauris.

Balslev, Sivan. 2020. *Iranian Masculinities: Gender and Sexuality in Late Qajar and Early Pahlavi Iran.* Cambridge: Cambridge University Press.

Baron, Ava. 2006. "Masculinity, the Embodied Male Worker, and the Historian's Gaze." *International Labor and Working-Class History* 69:143–60.

Bell, Robert Joseph. 2015. "Luti Masculinity in Iranian Modernity, 1785–1941: Marginalization and the Anxieties of Proper Masculine Comportment." MA Thesis, Graduate Center, City University of New York.

Chehabi, Houchang E. 1993. "Staging the Emperor's New Clothes: Dress Codes and Nation-Building under Reza Shah." *Iranian Studies* 26 (3–4): 209–29.

———. 1995. "Sport and Politics in Iran: The Legend of Gholamreza Takhti." *The International Journal of the History of Sport* 12:48–60.

Connell, R. W., and James W. Messerschmidt. 2005. "Hegemonic Masculinity: Rethinking the Concept." *Gender and Society* 19:829–59.

Cronin, Stephanie. 1997. *The Army and the Creation of the Pahlavi State in Iran,* 1910–1926. London and New York: I.B. Tauris.

———. 2006. *Tribal Politics in Iran: Rural Conflict and the New State, 1921–1941.* London: Routledge.

———. 2007. *Subalterns and Social Protest: History from Below in the Middle East and North Africa.* London: Routledge.

———. 2010. *Soldiers, Shahs and Subalterns in Iran: Opposition, Protest and Revolt, 1921–1941.* New York: Palgrave Macmillan.

Cronin, Stephanie, ed. 2003. *The Making of Modern Iran: State and Society under Reza Shah, 1921-1941.* London: Routledge.

Ehsani, Kaveh. 2003. "Social Engineering and the Contradictions of Modernization in Khuzestan's Company Towns: A Look at Abadan and Masjed-Soleyman." *International Review of Social History* 48:361–99.

Ghoussoub, Mai, and Emma Sinclair-Webb, eds. 2000. *Imagined Masculinities: Male Identity and Culture in the Modern Middle East.* London: Saqi Books.

Gölz, Olmo. 2021. "Racketeers in Politics: Theoretical Reflections on Strongman Performances in Late Qajar Iran." In *Age of Rogues: Rebels, Revolu-*

tionaries and Racketeers at the Frontiers of Empires, edited by Ramazan Hakkı Öztan and Alp Yenen, 120–47. Edinburgh: Edinburgh University Press.

Hammad, Hanan. 2016. *Industrial Sexuality: Gender, Urbanization, and Social Transformation in Egypt*. Austin: University of Texas Press.

Jacob, Wilson Chacko. 2011. *Working Out Egypt: Effendi Masculinity and Subject Formation in Colonial Modernity, 1870–1940*. Durham: Duke University Press.

Klubock, Thomas Miller. 1996. "Working-Class Masculinity, Middle-Class Morality, and Labor Politics in the Chilean Copper Mines." *Journal of Social History* 30:435–63.

Koyagi, Mikiya. 2021. *Iran in Motion: Mobility, Space, and the Trans-Iranian Railway*. Stanford: Stanford University Press.

———. 2009. "Moulding Future Soldiers and Mothers of the Iranian Nation: Gender and Physical Education under Reza Shah, 1921–41." *The International Journal of the History of Sport* 26:1668–1696.

Mahbubi-Ardakani, Hoseyn. 1978. *Tārikh-e Mo'assesāt-e Tamaddoni-ye Jadid dar Irān, Jeld-e Dovvom*. Tehran: Mo'asseseh-ye Enteshārāt va Chāp-e Dāneshgāh-e Tehran.

Malakuti, Mojtaba. 1948. *Rāh Āhan-e Irān*. Tehran: Chāpkhāneh-ye Khāndanihā.

Marashi, Afshin. 2008. *Nationalizing Iran: Culture, Power, and the State, 1870–1940*. Seattle: University of Washington Press.

Meyer, Stephen. 2016. *Manhood on the Line: Working-Class Masculinities in the American Heartland*. Urbana: University of Illinois Press.

Sato, Tsugitaka, et al. 1994. *Islam Shakai no Yakuza: Rekishi wo Ikiru Ninkyo to Burai*. Tokyo: Dai San Shokan.

Schayegh, Cyrus. 2009. *Who Is Knowledgeable Is Strong: Science, Class, and the Formation of Modern Iranian Society, 1900–1950*. Berkeley: University of California Press.

Vejdani, Farzin. 2015. *Making History in Iran, Education, Nationalism, and Print Culture*. Stanford: Stanford University Press.

Yildiz, Murat. 2015. "'What is a Beautiful Body?' Late Ottoman 'Sportsman' Photographs and New Notions of Male Corporeal Beauty." *The Middle East Journal of Culture and Communication* 8:192–214.

"A Sufism for the Age of Electricity":
The Early History of *Pishāhangi* (Scouting) in Iran

Afshin Marashi

THE ANNUAL MILITARY PARADE commemorating the coup d'état that brought Reza Khan (after 1925, Reza Shah Pahlavi) to power in 1921 took place according to its regularly prescribed schedule on the 3rd of Esfand, 1313 (February 22, 1935). As recalled by 'Ali Asghar Hekmat (1893–1980) – the scholar, diplomat, and cabinet minister who served as one of the chief architects of the cultural policies of the Reza Shah period – the 1935 military parade was notably different than the ones that preceded it.[1] As in previous years, the military parade took place on the equestrian field at the Maydān-e Jalālieh near the center of the capital city, not far from the newly inaugurated University of Tehran.[2] Also as in previous years, the 3rd of Esfand military parade featured a choreographed procession of soldiers and cadets from the various branches of Pahlavi Iran's armed forces. What distinguished the 1935 military parade from its predecessors, however, was the addition of adolescent scouts from the newly reorganized and expanded Iranian Scouting Organization (Sāzmān-e Pishāhangi-ye Irān).[3]

As Hekmat later recalled, the Iranian scouts were the final group to march past the tented viewing platform where Reza Shah – along with a host of other military and political dignitaries, including the new prime minister Mohammad 'Ali Foroughi and 'Ali Asghar Hekmat himself – stood to review the procession. According to Hekmat, Reza Shah was visibly moved while viewing the parade of approximately one thousand Iranian youths dressed in uniform, including brimmed military-style hats and triangular neckerchiefs that were characteristic of scouting organizations throughout the world. "Tears of emotion gathered

---

1. Hekmat 1976, 75, 84–85. For the biography of Hekmat, see Safā'i 1976, 94–110; Milani 2008, 1:181–85.

2. The Maydān-e Jalālieh was later refurbished and renamed Pārk-e Farah in 1966 and since 1980 has been known as Pārk-e Lāleh.

3. For the history of the Iranian Scouting Organization, see Delfāni 2003; Āshnā 1371/1992: 2–24; Sadi 1966, 2:169–72; Balslev 2019, 260–80; Arasteh 1969, 109–112; Elwell-Sutton 1944, 130–135; Banani 1961, 107; Schayegh 2002, 341–69; Chehabi 2014, 64–65; Koyagi 2009, 1668–1696. For the history of Iranian scouting in the post-WWII era, and the work of its principal leader in this period, Hossein Banā'i, see Yaghoubian 2014.

in his majesty's eyes,"[4] Hekmat remembered, as Reza Shah stood on the platform and viewed the youthful scouts marching in goose step, waving Iranian flags, hoisting banners adorned with scouting insignia, and proudly chanting in unison the Iranian scouting organization's pledge of allegiance to "God, Shah, and Nation." As Hekmat recounted this episode, it was at the conclusion of the procession that the clearly moved Shah turned to the newly appointed Prime Minister, Mohammad 'Ali Foroughi, and referring to Hekmat, decreed, I was going to wait until Nowruz to promote this man, however, his promotion to the rank of Minister of Education must instead take place effective today."[5]

Hekmat's promotion to the rank of Minister of Education was in fact a reward for the work that he had completed since the fall of 1934 to expand and formalize the Iranian Scouting Organization. Until that time there had been conflicting views about scouting's usefulness as part of Iran's nation-building project and the movement had gained little momentum. Things only changed in October of 1934 when Hekmat – while still in the position of interim Minister of Education – was approached by a pair of Iranian army officers and tasked to formalize the Iranian scouting organization.[6] The new impetus to expand Iranian scouting came after Reza Shah's trip to Kemalist Turkey in June and July of 1934, where he witnessed the Turkish republic's impressively organized and officially sponsored Turkish Scouting Federation (Türkiye Izcilik Federasyonu).[7] It was this experience that likely led the shah to see the virtues of scouting and to issue his decree to expand Iran's scouting movement along similar lines.

Hekmat had been one of the few proponents of scouting within the Iranian government prior to Reza Shah's decision to expand it, and despite intermittent objections and obstacles, had since the mid-1920s persistently advocated for its growth as part of the initiatives managed by the Ministry of Education.[8] For this reason, when the decision was made to expand Iranian scouting in the fall of 1934, 'Ali Asghar Hekmat was seen as the natural choice to spearhead the effort. Once assigned the task, Hekmat wasted no time, and within just a few months the results were so successful that by the time of the military parade in February of 1935 Reza Shah chose the occasion to reward Hekmat by officially promoting him to the rank of minister.

From that moment on, and until the abdication of Reza Shah in Septem-

---

4. Hekmat 1976, 84.

5. Hekmat 1976, 75.

6. Hekmat 1976, 84.

7. For the history of scouting in Turkey see, Uzgören 2000. For the role of scouting during Reza Shah's state visit to Turkey see, Marashi 2003, 107; Delfâni 2003, 39. Reza Shah's visit to Turkey also had an important effect on subsequent dress code policies in Iran, see Chehabi 1993, 215.

8. Hekmat 1976, 79; Āshnā 1992, 4; Delfâni 2003, introduction: 33.

ber of 1941, the Iranian scouting movement grew rapidly, becoming another of the primary means by which the cultural policies of nation-building were promoted within Iran. Like other aspects of the nation-building project, scouting was a state-led project designed to forge a unified sense of belonging among Iranians through the erosion of regional, religious, linguistic, and sectarian divisions, and the simultaneous promotion of a shared sense of national identity and territorial belonging.[9] To achieve these goals, scouting's methods often echoed techniques of military discipline promoting structures of allegiance that connected soldiers and subjects to the state and to the shah. Once formalized within the Ministry of Education, the scouting movement therefore became the most concerted means for instilling these bonds of national belonging and political loyalty in the youth-aged Iranian population.

It would, however, be overly simplistic to reduce the history of Iranian scouting to a project of authoritarian nation-building designed to indoctrinate children into the cult of monarchy and nationalism. The global history of scouting, and the history of Iranian scouting in particular, suggests that the movement represented something more socially, culturally, and politically complex. As the foregoing will detail, the early promoters of Iranian scouting saw it as a pedagogical tool to rear young Iranians into a new understanding of civic virtue that could be compatible with a universalized culture of modernity. The international scouting movement's mottos of "be prepared" and "do one good deed each day" became part of this ethos of civic virtue that was central to the mission of Iranian scouting and to Iran's cultural project of modernity and nationalism. This new cultural project was also rooted in newly ascendant conceptions of *secularism* and *national selfhood* that now redefined premodern ethical-moral systems as part of the rightful domain of state jurisdiction.[10] In addition to politics and ideology, therefore, scouting was also – from the viewpoint of its Iranian advocates – rooted in a larger effort of constructing a new moral-ethical system of Iranian nationhood that drew inspiration from early twentieth century theories of pedagogy, child development, and social psychology. The construction and promotion of this new moral-ethical system naturally encroached on cultural terrains long monopolized by Shi'i Iran's clerical establishment, and this cultural encroachment in turn had obvious political implications. From the point of view of Iran's modernizing social and cultural reformers, however,

---

9. There is a large literature on the connections between the global history of the scouting movement and nationalism during the twentieth century. See for example, Proctor and Block eds. 2009; Macdonald 1993; Jordan 2016; Honeck 2018; Pryke 1998.

10. For the imposition and implications of modern-national conceptions of "secularity and selfhood" see Mahmood 2015, 2–3.

encroaching on this terrain was necessary to achieve the larger liberal-national goal of constructing a version of Iranian culture rooted in modern civic virtues that could transcend ethnic, linguistic, religious, and regional divides.[11] The early history of scouting in Iran therefore reflected broader tensions between the interwar political history of nation-building from above, and Iran's project of building a modern, liberal, and pluralistic society bound together by a common national identity and shared civic culture.

The Early History of Iranian Scouting

Scouting in Iran emerged relatively late when compared to its counterparts in other parts of the Middle East. As a global phenomenon, scouting had its beginning through the work of Robert Baden-Powell (1857–1941).[12] A general in the British army (receiving a knighthood in 1909 by King Edward VII and eventually the title of baron by George V in 1929), Baden-Powell was a veteran of numerous British military campaigns, most notably the Second Boer War in South Africa. Drawing on his military experience, in 1908 Baden-Powell published the first edition of *Scouting for Boys*, a handbook of practical outdoor skills and crafts intended for a readership of adolescent boys.[13] The book quickly spawned local "scout troops" organized around the teaching, learning, and practice of scouting skills. *Scouting for Boys* also became an international best-seller, first in the English-speaking world, and soon elsewhere through a steady stream of translations and local editions.[14]

In the Middle East the book also found a wide-ranging readership, initially – not in Iran – but in the Ottoman Empire. Ottoman-Turkish and Armenian translations both appeared not long after the initial 1908 publication of the book.[15] By the late 1920s Latinized-Turkish and Arabic translations also appeared in succession. The proliferation of locally organized scout troops, often

11. Delfāni describes this as a shared or collective culture (*farhang-e hamagāni*), see Delfāni 2003, introduction: 26.

12. For biographical details of Baden-Powell and a general history of the early scouting movement, see Reynolds 1950.

13. Baden-Powell 1908.

14. The first edition of 1908 went through five printings in the first year. Twelve more revised editions appeared in the UK by 1926. For the early publishing history of *Scouting for Boys*, see Reynolds, 24–28. The first enormously successful Boy Scouts of America version of the book, *A Handbook for Boys*, was published in 1910, and went through three editions and thirty-seven printings by 1927, to a total of almost three million copies. The cover image of the third edition of the *Handbook* was drawn by the American artist Norman Rockwell. For the publishing history of *A Handbook for Boys* see front-matter of the 1936 edition. See also https://historyofscouting.com/handbooks/boyscout_handbooks .htm.

15. Watenpaugh 2009, 89–105.

with formal affiliations to the World Organization of the Scout Movement – headquartered initially in London, and later moving to Paris and eventually Geneva – also spread quickly during the late-Ottoman and immediate post-WWI periods. In Istanbul, scout troops formed prior to WWI at Robert College (Boğaziçi University) and at the Ottoman Imperial High School (Galatasaray Lisesi). Beirut and Cairo also saw the growth of scouting, with troops at the Syrian Protestant College (American University in Beirut) and at the American University in Cairo. After the disruption of WWI, scouting again proliferated, both in Kemalist Turkey and in the newly established mandate states.[16]

As detailed by Keith Watenpaugh, in Mandate Syria and Lebanon scouting was primarily a middle class phenomenon, used by members of upwardly mobile segments of these societies as markers of participation in a global middle class culture. In the Levant, scouting also became a marker of sectarian and ethno-linguistic affiliation, with different sectarian communities adapting scouting to their own cultures and identities. For example, the Armenian scouting organization (Homenetmen) adopted the image of Mt. Ararat as part of their scouting insignia, and placed great emphasis on the use of the Armenian language. The region's Arabic-speaking Catholic population, by contrast, largely belonged to the Scouts de France (rather than the more secular and interfaith Les Éclaireurs de France) and incorporated the more familiar scouting insignia of the fleur-de-lis, combined with the Catholic cross, and utilized the French language. The Syrian Arab Scouts, moreover, known in Arabic as al-Kashshāfa al-ʿArabiyya al-Suriyya, was the scouting movement that largely represented the Arab Muslim middle class, promoted an ethical ideal tied to Muslim modernist ideas, and localized international scouting culture to Arab customs, including the use of the *keffiyeh* in place of the traditionally brimmed scouting headgear.[17] By the mid-1920s all of these Middle Eastern scouting organizations had already become substantially formalized.

The history of scouting in Iran came on the heels of these scouting movements in other parts of the region. The belatedness of Iranian scouting was the result of internal obstacles that delayed – until the mid-1930s – the movement's full incorporation into Iran's nationalization project. The most notable pioneering figure in the early history of Iranian scouting was Ahmad Khān Aminzādeh (Figures 1 and 2). While not all the details of his life are known, we know that Aminzādeh spent some years as a member of the Iranian expatriate community of Istanbul during the late-Ottoman period. It was in Istanbul that he attended the Ottoman Imperial Teacher's College, and where he first learned about

---

16. Watenpaugh 2009, 89–90.
17. Watenpaugh 2009, 93–97.

Figure 1. Ahmad Khān Aminzādeh. From
Āshnā 1992.

the scouting movement. By the early 1920s Aminzādeh had returned to Iran
and became the earliest proponent of scouting as part of the larger campaign
for social and cultural reform.[18] By 1925 he had formed a privately organized
Iranian scouting group, and by 1926 became the founder and co-editor of
the first Persian-language periodical devoted to scouting, *Pishāhangi-ye Irān*.[19]
Through Aminzādeh's efforts, the Dār al-Fonun also established a scout troop
as early as 1926. Likely in cooperation with Aminzādeh, the American mission-
ary-founded Alborz College also inaugurated scouting-related activities around
this time.[20] By the mid 1920s, the school's founder and long-serving president,
Samuel Jordan (1871–1952), hired Elgin Sherk (1882–1976) to serve as the
school's director of physical education, YMCA initiatives, and early scouting
activities.[21]

18. Delfāni 2003, introduction: 29–34; Āshnā 1992, 3–5; Balslev 2019, 261–62; Hekmat 1976,
79.

19. *Pishāhangi-ye Irān* appears to have published six issues between 1926 and 1927. I am grateful
to Ashkan Rezvani Naraghi (1983–2020) for his assistance in obtaining digital copies of these issues
from the University of Tehran's Central Library.

20. Balslev 2019, 261; Āshnā 1992, 3; Moniri n.d.

21. Saleh 1976, 177,185; Āshnā 1992, 3. Jordan and Sherk had also worked to establish an organization called the "Iran Youth Association" in 1924, which like the YMCA and the Boy Scouts
had as its goal to "refine the morals of Iranian youth." See https://baskervilleinstitute.org/wp-content
/uploads/2020/12/JordanLetter.pdf.

Figure 2.   Ahmad Khān Aminzādeh, seated second from left. Courtesy D. Yaghoubian.

During this early period, however, there were conflicting views about the nature and usefulness of scouting in Iran. While there were active discussions about the best strategies for social and cultural reform, most of the discussions that focused on children's education prioritized basic literacy and subject-matter knowledge.[22] When scouting was discussed in this period, it was usually as part of discussions of the benefits of physical education. The most influential person in debates regarding physical education in the mid-1920s was Mir Mehdi Khān Varzandeh (1880–1982).[23] Like Aminzādeh, Varzandeh had also lived and studied in Istanbul in the late-Ottoman period. Varzandeh had, by contrast, gone on to Belgium, where he studied the new science of physical education at Brussell's École normale de gymnastique et d'escrime (ENGE).[24] Trained in the Swedish school of gymnastics, based on the methods developed by Per Henrik Ling (1776–1839), Varzandeh became an advocate for a model of physical education in Iran that emphasized holistic methods of promoting harmony between mind and body. Following Ling's theories, Varzandeh promoted a program of physical education that emphasized gymnastics, calisthenics, and fencing, which he believed would be most successful in combating – echoing the then current lan-

22. Delfāni 2003, introduction: 31.

23. For the life and work of Mir Mehdi Varzandeh, see Chehabi 2014, 55–72; Balslev 2019, 246–47; Sadri 1961, 138–39.

24. Chehabi 2014, 55. The École normale de gymnastique et d'escrime was originally founded in 1885 as École normale de escrime (fencing), in 1894 it expanded its program to include both gymnastics and fencing. For the history of the school see Delheye 2003, 335–57.

guage of Social Darwinism – the condition of national degeneracy.[25] Despite their occasional collaborations, it was ultimately Varzandeh's Swedish model of physical education that prevailed over Aminzādeh's scouting methods for most of the period between the mid-1920s and the mid-1930s.[26]

While disappointed, Aminzādeh and the small group of scouting enthusiasts whom he had cultivated inside Iran, were not immediately discouraged. The challenge, they concluded, was that scouting remained poorly understood. The public itself knew little of scouting, and teachers, educational policy makers, and the growing cadre of school administrators were unfamiliar with what Aminzādeh and others felt were the benefits of scouting. There were also culturally conservative critiques that posed obstacles to scouting, voiced by some segments of the *'ulamā'*, who felt that scouting encroached on social and ethical disciplines that were already prescribed within Islamic tradition. Others questioned scouting's practice of removing adolescent boys from the proximity and supervision of family, to be relocated to rural and mountain regions accompanied only by unknown male adults.[27] For these and other reasons, between 1925 and 1934, with few exceptions, the leadership of the Ministry of Education was steadfast in refusing to endorse scouting. A letter by Aminzādeh written in 1927 to the ministry requesting funds – including to pay Iran's membership dues to the World Organization of the Scouting Movement – was tersely denied.[28] Another letter written in 1928 by the Ministry of Education to administrators of the Shahpour High School in the Gilan province, which had established a scout troop by their own initiative, rebuked the schools' leadership, stating that scouting is a private club activity that is "entirely prohibited in schools."[29]

Promoting *Pishāhangi*

To combat the resistance to scouting, Aminzādeh and a small group of other scouting supporters – including 'Ali Asghar Hekmat, then a mid-level Ministry of Education official – began a campaign of publishing articles in progressive-minded newspapers and journals. Their goal was to introduce scouting to influential segments of the Iranian public, advocate for its benefits, and counter the prevailing criticisms and misconceptions that many had about scouting.

25. Chehabi 2014, 61–63. For discussions of combatting "degeneracy" through sports see also, Balslev 2019, 254–57; Schayegh 2002, 357–58.

26. Balslev 2019, 261–62. Aminzādeh and Varzandeh had in fact occasionally collaborated between 1920 and 1925 in establishing the "Anjoman-e Varzesh" and the "Anjoman-e Pishāhangi," see Delfāni 2002, introduction: 29–30 and Āshnā 1992, 3.

27. Balslev 2019, 266; Āshnā 1992, 8.

28. Delfāni 2003, introduction: 32, documents: 72–73.

29. Delfāni, introduction: 34, documents: 17.

Aminzādeh, Hekmat, and others also felt the need to argue for the compatibility of scouting with long-established traditions within Iran's national heritage.

Hekmat was the first to make the case for scouting, in an article published in the Ministry of Education's main journal, *Ta'lim va Tarbiat*, in 1925.[30] It was in this article that Hekmat became the first person to advocate for the use of the Persian word *pishāhang* as the equivalent for "scout." "Recently," he began the article, "the English word *'boy scout'* has been heard a great deal,"[31] referring to debates taking place within Iran's progressive-minded circles. This word, he continued, had entered the Persian language as a direct linguistic borrowing without much understanding of its meaning. He went on to describe how the scouting movement in the Arab world had already adopted its own terminology for scouting. Showing his awareness for scouting developments in other parts of the region, he states, "the Arabs have translated it [scout] as *al-kashshafā*."[32] Writing in 1925, Hekmat was perhaps correct to assume that the readers of the journal would likely be more familiar with the Arabic language than English. He then introduced several similar Persian words to provide a fuller definition of the term for Persian readers, including *talāyeh-ye sepāh* (military vanguard) and *pish-qarāvol* (guard, watchman, sentinel). Along with these terms, Hekmat also introduced the word *pishāhang* (herald, forerunner, precursor), which he argued is the most approximate linguistic equivalent of the English term *scout*. Referring to the compound expression *boy scout*, he concluded by saying, "... on the basis of the forgoing assessment, we propose the term *javān-e pishāhang* as its equivalent."[33] Significantly, Hekmat substituted the gender-neutral word *javān* (youth) for the English original *boy*, suggesting that from its beginning the leadership of the Iranian movement saw scouting as an activity intended for both adolescent boys and girls.[34]

Hekmat went on to give a brief summary of the history of scouting, its aims and objectives, and introduced Robert Baden-Powell to his readers. The scouting movement, he correctly states, began a generation earlier, "after the wars in Transvaal,"[35] referring to the consolidation of British sovereignty in Southern Africa after the Boer Wars of the 1880s and 1890s. Despite this military context, he is quick to emphasize, scouting's main goal is not to provide military training to young people, but is instead intended, "for the rearing/teaching [*tar-*

30. Hekmat 1925, 34–36.
31. Hekmat 1925, 34.
32. Hekmat 1925, 34.
33. Hekmat 1925, 34. See also Hekmat 1976, 79–80.
34. For the specifically female gendered politics of the Iranian Girl Scouts movement, see especially Koyagi 2009, 1678–81.
35. Hekmat 1925, 35.

biat] of young people and familiarizing them with the principles of diligence [*saʻi*], action [*ʻamal*], and self-reliance [*ʻetemād bar nafs*]."[36] The scouting organizations established by Baden-Powell around the world, Hekmat argued, "are in truth moral and ethical campaigns"[37] that grew out of their original military context. Rather than simply instilling martial skills, scouting's purpose is to instill an ethic of social responsibility and group solidarity in young people, in particular with respect to a shared commitment to "God and the homeland."[38]

The article does not go into great detail to describe the specific activities, games, and skills that scouts learn and practice, but he does give a summary of the "ten scouting laws" (*dah qānun-e pishāhangi*) that serve as the basis of the ethical virtues of the scouting movement: good character, loyalty, helpfulness, tolerance, courtesy, kindness towards animals, obedience to parents and scout masters, perseverance, thrift, and purity in thoughts, words, and deeds.[39] As he emphasized, the value of scouting is that these civic virtues are not imposed by force, but are instilled through what he described as a "method of action" (*osul-e ʻamal*). This method serves as the basis of the crafts, outdoor activities, and participation in games, which he suggests, help scouts to naturally develop bonds of social solidarity rooted in the civic virtues enshrined in the ten scout laws. He concludes the article by saying "in the end this organization rears young people through work, effort, diligence, good deeds, alleviation of suffering [in others], conscientiousness, and self-reliance."[40] In addition to the more familiar political goals of building loyalty to the Pahlavi monarchy, for Hekmat and the other early promoters of scouting, Iran's nation-building project also necessitated the promotion of these civic virtues among the school-aged population.

Hekmat's brief introduction to scouting in 1925 was perhaps the earliest effort to familiarize Iranians with the social benefits of scouting's ethical principles. What is just as important, however, is his attempt to authenticate scouting by emphasizing its compatibility with traditions found within Iran's own cultural heritage. His linguistic arguments for adopting the pure Persian word *pishāhang* as the preferred term for "scout" was part of this effort to authenticate and normalize scouting for Iranians.[41] In later writings, he also makes comparisons between scouting and the pre-modern *javānmardi/fotuwwat* (chivalry)

---

36. Hekmat 1925, 35.
37. Hekmat 1925, 35.
38. Hekmat 1925, 35.
39. Hekmat 1925, 36.
40. Hekmat 1925.
41. For a more detailed lexicology of this word in Persian literary history see Dehkhodā, *Loghat-nāmeh*, 13:707.

and *zurkhāneh* (house of strength) traditions, as well as the *pahlavān* (heroic) tradition of the *Shāhnāmeh*.[42]

Like Hekmat, Amin Khan Aminzādeh also saw the importance of emphasizing scouting's compatibility with Iranian culture, in large part as an effort to preempt criticisms that scouting was an alien activity of British and American extraction. Of particular importance for Aminzādeh was to highlight scouting's compatibility with Islam. In the short-lived scouting periodical that he founded in 1926, *Pishāhangi-ye Iran*, the first such periodical published in Persian on the subject, Aminzādeh included a multi-part series of articles addressing this topic.[43] The six extant issues of the journal include articles written by the progressive-minded Shi'i cleric Shaykh Hassan Hā'eri-Māzandarāni. The articles by Shaykh Hassan extol the value of scouting by emphasizing its compatibility with Iran's Islamic and Shi'i traditions. Echoing some of Hekmat's arguments, Shaykh Hassan begins by highlighting scouting's emphasis on useful and practical activities, what in his phrasing he calls an educational method based on action (*tarbiat-e 'amali*). "Those who know the Islamic authorities and who have studied the laws of Islam … know that they have always placed emphasis on training/practice (*tamrin*)."[44] The practical skills that can be developed from this method of education, Shaykh Hassan argues, can have immense benefits for the community.

To further elaborate on this idea, Shaykh Hassan included a discussion of the concepts of *sabaq* and *ramāyah*, usually translated from Arabic as competitive horse or camel racing and archery. He reviews the arguments surrounding these concepts within Islamic jurisprudence to make the case for scouting's permissibility by the logic of creative analogy (*ejtehād*). Conservative interpreters of the tradition, he states, unambiguously frown upon activities that could be associated with gambling, or the placing of bets on the outcome of competitive activities. Horse and camel racing, as well as competitive archery – activities that were common in the social milieu of early Islamic history – could therefore be seen as prohibited from the standpoint of a conservative reading of Islamic law. As Shaykh Hassan points out, however, there are numerous traditions within Islamic jurisprudence that explicitly exempt horse and camel racing, and

42. Hekmat 1976, 75–76. For the history of the *zurkhāneh* see also Chehabi 2019, 395–421. See also Bayzā'i-Kāshāni 1958. For the *javānmardi* tradition in premodern and modern Iran, see Adelkhah 1998, 33–35.

43. The editors of *Pishāhangi-ye Iran* are listed as Ahmad Aminzādeh, Ahmad Ārām, and Mohammad Sādeq Hosseini. Another associate of Aminzādeh, Rezā Akhavi, was also associated with the journal.

44. Hā'eri-Māzandarāni 1926, 26–27.

archery, from the category of prohibited activities. In both the early history of Islamic law, and in later Usuli Shi'i jurisprudence, Shaykh Hassan details that the value of archery and horsemanship is recognized.[45] The traditional legal arguments for authorizing these activities, he goes on, are based on the principle that both activities promote disciplines and training that are necessary for the development of martial skills associated with *jihad*.

Following this logic, Shaykh Hassan continues, the *tamrin* – practice, training, skills, exercise, and repetitive drills – associated with scouting, can be seen as analogous to the warrior skills acquired through horsemanship and archery, and should therefore be considered permissible. He makes this point very clear, when he argues in reference to one of the canonical texts of Islamic law, "if I were to translate the book *Sabaq wa Ramāyah*, which is one of the most important works of Islamic law, into Persian, I would title the book *Pishāhangi*."[46] According to Shaykh Hassan's legal reasoning, scouting is therefore a modern method of instilling skills and disciplines that have always been central to Islam's success in the world. He states, it was precisely this educational method of action (*tarbiat-e 'amali*) – that horsemanship and archery have in common with scouting activities – that enabled early Islamic history to develop the skills necessary to extend its reach, "in the east to the Indus River, in the west to Marakesh and Algeria, in the north to Anatolia, and in the south to Najd."[47]

Hekmat and Shaykh Hassan's reasoning to promote scouting differ from one another in significant ways. Whereas Hekmat emphasized the civic virtues that scouting promotes, Shaykh Hassan's arguments for scouting rest on more familiar martial arguments. Nevertheless, both agree that scouting should be authorized as part of the larger campaign to politically strengthen and socially develop Iran. In subsequent years, this ambiguity between scouting's ethical-civic virtues and its military-political usefulness will continue to reflect an unresolved tension regarding scouting's role in Iran's nation-building project.

The Expansion of the Iranian Scouting Movement

As a result of the collective efforts of scouting's Iranian promoters, as well as the decree by Reza Shah to elevate Hekmat to the position of Minister of Education, from the spring of 1935 the Iranian scouting movement experienced rapid growth. The result was a new emphasis on the importance of scouting as part of the larger goals of youth education, as well as substantially increased public resources now devoted to the scouting movement. The institutional organiza-

---

45. Hā'eri-Māzandarāni 1926, 26–27.For similar discussions relating to differing interpretations of sports and gaming in Islamic law, see Chehabi 2002, 389.

46. Hā'eri-Māzandarāni 1926, 26.

47. Hā'eri-Māzandarāni 1926, 26.

tion of scouting also grew from its status as a private club activity to becoming a fully incorporated department within the Ministry of Education. While still in the role of interim Minister of Education in 1934, Hekmat had already established the National Association for Physical Education (Anjoman Melli-ye Tarbiat-e Badani), and placed it under the directorship of (Adib al-Saltaneh) Hossein Sami'i.[48] It was in this period that the goals of physical education made a decisive shift from Varzandeh's holistic mind-body Swedish methods to a new emphasis on competitive sports and the moral-ethical teachings of scouting.[49] In the spring of 1935, Hekmat as the newly appointed permanent minister, added "scouting" to the association's name, which now became known as the Association for Physical Education and Scouting (Anjoman-e Tarbiat-e Badani va Pishāhangi). By October of 1935 it became just as common to see the order of these two terms reversed, and the department was often referred to as the Association for Scouting and Physical Education. Still later the scouting and physical education divisions were separated to become separate offices within the Ministry of Education.[50]

During this period Hekmat also began drafting a series of directives and founding documents detailing the structure, organization, functions, and goals of the scouting organization. Some of these documents had been in draft form for years, others were now newly prepared to formally establish the scouting organization.[51] Collectively the documents make clear that for Hekmat, scouting's primary political and cultural objectives were the following:

1. overcoming regional and tribal differences,

2. overcoming social divisions based on local customs and habits,

3. promoting patriotism with the goal of preventing secessionist movements,

4. promoting physical health,

5. encouraging young Iranians to represent their national culture via participation in international scouting events, and

---

48. Delfāni 2003, introduction: 34; Chehabi 2014, 66; Schayegh 2002, 351; Hekmat 1976, 79; Sadiq 1966, 2:170.

49. Chehabi 2014, 66–67. Chehabi describes this shift in the methods of physical education as a transition from "the Swedish method" to the victory of the "Anglo-Saxon notion of competitive games." Along with the new emphasis on competitive sports, the new Anglo-Saxon model also marked the victory of scouting as a new method for moral-ethical training of children. Despite the new expansion of scouting in this period, its principal Iranian founder, Amin Khān Aminzādeh, had already emigrated to Iraq by this period, see Delfāni 2003, introduction: 33–34; Āshnā 1992, 5.

50. Delfāni 2003, introduction: 79; documents: 26–27.

51. Sadiq 1966, 2:170; Delfāni 2003, documents: 6–15, 24–26; Āshnā 1992, 5.

    6. the use of scouting as a way of encouraging other Iranians to adopt other aspects of the Pahlavi nation-building project.[52]

As Hekmat described in his memoir of the Reza Shah years, these overarching goals of the scouting movement were intended to promote the broader nationalizing cultural policies of the Pahlavi monarchy. The policies were intended, as he wrote, to help build an Iranian national culture comprised "of a single cloth" (*yekpārchegi*);[53] and referring to Reza Shah, he explained, "from the beginning of his rule, he worked to consolidate this unity and *yekpārchegi* of Iran."[54] Significantly, Hekmat and other advocates of Reza Shah's nation-building policies, did not see scouting's goals and methods as part of a project of authoritarian nationalization. Hekmat was to argue clearly that the goals of Iran's nation-building project was to integrate – for the purpose of making equal – all the varied peoples of Iran as part of a shared culture of civic participation. For Hekmat and others, the principle of cultural nationalization and *yekpārchegi* was not inconsistent with the project of promoting a new moral-ethical system rooted in notions of citizenship, civic virtue, and social solidarity. This idealized notion of integrative nationalism no doubt also produced elision and marginalization, but it also produced some surprisingly creative efforts to produce a liberal vocabulary of Iranian nationalism. While invoking the seemingly divisive category of race in a chapter titled *vahdat-e nezhād* (racial unity), for example, Hekmat reveals that his understanding of race appears to be impressively malleable to include a civic ideal. Referring to Turks, Arabs, Kurds, Armenians, Jews, and others living within Iranian territories, he wrote that "all of the peoples of Iran, regardless of lineage [*dudmān*] or extraction [*tabār*] will be considered as pure [*khāles*] Iranians ... [and] are the common inheritors of the Achaemenid and Sassanian heritage."[55]

To carry out these efforts Hekmat assembled a team to lead the newly formulated Association for Scouting and Physical Education. In addition to Hossein Sami'i, Hekmat also appointed 'Isā Sadiq, a graduate of Columbia University's Teacher's College and the founding chancellor of the University of Tehran. According to Sadiq's memoir, the leadership team of the association tasked him to hire an expert to manage the expansion of both physical education and the scouting organization in Iran. Sadiq consulted with William F. Russell (1890–1956), his former professor, dean of Columbia University's Teacher's College, and expert in building new national education systems to promote democracy

52. Delfāni 2003, introduction: 35.
53. Hekmat 1976, 130.
54. Hekmat 1976, 141.
55. Hekmat 1976, 141.

Figure 3. Bahā' al-Din Pāzārgād. From
https://www.wikidata.org/wiki/Q5872334.

in modernizing societies.[56] Russell recommended Thomas R. Gibson, an American who like Sadiq had also recently graduated from the teacher's college at Columbia University. In addition to his advanced degree in education Gibson also had experience with the Boy Scouts of America.[57]

Gibson arrived in Tehran in the fall of 1934, not long after Hekmat had received the directive to expand Iran's scouting movement. In addition to Gibson, the association also hired several local Iranian scouting enthusiasts, including Amir Birjandi, Hossein Banā'i, and Bahā' al-Din Pāzārgād (Figure 3), to serve as Gibson's Persian-speaking deputies.[58] This became the team who led the efforts to develop the core group of Iranian scouts in preparation for the February 1935 military parade. Gibson and his team also understood that in order to achieve the association's goal of expanding the scouting movement on a nationwide scale, the ministry would need to make substantial investments in

56. For Russell's most important works in this area, see Russell 1918, and Russell 1924.

57. Sadiq 1966, 2:171; Delfāni 2003, documents: 27; Āshnā 1992, 5; Balslev 2019, 262.

58. Sadiq 1966, 2:171; Delfāni 2003, introduction: 36–38; Hekmat 1976, 79; Āshnā 1992, 5. Hekmat's memoir is the only source that mentions Birjandi and Banā'i in this context. The others emphasize the role of Pāzārgād as Gibson's primary deputy, although some sources give his name as Hesām al-Din Pāzārgād or Bahā' al-Din Hesāmzadeh rather than Bahā' al-Din Pāzārgād (1899–1969), the journalist, poet, author and translator of numerous works. On name changes in this period, see Chehabi 2020.

Figure 4. Manzarieh Park Scout Master Training Camp, 1935. Thomas Gibson second row center. Courtesy D. Yaghoubian.

facilities, programs, and training materials. These would be essential to recruit a large enough cadre of scout masters who would then serve as leaders, mentors, and guides for the scout troops that were to be established throughout Iran.

The most substantial early investment was the purchase of numerous tracts of land to establish sites for training camps and other scouting activities. Their first purchase was Manzarieh Park, a six-hundred-acre tract of land north of Tehran in the bucolic foothills of the Alborz mountains. The park was inaugurated in the summer of 1935 and was initially used to provide a fifteen-day training program for eighty-four participants selected as part of the first leadership group of scout masters (*morabi*) (Figure 4).[59] In the following years the summer training camps at Manzarieh Park became a regular program for producing scout masters from the various cities, towns, and provinces throughout Iran.[60] Requirements for recruitment into the leadership program were also established during this period. The competitive program required meeting the following minimum criteria:

59. Sadiq 1966, 2:171–72; Delfāni 2003, introduction: 36; Āshnā 1992, 6.

60. The documents that Mahmud Delfāni includes in his *Asnād-e Sāzmān-e Pishāhangi* suggests that the troops in Isfahan, Hamedan, Khorramshahr, Abadan, Yazd, Shiraz, and Zanjan were particularly active. Other sources suggest that the Mazandaran region also had active scout troops. In addition to the training program at Manzarieh park in Tehran, regional scout camps and field excursions were also held in the provinces, including a significant one at Takht-e Jamshid near Shiraz in 1938. See Delfāni 2003, documents: 98–100.

Figure 5.　Muhammad Reza Pahlavi as Chief Scout, Manzarieh Park, 1936. Hekmat at right, holding hat. From Pāzārgād 1936.

1. must be at least twenty years old,

2. must demonstrate good character (*akhlāq-e nik*),

3. must be able to devote two afternoons per week, and occasionally complete days, to scouting activities, and

4. must be devoted to the education of children.

The return to Iran of the young prince Muhammad Reza Pahlavi, after completing boarding school in Switzerland, also helped to promote the activities of the Iranian Scouting Organization. The seventeen-year-old prince was now appointed as the honorary president and chief scout of the organization and participated in the training camp at Manzarieh Park in the summer of 1936 (Figure 5).[61] Also participating in the rapidly expanding scouting organization was princess Shams Pahlavi (1917–1996), who like her brother was appointed as the chief scout of the newly organized Iranian Girl Scouts organization.[62]

In addition to the establishment of the training camp at Manzarieh Park, Hekmat also acquired tracts of land in various quarters within Tehran to be used

---

61. Delfāni 2003, introduction: 36–37; Elwell-Sutton 1944, 131.

62. Delfāni 2003, introduction: 60–63. Between 1935 and 1937 sixty female scout masters were trained to grow the Girl Scout organization. Accoording to Delfāni, by 1940 there were approximately 3500 girl scouts in Iran.

as public facilities for regular scouting and sports activities. The largest of these became the Maydān-e Amjadieh, built on land of the former Bāgh-e Amjadieh, purchased from Mehdi Qoli Hedāyat, near the former northern gate of the city, the Darvāzeh-ye Dowlat.[63] Once acquired by the ministry, the Amjadieh facility quickly evolved from an open field to become Iran's first modern stadium, complete with bleachers, stands, and other facilities capable of accommodating thirty thousand spectators. In the following years, Amjadieh Stadium became the primary location for larger sporting and scouting activities in the capital city (Figures 6 and 7).[64] Other smaller facilities were also established in other parts of Tehran, and gradually in other cities and towns throughout the provinces. As Hekmat described, the goal of the Ministry of Education was ultimately to make scouting and sports facilities publicly available to all young people in the neighborhoods where they lived and went to school.[65]

In addition to facilities, Gibson and Pāzārgād also understood that in order to train the necessary cadre of leaders the scouting association also needed to publish a definitive Persian-language scout handbook. Such a book would serve as a tool for scout masters, as they learned the foundations of scouting and began teaching its principles to young Iranians. Bahā' al-Din Pāzārgād was assigned the task of producing such a manual, and by June of 1936 published a six-hundred page scouting compendium, titled *Pishāhangi-ye Irān*.[66] As with the earlier Turkish, Armenian, and Arabic scouting movements, Pāzārgād drew liberally from scouting materials published by international scouting organizations to produce his Persian-language scouting compendium. Likely drawing on Thomas Gibson's association with the Boy Scouts of America, in Pāzārgād's case it is clearly the 1935 third revised edition of the *Handbook for Boys*, published by the Boy Scouts of America, that Pāzārgād drew from in producing his Persian-language edition of the book.

Significant portions of Pāzārgād's *Pishāhangi-ye Irān* are direct translations or very close adaptations of the 1935 *Handbook for Boys*. Discussions of the twelve scout laws, what Pāzārgād calls the twelve *manesh*, and the scout pledge, or *sogand*, are for example close translations – often with the same accompanying facsimile illustrations – from the *Handbook for Boys*.[67] Other examples, such

63. Hekmat 1976, 81; Delfāni 2003, introduction: 37.

64. Āshnā 1992, 6. The site was used as a sporting and scouting field from 1934 and was expanded into a stadium in 1939. Ajmadieh Stadium was eventually replaced as a venue for larger events by the construction of the 80,000 seat Aryamehr Stadium in 1971. After the 1979 revolution, Ajmadieh Stadium continued to be used as a venue for various events but was renamed Shahid Shirurdi Stadium.

65. Hekmat 1976, 81.

66. Pāzārgād 1936. An earlier partial portion appears to have been published by late 1935.

67. Pāzārgād 1936, 171–76, for example is adapted from the *Handbook for Boys* (New York: Boy Scouts of America, 1935), 34–37.

Figure 6.   Iranian Boy and Girl Scouts at Amjadieh Stadium, 1936. The author's collection.

Figure 7.   Iranian Girl Scouts, 1936. The author's collection.

as details of scouting signage, uniforms, games, drills, camping activities, and skills associated with the earning of merit-badges (*neshānhā-ye shāyestegi*) are also directly adapted from the Boy Scouts of America's handbook.[68] Pāzārgād

68. Pāzārgād 1936, 203–63, for details of scouting signage and uniforms; chapter 9, 325–58 gives detailed descriptions of scouting games; merit badges are described in chapter 12, 580–88; camping skills are described in chapter 13, 589–607.

also goes into substantial detail to provide scout masters-in-training step-by-step instructions for establishing a scout troop, adopting a scouting curriculum, and planning a program of activities for the elementary level (ages 7–12) of the "cub scouts," which he renders into Persian as the *shir bachegān* (literally, lion cubs).[69]

What is most original about Pāzārgād's manual, however, is not the instructional materials contained in the compendium, which were largely derivative of other sources. Rather it is the extended introduction of *Pishāhangi-ye Irān* that represents Pāzārgād's own account of the value of scouting in the context of Iran's social and cultural reform movement. Like Hekmat and Shaykh Hassan's arguments a decade earlier, Pāzārgād writing in the mid-1930s also invokes the similarities between scouting and strands of tradition within Iran's cultural heritage. Following his predecessors, Pāzārgād also alludes to the *pahlavān, javānmardi*, and *adab* traditions.[70] In Pāzārgād's case, however, it is the Sufi tradition that he sees as the closest parallel to the scouting movement. He argues that like Sufism, the goal of scouting is to emphasize principles of ethics and morality (*masālak-e akhlāghi*), and to find techniques, methods, and disciplines for instilling these principles "into the hearts" of children.[71] "If we look at the history of Sufism," Pāzārgād writes, "we will notice that this group's goal was the refinement [*tasfieh*] of hearts [*qolub*] and the cultivation [*tahzib*] of souls/selfhood [*nofus*]."[72] In Sufism, he continues, this ethical cultivation is instilled through practices and disciplines (*zekr*) that he describes as "ceremonies [*marāsem*] and procedures [*tashrifāt*]."[73] What is significant for Pāzārgād is Sufism's synthesis of various disciplinary techniques with the goals of ethical and moral refinement. This synthesis, he believes, is lacking in the current methods of instruction in Iran's educational system. He argues instead that scouting – like Sufism – provides the ideal combination of pedagogical and disciplinary methods required to creatively construct and disseminate the ethical principles and civic virtues necessary for the Iran's nation-building project.[74]

Pāzārgād also invokes novel scientific theories to support his argument for the benefits of scouting, describing it as a system based on "progressive psycho-

69. Pāzārgād 1936, 25–26. He also gives a detailed explanation of the choreography surrounding the cub scout initiation ceremony, see 41–47, 245–52.

70. Pāzārgād 1936, 31.

71. Pāzārgād 1936, 10.

72. Pāzārgād 1936, 11.

73. Pāzārgād 1936, 11.

74. The connections between these *productive* rather than *repressive* uses of scouting techniques, and Foucault's notions of biopolitics/biopower, governmentality, and technologies of the self, are striking. For more detailed discussions see Schayegh 2009, 8; Meftahi 2016..

logical principles."[75] In describing scouting activities designed to instill virtues such as fairness and cooperation, for example, he argues that new theories of pedagogy suggest that rather than rote memorization, or systems of punishment and reward, civic virtues can best be instilled through games, or as he puts it, through play (*bāzi*). "[T]he word play (*bāzi*) is generally understood in our country as having a small or limited meaning," he writes "... but this play [*bāzi*] does have a more serious meaning and purpose because it works to produce the essential foundation of ethics and the spirit/psyche [*ruh*] in boys and adolescents."[76] Elsewhere in the same text he also draws on specific early twentieth-century psychological theories, such as the then vogue of Pelmanism, which argued for brain exercises and "mind games" as a method of enhancing cognitive function.[77] Scouting is based on these same advanced scientific principles, he argues, combining the latest psychological and pedagogical theories to promote civic, ethical, and national goals. He acknowledges that the difference between Sufism and scouting is Sufism's otherworldly orientation. Despite this distinction, when combined with Sufism's emphasis on disciplinary practices of the self, Pāzārgād states that scouting's focus on the modern-material world can make the *pishāhangi* movement "a Sufism for the age of electricity."[78] This emphasis on science alongside his invocation of Sufism also suggests that for Pāzārgād – and for the Pahlavi state more generally – Iran's nationalization project was not shy to claim for itself the authority to speak in the name of science, morality, culture, the nation, and Islam itself. As the Pahlavi state became increasingly consolidated and ambitious by the mid-1930s, the role of scouting was increasingly viewed as having a moral authority that could be used as a political tool in the culture wars that defined the still contested status of the nation.

CONCLUSION

The work of Pāzārgād, Gibson, Hekmat, and others met with remarkable success in formalizing and expanding the scouting movement in Iran during the final years of Reza Shah's reign. The production of an Iranian version of the scouting handbook, the training of cadres of new scout masters, the building of camps such as Manzarieh Park, and facilities like Amjadieh Stadium, all led to a tremendous increase in the number of young Iranians who participated in the movement. Between the fall of 1934 and February of 1935, the Iranian scouting

---

75. Pāzārgād 1936, 9. Rather than use the Persian term *ravānshenāsi*, which was likely not yet in regular usage, he transposes the term "psikulujiki" directly into Persian characters.
76. Pāzārgād 1936, 56, 16–18.
77. Pāzārgād 1936, 18.
78. Pāzārgād 1936, 11.

organization managed to train approximately 1,000 scouts.[79] The following year
the numbers had risen to 3,000; by 1937 to 21,000; and by 1940 reached 38,000
Iranian boy and girl scouts.[80] In 1937 the Iranian scouts also rejoined the World
Scout Organization after a decade of lapsed membership, and for the first time
participated in the fifth World Scouting Jamboree, held in Vogelenzang, the
Netherlands, in July and August of that year.[81] The following year, in 1938, the
Ministry of Education decreed that one year of participation in scouting activities would become a requirement for matriculation from Iran's high schools.
Scout offices were now increasingly established in schools throughout Iran,
tasked to coordinate scouting activities and to incorporate scouting principles
into the standard curriculum.[82]

This record of success, however, came at the cost of increasingly politicizing
the Iranian scouting movement. The goals of scouting were always articulated
in a language that combined the principles of civic virtue with the aspirations of
nation-building. Combining these two goals meant that it was the Iranian state
– in the form of the Pahlavi monarchy – that increasingly claimed for itself the
authority to adjudicate matters of culture, identity, ethics, and morality. Claiming the authority to speak for the nation also meant that the Pahlavi monarchy
intended to encroach on cultural terrains traditionally monopolized by Iran's
Shiʻi clerical establishment. The Iranian scouting organization's invocation of
pishāhangi's moral-ethical virtues was therefore not only part of a project of
fostering a civic culture in modern Iran but was also a direct challenge to traditional institutions of moral and cultural authority. Nowhere is this clearer than
in the Pahlavi state's utilization of the newly formed Iranian Girl Scouts as part
of the ceremonies surrounding Reza Shah's decree to ban the veil in January of
1936.[83] The role of scouts in promoting other aspects of sartorial reform and
new regulations for the licensing of the *ʻulamāʼ* also suggested that the scouting
movement's goals were not only tied to the goals of promoting civic virtue, but
to the state-led politics of cultural engineering.[84] Like much else in the twentieth-century history of Iranian nationalism, the scouting movement therefore
reflected the tensions between the political imperatives of nation-building from
above and the progressive moral-ethical ideals of engendering a civic and liberal
culture in modern Iran.

79. Delfāni 2003, introduction: 36.
80. Delfāni 2003, 41.
81. Delfāni 2003, 39.
82. Delfāni 2003, 55–56.
83. Delfāni 2003, 59; Hekmat 1976, 87. See also, Chehabi 2003, 193–210; Koyagi 2009, 1680.
84. Delfāni 2003, introduction: 65.

Works Cited

Adelkhah, Fariba. 1998. *Being Modern in Iran.* London: Hurst.

Arasteh, A. Reza. 1969. *Education and Social Awakening in Iran, 1850–1968.* Leiden: Brill.

Āshnā, Hesām Aldin. 1371/1992. "Pishāhangi dar Irān: Bargi az Siāsat-e Farhangi-ye Dowreh-ye Rezā Shāh, 1304–1320." *Ganjineh-ye Asnād* 2:2–24.

Baden-Powell, Robert. 1908. *Scouting for Boys: A Handbook for Instruction in Goo Citizenship.* London: Horace Cox.

Balslev, Sivan. 2019. *Iranian Masculinities: Gender and Sexuality in Late Qajar and Early Pahlavi Iran.* New York: Cambridge University Press.

Banani, Amin. 1961. *The Modernization of Iran, 1921–1941.* Stanford, CA: Stanford University Press.

Chehabi, Houchang. 1993. "Staging the Emperor's New Clothes: Dress Codes and Nation-Building under Reza Shah." *Iranian Studies* 26:209–33.

———. 2002. "A Political History of Football." *Iranian Studies* 35:371–402.

———. 2003. "The Banning of the Veil and Its Consequences." In *The Making of Modern Iran: State and Society under Riza Shah*, edited by Stephanie Cronin, 193–210. London: Routledge.

———. 2014. "Mir Mehdi Varzandeh and the Introduction of Modern Physical Education in Iran." In *Culture and Cultural Politics Under Reza Shah,* edited by Bianco Devos and Christoph Werner, 55–72. London: Routledge.

———. 2019. "Gender Anxieties in the Iranian Zūrkhāneh." *International Journal of Middle East Studies* 51:395–421.

———. 2020. *Onomastic Reforms: Family Names and State Building in Iran.* Boston: Ilex Foundation.

Delfāni, Mahmud. 2003. *Asnād-e Sāzmān-e Pishāhangi-ye Irān Dar Dowreh-ye Rezā Shāh.* Tehrān: Sāzmān-e Asnād.

Delheye, Pascal. 2003. "La Patrie régénérée? Clément Lefébure, L'Ecole normale de Gymnastique et d'Escrime de l'Armée et la percée de la gymnastique suédoise en Belgiquie, 1885–1908." *Cahiers de L'INSEP (Institut national du sport, de l'expertise et de la performance),* Hors-Série: 335–57.

Elwell-Sutton, L.P. 1944. *Modern Iran.* London: Routledge.

Hā'eri-Māzandarāni, Shaykh Hassan. 1926. "Pishāhangi va Masādar-e Islāmi." *Pishāhangi-ye Iran* 1:26–27.

Hekmat, 'Ali Asghar. 1925a. "Javānān-e Pishāhang, Al-Kashshāfa, Boy-Scout." *Ta'lim va Tarbiat* 1:34–36.

———. 2535/1976. *Si Khātereh az ʿAsr-e Farkhondeh-ye Pahlavi*. Tehrān: Vahid.

Honeck, Mischa. 2018. *Our Frontier is the World: The Boy Scouts in the Age of American Ascendency*. Ithaca: Cornell University Press.

Jordan, Benjamin René. 2016. *Modern Manhood and the Boy Scouts of America*. Chapel Hill: University of North Carolina Press.

Koyagi, Mikiya. 2009. "Moulding Future Soldiers and Mothers of the Nation: Gender and Physical Education under Reza Shah, 1921–1941." *International Journal of the History of Sport* 26:1668–1696.

Macdonald, Robert H. 1993. *Sons of the Empire: The Frontier and the Boy Scout Movement, 1890–1918*. Toronto: University of Toronto Press.

Mahmood, Saba. 2015. *Religious Difference in a Secular Age: A Minority Report*. Princeton: Princeton University Press.

Marashi, Afshin. 2003. "Performing the Nation: The Shah's Official State Visit to Kemalist Turkey, June to July 1934." In *The Making of Modern Iran: State and Society under Riza Shah, 1921–1941*, edited by Stephanie Cronin, 99–120. London: Routledge.

Meftahi, Ida. 2016. *Gender and Dance in Modern Iran: Biopolitics on Stage*. London: Routledge.

Milani, Abbas. 2008. *Eminent Persians*. Syracuse, NY: Syracuse University Press.

Moniri, Sayyed Hāshem. n.d. "Kārvāzhehhā-ye Pishāhanghā-ye Dowreh-ye Rezā Shāh." Institute for Iranian Contemporary Historical Studies. http://www.iichs.ir/News-20156.

Pāzārgād, Bahā' al-Din. 1936. *Pishāhangi-ye Iran*. Tehrān: Ketābkhāneh-ye Markazi.

Partov-Bayzā'i-Kāshāni, Hosayn. 1958. *Tārikh-e Varzesh-e Bāstāni-ye Irān, Zurkhāneh*. Tehrān: Haydari.

Pishāhangi-ye Irān. Tehran: 1926–1927.

Proctor, Tammy M. and Nelson R. Block eds. 2009. *Scouting Frontiers: Youth and the Scout Movement's First Century*. Newcastle: Cambridge Scholars Publications.

Pryke, Sam. 1998. "The Popularity of Nationalism in the Early British Scout Movement." *Social History* 23:309–24.

Reynolds, E. E. 1950. *The Scout Movement*. London: Oxford University Press.

Sadiq, ʿIsā. 1966. *Yādgār-e ʿOmr*. Tehran: Amir Kabir.

Safā'i, Ebrāhim. 1976. *Rezā Shāh Kabir dar Ā'ineh-ye Khāterāt*. Tehrān: Vezārat-e Farhang.

Saleh, Ali Pasha. 1976. *Cultural Ties Between Iran and the United States.* Tehran: Bistopanj-e Shahrivar.

Schayegh, Cyrus. 2002. "Sports, Health, and the Iranian Middle Class in the 1920s and 1930s." *Iranian Studies* 35:341–69.

———. 2009. *Who is Knowledgeable is Strong: Science, Class, and the Formation of Modern Iranian Society, 1900–1950.* Berkeley: University of California Press.

Uzgören, Gökhan. 2000. *Türk Izcilik Tarihi.* İstanbul: Papatya Yayıncılık.

Watenpaugh, Keith. 2009. "Scouting in the Interwar Arab Middle East: Youth, Colonialism, and the Problems of Middle Class Modernity." In *Scouting Frontiers: Youth and the Scout Movement's First Century*, edited by Tammy M. Proctor and Nelson R. Block, 89–105. Newcastle: Cambridge Scholars Publications.

Yaghoubian, David. 2014. *Ethnicity, Identity, and the Development of Nationalism in Iran.* Syracuse: Syracuse University Press.

Secular State and Religious Endowments:
The Administration of *Owqāf* under Reza Shah

Christoph U. Werner

ALREADY IN THE LATE QAJAR PERIOD a newly emerging modern administration in Iran attempted to exert some control over the large number of religious endowments (*vaqf*, pl. *owqāf*), their income, land, properties, buildings, and infrastructure. This was not necessarily carried out in opposition to the Shiite clergy who equally had an avid interest to clarify complicated ownership issues, to end litigations and disputes, and to involve state authorities in the upkeep of mosques, madrasas and religious places. The ministry in charge of endowments continued its activities through the Constitutional period into the early years of Pahlavi rule. Only gradually, the new Pahlavi state began to issue new ordinances, laws, rules, and guidelines with the aim of asserting a more comprehensive control over endowments and their funds. This included the systematic registration of endowments and properties, the appointment of guardians and administrators, and increasingly the direct management of *owqāf* and redirecting their revenues. The present article follows these attempts through the 1920s and 30s in a close reading of legislative efforts and a particular emphasis on one hitherto neglected administrative manual (*dastur*) issued and published during this time. Furthermore, we want to find out more on how the new Pahlavi administration approached the question of endowments, what challenges the ministries, departments, and offices faced in practice, and their intrinsic motives. The debate over endowments, together with the legislation and administrative re-organization involved, sheds light on wider questions of modernization in Iran and the nature of the authoritarian policies of the first Pahlavi period. How much actual power did Reza Shah and the technocrats in his closer circle wield in practice when it came to concrete administrative measures?

The modernization efforts of the Reza Shah period have been portrayed as addressing the army and gendarmerie, tackling cultural affairs including new dress codes, and being supported by an overall technocratic, secular, and nationalist stance.[1] The state's attempt to exert domination over all aspects of Iranian society became more pronounced in the 1930s and education on all

---

1. Cronin 1997; Cronin, ed. 2003; Marashi 2008.

levels was of major importance to form and strengthen a new bourgeoisie and middle class.[2] One of the outward signs and markers of the growing presence of Pahlavi cultural and administrative policies was the issuance, publication, and distribution of regulations, manuals, and guidelines on almost every imaginable issue and topic. Regulations (*nezāmnāmehs*) and statutes (*āyinnāmehs*), neatly arranged in Western-style paragraphs, spelled out ordinances and rules for administration and public to follow. They accompanied legislation and new laws that were drafted and issued systematically in the late 1920s and early 1930s. Quite often, these regulations were representative of what the Pahlavi expected from its citizens and demonstrative of its intentions, detailing and explaining legislation. With regard to administration, it often laid out what government institutions were supposed to do, rather than what they were actually capable of carrying out and implementing.

The question of religious endowments (*owqāf*) and the wider field of issues related to the institution of *vaqf* was of utmost importance to the nascent Pahlavi state. At first glance, this appears to be contradictory. Why should a modernizing, strongly nationalist and self-declared secular state care much about religious endowments? The fact is that *vaqf*, whether private or public, permeated Iranian society as a religious, social, and economic institution.[3] It was linked to buildings such as mosques and madrasas, urban structures such as the major bazaars and huge tracts of agricultural land including whole villages, with their irrigation systems and water canals (*qanāts*). For centuries, *vaqf* had been an established way to both secure and transfer private and public wealth, and to provide lasting funds for religious, cultural and educational activities. Especially during the Qajar period, endowments had multiplied and expanded widely. They were established in place of normal inheritance, but they also funded religious rituals and practice, from mourning ceremonies for the Shiite Imams (*ta'ziyeh*) to pilgrimage and burials.[4]

Vaqf thus appears more often as a topic in public discourse than one would perhaps imagine in the midst of a rapidly modernizing country. This is true for Iran as well as for most other Islamic or Islamicate countries during the nineteenth and early twentieth centuries – perhaps with the crucial difference that there was no colonial administration in Iran that would have tried to introduce Western-style legislation on endowments. Iran was thus confronted rather late with the challenge of how to deal with religious endowments within a modern

2. Devos and Werner eds. 2014.

3. Werner 2015, 35–51. A contemporary overview from an Iranian-Islamic perspective, Modarres 1385/2006.

4. Werner 2000, 97–146.

legal framework and in a very short time.[5] Looking closely at *vaqf* as a case study for legal transformation is thus a way to identify similar issues in other fields. Questions related to *owqāf* also highlight continuities from the era of Nāser al-Din Shāh (1848–96), to the Constitutional Revolution (1906–11), the coup d'état 1921, and the establishment of Pahlavi rule.

There is another reason why the issue of *owqāf* is so relevant for the first Pahlavi period. It contributes to our understanding of the relation between Shiite Islam and the authoritarian Pahlavi state and the urgent need to differentiate. Often, the state's approach towards *vaqf* is reduced to a confrontation between a traditional, even backward, Islamic clergy and the secularization politics of a modernizing government. *Vaqf* appears therefore in the literature in more or less stereotyped contexts. *Owqāf* are presented as the major source of income for the Shiite ulama.[6] State control over *owqāf* is seen as an integral part of Reza Shah's attempt to weaken or eliminate the ulama's economic base.[7] In the field of education, *owqāf* are linked exclusively to traditional religious education, to madrasas and *maktabs* (traditional primary education) and thus as an impediment to establishing modern education. Yet another instance where *vaqf* is frequently mentioned, is the larger issue of land reform and the overall necessity to make agricultural land arable and profitable.[8] This becomes crucial in the land reform discussions of the 1960s, but is present already in the discourse of the Reza Shah period. So *owqāf* appear mostly in conjunction with Shiite clergy, with education and with land reform. Dealing with *owqāf* is portrayed as an integral part of Reza Shah's secularizing and anti-religious politics and often introduced in sweeping and generalizing statements.[9]

Other aspects that actually informed the legal discussion at the time, are often ignored. The most pressing among them was how to deal with endowments lacking an acknowledged guardian or supervisor. And, in conjunction with this, how to register such properties as part of the overall state effort to record property titles. *Owqāf* might comprise a dilapidated religious building inside the bazaar, a water supply channel (*qanāt*) that urgently needed upkeep, a village whose ownership was contested among various descent groups, or a religious school that had fallen out of use, but could be re-employed for other purposes.

How could bureaucracy help to solve such practical challenges – without completely antagonizing traditional elites? Was bureaucratizing *owqāf* a way

5. There are numerous studies on *vaqf* in colonial contexts; examples are Kozlowski 1985; Kogelmann 1999; Pianciola and Sartori 2007, 475–98.

6. Algar 1969, 14.

7. Hiro 1985, 27.

8. Still valid, Lambton 1953, 230–37.

9. Boroujerdi 2003, 156.

to cut through the myriad of unresolved lawsuits, to locate and repair abandoned religious buildings and infrastructure, and to repurpose ownerless landed properties? Or were such arguments simply a pretext to disown the clergy, to amass land holdings for the state and ultimately to make room for rural and urban development? Such conflicts existed and recent studies, based on archival sources have shown the reaction of the clergy to attempts to disinvest them from traditional holdings.[10] Both perspectives are valid and the state's outlook on *owqāf* combines various, often contradictory aims, even today. The present article takes the perspective of the developing and growing *vaqf* bureaucracy and thus reflects their view.

The files and archives of Iran's current organization in charge of *vaqf*, the Sāzmān-e owqāf va omur-e kheyriyeh, remain difficult to access, because of a very special dilemma the Islamic Republic of Iran finds itself locked in. The Islamic Republic is obliged by Islamic law and its own ideology to uphold the principle of theoretical eternity of *vaqf* and the inviolability of endowed properties. On the other hand, acknowledging the common good (*maslahat*) does not allow their organizations to ignore the realities on the ground. Recalling or revoking private ownership of whole urban quarters and city structures, because land has been *vaqf* at some point, is not realistic. In practice, however, the employees and clerks of the Sāzmān-e owqāf are still busy sorting, evaluating, and registering *vaqf*-related ownership questions, analyzing documents and dealing with very basic problems. Finding guardians and supervisors for abandoned or "muddled" endowments remains time-consuming. In fact, not much has changed in the last hundred years – and the "Research Departments" that we will encounter later on in this article are still working on similar issues as in the early 1920s and 30s.[11]

Having said this, one must accept that also in the Pahlavi period the state's interference in *owqāf* was not always guided by the intention to usurp or appropriate, but was often essential to solve practical problems. It was up to the new bureaucracy to sift through layers of contradictory statements made in front of religious courts. Once *vaqf* properties had been treated as private inheritance by families for decades, how could the original intention of an endowment be restored? What to do when landed *vaqf* properties continued to produce revenues, but the original purpose had disappeared? Many such problems have their

10. Sha'bānipur, Ahmadvand and Foruzesh 1398/2019, 113–33.

11. Based on observations of my own field research in both the central and local offices of the research offices of the Sāzmān-e owqāf in the 1990s, information from researchers who are presently working there, and research publications in the journal *Vaqf: Mirās-e jāvidān*, as well as other publications sponsored by this organization.

origin in the Qajar period and are intimately linked to the changing social, economic and legal landscape of late nineteenth-century Iran.[12] In that way, *vaqf* issues can be seen as an indicator of large-scale transformational processes that go beyond the question of *owqāf* and religious affairs proper. Since the issues at stake did not disappear with the demise of the Qajar dynasty, the nascent Pahlavi state administration had to pick up on many of these unresolved issues.

Legislation, Parliamentary Debates and the Institutionalization of *Vaqf* Affairs

Dealing with endowments, their properties, their administration, income, and expenditures, presented an enormous challenge to the emerging modern state and government from the late Qajar period on, till the allied occupation of Iran in 1941 and beyond. Seen as a long-term process, it continues up to the present day, with familiar tasks carried on throughout the two Pahlavi periods of rule without a major cessation, straight into the Islamic Republic.

Creating a timeline of efforts in the field of legislation and administrative reform on *vaqf* affairs is crucial to understand the complexities of the process in the early Pahlavi period.[13] Analyzing a similar development, Houchang Chehabi has been following the intricate and complicated paths of legislature and parliamentary discussions on introducing Iranian family names (*sejell-e ahvāl*) and the ban on the use of traditional titles; a process that lasted over ten years, up until 1314 (1935).[14] Far from a simple authoritative order by Reza Shah, such efforts involved complicated negotiations and close cooperation between various ministries, institutions, and offices. One must be careful not to take pronouncements in the nationalist and modernist press as factual evidence. Instead, press declarations are meant to propagate a political agenda yet to be accomplished. When Mohammad Faghfoory, citing an article from the newspaper *Ettelāʿāt*, declares: "In 1312 Sh./1933, the government implemented another measure aimed at the destruction of the economic foundations of the ulama's power – it took control of the administration of the *awqāf* (pious endowments)," he not only reiterates the topos of *owqāf* and clergy, he also confuses implementation and announced intention.[15] The chronological sequence shows that it took two more years to get the desired *vaqf* law ratified by the Majles (parliament). The ulama's influence might have been weakened as a result, but it certainly did not

12. As an example of the intricacies of Qajar legal issues, see Kondo 2003, 106–28.

13. An excellent summary and discussion is ʿAbbāsi, Qāsemkheyli and Divkalāyi 1401/2022, 89–105.

14. Chehabi 2012, 84–114.

15. Faghfoory 1993, 288–89.

mean the destruction of their economic foundations – in fact, one might argue that it also took a large burden off the clergy's shoulders and allowed them to concentrate on other sources of income and social influence.

During the Qajar period no state administration in charge of endowments existed, whether private or public, at least none that had practical competences or authority. As other ministries created during the period of Nāser al-Din Shāh, the Ministry of Pensions and Vaqf Affairs (Vezārat-e vazāyef va owqāf) established in 1275q/1850 and placed under the direction of Mirza Fazlollāh Nasir al-Molk had very limited powers and was primarily of a symbolic nature.[16] Its denomination at that time did not include any mention of culture or education; the term *vazāyef* referred to stipends also paid to members of the Shiite clergy, hence the connection to endowments (*owqāf*). There was, however, an increasing awareness of the importance of the issue of endowments under Mozaffar al-Din Shāh and its potential for state finances. This was partly inspired by the independent policies of major endowment complexes, such as the Āstān-e Qods-e Razavi in Mashhad, which tried to compile new registers and modernize their administration.[17] Still, no concrete measures were initiated by the Qajar state prior to the Constitutional Revolution.

The first major new step in this direction occurred within the legislative period of the second Majles, that lasted from 1909–11. With the establishment of a new Ministry of Education, Endowments and Fine Arts (Vezārat-e ma'āref va owqāf va sanāye'-e mostazrafeh) in 1910,[18] *vaqf* affairs found a new home. That this was not just another empty promise becomes immediately apparent from the ministry's new administrative law (*qānūn-e edāri*), dated 28 Sha'bān 1328q (4 September 1910). The relevant paragraph §6 specifies the formation of a Vaqf Bureau (Edāreh-ye owqāf) as part of the ministry, with a wide range of obligations and tasks. The new department was in charge of evaluating and compiling all *vaqf* deeds in Iran, supervising the activities of guardians and administrators, directly managing the endowments linked to the acting ruler (*soltān-e 'asr*), controling expenditures of endowments along the original directives, especially if destined for educational purposes, and overseeing endowments without a guardian (*motevalli*).[19] We will get back to this important law with a detailed discussion of a later instructional handbook, specifying and amending these rough outline some twenty-five years later.

After the coup d'état in 1921 and under the new government with Reza

---

16. Bakhash 1971, 154.
17. Werner 2015, 104–6.
18. Banani 1961, 90.
19. Werner 2015, 136–37; Persian text and translation "Owqāf," 1273–1278.

Khan this ministry continued its work under the same name, together with its *owqāf* department.[20] Further specifications were added in a set of regulations (*nezāmnāmeh*) in 1303/1925, although only a few paragraphs dealt directly with *vaqf* issues.[21] The comprehensive Civil Code (Qānun-e madani), initiated as the keystone of Iran's new laws by the minister of justice 'Ali Akbar Dāvar, was a big step forward in drafting an overarching set of modern legislation – despite its reliance on classical manuals of Shiite law in large sections.[22] The Qānun-e madani from 1307/1928 also included references to *vaqf*, which for the first time were now codified law (in §55–91). More important, and of higher practical relevance, was however the "Law on the registration of documents and property deeds", the Qānun-e sabt-e asnād va amlāk-e Irān from 1310/1932, again with explicit mention of *vaqf* deeds (§27–31).[23] In many ways this laid the foundation for any further legislation on *owqāf*, as the tasks of the Vaqf Bureau (Edāreh-ye owqāf) in the Ministry of Education and Endowments could not reasonably be carried out without a systematic registration of property titles.

Even in the 1930s, more than twenty years after the initial establishment of the Ministry of Education and Endowments and its *owqāf* department, there still was no definite legislation on *vaqf*, despite numerous efforts in that direction. What had caused such delays? And why was it so difficult to draft a distinct and all-encompassing *vaqf* law in Iran that could have served both the administration and the public?

In fact, the legislative process on a separate *vaqf* law had begun simultaneously to the work on the Civil Code in 1307/1928. In an admirable and painstakingly detailed outline, Mahdi 'Abbāsi and his colleagues have traced these efforts in a recent article that offers a fascinating look into legislative procedure and the role of the parliament in the Reza Shah period.[24] A first step in early 1928 had been to create an administrative division for the country's endowments in eight regions (Tehrān, Gilān, Āzarbāyjān, Ekbātān, Kermān, Fārs, Esfahān and Khorāsān). A first draft (*lāyeheh*) of a new *vaqf* law was prepared in December of that year. Simple and straightforward in ten paragraphs, it pro-

20. The Persian name remained the same, the English and French designations shifted around that time, which sometimes causes confusion in the secondary literature. The same is true for various renderings of the term *edāreh*, I use bureau, department or office, depending on the context.

21. With cabinet approval, dated 30 Hut 1303 (1 March 1925), "Nezāmnāmeh-ye edāri-ye Vezārat-e Ma'āref", 26–35.

22. For further background, Arjomand 2016, 263–73.

23. The full text of this law (as ratified on 26 Esfand 1310 (17 March 1932) is available online on www.mashruteh.org and the website of the Iranian Parliament.

24. 'Abbāsi, Qāsemkheyli, and Shojā'i Divkalāyi 1401/2022, 92–93. The following summarizes their excellent research which itself is based on relevant news items in the newspaper *Ettelā'āt* as well as parliamentary and governmental announcements.

posed to grant the state far-reaching control over all endowments with a clear division into two categories: endowments under direct control of the ministry and those with an accredited guardian (*motevalli*) supervised by the ministry. The draft, however, did not even make it to parliament and was already halted on the cabinet level. A year later, in December 1930 a new draft was compiled that was much more exhaustive and spelled out further powers to be given to the ministry and its *owqāf* department, such as redirecting funds and raising large administrative fees. For the first time, cultural policy aims are mentioned: the renovation and upkeep of holy shrines and national monuments as well as investment in new primary and secondary schools. Again, the draft apparently faced early opposition within the cabinet and from representatives before it was even submitted formally to the Majles.

For two years, the project was stalled, until in 1311/1932 Reza Shah took an interesting step forward: the shah himself sought support from leading Shiite scholars. If reports are correct, he charged Seyyed Mehdi Farrokh (Moʿtasam al-Saltaneh), at that time deputy (*moʿāven*) in the Ministry of Education to get in touch with Ayatollah ʿAbd al-Karim Hāʾeri Yazdi for clarification of Islamic legal opinions on *vaqf*. In particular, Farrokh was to inquire about the legal permissibility of redirecting funds to new purposes, for example modern education. The legal details concerned the term *majhul al-masraf*, a *vaqf*, with unknown, forgotten or undefined purpose (for example, nobody knew anymore on what to spend the income of an endowment) and the case of testamentary endowments, which had become popular and widespread in Qajar Iran.[25] In a context where the *vaqf* policy of Reza Shah and his administration is usually considered to have been clearly directed against the Shiite clergy and their interests, this move might come as a surprise. It clearly shows, however, that the legal and practical problems involved in drafting *vaqf* legislation surpassed the assumed ideological bias. Reza Shah felt the double need to receive both legal backing from the Shiite ulama in Qom for his reform projects and practical advice on Islamic legal terminology and possible pitfalls.

With some issues cleared, a new draft law in fourteen paragraphs was prepared in Ordibehesht 1311 (April-May 1932) for the cabinet and a month later sent to the Ministry of Finance. For reasons unknown, the draft law got stuck again. In the meantime, Amir Shahidi, the director of the General Vaqf Bureau (*edāreh-ye koll-e owqāf*) set up a new organizational structure and created four major divisions, a bureau for general affairs, a bureau for the provincial

---

25. ʿAbbāsi, Qāsemkheyli, and Shojāʿi Divkalāyi, 1401/2022, 93 (here to be corrected: the minister of education at that time was Yahyā Qarāguzlu). On testaments and *vaqf* see Christoph Werner 2005, 211–26.

<table>
<tr><td colspan="4" align="center">Vaqf Legislation, Parliamentary
Debates and Administrative Guidelines and Instructions</td></tr>
<tr><td>Date</td><td>Title / Topic</td><td>Title / Topic (original)</td><td>Institution/Type</td></tr>
<tr><td>1328q Sha'bān 28
1910 September 4</td><td>Administrative Law of the Ministry of Education, Endowments and Fine Arts</td><td>Qānun-e edāri of Vezārat-e Ma'āref va owqāf va sanāye'-e mostazrafeh)</td><td>Parliament
Second Majles</td></tr>
<tr><td>1303 Esfand 10
1925 March 1</td><td>Administrative Regulations for the Ministry of Education, Endowments and Fine Arts</td><td>Nezāmnāmeh-ye edāri-ye Vezārat-e Ma'āref va owqāf va sanāye'-e mostazrafeh</td><td>Cabinet
Nezāmnāmeh</td></tr>
<tr><td>1307 Ordibehesht 18
1928 May 8</td><td>Civil Code</td><td>Qānun-e madani</td><td>Cabinet/Parliament</td></tr>
<tr><td>1312 Shahrivar 1
1933 August 23</td><td>Presentation of a draft law on vaqf by the acting minister of the Ministry of Education and Endowments ('Ali Asghar Hekmat)</td><td>Taqdim-e lāyeheh-ye owqāf az taraf-e Āqā-ye kafil-e Vezārat-e Ma'āref va owqāf</td><td>Parliament
Mozākerāt-e Majles, session 29</td></tr>
<tr><td>1312 Shahrivar 15
1933 September 6</td><td>First reading of the amended draft on vaqf law</td><td>Showr-e avval-e lāyeheh-ye takmil-e Qānun-e owqāf</td><td>Parliament
Mozākerāt-e Majles, session 31</td></tr>
<tr><td>1312 Shahrivar 19
1933 September 10</td><td>First reading of the amended draft on vaqf law, 2nd part</td><td>Baqiyeh-ye showr-e avval-e lāyeheh-ye takmil-e Qānun-e owqāf</td><td>Parliament
Mozākerāt-e Majles, session 32</td></tr>
<tr><td>1312 Bahman
1934 Jan. – Feb.</td><td>Manual of "Administrative Instructions on Endowments"</td><td>Dastur-e edāri-ye owqāf</td><td>Ministry
Vezārat-e Ma'āref va owqāf</td></tr>
<tr><td>1313 Āzar 11
1934 December 2</td><td>First reading of the report of the Ministry of Education commission on vaqf legislation</td><td>Showr-e avval-e khabar-e kumisiyun-e Ma'āref rāje' be owqāf</td><td>Parliament
Mozākerāt-e Majles, session 110</td></tr>
</table>

1313 Dey 1 1934 December 22	Remaining reading of the revised draft of the *vaqf* law	Baqiyeh-ye showr-e lāyeheh-ye tajdid-e nazar dar Qānun-e owqāf	Parliament Mozākerāt-e Majles, session 115
1313 Dey 3 1934 December 24	Remaining second reading and ratification of the draft of the *vaqf* law	Baqiyeh-ye showr-e sāni va tasvib-e lāyeheh-ye owqāf	Parliament Mozākerāt-e Majles, session 116
1313 Esfand 4 1935 February 23	Appointment and presentation of 'Ali Asghar Hekmat as Minister of Education and Endowments	Mo'arrefi-ye Āqā-ye Mirzā 'Ali Asghar Khān Hekmat be samt-e Vezārat-e Ma'āref va owqāf	Parliament Mozākerāt-e Majles, session 125
1314 Ordibehesht 13 1935 May 4	Implementing Regulations on the 1934 *vaqf* law	Nezāmnāmeh-ye Qānun-e owqāf	Cabinet Nezāmnāmeh

branches, an accounting bureau (*edāreh-ye mohāsebāt*), and a research bureau (*edāreh-ye tahqiq-e owqāf*). The parliament was not pleased to see such steps without proper legislation in place. In order to speed things up, a commission was formed (including members from other ministries and representatives of parliament). Finally, on 1 Shahrivar 1312 (24 August 1933) a draft was sent for deliberation to the Majles in its twenty-ninth session. Readings took place in the thirty-first and thirty-second sessions on 15 and 19 Shahrivar 1312 (6 and 10 September) respectively.[26] The law was not ratified by parliament and Reza Shah appointed 'Ali Asghar Hekmat as interim minister (*kafil*) of the Ministry of Education and Endowments on 26 Shahrivar 1312 (17 September).[27]

Again, a commission was set up to mediate different positions. The report of the commission was presented to the Majles in its 110th session on 11 Āzar 1313 (2 December 1934) together with a new draft law in ten paragraphs. This draft was discussed in its final revised version in its second reading and ratified on 1 and 3 Dey 1313 respectively (22 and 24 December 1934). The new law was a milestone for the future of endowments and *vaqf* policy in Iran. Its contents have been discussed and summarized in the literature, but the extremely complicated and path towards it has not been treated and discussed adequately.[28]

26. Full text available on www.mashruteh.org.

27. His formal appointment as *Vazir-e Ma'āref va owqāf* only took place on 4 Esfand 1313 (23 February 1935).

28. The full text of the law in "Owqāf" (*Irānshahr*), 1375 (and online); a translation can be found

The whole process was only completed some months later, when the Ministry of Education and Endowments issued the official Implementing Regulations to complement, annotate, and detail the *vaqf* law in its Nezāmnāmeh-ye Qānun-e owqāf of 13 Ordibehesht 1314 (4 May 1935).[29] The table on the next page shows the long and arduous journey towards *vaqf* legislation.

There is no place here to enter the parliamentary debates on *vaqf* legislation in detail.[30] However, even a short glance shows that these debates were extremely focused and serious. The delays in the legislative process mentioned above were not motivated by obstructionism or fundamental opposition; to the contrary, the questions and answers show an in-depth familiarity with the issues involved and provide exhaustive, and surprisingly constructive criticism. Thus even in the final second reading of the *Qānun-e owqāf* on 1 Dey 1313 (22 December 1934), two days before the final vote and ratification of the law, Seyyed Esmāʿil ʿErāqi, the representative from Arāk, posed a far-reaching opening question to the interim minister ʿAli Asghar Hekmat. Politely, but insistent, he asked the minister to clarify his understanding of the term "unknown guardianship" (*majhul al-towliyeh*). Could it not be, he states, that the stipulations of a *vaqf* deed allow two or three persons to be qualified as guardian (*motevalli*) – in which case the right *motevalli* would also be unknown, allowing ministerial authority to take over? Or, he continues with a similar hypothetical question on the distinction between a public and a private endowment, arguing that the borderlines in traditional judicial terms are often vague. The example he provides is that of a private *vaqf* of properties to the benefit of the descendants of the founder, albeit with certain conditions (*shart*), such as that they would have to donate funds on the reading of Shiite eulogies (*rowzeh-khvāni*), or send a certain number of believers on pilgrimage, or provide fifty coats to beggars a year. Clearly, the ownership character of such an endowment remains that of a private vaqf (*khāṣṣeh*), while simultaneously featuring aspects of a public good *vaqf* (*ʿāmm*). In short, the rigid and binary text of the law would again give the ministry too much room to prioritize its own prerogatives.

The interim minister in his response demonstrates equally a high level of competence and refers to the excellent work of the legal commission that had helped in drafting the law. He stresses that for the second question, the ministry is concerned with supervision (*nezārat*) and the control of long-term rents,

---

in de Janssens 1952, 67; reproduced in Werner 2015, 138–39. A full discussion and paraphrase in simplified Persian in ʿAbbāsi, Qāsemkheyli, and Shojāʿi Divkalāyi 1401/2022, 94–95. A discussion of major points in Akhavi 1980, 55–59.

29. Available at www.mashruteh.org and the website of the Iranian Parliament.

30. The debates are extensive. Further research will attempt to identify protagonists and motives in more detail.

even in the case of apparent public-good endowments, without putting to question the actual character of an endowment. As to the first question, he replies that specially to alleviate such misunderstandings, the expression "or persons" (*yā ashkhās*) has been added to the original formulation.

But not only Hekmat as interim minister of the Vezārat-e Maʿāref va owqāf participated in this session. The minister of justice (*vazir-e ʿadliyeh*), at this time Mohsen Sadr, as the successor of ʿAli Akbar Dāvar, took active part in the debate as well and defended the new law. He justifies this intervention stating that the draft had been drawn up with the active participation and in consultation with the Ministry of Justice. In particular, he explains again the terms *majhul al-towliyeh* and *maʿlum al-towliyeh*, unknown and known guardianship of endowments in all its practical consequences. The necessity to dispel concerns by representatives of the Majles that a too liberal interpretation of "unknown" would enable the Ministry of Education to appropriate endowments under a simple pretext is tangible in the discussion.

Legislative procedure was open and transparent and the long and complicated history of drafting a new *vaqf* law proves that the parliament even in the thirties played a critical and constructive role in the process. The widely held image of an unrestrained authoritarian government – at least in this case – needs to be adjusted.

ADMINISTRATIVE PERSPECTIVES:
THE *DASTUR-E EDĀRI-YE OWQĀF* OF 1312/1934

The manual "Administrative Instructions on Endowments," or simply *Dastur-e edāri-ye owqāf*, published and distributed in Bahman 1312 (January 1934) offers fascinating insights into the administrative reality concerning endowments in the early 1930s.[31] This manual was published by the Ministry of Education and Endowments on the initiative of the interim minister, ʿAli Asghar Hekmat. A small imprint at the end carries his signature and affirms that the manual is valid from a month after its publication, from Esfand 1312/February 1934 onward. The *Dastur-e edāri* thus precedes both the new Vaqf Law from December 1934 and the following Implementing Regulations (*Nezāmnāmeh*) from 13 Ordibehesht 1314 (4 May 1935).

Whereas the Vaqf Law of 1313/1934 and the following *Nezāmnāmeh* of

---

31. Vezārat-e Maʿāref va Owqāf, *Dastur-e edāri-ye owqāf* (Tehrān: Matbaʿeh-ye Berukhim, Bahman 1312/January-February 1934). The *Dastur-e edāreh-ye owqāf* has not been mentioned or used until now in the research literature on *owqāf* in the Reza Shah period, whether inside or outside of Iran. Thanks to the digitization efforts of the Central Library of the University of Tehran, under its former director Rasul Jaʿfariyān, this manual has now become available.

1314/1935 mirror an external perspective on the administration of endowments, primarily concerned with granting more extensive powers and authority to the Ministry, the *Dastur-e edāri-ye owqāf* is, despite its published and public character, an internal manual that reflects to a large degree the actual challenges the working administration had to confront in their daily routines. We immediately understand that here was a huge personnel problem within the *vaqf* department. Tasks and duties entrusted to the *vaqf* department required an intimate understanding of Islamic legal terminology and practice, whereas probably few of the employees and clerks at that time had had such training. In practical terms it involved reading and understanding historical *vaqf* deeds, legal documents and records of previous ownership, dispute,s and court proceedings.

The preliminary, transitional, and programmatic character of this manual is not immediately apparent. It was preliminary and transitional, because it expresses the impatience and urgency felt by the interim minister Hekmat, who was not yet officially appointed. Only more than a year later and only after the successful implementation of the new Vaqf Law, was he officially introduced as the new minister of education to the parliament.[32] At the same time, the *Dastur-e edāri* was based on the outdated administrative law of the Ministry of Education from 1328q/1910 and could not yet incorporate the new *vaqf* legislation that was still caught up in parliamentary debates. This manual was not part of official legal governmental publications such as laws, decrees, or regulations, but an almost private ministry publication. This is the reason why it has escaped the attention of researchers who mainly follow the official state announcements of *Qavānin-o moqarrarāt* and parliamentary decisions and protocols – where this booklet does not appear. Further, it was programmatic in so far as it laid out what the tasks and organizational structure of the Edāreh-ye owqāf should be, rather than what they essentially were or what the *vaqf* bureaus were actually able to accomplish.

The *Dastur-e edāri-ye owqāf* consists of five chapters (*fasl*) and an appendix. The appendix, under the heading of a conclusion (*khātemeh*), is actually a collection of all relevant laws and legal ordinances relevant to the Owqāf Bureau. It contains verbatim citations of the administrative paragraphs §6 and §7 from the 1910 law, detailing the administrative structure of the Vezārat-e Ma'āref va owqāf; the relevant paragraphs §27 to §31 from the Law on Document Registration (*Qānun-e sabt-e asnād*), and the respective Implementing Regulations on the Registration of Documents and Properties (*Nezāmnāmeh-*

---

32. "Mo'arrefi-ye Āqā-ye Mirzā 'Ali Khān Hekmat be samt-e Vezārat-e Ma'āref va owqāf," *Mozākerāt-e Majles-e Shurā-ye Melli, dowreh-ye qānungozāri-ye nohom, 4 Esfan*d *1313 neshast 125*: p. 1722, available at www.mashruteh.org.

ye sabt-e asnād va amlāk) with paragraphs §14 to §16 and §46, as well as the main paragraphs from the Civil Code (*Qānun-e madani*) in its version from 1307/1928 with paragraphs §66–67, §75, §77, §79–84, §86, §88–91 dealing with *vaqf* issues; paragraphs §65 and §66 of the Law on Judicial Organisation (*Qānun-e osul-e tashkilāt-e ʿadliyeh*); and finally the concluding paragraph §12 of the 1328q/1910 law that concerns the endowments under the direct control of the Ruler of the Age.

Starting from the appendix, it is obvious that the *Dastur-e edāri* is also a small legal vademecum, that tried to assemble all relevant laws and regulations from various ministries and organizations. We notice the number of governmental organisations involved: the Ministry of Justice and the new organizations for the Registration of Documents and Properties feature next to the Edāreh-ye owqāf as part of the Ministry of Education.

The short preface states the main purpose of this manual: "Paragraph 6 of the administrative law of the Ministry of Culture and Endowments has laid out the tasks related to endowments of this ministry, especially the assignment to prepare a comprehensive list of all endowments and to supervise the activities of guardians (*motevalliyan*) and administrators (*motesaddiyan*) and to prevent them from misappropriating funds. While various circulars have spelled out the duties of the subordinate offices to a certain degree, the following instructions are now communicated, so that everyone shall have a coherent and practical instructional handbook in his hands and can discern his duties without recourse to the central office."[33]

Apparently there had been growing uncertainty among the employees of the central bureau and the local branches of the *vaqf* bureaus regarding their exact duties and how to go about them. The first chapter deals with the question on how to compile various registers (*daftar*, pl. *dafāter*) and what information to include. In contrast to traditional lists and account keeping, which were composed in a special form of accountancy script (*siyāq*), the new registers follow a western tabular model with numbered lines and columns. Crucial is the number of each file (dossier, *dusiyeh*), which allows cross-referencing. The bureaus are to prepare a register of endowed properties (*daftar-e raqabāt*), a register of endowments (*daftar-e mowqufāt*), a separate register of properties under the direct administration of the Vaqf Bureau (*daftar-e raqabāt-e motesarrefi-ye edāreh*). and for the endowments which have an external guardian or administrator, a register of yearly accounts has to be compiled as well (*daftar-e surat-hesāb-hā*). Crucial is a close examination of all *vaqf* deeds and related documents (*tahsil-e madārek*), in the original or as copy – all documents have to carry the number

33. *Dastur-e edāri-ye owqāf,* 1.

of the endowment register on their back, so that easy reference to the documentation is possible.

For the year 1312/1933–34, that is the actual year of the publication of this instruction handbook, special care should be taken of endowments for traditional religious schools (that is, *madresehs*). A full report on yearly income and expenditures on teaching for religious sciences in the field of literature and theology (*ma'qul-o manqul*) has to be compiled and submitted. This is a clear indication that beyond administrative regulations, the new interim minister also followed a political educational agenda of his own.[34]

The second chapter details the task of administrative supervision the Vaqf Bureau has to carry out for all endowments. A yearly budget report for every single endowment has to be compiled and verified against the original *vaqf* deed and its specifications. Again, documents with an external guardian or supervisor are separated from those endowments under the supervision of the Vaqf Bureau, where expenditures are unknown (*majhul al-masraf*), not feasible (*mote'azzar al-masraf*), or destined for general pious deeds or welfare (*mabarrāt-e motlaq*). Once again, all necessary tabular columns are specified in detail. The budget reports from external supervisors (*motesaddiyan*) also have to follow these regulations; their financial reports have to match the pre-submitted budgets for the year.

In the third chapter, various other regulations are mentioned; in fact, it is in this chapter that the reality becomes visible and a number of problems and challenges are discussed. This stands in contrast to the apparently simple and mechanical tasks listed above, where everything can and should be placed into neat columns. Most of the issues treated here are related to conflicts, the numbers and extent of which must have been overwhelming. To quote the opening paragraph §9 of this chapter in full:

> One of the tasks of the *vaqf* bureaus according to §6 of the Administrative Law of the Ministry of Education and Endowments [see above] is to comprehensively study all the *vaqf* deeds of the Iranian realm. It is necessary to take this extremely seriously and to get a full list of all endowments under their jurisdiction. It might be necessary to make use of and enlist the support of the Office for Finance and the Office for the Registration of Documents. In case someone refuses to submit documents, it is necessary to inform the public prosecutor or his deputy, so that they can prepare a charge."[35]

---

34. Still valid for a comprehensive survey of educational policies, Matthee 1993, 313–36.
35. *Dastur-e edāri-ye owqāf*, 7.

The idea to prepare a comprehensive list of all endowments in Iran is obviously unrealistic, given the actual capabilities of the Vaqf Bureau. Equally, it is not surprising that many individuals had very little interest in cooperating with the Vaqf Bureau, for fear of usurpation, appropriation, or interference. Often, there might also have been practical problems to submit the necessary documents. Opposition also came from the guardians or administrators of endowments, who were either not able or willing to submit the required financial budget reports (§10), although the manual threatens their expulsion or exclusion from further involvement in the affairs of their endowments. Apparently, a large number of administrators had not even yet registered the endowments under their control or lodged an official complaint with regard to their ownership (§11). They are exhorted to do so urgently until the end of the year 1313 (1935). What happened if *vaqf* properties were damaged as a result of a public road being expanded or for other causes? This also was a recurring challenge for the Vaqf Bureau (§12) as were a large number of new or ongoing court cases and legal suits. Costs for legal representation had to be covered from the proceeds of the respective endowment; in every single case reports had to be written and submitted (§13 and §14). Particularly troublesome were plaintiffs from among the endowments' beneficiaries (*mowquf 'aleyhom*) in case of private endowments. The bureaus are advised to respect the rights of legal beneficiaries, but to abstain from interfering in any other claims for fees or stipends and pass those on to the judiciary (§15).

By now it must have become clear how important the newly established research units (*davā'ir-e tahqiq-e owqāf*) within the *vaqf* bureaus were. Their tasks and duties, as well as their composition and personnel requirements are detailed in chapter four. Quite surprisingly, given the enormous scope of their work, these units in both the central office and the local branches were quite small. The teams were composed of a unit head and two members, with a minimum age of thirty required to guarantee a certain experience and seniority; and at least one of them was required to have had training as an accountant (§17). On the other hand, their range of work was wide: they were supposed to mediate conflicts between guardians, administrators, and employees of endowments, while at the same time they had to evaluate all written documents related to respective endowments. They had to check the balance sheets and distinguish *vaqf* properties from personal ownership. In addition, they were in charge of handling requests and petitions (*'arzhāl*) and verify submitted documents – to a degree where they appear to have had a wide range of judicial powers, including the enforcement of outstanding payments or deficits from submitted account sheets (§41-§43). It is in this chapter where we realize that the guidelines imagine a gigantic bureaucratic apparatus that would have needed to be at least ten times the actual size in order to only scratch the surface of the tasks scheduled for them. The final chapter five of the manual returns to administrative basics and lists the costs for stamps and fees, and the income generated through them.

Altogether, this instructional manual is short and compact, with a total of twenty pages, of which five are reproductions of laws and legal ordinances in the appendix. It is still based on the administrative law of the Vezārat-e maʿāref va owqāf from the Constitutional Period. However, it already displays the new élan of the interim minister, ʿAli Asghar Hekmat, and his plans for the further development of the administrative units of the *vaqf* bureaus. His emphasis on deadlines – by the end of 1313 (spring 1935) all endowments were to have been registered – and the particular urgency to examine the budgets of endowments dealing with traditional religious schools are proof of his new policies. That Hekmat meant business can also be gleaned from his recourse to judicial and executive measures. Supervisors could be dismissed, misappropriations were to be persecuted and bothersome plaintiffs should be ignored. The instructional manual is an odd composition: on one hand, it describes basic administrative layout tasks, lists to be compiled, columns to be filled, stamps for fees to be sold; on the other hand, it details problems and challenges that clearly surpass the capacities of the *vaqf* bureaus and their research units. To register the totality of all *vaqf* deeds in Iran, including additional documents, to supervise and control yearly budget sheets, and to manage law suits and disputes and various levels was far beyond even what later administrations could achieve. The registration might have been at least partly manageable, the budget controls pointed out the enormous challenges ahead, and only the new *vaqf* law that was passed two years later and its implementing regulations could guarantee the legal basis for such matters.

In all of that, Reza Shah was rather absent, due to the concerted action of ministers, high-level technocrats, and legal experts who helped to advance a practical agenda to focus on the income from endowments and new legal structures. The initiated process was interrupted by the world war and other affairs took precedence and the issue of *vaqf* affairs was only to surface on a larger scale again in the context of the land reforms of the 1960s.

CONCLUSION

The question of endowments (*owqāf*) in the first Pahlavi period under Reza Shah continues to be portrayed in a stereotyped framework of conservative ulama against a modernist state. The primary aim of Pahlavi politics, in such a perspective, was to weaken the Shiite clergy and strengthen the secular and authoritarian government. As soon as one moves beyond such overly simplified perceptions of Pahlavi policies, one must differentiate and to allow for a multiple and often diverse set of motives. Such a shift is not revisionist, but outlines the need to read and understand the state protagonists' motivation from their own background in the 1920s and 30s, instead of through the later, often distorted lens of binary opposition from the second Pahlavi period – even more so when an anti-Islamic perspective is added after the Islamic Revolution. To look at endowments from a pragmatic administrative perspective, through the eyes of the administration and the legislators involved, allows a new and necessary adjustment. It is worth noting that such adjustments are supported, if not initiated, by recent source-oriented studies published in Iran. ʿAbbasi and his colleagues consequently stress the need to finance and fund new educational institutions, primary and secondary schools, as the dominant driving force behind the Ministry of Education's *vaqf* policies.[36]

Applied *vaqf* administration in the 1930s might at first glance appear as a highly arcane and specialized subject. In contrast to much more symbolic and visible cultural politics such as dress codes, military reforms, or nationalist architecture and celebrations – in the year 1934 we are witness to the *Shāhnāmeh* memorial events that were widely publicized – it is indeed very much a down-to-earth and pragmatic issue. Still, for the politicians of the day – and the personal investment from individuals such as the minister of education, ʿAli Asghar Hekmat, is a clear indication – this was a political field that was of utmost importance. It was tied to financial affairs and the emerging educational sector as well as a growing awareness of the necessity to actively safeguard the numerous sites of cultural heritage (and to provide adequate funding for them). For someone like Hekmat, *vaqf* legislation was as crucial and deserving of his attention as the establishment of the University of Tehran or the Ferdowsi anniversary celebrations.

Taking a closer look, we have seen that in contrast to the standard image of Reza Shah as an authoritarian ruler with almost absolute powers, he was not able in the early 1930s to get his *vaqf* legislation through parliament without compromises. His ministers had to answer numerous questions to critical and technically well-informed Majles representatives. The parliamentary debates on the various drafts of the law were exhaustive and filled many pages of parliamentary proceedings. In addition, *vaqf* legislation alone did not solve the numerous challenges the slowly evolving administration from the Vaqf Bureau (Edāreh-ye owqāf) was facing. New sub-divisions had to be created, the provincial offices had to cooperate with the central office, a new research department was estab-

---

36. ʿAbbāsi, Qāsemkheyli, and Shojāʿi Divkalāyi 1401/2022, 102.

lished, and registers and lists had to follow clear structures and new layouts. This points toward continuities: the first Pahlavi ruler and the nascent administration inherited the problems concerning the management of endowments from the late Qajar period. Equally, the crucial task of creating inventories, sifting through endowment deeds, additional files, and court cases was not to be completed in a couple of years. The Sāzmān-e owqāf va omur kheyriyeh of the Islamic Republic with its local and regional branches continues to read through deeds and documents, to evaluate legal issues and disputes related to *owqāf*, placing state interests above individual grievances.

For the Reza Shah period, *vaqf* legislation and administration is an excellent case study. It demonstrates the intertwined issues of legislation, parliamentary debates, administration, and actual practice. The administration had to define tasks and create new structures and divisions. It had to organize and adjust responsibilities between different ministries and organizations, and to spell out the relation between the center and the peripheries. From the start, it was obvious that *vaqf* issues were local affairs that needed local expertise and knowledge within regional branches – centralized efforts would not be successful. Understanding the legislative and administrative processes surrounding *owqāf* in the first Pahlavi period is crucial to acquiring a more nuanced understanding of the modernizing strategies in Iran of the 1930s.

WORKS CITED

'Abbāsi, Mahdi, Rezā Shajari Qāsemkheyli and Seyyed Hasan Shojā'i Divkalāyi. 2022/1401. "Sāzmāndeh-ye nezām-e owqāf va ahdāf-e āmūzeshi-ye ān dar 'asr-e Pahlavi-ye avval," *Pazhuheshhā-ye Tārikhi (Eṣfahān)* 58, new series 14:89–105.

Akhavi, Shahrough. 1980. *Religion and Politics in Contemporary Iran: Clergy and State Relations in the Pahlavi Period*. Albany: State University of New York Press.

Algar, Hamid. 1969. *Religion and State in Iran 1785–1906. The Role of the Ulama in the Qajar Period*. Berkeley: University of California Press.

Arjomand, Saïd Amir. 2016. *Sociology of Shi'ite Islam. Collected Essays*. Leiden: Brill.

Bakhash, Shaul. 1971. "The Evolution of Qajar Bureaucracy: 1779–1879." *Middle Eastern Studies* 7:139–68.

Banani, Amin. 1961. *The Modernization of Iran, 1921–1941*. Stanford: Stanford University Press.

Boroujerdi, Mehrzad. 2003. "Triumphs and Travails of Authoritarian Modernisations in Iran." In Cronin 2003, 146–154.

Chehabi, Houchang. 2022. "The Reform of Iranian Nomenclature and Titulature in the Fifth Majles." In *Converging Zones: Persian Literary Tradition and the Writing of History. Studies in Honor of Amin Banani*, edited by Wali Ahmadi, 84–114. Costa Mesa: Mazda.

Cronin, Stephanie. 1997. *The Army and the Creation of the Pahlavi State in Iran, 1910–1926*. London: I.B. Tauris.

Cronin, Stephanie ed. 2003. *The Making of Modern Iran: State and Society under Riza Shah, 1921–1941*. London: Routledge.

Devos, Bianca and Christoph Werner, ed. 2014. *Culture and Cultural Politics Under Reza Shah. The Pahlavi State, New Bourgeoisie and the Creation of a Modern Society in Iran*. London: Routledge.

Faghfoory, Mohammad H. 1993. "The Impact of Modernization on the Ulama in Iran, 1925–1941." *Iranian Studies* 26: 288–89.

Hiro, Dilip. 1985. *Iran under the Ayatollahs*. London: Routledge and Kegan.

Janssens, G. Busson de. 1952. "Les wakfs dans l'islam contemporain." *Extrait de la Revue des Études islamiques*, année 1951. Paris: Librairie Orientaliste Paul Geuthner.

Kogelmann, Franz. 1999. *Islamische fromme Stiftungen und Staat: Der Wandel in den Beziehungen zwischen einer religiösen Institution und dem marokkanischen Staat seit dem 19. Jahrhundert bis 1937*. Würzburg, Ergon.

Kondo, Nobuaki ed. 2003. *Persian Documents*. London: Routledge, 2003.

Kozlowski, Gregory C. 1985. *Muslim Endowments and Society in British India*. Cambridge: Cambridge University Press.

Lambton, Ann K. S. 1953. *Landlord and Peasant in Persia: A Study of Land Tenure and Land Revenue Administration*. London: Oxford University Press.

Marashi, Afshin. 2008. *Nationalizing Iran: Culture, Power, and the State, 1870–1940*. Seattle: University of Washington Press.

Matthee, Rudi. 1993. "Transforming Dangerous Nomads into Useful Artisans, Technicians, Agriculturists: Education in the Reza Shah Period." *Iranian Studies* 26:313–36.

Modarres, Mohammad Aminiyān. 1385/2006. *Vaqf: az didgāh-e hoquq va qavānin*. Mashhad: Bonyād-e Pazhuheshhā-ye Eslāmī.

"Nezāmnāmeh-ye edāri-ye Vezārat-e Ma'āref va owqāf va sanāye'-e mostazrafeh." *Ta'lim va tarbiyat* 1,1 (dowreh-ye avval, no. 1), Farvardin 1304/1925:26–35.

Pianciola, Niccolò and Paolo Sartori. 2007. "Waqf in Turkestan: the Colonial Legacy and the Fate of an Islamic Institution in Early Soviet Central Asia, 1917–1924." *Central Asian Survey* 26:475–98.

"Owqāf" in *Irānshahr: Nashriyeh-ye shomāreh-ye 22 Kumisiyun-e melli-ye Yunesku dar Iran (=Unesco-Iran)*, volume 2, Tehran: 1343/1964.

Shaʿbānipur, Shahnāz, ʿahnā Ahmadvand and Sinā Foruzesh. 1398/2019. "Vākonesh-e ʿolamā be seytareh-ye hokumat-e Pahlavi bar owqāf (bā taki-yeh bar asnād)." *Pazhuheshnāmeh-ye Tārikh-e Eslām* 9:113–33.

Werner, Christoph. 2000. *An Iranian Town in Transition: A Social and Economic History of the Elites of Tabriz, 1747–1848.* Wiesbaden: Harrassow-itz.

———. 2005. "Pious Merchants: Religious Sentiments in Wills and Testaments." In *Religion and Society in Qajar Iran*, edited by Robert Gleave, 211–26. London: Routledge.

———. 2015. *Vaqf en Iran: Aspects culturels, religieux et sociaux.* Paris: Assoc. pour l'avancement des études iraniennes.

A Modern Tale from the *Arabian Nights*?: The Wedding of the Iranian Crown Prince Mohammad Reza Pahlavi and the Egyptian Princess Fowziyeh in 1939

Bianca Devos

WHEN THE OCEAN LINER *MOHAMED ALY EL KEBIR* of the Pharaonic Line set sail from Port Said in fine weather on 3 April 1939, the newly-wed royal couple stood at the railing and gazed back at the Egyptian coast and the crowd that had gathered there to bid them farewell. Sailing at fifteen nautical miles per hour through the Suez Canal, Iranian Crown Prince Mohammad Reza and Princess Fowziyeh, sister of the young king Faruq of Egypt, headed towards further celebrations and their future together in Iran.[1] Their marriage was not a love match, but a political union between royal houses of two Islamic countries. As the wedding was not only a diplomatic act between Iran and Egypt, but also a media event, representatives of the press were on board as well. Particularly for the Iranian side, which had initiated this marriage, it was an event of great propagandistic significance.

At the end of the 1930s, Iran had achieved some successes on its way to progress and national independence and entered the foreign policy arena more self-confidently than before, demanding recognition.[2] The international attention the wedding attracted provided an opportunity to present itself as a modern nation state.[3] After eliminating possible political rivals within the country, Reza Shah had consolidated his position as an autocratic ruler, and the institutionalization of his dynasty gained in importance. In this phase of transition from "nationalism to dynastic nationalism,"[4] the wedding drew attention to the crown prince as the guarantor of the Pahlavi dynasty's survival. At the same time, the country had reached a point where the state's ambitions went beyond mere censorship so that education of the public was on the agenda. Its efforts culminated in the foundation of the Sāzmān-e Parvaresh-e Afkār (Organization for Public Enlightenment) in January 1939, only three months before the wed-

---

1. "Naẓrat al-widāʿ ilā ash-shāṭiʾ al-miṣrī," *al-Ahrām*, 5 April 1939, 1, 8.

2. In 1937, Iran signed the Saadabad Pact, a nonaggression treaty between its neighboring countries Iraq, Turkey and Afghanistan.

3. Amin 2002, 136.

4. Ansari 2008, 71.

ding.[5] This institution pursued a comprehensive approach in order to exploit a broad repertoire of media influence, be it through the press, radio, music or cinema and theatre.[6] But since there was no radio in Iran at the time of the royal wedding, the press, as the medium with the greatest reach, gained the leading role in reporting the event and disseminating the official narrative.[7]

This article examines the wedding and its press coverage with the aim of outlining the layers of the official narrative and its implementation in the Iranian press. The wedding was an exceptional affair for the newspapers. As a joyous event of high political significance, with bride and groom as two handsome protagonists and lavish festivities attended by high-ranking international guests, it held great journalistic potential, not only for the Iranian press. For Western media, the event promised to be a modern fairy tale from the *Arabian Nights*. The Iranian journalists, however, acted under the particularly watchful eye of the state censors and were under great pressure in view of the great propagandistic importance of the event. Therefore, they subordinated their own journalistic or entrepreneurial interests to the state's expectations of reporting. In this regard, considering the coverage of the wedding as a case study will show certain characteristics of Iran's press of the 1930s less clearly, though they were nevertheless present. Predominant are the propagandistic imperatives. The press campaign around the wedding was immense and had two peak moments, at least in Iran's largest daily, *Ettelāʿāt* (Information). Before the extensive coverage of the wedding started in spring of 1939, a first wave of frontpage articles occurred on occasion of the engagement in May 1938. Both phases will be considered in this article, with a focus on the reporting of the actual wedding in 1939 and complemented by a comparative glimpse into Egyptian newspapers and their coverage of the event.

Diplomacy and Wedding Planning

The crown prince had returned from his Swiss boarding school in 1936 and had completed his training at the Iranian military academy. The time seemed ripe to look for a proper bride. As the primary aim was to ensure the continuation of the Pahlavi dynasty, the bride should be suited to be Iran's future queen. While looking for an appropriate candidate from the Iranian aristocracy, the idea came

---

5. The founding charter is dated 2 January 1939. Marashi 2008, 104–9.

6. Seven commissions were formed within the Sāzmān-e Parvaresh-e Afkār, for the press, public speeches, performances (in theatres and cinemas), music, radio, textbooks, and for social activities. Mahmud Delfāni 1375/1996, 1–4.

7. The first radio station in Tehran (Rādiyo-ye Tehrān) broadcast its program only on 4 Ordibehesht 1319 (24 April 1940). Vezārat-e farhang va ershād-e eslāmi, ed. 1379/2000, 7. On the radio see also Amin 2014, 279–81.

up to marry the crown prince to a woman from another Islamic royal house.[8] Iran's representatives in Islamic countries were asked to make suggestions. The proposal of Ahmad Rad, envoy in Cairo, proved to be particularly interesting: Fowziyeh, the younger sister of the Egyptian king Faruq, promised to be a good choice.[9] A delegation led by Prime Minister Mahmud Jam was commissioned to travel to Cairo and propose to the princess.[10] On 5 Khordad 1317 (26 May 1938) the court announced the engagement of Mohammad Reza and Fowziyeh.[11]

Regarding the succession to the throne, however, there was a constitutional challenge: Article 37 of the Iranian constitutional supplement stipulated that the mother of the future heir to the throne had to be Iranian (*irāni al-aṣl*). Since Fowziyeh had no Iranian ancestry to claim, the interpretation of the term was used and its meaning extended to include not only a native Iranian, but also a woman who had been granted Iranian citizenship before marrying the shah or the crown prince, at the suggestion of the government and with the approval of parliament. The procedure was initiated under the auspices of the minister of justice, Ahmad Matin Daftari, in order to overcome this obstacle quickly.[12] Fowziyeh was granted Iranian nationality on 7 February 1939.[13]

A direct political consequence of the prospective marriage was the expansion of diplomatic relations between Egypt and Iran. In Autumn 1938, the legations (*sefārat-khāne-hā*) of both countries were elevated to embassies (*sefārat-hā-ye kobrā*).[14] However, the diplomatic recognition of an increased powerful position brought about by such an elevation was not welcomed unreservedly by all. The British as the former protectorate power viewed the rising Egyptian self-confidence with some unease. After Great Britain had abolished the protectorate in 1922 and declared Egypt independent, it had agreed to Egypt's entry into the League of Nations only in 1937, so that it could open consulates and

8. Matin Daftari reports that the idea came from Reza Shah himself. ʿĀqeli 1371/1992, 138–39.

9. ʿĀqeli 1371/1992, 139.

10. Other members of the delegation were Mohaddab al-Dowleh Nafisi, chamberlain of the crown prince (*pishkār-e valiʿahd*), Dr. Qāsem Ghani, member of parliament, Dādmarz, head of the prime minister's office, Gholamrezā Rashid Yasemi, university professor and court translator. ʿĀqeli 1371/1992, 140.

11. "Bozorgtarin mozhde-ye massarat-bakhsh," in *Ettelāʿāt* 3490, 5 Khordād 1317 (26 May 1938), p. 1.

12. Bāstāni Pārizi, 13, 1982/1361 (*sizdah*). Amin 2002, 136. As Matin Daftari was the driving force behind the passage of the law, he included a more detailed account of the procedure in his memoirs. His involvement was later held against him by his critics. ʿĀqeli 1371/1992, 142–43, 152.

13. R. 1939, 161 (Firmano dello Scià per il conferimento della nazionalità persiana alla Principessa egiziana Fawziyyah).

14. The first Egyptian ambassador to Iran was ʿAbd al-Laṭīf Ṭalʿat Baik, the first Iranian ambassador to Egypt was ʿAli Akbar Bahman. ʿĀqeli 1371/1992, 145–146. Also see R. 1939, 162 (La Legazioni rispettive della Persia e dell'Egitto elevate al rango di Ambasciate).

embassies worldwide.[15] Now, the British ambassador in Egypt, Sir M. Lampson, feared that the Egyptian state would elevate the legations of other countries, such as Germany, Italy, and France, as well.[16] The marriage thus was part of the overall Egyptian and Iranian ambition for national self-determination and international recognition. For Iran, the wedding offered an opportunity to present itself as a sovereign nation on the international stage and to end the hitherto small presence of the ruler or other members of the royal family in foreign politics. Apart from his trip to Turkey in 1934, Reza Shah made no further state visits during his reign. Therefore, the Iranian crown prince's trip to Egypt was of special significance, particularly since he traveled overland to the Mediterranean coast through Iraq, Syria, and Lebanon, where he was received with military honors.

With international media attention on the wedding behind them, it was essential for both states to take advantage of the public stage. Given its enormous propaganda potential, the wedding followed an elaborate schedule, which went far beyond the actual wedding ceremony. This included a meticulous timetable for the crown prince's journey to Egypt, the program during his stay there, the couple's return journey to Iran and the celebrations in Tehran.[17] On 24 February 1939, Mohammad Reza left Tehran at eight in the morning, crossed the border into Iraq on 26 February, traveled from Baghdad to Syria on 1 March, and on the same day to Lebanon, where he boarded the Egyptian royal yacht *al-Maḥrūsa* two days later to sail to Alexandria. The royal yacht was escorted by the two cruisers *al-Amīr Fārūq* and *al-Amīra Fawziyya*, greeted with twenty-one gun salutes on entering Egyptian waters and escorted by squadrons of the Royal Egyptian Air Force.[18] During the crown prince's month-long stay in Egypt, military parades and festive receptions were held in his honor, as well as numerous dinners and balls. The program also included visiting various institutions, sightseeing, and attending the opera. The wedding itself was a brief, formal act on the morning of 15 March 1939 (24 Esfand 1317) at the 'Abdin Palace.[19] However, its date had great symbolic power, as it was the day of Egyptian independence after the end of the British protectorate and at the same time Reza Shah's birth-

15. Pink 2014, 189, 194.

16. Therefore, he warned Egypt's prime minister against such a step and pointed out that unlike Great Britain and Iran, there were no treaties or dynastic relations with the other countries that would justify such a step. Sir M. Lampson to Viscount Halifax, Cairo, 3 March 1939 (J 1025/202/16). FO 407/223 *Further Correspondence respecting Egypt and Sudan*, Part CXXV, January to June 1939.

17. *Ettelā'āt* published the entire program on more than three pages. "Barnāmeh-ye 'arusi-ye vālā-hazrat homāyun vali'ahd bā vālā-hazrat shāhzādeh khanom Fowziyeh," *Ettelā'āt*, 4 Esfand 1317 (23 February 1939), 5–7. The program in Egypt can also be found at Sabit 1993, 93–101.

18. "Barnāmeh-ye 'arusi," *Ettelā'āt*, 4. Esfand 1317 (23 February 1939), 5–6. Sabit 1993, 94.

19. Sabit 1993, 97.

day, which was already celebrated with great state festivities in Iran.[20] After a ceremonial farewell, the wedding party, including Fowziyeh's mother and three younger sisters, set off from Port Said on 3 April 1939 for Iran.[21] On board the *Mohamed Aly El Kebir* there was a colorful entertainment program with cinema, orchestra, and evening parties.[22] Photographs of the illustrious travel party convey a sense of cheerfulness and leisure in the ship's well-groomed, luxurious surroundings.[23] During its passage through various territorial waters, the ocean liner was escorted by ships from the respective country, first by Italian, then by British, and finally by Iranian ships in the Persian Gulf. On 15 April 1939, the wedding party disembarked at Bandar-e Shāhpur in Iran, where they were given a ceremonial welcome, and then set off for the capital, Tehran, onboard the newly completed Trans-Iranian Railway.[24]

The timing for this journey could not have been better: Only a few months earlier, on 6 August 1938, the crown prince had accompanied his father to Sefid Cheshmeh station for the ceremonial completion of the Trans-Iranian Railway, the jewel in the crown of the Pahlavi state's ambitious modernization and nation-building program.[25] Unlike the railroads of other countries in the region, it was not built by colonial powers but by the state, largely financed through taxation. Accordingly, the Pahlavi state narrative presented the railroad as a national project and the censors were quite sensitive about its representation.[26] Conveying the image of Egypt and Iran as two modern nation states was one of the main concerns in planning the celebrations. Technology, as the epitome of progress, naturally played an extraordinary role. Electric lighting was a first component of an appropriate staging of the event. It created a festive atmosphere in the evening, particularly the colorful lights on board *Mohamed Aly El Kebir*, reflected by the sea.[27] During the festivities in Tehran from 22 April to 25 April 1939, a festival of lights was held to bring the splendor of progress to the capital.[28] Since those in charge for the program on the Iranian side wanted

20. Ansari 2008, 72–73.

21. "Barnāmeh-ye 'arusi," *Ettelā'āt*, 4. Esfand 1317 (23 February 1939), 6. Sabit 1993, 98–99.

22. 'Abbās Mas'udi, "Gozashtan-e keshti az āb-hā-ye Mesr," *Ettelā'āt*, 7 Farvardin 1318 (28 March 1939), 1.

23. Sabit 1993, 42–48.

24. "Barnāmeh-ye 'arusi," *Ettelā'āt*, 4. Esfand 1317 (23 February 1939), 6.

25. "Ā'in-e bā shokuh-e goshāyesh-e rāh āhan-e sarāsar-e keshvar," *Ettelā'āt*, 5 Shahrivar 1317 (27 August 1938), 1.

26. Koyagi 2021, 6.

27. "Wali 'ahd Īrān fī ṭarīqihi ilā Miṣr safarihi min Baghdād āms wa waṣulihi ilā Sūriyya," *al-Ahrām*, 1 March 1939, 8. Mas'udi, "Gozashtan-e keshti," 1.

28. "Khabarhā-ye dākheli – moqaddamāt-e jashn va cherāghāni," *Ettelā'āt*, 21 Farvardin 1318 (11 April 1939), 2.

to be on a par with the Egyptians, but did not have the same resources, they had to rely on the help of the Tehrani people. For instance, for a modern setting automobiles were essential, but the state did not have enough at its disposal. Therefore, it confiscated all the private cars available in the capital and returned them after the celebrations.[29]

For the ceremonial welcome in Tehran, the exact route of the wedding party was announced in the press so that residents could decorate along the route through the city.[30] Local institutions erected festive arches.[31] To decorate them, clever businessmen sold large-format posters with portraits of the bride and groom.[32] Electric lanterns and other decorative items were also advertised.[33] For fashion-conscious women, who wanted to wear the right clothes when greeting bride and groom at the roadside, stylish hats were on offer.[34] Also, special flags for the cheering crowd were available everywhere for 30 dinars. The official "decoration commission" (*komisyun-e taz'ināt*) had approved them, on one side the Egyptian flag and on the other the Iranian.[35] The government also issued of a set of stamps to mark the wedding.[36] All in all, state supervision of the whole event was extensive.

However, despite all the meticulous planning, things still went wrong. Matin Daftari, who was a member of the crown prince's delegation, reports in his memoirs of embarrassing moments for him and his Iranian fellow travelers. After lavish receptions and exquisite hospitality in Egypt, in Iran the traveling party was confronted with some mishaps. He complained that once in Iran there was much disorder in the reception of the Egyptian and other foreign guests, which was sometimes unbearable and disgraceful. Due to heavy rainfall and unusually cold weather, the preparations in Tehran were not completed in time, so that the arrival of the traveling party had to be postponed by one day at short notice. However, only the guests of honor were provided with temporary accommodation in railway bungalows in Ahvaz, while the rest of the group had

29. Maillart 1947, 66.

30. "Barnāmeh-ye 'arusi-ye vālā-hazrat homāyun vali'ahd bā vālā-hazrat shāhzādeh khanom Fowziyeh," *Ettelā'āt*, 2 Bahman 1317 (22 February 1939), 1.

31. "Yeki az tāq-hā-ye nosrat-e jāleb-e tavajjoh va zibā ke dar khiyabān-e Pahlavī bar pā shode bud," *Ettelā'āt* 8 Ordibehesht 1318 (29 April 1939), 1.

32. "Āgahi, no 555, Kālā-ye Irān," *Ettelā'āt*, 21 Farvardin 1318 (11 April 1939), 2.

33. "Barā-ye Jashn-e 'arusi-ye vālā-hazrat-e homāyun-e velāyat'ahd," *Ettelā'āt* 22 Farvardin 1318 (12 April 1939), 2.

34. "Khedmat be-'arusi – Sālon-e kolāh-duzi-ye shik," *Ettelā'āt*, 19 Farvardin 1318 (9 April 1939), 1.

35. "Khabar-hā-ye dākheli: Parcham-e Irān va Mesr," *Ettelā'āt*, 24 Farvardin 1318 (14 April 1939), 2. "Parcham-hā-ye dasti," *Ettelā'āt*, 24 Farvardin 1318 (14 April 1939), 2. "Parcham-e Irān va Mesr," *Ettelā'āt*, 25 Farvardin 1318 (15 April 1939), 1.

36. Siebertz 2014, 179.

to spend the night in the train compartments. In addition, Matin Daftari was ashamed of the ordinary food on board the train, served on simple tin-plates by untrained staff. Since the dining car was not yet fully equipped, the food was cooked outside the train, so that the train had to stop for the meals.[37] Matin Daftari was certainly a particularly critical observer of the entire wedding celebrations; after all, he was a key figure in the state's new systematic propaganda efforts as he headed the *Sāzmān-e Parvaresh-e Afkār*.[38]

JOURNALISM BETWEEN SENSATION AND CENSORSHIP: REPORTING THE WEDDING

As the wedding was an affair of utmost importance, its press coverage was a sensitive matter. The members of the crown prince's entourage on his trip to Cairo were handpicked und included ʿAbbās Masʿudi, editor of Iran's largest newspaper, the *Ettelāʿāt* (Information), and the country's only French-language newspaper, *Journal de Téhéran*, whose readership included, in particular, foreigners living in Iran.[39] With these two periodicals, Masʿudi's reports achieved the widest reach in the Iranian press. Moreover, he was a journalist who had already proved his loyalty as a press representative during Reza Shah's visit to Turkey in 1934.[40]

Masʿudi had founded his newspaper in 1926. Initially published only in Tehran, the paper soon became the country's daily with the highest circulation and a nationwide distribution. Coming from a traditional bazaar background, Masʿudi followed an explicit entrepreneurial approach to his newspaper. For him, journalism was less a vocation than a business, apparent in his sense of profitable investments, such as the import of Iran's first rotary printing press. He also implemented sales-promoting journalistic innovations, such as recent photographs or entertaining columns in his paper. Given his pioneering role in the history of the Iranian press, Masʿudi is sometimes referred to as the "father of modern Iranian journalism." In the increasingly restrictive environment

37. ʿĀqeli 1372/1992, 147–48.

38. Durbeyki 1382 (2003), 137–44. Devos 2012, 106–9.

39. Members of the delegation were Hasan Esfandiyāri, speaker of the majles, Ahmad Matin Daftari, minister of justice, Mozaffar Aʿlam, minister of foreign affairs (returned in Iraq), ʿAli Asghar Moʾaddab Nafisi, the crown prince's chamberlain, Mohammad ʿAli Moqaddam, director general of the Ministry of Foreign Affairs, Ghāsem Ghani, member of parliament, Abdollāh Foruhar, second secretary of Iran's ambassy in Egypt, ʿAli Izadi, chief secretary of the crown prince's office, and three adjutants, Colonel Moʿtazzadi, Captain Qadimi, and Captain Esfandiyāri. Majid Movaqqar, editor of the country's oldest daily, *Iran*, joined the delegation in Iraq. ʿĀqeli 1372/1992, 146. The members of the delegation on departure in Tehran were listed on the front page of *Ettelāʿāt*, 5 Esfand 1317 (24 February 1929), 1.

40. Devos 2012, 137.

for the Iranian press during Reza Shah's rule, his entrepreneurial approach and his interest in news journalism proved remarkably successful. As a state-trusted journalist, Mas'udi accompanied the crown prince on his trip to Egypt.[41] But on this journey, he was not just an agent of official state propaganda; he clearly had his own economic agenda and seized the opportunity to provide his paper with exclusive cover stories and photographs from such an illustrious event.

Being on the scene gave him an advantage over the other newspapers to supply his editorial staff with the latest news from Cairo by means of telegrams. These telegraph messages were published in large numbers in various sections, such as the domestic news or the especially created sections "Telegrams from Cairo."[42] The field of news journalism was *Ettelāʿāt*'s great strength. Alongside the standard way to present news content, the paper created a special column called "letter from Egypt" (*nāmeh-ye Meṣr*), signed by 'Abbās Mas'udi. These articles were less up to date than the telegrams, and were less concerned with recounting events, but rather with expanding and contextualizing what had been reported. As the subjectivity of the journalist was also more apparent, they were more in the nature of a reportage..[43] In addition to currency, this use of diverse journalistic forms gave authenticity to the coverage of the wedding. This is especially true for the pictures, taken in Egypt and published in the weeks after Mas'udi's return to Iran. For the *Ettelāʿāt*, pictures were an important means to attract readers, as the paper's financing was based on sales figures and advertising revenues. Photographs from the royal wedding made the daily more light-hearted and entertaining than usual and promised to attract a larger audience; so its editor decided to publish special issues with a larger amount of pictures or regular issues with an increased number of pages.[44] As *Ettelāʿāt*'s coverage of the wedding was primarily propaganda oriented, it had the character of a campaign, but it was also, to a certain degree, economically motivated.

The main part of the press campaign covered the entire wedding celebrations in Egypt and Iran, a period roughly from February to April 1939 and some time afterwards. The campaign's first part occurred on the occasion of Fowziyeh's and Mohammad Reza's engagement and was intended to prepare the public for the upcoming wedding. It was indeed a considerable prelude, with front page articles and pictures running for weeks, from May to July 1938.

41. Devos 2012, 117–21, 126–28, 132–43.

42. In a neutral, impersonal form, they reported, sometimes in minute detail, on the events of the day or the previous day.

43. Already from the end of the 1920s onwards, Mas'udi regularly relied on this journalistic form to report on his numerous travels inside as well as outside Iran. Devos 2012, 137.

44. "Resāleh-ye makhsus-e *Ettelāʿāt* be-eftekhār-e jashn-e 'arusi," *Ettelāʿāt*, 27 Farvardin 1318 (17 April 1939), 1. "Enteshār-e ruznāmeh-ye *Ettelāʿāt* be-towr-e fowq ol-'ādeh," *Ettelāʿāt* 2 Farvardin 1318 (23 March 1939), 1.

Like the second part of the campaign, the first stage was marked by news and reports about the journey of the Iranian delegation to Egypt in order to arrange the engagement. However, it had a slightly different character than the later coverage of the wedding. With none of its reporters to accompany the delegation, *Ettelāʿāt* had no regular daily news from Cairo and published more articles with background information on Egypt, reflections on the forthcoming union or reports on international reactions to this engagement instead. As a result, an otherwise rather rare journalistic genre found its way onto the front page: the interview. A reporter from *Ettelāʿāt* interviewed delegation member Qāsem Ghani after his return from Cairo about his visit to the famous and pioneering author of modern Egyptian literature, Taha Husain.[45] In terms of content, the interview fitted into the overarching trend of the first phase of this press campaign, the emphasis on the cultural connection between Iran and Egypt. What is also noticeable in this phase is the significant number of excerpts and summaries from Egyptian newspapers that had been translated into Persian. *Ettelāʿāt* had a journalistic interest in the Egyptian press, which had emerged in a different context, namely a colonial milieu with considerable European and non-Muslim stimuli. Building on a rich tradition and greater political freedom, Egypt's press between the two world wars was dynamic and popular with readers beyond the country's borders.[46] Apart from their transnational reach, Egyptian newspapers were more differentiated and more professionalized than their Iranian counterparts.

In this article, one example from the Egyptian press will be used for comparisons with the *Ettelāʿāt, al-Ahrām* (The Pyramids).[47] The comparison between these newspapers is reasonable as they were both the leading and most widely circulated dailies in their countries. Both were committed to neutrality, especially towards the ruling house. Therefore, both distinguished themselves particularly through news journalism and not through opinion press. Moreover, both were more oriented towards profitability compared to other periodicals in their country.[48]

Egypt and Iran – Facets of the Union

When *Ettelāʿāt* announced the royal engagement on 26 May 1938 (5 Khordad 1317), the central motifs of its coverage were already apparent. The emphasis on the joy of the people and their positive feelings toward the royal family was predominant. The betrothal was declared the greatest good news for the Iranian

45. "Odabā-ye Meṣr va ehsāsāt-e ānhā dar-bāreh-ye Irān," *Ettelāʿāt*, 26 Tir 1317 (17 July 1938), 1.
46. Ayalon 1995, 74–75.
47. The first issue was already published in 1876. Ayalon 1995, 42–43.
48. For *al-Ahrām*'s characteristics see Ayalon 1995, 81.

nation, especially since it was a union of Iran's crown prince with a member of a famous royal family of noble lineage. [49] Another constant feature was the focus on the connections and similarities between Iran and Egypt as representatives of two of the world's ancient civilizations, both in the process of restoring their old greatness under the leadership of a capable and popular ruler, who was committed to progress. The reform efforts of Muhammad Ali Pasha, Fowziyeh's ancestor, were particularly highlighted. The couple themselves were less in the center of attention. The paper mentioned the crown prince's popularity and projected a vague idealized image of Fowziyeh as a princess beloved by her father, fully educated and morally charming. [50]

A comparison of the engagement announcements in the two newspapers, *Ettelāʿāt* and *al-Ahrām*, reveals other basic lines of reporting. Both newspapers published the announcement of the engagement on their front page on two consecutive days, conveyed their congratulations and looked forward to the intensifying relations between the two countries. [51] *Al-Ahrām* also mentioned Fowziyeh's noble royal upbringing, good manners and beauty, and differed from the *Ettelāʿāt* in several respects: The two news items about the engagement appeared in *al-Ahrām* slightly earlier than in *Ettelāʿāt*, namely already on 24 and 25 May 1938. Moreover, they focused more on the protagonists of the engagement, Mohammad Reza and Fowziyeh, and presented them more clearly as individuals, for instance by providing more biographical "hard facts" about them. In addition, *al-Ahrām* published portrait pictures of the crown prince and the princess – which is not surprising given the significantly higher number and greater variety of photographs published in the Egyptian paper in general. And finally, *al-Ahrām* also reported on international reactions to the announcement of the engagement, including very concise press reviews of articles in European newspapers. Overall, the Egyptian press appeared more professional, international and uncensored than its Iranian counterpart, but throughout their coverage of the wedding, they shared common themes.

The beloved royal family

The love for the country and its monarch was a crucial element of Pahlavi state propaganda, found on the pages of Iranian newspapers for decades to come. *Ettelāʿāt* celebrated the union with the Egyptian royal family enthusiastically

49. "Bozorgtarin mozhdeh-ye massarat-bakhsh," in *Ettelāʿāt*, 5 Khordād 1317 (26 May 1938), 1.
50. "Bozorgtarin mozhdeh-ye massarat-bakhsh," in *Ettelāʿāt*, 5 Khordād 1317 (26 May 1938), 1.
51. "Al-Khuṭbat al-malikiyyat al-maymūna," *al-Ahrām*, 24 May 1938, 1. "Al-Khuṭbat al-malikiyyat al-maymūna" *al-Ahrām*, 25 May 1938, 1. "Bozorgtarin mozhdeh-ye massarat-bakhsh," in *Ettelāʿāt*, 5 Khordād 1317 (26 May 1938), 1. "Mellat-e Iran nāmzadi-ye vālā-hazrat velāyatʿahd-e mahbub-e khod rā jashn khvahad gereft," *Ettelāʿāt*, 6 Khordād 1317 (27 May 1938), 1.

and left no doubt that the Iranian people was overjoyed by the wedding. The paper celebrated the union with the Egyptian royal family enthusiastically. Likewise, *al-Ahrām* reported on the joyful mood in Egypt when the Iranian crown prince arrived. The enthusiasm of the Egyptians was hardly less, if *al-Ahrām* is to be believed. It described how the hearts of sixteen million Egyptians beat faster, when the Iranian crown prince, "Shāhbur", arrived in Egypt on 3 March 1939. Young and old rejoiced and celebrated on the occasion of the happy event.[52]

Criticism of the celebrations in various sections of Egyptian society was not covered in the press, but in the confidential reports sent by the British ambassador Sir Miles Lampson to Viscount Halifax in the same day. According to him, many Egyptians felt that the countless celebrations during the crown prince's month-long stay were disproportionate, especially since King Faruq's own wedding had been celebrated for only three days. Moreover, some criticized the waste of time that would have been better invested in preparations for defense in view of a looming war.[53]

Militarism

Militarism was another motif prevalent in the event's coverage. Although the wedding was a festive occasion and in several respects a counterpoint to war, the celebrations had a military undertone throughout. The ceremonial greetings and farewells were, of course, military in character. Reviews of scouts and military cadets at 'Abdin Square in Cairo and Amjadiyeh Circuit in Tehran, visits to Egypt's military academy and the Muhammad Ali barrages, a Cairo police tournament, an Iranian military air show and, last but not least, the large military presence all contributed to the militaristic atmosphere. The official schedule included a military program parallel to the representative festivities, which was announced separately in the *Ettelāʿāt*.[54] When the paper published a report on a military parade in Cairo, it embedded a brief history of the Egyptian military and described its current situation.[55]

The crown prince furthermore appeared in uniform on all official occasions – even at the opera – while King Faruq wore a dinner jacket.[56] During his trip and stay in Egypt, the press did not publish a single picture of him in any attire

---

52. "Marḥaban bi-al-ḍayf al-karīm" and "Ahlan bi-akram wāfid," *al-Ahrām*, 3 March 1939, 1.

53. Sir M. Lampson to Viscount Halifax, Cairo, 3 March 1939 (J 1025/202/16). FO 407/223 *Further Correspondence respecting Egypt and Sudan*, Part CXXV, January to June 1939.

54. A three-hundred-strong military delegation had traveled from Egypt to Iran and military dignitaries were invited to all the festive dinners. "Barnāme-ye neẓāmi", *Ettelāʿāt*, 4. Esfand 1317 (23 February 1938), 4.

55. "Mosābeqe-ye shamshir-bāzi dar pishgāh-e aʿlāhazrat pādshāh-e Meṣr va vālā-ḥażrat," *Ettelāʿāt* 8. Farvardin 1318 (29 March 1939), 1.

56. "Dar Operā-ye Saltanati," *Ettelāʿāt*, 4. Farvardin 1318 (25 March 1939), 1.

other than his uniform – not even on the official wedding photo.[57] The bride also received military honors by having a regiment named after her.[58] Furthermore, a march was composed for her on the occasion of the wedding, and the *Ettelāʿāt* printed the notes and lyrics for its readers.[59] Closely linked to the military dimension were the aspects youth, power and strength – essential elements of the ideological orientation of the Pahlavi state and all aspects that the couple embodied.[60] Therefore, they attended a wide variety of sporting events such as an international tennis tournament, the World Table Tennis Championships, nocturnal horse races or swordplay in Egypt, or a show of modern and traditional sports in Iran.[61]

Cultural ties

Culture was seen as the essential unifying element between Egypt and Iran, both in terms of modern education and science and in terms of the rich cultural heritage that both countries could draw on. These two aspects were reflected in the official program of the crown prince in Egypt: Alongside all the military parades, ceremonial receptions and dinners, there were several cultural highlights. Mohammad Reza not only went to the opera with his hosts, but also visited the country's museums, collections, and universities, and of course, a sightseeing tour to the pyramids was also on the agenda.

The pre-Islamic heritage linked the two countries and gave them a special place in human history. It was used by both of them to legitimize their quest to regain their former greatness, now as modern nation states. Both the Egyptian and Iranian press highlighted their cultural heritage as the most important link between the two nations and referred recurrently to pre-Islamic times in their articles and sometimes in their photographs. Neither of the two papers published photos from the visit to the pyramids, but in May 1939, the front page of *Ettelāʿāt* carried two pictures of the young couple's visit to Iran's Archaeo-

---

57. This was not lost on the British ambassador, who, despite his generally positive attitude towards Mohammad Reza, was dismissive of the fact in his report. Sir M. Lampson to Viscount Halifax, Cairo, 3 March 1939 (J 1041/1/16). FO 407/223 *Further Correspondence respecting Egypt and Sudan*, Part CXXV, January to June 1939. As photographs from Egypt show, the crown prince sometimes wore civilian clothes on private occasions. Sabit 1993, 29.

58. ʿĀqeli 1371/1992, 151.

59. The text was written by Malek osh-Shoʿarā Bahār. "Sorud-e Fowziyeh," *Ettelāʿāt*, 8 Ordibehesht 1318 (29 April 1939), 4.

60. Schayegh 2002, 341.

61. Chehabi 2006.

logical Museum.[62] In terms of content, however, these references were mostly of little substance and appeared more as lip service to the official ideological imperatives, sometimes just mentioning events like lectures on ancient Iran.[63] Actual content related to ancient history found its way into press articles only to a limited extent.

Overall, however, the Islamic heritage was more present, both in terms of history and literature.[64] The Egyptian cultural magazine *ar-Risāla* (The Message) published several articles on Iran, including multi-page pieces on its history, climate, culture, and recent reforms. While the historical greatness in pre-Islamic times was highlighted as the great parallel between the two countries, Iran's Islamic cultural heritage received more attention. For example, Nezām ol-Molk's *Siyāsatnāmeh* was prominently featured in an article.[65] In the context of the intense debate in the Egyptian press on national identity and other political issues, the new relationship between the two countries appeared, with anti-imperialist undertones, as an empowerment of the East vis-à-vis the West.[66] The "renaissance of the Islamic East" was also thought of and described in ethnic categories as a new bond between the Semitic and the Aryan.[67]

The Islamic heritage as a common basis allowed cultural interaction, for example in the field of language and literature. Immediately after the engagement, Fowziyeh began learning Persian from a distinguished member of Cairo's vibrant Iranian community.[68] The Iranian crown prince, however, did not speak Arabic, so during his visit to al-Azhar the speech of the rector Muḥammad Muṣṭafā al-Marāġī had to be translated into French. As a consequence, Persian was included in al-Azhar's curriculum, where also attempts at an ecumenical

62. The picture showed Mohammad Reza and Fowziyeh listening attentively to the explanations of André Godard, the head of Iran's General Antiquities Service, Vālā-hażrat homāyun velāyatʿahd va vālā-hażrat homāyun Fowziyeh Pahlavi," *Ettelāʿāt*, 8 Khordād 1318 (30 May 1939), 1.

63. For instance, a speech by the editor of the Persian-language journal *Chehrenemā* in Cairo was announced. "Mūzeh-ye āsār-e eslāmī dar Qāhere [nāme-ye Mesr - yād-dāsht-hā-ye mosāferat]," *Ettelāʿāt*, 10 farvardin 1318 (31 March 1939), 1.

64. Hanan Hammad's observations on the mutual perception and "East-East interaction," particularly Iran's interest in modern Egypt and the Egyptian interest in medieval Iran also apply to the coverage of the wedding. Hammad 2014, 275–96.

65. ʿAbd al-Wahhāb ʿAzzām, "Kitāb as-siyāsat li-l-wazīr Niẓām al-Mulk." *ar-Risāla* 3 April 1939, 657–58.

66. Muḥammad Fahmī ʿAbd al-Laṭīif, " Bayna Miṣr wa Īrān," *ar-Risāla*, 13 March 1939, 513–14.

67. Ibn ʿAbdul Malik, "Risālat Āmir al-muʾminīn al-Fārūq ilā ash-shabāb," *ar-Risāla* 13 March 1939, 480–81.

68. "Vālā-hażrat shāhzāda ḫānum Fowziyeh zabān-e Fārsī taḥṣīl mīkonad," *Ettelāʿāt* 23 Khordād 1317 (13 June 1938), 1. In Egypt, a Persian grammar dedicated to princess Fowziyeh was published. Brunner 1996, 88. For more on the Iranian community in Egypt see Yadegari 1980.

rapprochement between Sunnis and Shiites were made in the following years.[69] In his conversation with Qāsem Ghani in Cairo in 1938, Taha Husain reported on his efforts to establish a chair for Persian language at Cairo University's Faculty of Literature, whose dean he was at that time. He emphasized that the Iranians had been able to introduce their own thoughts into all fields of Islamic culture, such as literature, science, philosophy, and politics, since from the beginning they had sought access to everything Arabic.[70] This was true at least regarding classically educated Iranians, who were proficient in Arabic. Hasan Esfandiyāri, speaker of the Iranian parliament and member of the crown prince's entourage in 1939, gave an example of his knowledge by writing a *qasida* in Arabic in praise of Egypt and in gratitude for its precious gift to Iran, that is, Fowziyeh.[71]

The Bride

Fowziyeh, the young, beautiful, smartly dressed, well-educated bride, was the epitome of the modern woman and as such regularly covered in the press. The Egyptian and Iranian press published portraits of the young princess on their front pages, and later also recent pictures of her on official occasions. The first prominently placed portrait photograph of Fowziyeh appeared in *al-Ahrām* alongside the announcement of the engagement in May 1938 – or at least the paper intended to publish a picture of her. Instead, the editors mistakenly printed a picture of Faiza, Fowziyeh's younger sister.[72] King Faruq's sisters were apparently not much in the public eye, which would explain the confusion between the two sisters. It was not until a few weeks later, on 11 July 1938, that the *Ettelā'āt* newspaper published the first picture of Fowziyeh.[73] Aware of the sales-promoting effect, the paper announced the publication of a newer, charming photograph of the princess for the following day.[74]

As a little-known member of Egypt's royal family at the time of the wedding, even within her home country, Fowziyeh stirred people's imagination. For instance, a female contributor to the magazine *ar-Risāla* dedicated her article to

69. Brunner 1996, 86–87, 95–106, 215–32.

70. "Odabā-ye Meṣr va eḥsāsāt-e ānhā dar-bāre-ye Irān," *Ettelā'āt* 26 Tir 1317 (17 July 1938), 1.

71. *Al-Ahrām* published the *qasida*. "Miṣr tudiʿ al-āmirayn al-karīmayn," *al-Ahrām*, 4 April 1939, p. 3. There was more poetry written on the occasion. Bayat and Baktiari 2002, 322.

72. The paper corrected its mistake and printed the correct photo the next day. "Al-Khuṭbat al-malikiyyat al-maymūna," *al-Ahrām*, 25 May 1938, 1.

73. *Ettelā'āt*, 20 Tir 1317 (11 July 1938), 1. Thus, she appeared in the press earlier than suggested by Amin, though not in ceremonial action. Amin 2002, 136, 282.

74. The next day, a large, up-to-date portrait of Fowziyeh graced its front page. *Ettelā'āt*, 20 Tir 1317 (11 July 1938), 1.

the "Princess of the Nile" and expressed rather lyrically her own feelings about the royal wedding, praising Fowziyeh and her future as a wife.[75] The Iranian press dealt with Fowziyeh in a comparable way: In the first part of the press campaign on occasion of the engagement in 1938, several articles were devoted to her, at least at first glance. But even if an article named her in the headline, it could be limited to general wishes and expectations of her.[76] Throughout the wedding festivities in 1939, she was much overshadowed by the male protagonists, first and foremost by the groom, but also from her brother and her father-in-law. When, following Egyptian tradition, the youngest daughter of an eminent tribal leader from Alexandria brought henna for the royal bride to the court in Cairo, *Ettelāʿāt* described how the crown prince received the tribal princess and her magnificently decorated camel caravan, while Fowziyeh was not mentioned in the article.[77] Overall, she retained a marginal role, which only changed to some extent towards the end of the official wedding program, when she took a more active part in various representative events.

The journalistic potential of the Egyptian princess as bride in a fairytale wedding did not go unnoticed by the Western press. And again, it was not Fowziyeh as a person who was of interest, but she was rather used for the projection of Orientalist stereotypes. A blatant example was found in an article in the British tabloid *Daily Sketch*, published on the occasion of the engagement. The article described how the princess's life would change after the wedding: She would have to give up all the sports she loved: tennis, swimming, skiing. While she had been unveiled until now, afterwards she would have to hide her beautiful face behind a veil and live her life in the seclusion of the harem. *Ettelāʿāt*'s reaction was fierce. It published a big lead on its front-page on 11 June 1938, in which the author was stunned by the dramatic foreign ignorance of the achievements of Iran's national women's movement launched by the state three years earlier. He felt particularly offended by the question of veiling and lamented the decline of the Western press in general.[78] It is remarkable that *al-Ahrām* had already mentioned the *Daily Sketch* article briefly on 25 May 1938, gave a very brief summary of its content and speculated that the British author had obviously given free rein to her imagination.[79] The reaction of *Ettelāʿāt* was much more vigorous in comparison and shows the Iranian sensitivities: Even an article

75. Zaynab al-Ḥakīm, "al-Amīra Fawziyya," *ar-Risāla*, 10 April 1939, 731–33.

76. "Vālā-hazrat shāhzādeh khānom Fowziyeh," *Ettelāʿāt*, 26 Khordād 1317 (16 June 1938), S. 1.

77. *Ettelāʿāt* reported also that the daughter of the tribal chief was dressed in tribal costume and accompanied the camel caravan in a car adorned in the colors of the Iranian flag. "Āʾin-e taqdim-e henna-ye ʿarusi", *Ettelāʿāt*, 6 Farvardin 1318 (27 March 1939), 1.

78. "In āzādi-ye qalam ast yā harj-o marj?" *Ettelāʿāt*, 21 Khordād 1317 (11 June 1938), 1.

79. "Khuṭbat malikiyyat al-maymūna," *al-Ahrām*, 25 May 1938, 1.

in the British tabloids was responded to in a long front-page article in Iran's largest daily newspaper. The vehemence of the reaction was certainly due to the fact
that Iran's advances made in previous years, though highly praised in the official
narrative, seemed to be ignored by Europeans, in particular the state's steps to
enforce the unveiling of Iranian women and promote the women's movement.
In addition, the Iranian press was well aware of the Shah's personal sensitivity to
negative press abroad; the country had already broken off diplomatic contacts
as a result.[80]

Also, artistic creation could be perceived as an insult to the nation. The ban
on the film "Leila, Daughter of the Desert" by the Egyptian director Bahiga
Hafez in 1937 shows how great Iranian sensitivity was towards popular media
even of other countries. The timing of the release of this film, about an Arab girl
who rejected the love of the Persian king, could not have been worse. Deeply
concerned about the international perception of their own country, the Iranians
protested officially and urged the Egyptian government to ban the film.[81] In an
official request to the Austrian Federal Chancellery, the Imperial Legation of
Iran justified its petition to prevent the screening as follows: "Ce film est une
invention de mauvais genre et il est totalement dépourvu de base historique. Il
porte atteinte à la dignité du passé et à l'honneur national de l'Iran."[82]

The Egyptian and Iranian press saw Fowziyeh as a modern woman at the
side of the crown prince. From the beginning, she was expected to serve as a role
model for Iranian women by living up to the ideal of a "mistress of the house"
and "lady of society."[83] In the period that followed, especially after the birth of
daughter Shahnāz in 1940, Fowziyeh took on the role of the loving mother of
the country. The magazine *Zabān-e Zanān* (Women's Voice), published by the
activist Sediqeh Dowlatābādi and a vital organ of Iran's women's movement,
featured a portrait of Fowziyeh on its first page, now the country's queen, with
her little daughter.[84]

In the end, Fowziyeh proved that she was a modern woman – more modern
than many would have wished. She went back to Egypt officially for health rea-

---

80. Devos 2012, 86.

81. Gharib 2019.

82. I am greatly indebted to Dr. Giorgio Rota (Institute for Iranian Studies, Austrian Academy of
Sciences) for pointing me to this file in the Austrian State Archives. ÖSTA/ADR, BKA/AA, NPA,
Liasse Persien (Iran) I/1, Zl. 1937/13–44246.

83. "Marḥaban bi-al-ḍayf al-karīm," *al-Ahrām*, 3 March 1939, 1.

84. *Zabān-e Zanān*'s mission was to educate mothers (*tarbiyat-e mādar*) *Zabān-e Zanān* no.1,
Āzar 1321 (December 1942), 1. Again 1945, the magazine published a picture of the royal family as
a symbol of how only parental love and affection brighten [the children's] lives. *Zabān-e Zanān* no. 1,
Farvardin 1324 (March 1945), 1.

sons, as Iran's climate did not seem to be beneficial to her.[85] Leaving her daughter behind she escaped from the arranged marriage, masterminded by Reza Shah, now himself in exile. Curiously, he once again played a crucial role, albeit unwillingly, in ending this marriage: In 1949, the Egyptian side used his corpse, by then in Cairo, as a bargaining chip for Iran's consent to the divorce.[86]

CONCLUSION

Fowziyeh's and Mohammad Reza's wedding had never been a romantic story in the Iranian and Egyptian press. Iran's daily *Ettelāʿāt* presented the wedding as a national triumph full of splendor and reported its events in a quite sober and prosaic way, lacking any emotional coloring or amorous anecdotes.[87] The Western press proved more amenable to the fairytale-like. As a result, even in the serious media, the coverage was reminiscent of the tabloid press. With a young, handsome crown prince and a beautiful princess, both royal children from two Oriental dynasties, the foreign press had all the ingredients it needed for a modern fairy tale from the *Arabian Nights*. It is not surprising, therefore, that certain aspects of the wedding were particularly highlighted in these reports. All of them gave special attention to the fact that the marriage was arranged, and bride and groom had never met before the wedding.[88] Describing it as "wedding without a bride"[89] as was customary in Egypt, Western media in general tended to emphasize the exotic nature of the wedding. At the same time, they highlighted the luxury of the celebrations and were interested in the exquisite jewelry given to the princess during the wedding.[90]

The censored Iranian press covered the wedding in line with the official narrative that the Pahlavi state wanted to propagate. *Ettelāʿāt* told the story of national advancement and progress in all its facets. The press painted a flawless picture of a self-confident, rising modern Iranian nation and joined in the eulogies to the shah, which is not surprising, as the reporting on the wedding

85. Bāstāni Pārizi 1361/1982, 33 (si-o seh).

86. Bāstāni Pārizi 1361/1982," 11 (yāzdah). Fowziyeh seems to have obtained an Egyptian divorce already in 1945. Kozhanov 2012, 487.

87. On this point, I cannot agree with Abbas Milani, who attributed "romantic accounts of the journey and the marriage" to ʿAbbās Masʿudi. Milani 2008, 2:397.

88. For example "Iranian Prince in Cairo meets Bride-to-Be, King's Sister, for First Time," in *New York Times*, 4 March 1939.

89. "Royal Wedding in Cairo 1919," *British Pathé*, , https://www.britishpathe.com/video/VL-VA66S7ELRIDLLZ289KEROKU5PUQ-CROWN-PRINCE-OF-IRAN-MARRIES-PRIN-CESS-FAWZIA-OF-EGYPT. The New York Times referred to religious reasons: "According to the strictest Moslem tradition the Prince and Princess have not yet met." "Iranians confirm royal betrothal," in *New York Times*, 11 June 1938.

90. For example, "Iranians confirm royal betrothal," in *New York Times*, 11 June 1938.

was particularly sensitive. At this politically important event, members of the royal family took center stage, while the state tightened its control over the press through new institutions to create a propaganda apparatus, for which the wedding may have emerged as something of a test case.

Nevertheless, this event opened up completely new thematic fields for the newspapers. Egypt in all facets became a relevant subject of reporting: its history, culture and customs and, of course, its progress. In addition, the newspaper was able to report on completely new groups of people, particularly the female members of the royal family, who had hardly ever appeared so prominently in the newspapers before. Despite the omnipresent praise of the ruler, the numerous travel reports, background articles and interviews provided a glimpse of those persons who were the true architects of this union and had conducted the negotiations in the forefront of the wedding and were members of the Iranian delegations to Egypt.[91] The exchange with the Egyptian press also broadened the Iranian journalists' horizons. The intensified examination of the more progressive Egyptian press and certainly also the personal contact with the Arab colleagues gave them new impulses. And in the end, the coverage probably had a positive effect on newspaper sales, as the wedding, even in its officially sanctioned form, held great fascination for the Iranian public.

The fascination with this wedding, even in its failure, continues. A recent example is Amir Hasan Cheheltan's latest novel *Eine Liebe in Kairo*.[92] It centers on the Iranian ambassador in Cairo, who was tasked with protracted negotiations in the wake of the separation. In the book an unnamed protagonist, who can be identified as the real-life ambassador Qāsem Ghani, left diary entries which inspired Cheheltan to use this source beyond the scholarly context and to write a novel with a love story – though not between Mohammad Reza and Fowziyeh.[93]

91. These were men like Mahmud Jam, Ahmad Matin Daftari or Qāsem Ghani.

92. Cheheltan 2022. An Egyptian example of a nostalgic and monarchist view on the wedding is a pricey coffee-table book which was published in 1993 under the title *1939, The Imperial Wedding (Royal Albums of Egypt)*, produced in 700 collector's copies. Sabit 1993.

93. *Khāterāt-e Doktor Qāsem Ghani*, ed. Mohammad ʿAli Sowti. And Ghani 1360–63/1981–84.

Works Cited

al-Ahrām. 1938–1939. Cairo.

Amin, Camron Michael. 2002. *The Making of the Modern Iranian Woman: Gender, State Policy, and Popular Culture, 1865–1946*. Gainesville: University Press of Florida.

———. 2014. "The Press and public diplomacy in Iran, 1820–1940." *Iranian Studies* 48:269–87.

Ansari, Ali. 2008. *Modern Iran: The Pahlavis and After.* Harlow: Pearson Longman.

ʿĀqeli, Bāqer. 1371/1992. *Khaterāt-e yek nakhost vazir, Duktur Ahmad Matin Daftari.* Tehran: Enteshārāt-e ʿelmi.

Ayalon, Ami. 1995. *The Press in the Arab Middle East: A History. Studies in Middle Eastern History.* New York: Oxford University Press.

Bayat, Asef, and Bahman Baktiari. 2002. "Revolutionary Iran and Egypt: Exporting Inspirations and Anxieties." In *Iran and the Surrounding World: Interactions in Culture and Cultural Politics*, edited by Rudolph P. Matthee and Nikki R. Keddie, 305–26. Seattle, London: University of Washington Press.

Bāstāni Pārizi, Mohammad Ebrāhim. 1361/1982. "Dar-bāreh-ye yāddāsht-hā-ye Doktor Ghani." In *Khāterāt-e Doktor Qāsem Ghani*, edited by Mohammad ʿAli Sowti. Tehran: Enteshārāt-e Kāvesh.

Brunner, Rainer. 1996. *Annäherung und Distanz. Schia, Azhar und die islamische Ökumene im 20. Jahrhundert.* Berlin: Klaus Schwarz Verlag.

Chehabi, Houchang. 2006. "Zur-ḵāna." *EIr.* online edition.

Cheheltan, Amir Hassan. 2022. *Eine Liebe in Kairo*, translated by Jutta Himmelreich. München: C. H. Beck.

Delfāni, Mahmud, ed. 1375/1996. *Farhang-e setizi dar dowreh-ye Rezā Shāh: Asnād-e montasher nashodeh-ye Sāzmān-e Parvaresh-e Afkār, 1317 – 1320 h.sh.* Tehran: Enteshārāt-e sāzmān-e asnād-e melli.

Devos, Bianca. 2012. *Presse und Unternehmertum in Iran: Die Tageszeitung Iṭṭilāʿāt in der frühen Pahlavī-Zeit.* Würzburg: Ergon.

Durbeyki, Bābak. 1382 (2003). *Sāzmān-e Parvaresh-e Afkār.* Enteshārāt-e markaz-e asnād-e enqelāb-e eslāmī. Tehran: Markaz-e asnād-e enqelāb-e eslāmi.

Ettelāʿāt. 1317–1318/1938–1939. Tehran.

Gharib, Ashraf. 2019. "Remembering Bahiga Hafez: Egyptian cinema pioneer". *ahramonline*, August 21. https://english.ahram.org.eg/NewsContent/5/32/344091/Arts--Culture/Film/Remembering-Bahiga-Hafez-Egyptian-cinema-pioneer.aspx.

Ghani, Qāsim. 1360–63/1981–84. *Yāddāsht-hā-ye Doktor Qāsem Ghani*, edited by Sirus Ghani. 11 vols. Tehran: Farzān.

Hammad, Hanan. 2014. "Relocating a Common Past and the Making of East-Centric Modernity: Islamic and Secular Nationalism(s) In Egypt and Iran." In *Rethinking Iranian Nationalism and Modernity*, edited by Kamran S. Aghaie and Afshin Marashi, 275–96. Austin: University of Texas Press.

Koyagi, Mikiya. 2021. *Iran in Motion: Mobility, Space, and the Trans-Iranian Railway.* Stanford, CA: Stanford University Press.

Kozhanov, Nikolay A. 2012. "The Pretexts and Reasons for the Allied Invasion of Iran in 1941." *Iranian Studies* 45:479–97.

Maillart, Ella K. 1947. *The Cruel Way.* London: William Heinemann.

Marashi, Afshin. 2008. *Nationalizing Iran: Culture, Power, and the State, 1870–1940.* Seattle: University of Washington Press.

Milani, Abbas. 2008. *Eminent Persians: The Men and Women Who Made Modern Iran, 1941–1979.* Syracuse: Syracuse University Press.

New York Times. 1938. New York.

Pink, Johanna. 2014. *Geschichte Ägyptens: Von der Spätantike bis zur Gegenwart.* München: C.H.Beck.

R., E. 1939. "Persia" *Oriente Moderno* 19: 161–62.

ar-Risāla. 1939. Cairo.

Sabit, Adel M., Maged M. Farag. 1993. *1939, The Imperial Wedding: Royal Albums of Egypt.* Cairo, Egypt: Max Group.

Schayegh, Cyrus. 2002. "Sport, Health, and the Iranian Middle Class in the 1920s and 1930s." *Iranian Studies* 35:341–69.

Siebertz, Roman. 2014. "Depicting Power: Reza Shahs Rule, Cabinet Politics and the Commemorative Stamp Set of 1935." In *Culture and Cultural Politics Under Reza Shah: The Pahlavi State, New Bourgeoisie and the Creation of a Modern Society in Iran*, edited by Bianca Devos and Christoph Werner. Abingdon: Routledge.

Mohammad, Yadegari. 1980. "The Iranian Settlement in Egypt as Seen through the Pages of the Community Paper: Chihrinima (1904–1966)." *Middle Eastern Studies* 16:98–114.

Vezārat-e farhang va ershād-e eslāmi, ed. 1379/2000. *Asnādi az tārikhcheh-ye rādiyo dar Irān. 1318–1345 h.sh.* Tehran: Sāzmān-e chāp va enteshārāt-e vezārat-e farhang va ershād-e eslāmi.

A Feminist-Proletarian Model for Iranian Football

Babak Fozooni

IN THE AUTUMN OF 2004, and following the publication of my first-ever study of Iranian football, I received a complimentary email from a Bostonian professor by the name of Houchang Chehabi. He wished to inform me that I was now the honorary member of an elite cabal of four researchers engaged in this niche scholarly pursuit. Apparently, what we lacked in relevance, numbers, and prestige we more than made up for by an unwarranted chutzpah. Perhaps it was his gentle way of telling me, "Kid, don't waste your life. This is not the way to fame and fortune. No one will ever read your work, and the abiding impression left on the handful who might accidently glance through the abstract would be one of pity." Alas, the follies of mid-life and an unhealthy obsession with football prevented me from heeding his sage advice.

In the ensuing years I came to rely heavily on Houchang's encyclopedic knowledge of global affairs in order to find my way through this complex arena. His wry, reflective sense of humor has acted as a shield against undue bias and preferentialism. Politically, Houchang and I express polar opposites, but somehow our affection for football, Star Trek, and the culinary delights of chelo-kebab has prevented the kind of falling out that is all too rife within the "Iranian community." I thus continue to benefit from his well-informed insights into the development of football in Iran.

According to Chehabi, the development of physical education and regulated sports are tied into modernism and the Constitutional Revolution of 1906. At a more personal level, Mir Mehdi Varzandeh (1880–1982) is credited with being the reformer who established modern sports in Iran, especially around 1925–1934. Varzandeh applied his knowledge of physical education gained in the neighboring Ottoman Empire, as well as Swedish calisthenics to found "a number of modern sports clubs, including Iran's first public swimming pool."[1]

After initial resistance to his plans, the more farsighted members of government supported his efforts in order to overcome the debilitating impact of famine, epidemics, and poor diet on the populace. The well-being of future wage-slaves and soldiers was becoming a paramount concern of state policy-makers.

---

1. Chehabi 2014, 65.

The "race" had to be revitalized and "degeneracy" reversed through a healthier life style.[2]

In 1934 the minister of education invited Thomas R. Gibson, a recent Columbia University graduate, to reorganize Iranian sports. The maneuver sidelined Varzandeh and his non-competitive European inspired calisthenics and replaced them with competitive Anglo-Saxon sports such as football. Chehabi notes that the "grounds for this victory [had] been prepared by Protestant missionaries,"[3] underlining the close ties between football, politics, and religion from the outset.

The continual interest in Varzandeh's legacy reaffirms the linkage between modernism and football. Chehabi has claimed that "in a very basic sense, football embodies modernity," while Buytendijk argues that football is technical culture valuing team work, and Bromberger demonstrates how football reinforces division of labor and collective planning, "very much in the image of the industrial world which originally produced it."[4]

This is a sensible starting point, but below I will argue that this is a picture in need of amendment. Using the insight of the Welsh Marxist Raymond Williams I will be arguing that football may still be dominated by the needs of the modernist capitalist nation-states but it simultaneously carries within its frame "residual cultural artifacts" (premodern features such as tribalism, honor, fair play, and shame), as well as "emergent cultural artifacts" (postmodern features including multiple identities, authenticity, and a workable mix of structure and flexibility).[5]

Periodization of Iranian Football

I have taken every precaution to make my periodization of Iranian football a fluid, yet rigorous conflation of markers. After much consideration I ultimately settled on a layered approach to periodization. For the sake of simplicity, I have referred to the first layer as "socio-political" and the second as "organizational." I feel no affinity for these terms and use them merely out of convenience. The socio-political approach utilizes key markers from the history, politics and economy of Iran, and the organizational approach borrows ideas from the evolution of the sport itself. Together these two approaches cover most milestones related to Iranian football.

The socio-political approach considers the internal and external influences on football. The internal dynamics of Iranian capital and state formation should

2. Chehabi 2014, 61, 63.
3. Chehabi 2014, 66.
4. Chehabi 2002, 372–73.
5. Williams 1977, 121–27.

be studied simultaneously, since the development of capitalism in Iran is closely linked to the metamorphosis of the state. For instance, the game was introduced into Iran at the beginning of the twentieth century, thus the date acts as a natural demarcation point. The year 1924 symbolizes a break with the political turmoil of the pre-Reza Khan period. After 1924 a period of relative stability allowed for capital accumulation and state formation to encourage sport. The 1979 marker represents yet another organic break, since the attitude of the Islamic regime regarding football was initially at odds with the Pahlavi dynasty. In additional to these internal markers, various external factors have affected Iranian politics disproportionately and these too require consideration. World War II contributed to an early example of regime change and a corresponding modernization of the state apparatus. Football became a catalyst for change. In 2022 the World Cup in Qatar provided another external battleground between rebels and reactionaries. The miserable defeat of the regime's propagandists in Qatar 2022 has completed the cycle, and we hold our breath in anticipation of future developments. Below I provide a thumbnail sketch for Iranian football based on socio-political considerations.[6]

SOCIO-POLITICAL FACTORS

Early origins: circa 1900–1924

The Constitutional Revolution (1905–11) heralded the modern era. The bourgeoisie was enjoying the fruits of a (relatively) free press, parliament, and trade. Right in the midst of this cultural renaissance, two paradigms conjointly introduced football into Iran: the first was premodern Christianity spearheaded by missionaries and, the second, Western modernism championed by sports instructors and diplomats. Faced with this eccentric game-cum-sporting activity, the response of the population was layered and somewhat contradictory. While the ruling class was intrigued and excited by the prospect of a relatively cheap instrument of social engineering, the working class responded with cautious curiosity. The middle class, as ever divided along secular-religious lines, reacted with predictable intellectual slavishness and ascetic disapproval respectively.[7]

Shaky modernist foundations: 1925–1940

This was a time of unstable ethnic and religious tensions exacerbated by peasant and working-class resistance to capital accumulation. In response, the ambers of modernism initially ignited during the Constitutional Revolution were re-

---

6. In this section I have borrowed heavily from an earlier text of mine: Fozooni 2004.
7. Fozooni 2004, 356.

ignited by Reza Khan. His autocratic reign lasted from 1925 to 1940, during which modernism was tasked with dragging Iran out of superstition and towards prosperity and progress. Football was a ready-made talisman. But before football could fulfil its duty, footballers had to be re-structured. The residual artisanship of a feudal outlook was to be replaced by disciplined minds and bodies that could operate as cogs of a well-oiled machine. The paraphernalia of football also expanded to include football association and cup competitions, friendlies against foreign teams, sporting weeklies, a brand new stadium built at Amjadi'yeh and better trained referees.

Post-war boom: 1941–1967

The early years of Mohammad Reza Pahlavi were characterized by the centralization and militarization of football. As I explain elsewhere, "Elite army teams promoted the country abroad while at home the game was used to augment state education. Sporting committees at both national and provincial levels were set up to systematize the promotion of football."[8] The national side were runners up in the 1951 Asian Games and secured qualification to the 1964 Tokyo Olympic Games. Nothing earth-shattering in the grander scheme of things, but success of sorts, nonetheless. The shah was rebuilding an "imagined community" (Benedict Anderson) and the creation of fan-identities and national style through footballing allegiances was deemed a necessary part of the process. As Pablo Alabarces has explained in relation to Argentinian football, "On the one hand, style has an ideological component, particularly in journalistic discussions; on the other hand, it is used as a way of educating the public aesthetically."[9] The uneven development of capitalism, the bad harvest of 1959–60, and the unproductive military budget led to a wave of riots in 1963. Once these riots were suppressed, the ruling class had the opportunity to reflect upon its lessons, and embark on a more scientific management of the economy.

"Golden-Age" interrupted: 1968–1978

This is the decade that supporters of the Pahlavi dynasty refer to in sentimental terms as the "golden-age of monarchy." Boulevards, dams, and factories were built with the oil bonanza. Luxury apartment blocks and huge shopping malls altered the landscape. Regarding football, Brohm even suggests that in order to overcome the difficulties of over-capitalization and over-production in traditional industries, capital is encouraged to invest in "marginal" industries such

8. Fozooni 2004, 360.
9. Alabarces 1999, 79.

as sport and tourism.[10] I am not in a position to verify this conjecture but it is certainly true that football saw the benefits of this rapid growth in terms of the import of foreign coaches and footballers. Clubs invested in youth policy and introduced new tactics that laid the foundations for supremacy in Asia. The national league was expanded in order to be more ethnically inclusive. Women's teams were set up. Football became a "spectacle" in the Debordian sense of the term.[11] The heavy-handed modernization process served to provide a fig leaf for the cracks that would eventually bring down the monarchy.

Islamic vicissitudes: 1979–2023

To suggest that the mullah-bourgeoisie's stance on football has been contradictory is to understate the degree of confusion that has characterized policy since the victory of the Islamic counter-revolution.[12] The instincts of the new ruling class compelled them to initiate an official anti-football campaign. As I put it elsewhere, "a new form of divine chauvinism, based on the fascist concept of

10. Brohm 1978, 134.

11. Debord 1967. The "spectacle" represents a set of social relations mediated by the image. Its most superficial manifestation may be in the form of mass media, which rigs the game against the proletariat and makes subversive ideas and discourses trivialized. For Debord the "concentrated" form of the spectacle revolved around a dictatorial personality and a cumbersome bureaucracy. In the 1970s Iran became a concentrated form of the spectacle, although it was also groping haphazardly towards "diffuse" forms of the spectacle. The latter is a more advanced form of capitalism and associated with commodity abundance. The diffuse spectacle achieves its aims through seduction rather than brute force.

12. Why do I refer to the events of 1978–81 as the Islamic counter-revolution? Simply put: an uprising from below was crushed and then its remnants were recuperated by a new Muslim ruling class. A historical analogy with Germany fascism in the early twentieth century is instructive. The similarities between the Islamic Republic and European fascism of the 1930s are not merely ideological. Once in power, the mullah-bourgeoisie was faced with the same structural problems as those which bedevilled German and Italian capitalisms in the 1930s. They chose the same mechanisms for overcoming the crisis. These included the destruction of autonomous proletarian organizations, the banning of strikes and a reversion to methods of *absolute* surplus value extraction. Writing on German Fascism, Alfred Sohn-Rethel has described this process accurately: "The switch to the terroristic control of absolute surplus value production by the [Nazi] state meant that the bourgeois elite had to smash not only the proletarian political organization but also the mass basis appropriate to their own previous control through relative surplus value production, mainly the unions and social democracy; these they had to replace with a different mass basis: that of National Socialism" (Sohn-Rethel 1987, 69–70). Even the route by which Islamic fascism won power mimicked their German counterparts. In Germany the proletariat was defeated from the inside by social democracy and only then the fascists pushed themselves to the head of the queue. In Iran too it was a combination of liberals and social democrats (with the occasional Leninist-Stalinist) that undermined the working classes before the Islamists twisted the knife in. In both countries the process had two distinct phases. The only difference is that in Germany the process took fifteen years (from 1918–33), whereas in Iran it was compressed into approximately four years (1978–81). See Barrott 2019.

folk, was replacing patriotism based on monarchical principles."[13] Football was tainted through association with the imperial regime and football gatherings would get canceled based on the flimsiest pretexts. The call of the terrace was also a direct challenge to the call for prayers, and the competition proved too fierce for the mullah-bourgeoisie. In 2023 the regime seems to have given up on football as a tool for shoring up its popularity. Instead, the new head of the Football Federation, Mehdi Taj, has banned dissent and instructed clubs to record fans during matches as a deterrent against protests. Despite concerted efforts to suppress it, class struggle continues to express itself in the form of chanting, gossiping, strikes, go-slows, sit-ins, pitch invasions, boycotts, riots, and the ever-increasing cycle of animosity directed towards the Islamic theocracy.

Organizational factors

The socio-political approach is useful but it ignores the fluctuating rhythms of the sport itself. Too much emphasis is placed on external and distal factors. It, therefore, needs to be augmented by an "organizational" form of periodization that takes into account the passage of football from Fordism to post-Fordism, and the individual athletes from Taylorism to post-Taylorism. This approach allows us to see football as an industry where constant evolution is a mechanism for survival. Once again, I beg the reader's indulgence to allow me to base this part of the discussion on a previous published text of mine from 2017, where I drew parallels between the economy, the army, and football.

The establishment of Fordist football and Taylorist footballers in Iran goes back to the shaky modernist foundations (1925–1940) of capitalism, when Reza Kahn sought to forge a disciplined workforce and army. According to Pouryan, the industrializing process in Iran began in the 1930s, an earlier starting point than assumed by most scholars.[14] Nile Green takes the starting point even further back by suggesting that the *imaginary* of Fordism was introduced into Iran in the 1920s through American travelogues.[15] In a way, this is what football did for the Iranian economy; it painted an imaginary that could be passed, kicked, and dribbled into reality.

Professional athletes too were manufactured in this period as perishable exchange values to promote, "the cult of duty for its own sake, the sense of sacrifice for the community, the ideology of the super-ego, obedience, discipline, etc."[16] Football becomes "a cultivation of muscular effort which makes a virtue of la-

13. Fozooni 2004, 364–65.
14. Pouryan 2017, 708.
15. Green 2016, 290–91.
16. Brohm 1978, 26.

bour and suffering." The project is stamped with the mark of heavy-handed bu-reaucratic capitalism "with its system of competitive selection, promotion, hier-archy and social advancement."[17] Football training becomes structurally similar to the Fordist production line and the body is assembled through the deadening impact of routinization. Those forms of capitalism that are not sophisticated enough to establish American Fordism must make do with a hand-me-down Russian version in the form of Stakhanovism.[18]

Using either Fordism or Stakhanovism, the footballer's body is trained to withstand the rigors and injuries of the sport in the same way the worker's body is initiated into the unnatural factory rhythm, and the soldier's body is Tay-lorized to march, hide, shoot, and strangle the enemy. When the body is Taylo-rised all superfluous movements are avoided, time is saved and production made consistent. Taylor himself "took sport as his starting point for his studies on the rationalization of productive human labour."[19] Elitist football offers up the su-perman as an ideal pursuit for development and progress. Top athletes become the servants of the state and promote the regime's official propaganda, until that is they rebel and become foci of resistance, as is the case in contemporary Iran.

In the "West" Fordism works exceptionally well, until it does not. Gradual-ly Fordism reaches its limits and the profits dry up. Post-Fordism is inaugurated to raise profitability. Small flexible manufacturing units are once again revived. Specialized niche products are produced based on just-in-time methods in or-der to increase consumption. New technologies invade every facet of football from diets to training to career-saving surgery.

Ironically the process that began with small manufacturing plants trans-forming into giant factories and then kick-starting football Fordism is itself reversed when "leisure technicians" enter factories to bring sport to the work-ers. Exercise, football, basketball, and other leisurely pursuits aim to keep the worker fit and the mind agile, thus boosting production. According to Brohm, the leisure technicians have now become direct agents of class exploitation by lengthening youth and the life of labor power.[20] This post-Fordism brings forth the post-Taylorized footballer. This new brand of footballer must learn to be

17. Brohm 1978, 41, 50.

18. Alexie Stakhanov (1906–1977) was a Russian miner who was reported to have set a new record by mining 227 tonnes of coal in a single shift. Beria, who was Stalin's chief of security, used Stakhanov to raise productivity levels among workers. Stakhanovism can be seen as a make-shift version of Ford-ism and Taylorism. There are many similarities between the manner in which football was introduced into Iran and Russia. I intend to draw parallels with Carles Viñas's *Football in the Land of the Soviets* (2022) in future research.

19. Brohm 1978, 107.

20. Brohm 1978, 91, 95.

flexible on and off the field, improve not only in terms of exhaustive, repetitive action but also qualitatively by diversifying their skill portfolio. Efficiency is now complemented by faster crosses into the penalty area, quality passing by midfield maestros, diversified attacking patterns, just-in-time dribbles and training that is tailor-made for each player. Defenders are taught how to defend freekicks by specialist coaches, while strikers have their shooting improved by computer software that scrutinize every subtle movement.

Competitive forms of capitalism have overseen the passage from Fordism to post-Fordism. The paradigm shift does not make them immune to crisis but allows them to absorb the shock and to relaunch their enterprise more efficiently. It is my argument that both the shah's regime and now the mullah-bourgeoisie failed because ultimately, they could neither recognize nor negotiate this paradigm shift. Football illustrates this failure performatively. The case of Qatar 2022 illustrates these conceptual distinctions and hopefully makes things clearer.

The teams attending the 2022 World Cup in Qatar can be categorized into three groups based on organizational principles: those that were playing fluent and attractive post-Fordist football (examples would include Argentina, France, England and Brazil); those who were stuck in a predictable and pedantic Fordist footballing paradigm (Iran and perhaps Wales fall into this category); and those who were brave enough to initiate the shift from Fordism to post-Fordism knowing full well that during the transition, they would be vulnerable (Morocco, Croatia).

Let me just remind the reader that these categorizations must not be taken as fixed or absolute. After all even Iran, as one of the weakest footballing sides in the tournament, was blessed with a few talented individuals who have been trained under post-Fordist management techniques to accomplish post-Taylorist feats on the pitch. Iranians sometimes refer to such foreign-based players derogatorily as *legionnaires*. Saman Ghoddos plays for Brentford in the Premier League; Mehdi Taremi plies his trade at Porto; and Sardar Azmoun has recently joined Bayer Leverkusen. Despite the availability of these strikers, Iran's Portuguese manager, Carlos Queiroz, has set up Team Melli defensively in the last three World Cups. This is a strategy closely aligned with the military notion of "defensive territoriality."

As I wrote elsewhere, "the doctrine of defensive territoriality is about bounded wholes, sacrosanct borders and sovereign national rights. It relies on excessive hierarchy for direction and is risk-averse to the point of tedium."[21] The idea is to camp out inside one's own territory with the occasional sortie beyond

21. Fozooni 2017, 185.

the half-way line to harass and hurry the increasingly frustrated opponent. It is a footballing philosophy ideal for mass defense and the odd counterattack. The squad is trained to tackle, head, and pass in a standard format and no deviation from Taylorist time-motion criteria are permitted. So while post-Fordist teams combine structure with flexibility, individual flair with multi-tasking, teams like Iran can only offer an unappetizing diet of Fordist predictability.

To sum up this section let me reiterate my position: I have offered a layered approach to periodizing Iranian football with the socio-political and organizational vectors imposed upon each other. I could have made things more complicated but frankly I am satisfied with this new periodization – it captures both distal and proximal influences on football without getting bogged down in nuanced economic arguments over the respective merits of neo- and post-Fordism. Furthermore, it has a robust ability to explain the relative stagnation of Iranian football.

The Working-Class Vector of Resistance

As an academic I enjoy the illusion of having use-value for my students and the larger global community. In reality I, myself and my labor-power are mostly exchange value, to be bought, sold and humbled in the market place. Thankfully the etiquette of university-based employment still requires a modicum of dignity to conceal the brutality of this process, although that too is fast disappearing these days.

Footballers, however, have no such protection, which is why they are routinely objectified, quantified, and paraded like a piece of meat in front of prospective purchasers. The lucky ones hire agents to mediate the alienation but riches, fame, and last-minute flights across borders in private jets to meet transfer deadlines do not conceal the reality of the degradation. One minute they are planning to adapt to a new manager's 3-4-3 formation; the next, they are signing a contract to spend the next two years of their lives in a different culture, pretending to learn a new language.

When it comes to footballers, the mullah-bourgeoisie and their bureaucratic hangers-on, do not stand on ceremonies. Footballers are naught but semi-conscious tools with the duty to perfect their skills for the glory of God, capital, and the state. A group of official researchers from Iran have come up with a statistical model for "valuing players as human capital in the Premiere Football League of Iran."[22] They claim their findings have simplified a fifteen-variable model to a more manageable five-variable model. By assigning a weight to the players' pre-

---

22. Keshtidar et al. 2017, 39.

vious team, and measuring the number of goals scored in the previous season, the number of matches in which they played, their age, and the number of representative international matches they participated in, a value is assigned. Adding up individual players provides another estimate for each club's total market value. For example, the successful Iranian club, Persepolis was worth around thirteen million Euros (compared to Real Madrid, approximately at 770 million Euros). Just to give another point of comparison, in the 2016–17 season, the Premiere Football League of Iran was valued at around 105 million Euros, while the English Premiere League was close to 4.8 billion euros.[23]

The point I am making is not about the quality, rigor, or credibility of this study or the monetary pattern that is emerging. A more fundamental issue is at stake: once the mullah-bourgeoisie realized they can make money out of football, their attitude toward the game softened. They ordered government statisticians and economists to upgrade football's infrastructure and design profit models for a relatively risk-free form of investment. Its plebian culture needed to be tamed, of course, and security had to be guaranteed at stadiums, but otherwise, football could be treated as any other industry with the potential to enrich its owners. The fans could become a steady stream of cash as consumers of one of the very few pleasurable commodities available as mass entertainment under the mullahs, and the best footballers can be exported with oil, carpets, and pistachios to balance the budget.[24] What the mullah-bourgeoisie had not counted on was an alliance between the denigrated fans and the exploited players, in opposition to the dictates of the regime.

Parts of this proletarian alliance between fans and players has been chartered by Mastaneh Shah-Shuja. In her outstanding book, *Zones of Proletarian Development*, she applies concepts from Mikhail Bakhtin to a weeklong series of Iranian football riots (21–27 October 2001), during the qualifying rounds for the 2002 World Cup. In terms of both content and style, the parallels to today's riots against the very same mullah-bourgeoisie are uncanny.[25]

Shah-Shuja's analysis revolves around a duality between proletarian *carnivalesque* (Bakhtin) and religious *spectacle* (Guy Debord). The carnivalesque turns the world upside down by challenging the given order of things. It "expresses the people's hopes of a happier future, of a more just social and economic

23. Keshtidar et al. 2017, 49.

24. In order to increase profit margins, the Babbage Principle is utilized. This is a method of reducing total labor cost by assigning only high-skill tasks (e.g., playing in European leagues) to high skill footballers, and by limiting low-skill tasks (playing inside Iran's borders), to lower paid workers. It is also a wonderfully convenient way of creating divisions among players themselves and between high paid players (who are denigrated as *legionnaires*) and the fans.

25. Shah-Shuja 2008, 121.

order, of a new truth."[26] The carnivalesque stands in opposition to what Debord called the spectacle, a set of capitalist relations mediated by the image.

As these two forces fought each other in the streets of Iran throughout September-October 2022, and shortly after, at the 2022 Qatar World Cup, the differences became clearer. The people employ folk humor to bring the mighty low. In the Middle Ages, during the Feast of Fools, "the clergy and nobility were parodied and ridiculed, their belief system subjected to the cruellest condemnations, but the parody was nearly always a *regenerative* one."[27] In Iran, both during the 2001 football riots and the ongoing 2022–23 riots, insulting the clergy and turban-flinging became a street sport, indulged by the fast and nimble but vicariously enjoyed by even the old and decrepit.

The carnival depends for its existence on group solidarity and protection. After all, this is not a tame, domesticated tourist attraction, it is the real deal. Football fans in 2001 and again in 2022–23 have been at the forefront of creating solidarity between the people. Occasionally they even provide protection against the security forces. Moreover, as Bakhtin suggests in *Rabelais and His World*, during the early Renaissance era, people "built a second world and a second life outside of officialdom."[28] This, I would argue following Shah-Shuja, is precisely what Iranians have been engaged in. Now suddenly the second life has burst into the public realm and the Islamic spectacle seems helpless in dealing with it.

These two lives, the people's carnival and the elite's spectacle come into conflict in many ways, for example through language. As Shah-Shuja makes clear, "gradually a vernacular Farsi (enriched by various ethnic dialects) is superseding the official Arabesque-Farsi monologue of the Muslim elite."[29] The role of football chants in creating these linguistic bridges between terrace-humor and political slogans is becoming clearer every day. Iranian intellectuals with their insufferable petty-bourgeois moralism may not want to see this, but the people feel, chant and embody the new dialogism instinctively. Cursing, grotesquery, vulgarity, satire, and irony have become tools enriching people's assault on religion and capitalism. Desacralization has become a proletarian tool for fighting tyranny. We owe a great deal of this to football fans and rap artists, who parody official language with skill and imagination.

Observers have referred to contemporary young rioters as "mad" or "irrational" because they scream hysterically and do not put forward any discernible de-

26. Shah-Shuja 2008, 122–23.
27. Shah-Shuja 2008, 124.
28. Shah-Shuja 2008, 128.
29. Shah-Shuja 2008, 128.

mands. The 2001 football rioters were criticized in the same manner. Shah-Shuja captures their "scream" in these terms, "An instance of this *madness* is witnessed in the seemingly irrational post-match Iranian demonstrations where traffic is brought to a standstill by youngsters who neither march in the traditional sense nor raise any demands. In fact, there is no attempt at negotiations – just youngsters screaming *hysterically* in unison."[30] Security forces cannot understand today's young rioters and they cannot linguistically engage with them. This is also the reason the state seems incapable of recuperating their actions.

One conscious and explicit form of rejection emerged in 2001 among football supporters regarding the culture of "official martyrs." The state had learned very early on how to turn its losses on the battlefield with Iraq into "sacred commodities" and parade them around for propaganda purposes. This strategy was influential for many years but during the 2001 football riots something new emerged. Probably for the first time in Iranian history, *necrolatry* (idolatry of death and dead people or what is also known as martyrdom-worship) was scorned en masse during the riots. This rejection has intensified during contemporary protests with banners and posters of Islamic martyrs routinely set alight.[31]

Shah-Shuja's summing up of the 2001 football riots is fresh and relevant still, "what profanities, curses, rhythm, intoxication, music, eating, grotesquery, and sexual transgressions point to is the dissolution of the clergy's concept of *etiquette*. With the demise of etiquette and decorum, hierarchy, fixed social categories and class distinctions are put under collective erasure ... representatives of God on earth are heckled and abused."[32] The 2022–23 uprising has its roots in a week of football carnivalesque, when new possibilities were introduced into the body politic by working-class football fans.

Many professional footballers have picked up on this dynamic. Take individual footballers who have bravely spoken out against the Islamic Republic. Voria Ghafouri plays for the club side Foolad. He has been called the Iranian Che Guevara due to his unwavering support for working-class people. His criticisms of politicians see him being interrogated by the Ministry of Sport and Youth on a regular basis. His support for the right of women to attend football matches perhaps elevates his politics above that of the macho Che. In response

---

30. Shah-Shuja 2008, 136. The "scream" of course refers to John Holloway's concept in *Change the World Without Taking Power: The Meaning of Revolution Today*, (Pluto Press: London, Sterling/Virginia, 2002), 1–10. This unsettling tactic also has parallels with the British Suffragettes in the early parts of the twentieth century.

31. Shah-Shuja 2008, 139.

32. Shah-Shuja 2008, 146.

to his social media support of the movement, Iranian fans chant his name at football matches.[33]

Another famous footballer under pressure for his views is the retired Ali Karimi, once over-generously known as the "Maradona of Asia." His outbursts against the regime have become increasingly political. In turn, the regime has blocked his candidacy to head the Iranian Football Federation. More recently his house was confiscated, and he was forced to go into exile after receiving death threats. He has since joined forces with political activists and celebrities aiming to overthrow the regime.

The list of rebel footballers who have turned against the state, at no small risk to their own security I might add, is long. I could have mentioned Nasser Hejazi or Ali Daei, or several other celebrity-footballers. The point I am trying to make, however, is about a movement's dynamism. In Iran there is today mutual support and admiration between footballers, fans, and oppositional journalists. The organic viability of this coalition has pushed football to the forefront of resistance to the regime.[34] In the process, Marx's old distinction becomes relevant again: a "class in itself" is becoming a "class for itself," and that is a metamorphosis even more attractive than football.[35]

The Feminist Vector of Resistance

In Anglo-Saxon countries "incels" are variously interpreted as a sexually immature minority, or the natural follies of youth, or another manifestation of toxic masculinity, or a right-wing conspiracy to recruit vulnerable youth, or a backlash of one sort or another against feminism. In Iran, incels are simply the ruling class.

Sexual alienation has deep roots in Iranian society.[36] In an analysis of gender anxieties in the Iranian *zurkhaneh* (traditional gymnasium), Chehabi goes right to the heart of this psycho-sexual problem. He argues that in zurkhaneh "athletes exercised in a homosocial milieu that occasionally allowed for same-sex relations. Beginning in the twentieth century, modern heteronormativity made such relations problematic, while gender desegregation allowed women to

33. Anonymous 2022.

34. Contrasting this politicized triad of rebel footballer-fan-critical journalist with neighboring Turkey is instructive. There, according to Irak Daghan, this coalition is not as durable or politically dynamic as in Iran. This lack of solidarity "may have blocked the Gezi movement from making further political gains." See Daghan 2018.

35. For an interesting Polish case study of this Marxist transition see, Grodecki and Kossakowski 2021.

36. See Afray 2009, or Floor 2008 for a comprehensive general introduction to the topic. My own contribution is more inclined toward a psycho-political understanding. See Fozooni 2006 and 2014.

enter them. After the Islamic Revolution of 1979, gender segregation was again imposed, while heteronormativity was maintained."[37]

The psycho-sexual male anxieties described by Chehabi were re-enacted in football through the construction of a homosocial space. This became a key battleground between incel-Muslims who having erected a wall around "their space" hid behind it, and women who endeavored to make the public realm, including football, more inclusive. The breaching of this homosocial space was achieved in stages. Below I will review some of its seminal moments.

When the national team returned from Australia after qualifying for the 1998 World Cup, women demanded to participate in the celebrations. By intermingling with male fans and breaking strict social taboos female fans had started a process that would culminate in a nation-wide social rupture with the Islamic Republic in 2022–23. Their actions took the security forces by surprise and imbued the celebrations with a carnival atmosphere. In the words of Thomsen, "Young women were seen brazenly pulling off their black scarves, dancing with men and in some cases drinking alcohol in defiance of Islamic law. The street party went on for hours and the authorities did not try to stop it."[38] Hierarchies were being inverted, and the most unruly and undomesticated section of the proletariat, young female football fans, were leading the charge.

At this stage, the participants were still testing the limits of the enclosure and learning the rules of the game. A few years later, in 2001, the weeklong riot discussed above allowed the proletariat the opportunity to perfect some of their street-occupying tactics. This was particularly useful for women because it allowed them to imagine a life without head-scarves and sexual segregation. As I wrote in an earlier text, "in a society where female sexuality and the reproduction of labour power are as heavily guarded as the tomb of Ayatollah Khomeini, any infraction is tantamount to full-blown rebellion."[39] Women had discovered the Achilles heel of the regime and were aiming arrow after arrow after it.

Through participation in football celebration, gossiping, protesting, and whenever possible, rioting, Iranian women were dismembering the pomposity of official Islamic culture. More terrifying still for the mullahs was the feedback loop that was established between struggles in the workplace over exploitation, and the wider world. This cycle of struggles is precisely what we witness today when teenagers' school-strikes turn into walk-outs by teachers, which results in oil workers demanding backpay, and that in turn leads to a protest outside the notorious Evin prison by families of the arrested protestors. The cycle of struggle has become autonomous.

37. Chehabi 2019, 395.
38. I. Thomsen, quoted in Fozooni 2007, 120.
39. Fozooni 2007, 118.

Women also impact football as players. Once they were granted permission to play futsal, they turned indoor leagues into a fortress. The punitive measures imposed on them by the clergy, and lack of training facilities, TV coverage, and investment has not diminished their enthusiasm. In 2015 and then again in 2018 Iran won the AFC Women's Futsal Asian Cup. Progress for the national football team has been slower, but even here there has been distinct signs of improvement. Iranian women are currently sixty-seven in the FIFA world ranking.

The underfunding of women's football has resulted in female football referees having to purchase their own uniforms, and footballers having to pay for transport costs to sport facilities. Head scarves and tracksuit bottoms and long-sleeved shirts are imposed on female footballers in order to desexualize them as far as possible and reduce the risk of touching, kissing, and hugging, which is part and parcel of the modern game. Even referees are not immune from such restrictions. When "Mahsa Ghorbani, a successful female referee and the first Iranian woman to referee a men's match, refused to wear the uniform designated for female referees from Islamic countries, she was blacklisted by the Iranian Federation."[40] The fear of the flesh, in particular an independently minded flesh, is terrifying to incel-Muslims.[41]

The most tragic moment of the battle over biopower and homosocial space is without a shadow of a doubt the case of Sahar Khodoyari, or as she was dubbed by the media, the "Blue Girl." She was a fan sentenced to six months in jail for trying to attend a football match. In deep despair, and knowing what fate awaited her in prison, she decided to take her own life instead. In a final act of defiance, Sahar set herself on fire outside of an Islamic "Revolutionary" Court in Tehran in 2019. This was a quiet moment of social rupture for large swathes of Iranian society; at first, they were stunned, then infuriated and finally convinced that the mullah-bourgeoisie must go. Sahar's death had a similar impact to the act of self-immolation by the Tunisian Mohamaed Bouazizi in 2011. It was a brief moment in time, when society collectively shakes itself out of stupor.

What all these examples of resistance underscore is the centrality of the female body in this struggle. In the words of Silvia Federici, "the body has been for woman in capitalist society what the factory has been for male wages workers: the primary ground of their exploitation and resistance."[42] For women supporting football is about so much more than the game itself: it is also about invading

40. Rezai 2022.

41. The latest manifestation of this battle over biopower is the verbal assault by the reactionary Muslim tinkerer, Abdul Karim Soroush, on the Iranian actress Golshifteh Farahani. It is noticeable how these patronizing attacks become more intense when the target is a young, beautiful woman. Beauty unsettles inadequate men. This episode speaks more to the inadequacies of incel-Muslims than anything else.

42. Federici 2004, 16.

the public sphere; guaranteeing birth control; resisting unwanted sexual imposition; fulfilling unmet erotic desires; and the refusal to work (especially since housework is unwaged and unacknowledged). Football allows women to both invade male homosocial space as well as construct exclusively female homosocial space. Within their own space, women find the opportunity to convene, exchange news, take advice, and form an autonomous viewpoint, away from the chattering of incel-men.[43]

Conflictual Musical Ideologies

So far, my model has traced the socio-political and organizational contours of change within Iranian football. I have also investigated two fault lines of resistance emerging against the mullah-bourgeoisie: a general proletarian and a more specific, feminist fault line.

In this section I would like to briefly discuss the competing musical ideologies around Iranian football. I will do so through a cursory investigation of anthems, ballads, and terrace chants. This is part of a "future-forming" study (Kenneth Gergen). The reader is advised not to expect primary data or empirical rigor, which only a fully-fledged study can produce. Once again social class is at the forefront of these battles, with two ideologies at loggerheads: the first is an upper-class "reactionary modernism" (Jeffrey Herf) promoted by both imperial Iran and Islamic Iran, and aimed at solidifying an "Irano-Islamic" worldview; and, then there is an oppositional ideology promoted informally by the working classes in their everyday footballing activities through chants, rap music, social media forums, and gossiping.

The notion of upper-class reactionary modernism can be linked to the Fordist phase of football discussed earlier. More specifically, it can be associated with the first three phases of football's development which ranged from roughly 1900–1967. During this period the upper class imports the technological and scientific dimensions of modernism and in a rather piecemeal and clumsy manner eliminates the old to make room for the new. What is filtered out is all the political liberties and artistic debates, experiments, and transgressions that make the advancements in science and technology feasible. Grand modernist architecture builds huge stadia, but training pitches are neglected. Foreign coaches are imported for brief stints and asked to perform feats of magic, but local coaches find training and employment opportunities fleeting. Tribes are asked to give up their tribal identity and replace it with national allegiance, but power and wealth become increasingly skewed in favor of the metropolis. Ide-

---

43. Federici 2004, 72.

ologies are also hastily pitched, patented and consumed by fans. One conduit of these ideological innovations is music.

Focusing on the achievements of Ali-Naqi Vaziri (1887–1979), a pioneer of modern Iranian music, Chehabi reminds us that Iranian music is "an arena in which the tensions between temporal and spiritual authorities, between modernizers and traditionalists, and between proponents of different types of modernization have played themselves out."[44] It must be underlined at the outset that despite genuine intra-classist rivalries, the Mosque and the state have jointly ruled Iranians for centuries. At times the mosque has had the upper hand, and at other times the state has partially eclipsed the mosque. This uneasy symbiosis is reflected in the various Irano-Islamic permutations that have been on offer to the people. This Irano-Islamic bricolage is arguably more an exercise in rhetoric than substance.

The top-down engineering of an Irano-Islamic culture can be observed through music. Towards the end of the nineteenth century military bands were set up and schools brought in foreign music experts. Patriotic hymns and marches (*surud*) were composed for the monarch and his courtesans. These played a crucial role in prefiguring the idea of an Iranian homeland (*vatan*). According to Chehabi, surud has "gained a new prominence in the Islamic Republic," strengthening my argument that an aspect of the current theocracy is monarchical in nature.[45]

The 1906 Constitutional Revolution may have been an overall failure but it did loosen the grip of organized religiosity sufficiently for some progress to seep through. One beneficiary was non-military music which took advantage of the upheavals to tentatively enter the public sphere. Ballads (a loose translation of *tasnif*) repaid the favor by mobilizing support for the constitutionalists. Thus the monarchical surud and the republican-inclined tasnif came to forge competing Irano-Islamic ideologies. The monarchist version of Irano-Islamism contained a stronger militaristic element and was supported by the introduction of music lessons in schools. Under Reza Khan the religious pole of this synthesis was increasingly Zoroastrainized. The republican wing of the elite had a closer organic connection to civil society and a sharper instinct for the politics of the street. However, at the end of the day, both wings of the elite pursued music instrumentally in order to cement their powerbase, and that meant imposing a reactionary modernism from above.

Surud, which under the Pahlavis regulated the pulse of the nation and pro-

44. Chehabi 1999, 147.

45. In these early days, in addition to surud, the operatic modality was also utilized to revive a decidedly statist form of Zoroastrianism. See Chehabi 1999, 143.

vided rhythm for Fordist football, has undergone two further changes. The first change came about when the mullah-bourgeoisie instructed official musicians to merge surud with the *nauha* "a type of metric song traditionally performed as part of the mourning rituals of Muharram."[46] This fusion was unstable from the outset since it merged the breezy rhythms of brass bands with the stupor of fatalistic mourning songs. Football fans rejected it instinctively. The second evolution was rather more promising, as a younger generation of singer-songwriters fused Iranian rap with surud and tasnif. One branch of this current is officially sanctified rap. So it is undeniable that one part of today's rap culture is proudly atavistic. However, another part of it represents a genuine, angry proletarian rupture with the mores and values of the status quo. Football was at the forefront of the progressive branch of rap culture.

As the background noise to all the national anthems and marching songs and official football terrace chanting, we must once again discuss the role of Iranian fascism, both under the Pahlavis and the mullah-bourgeoisie.[47] Imperial Iran (which is desperately engineering a comeback), based its brand of fascism on the discredited notion of an "Aryan" race. Aryanism, it has been argued, is a discursive strategy designed to "manage the trauma of the encounter with Europe."[48] For various historical and cultural reasons the mullahs preferred to base their rule on the equally discredited notion of the Islamic *ummah*.

The latest propaganda tool designed to strengthen the ummah is the uncommonly long song known as "Salaam Farmandeh" (Hail, Commander). The largest rendition of this hymn was performed at Azadi Stadium (Iran's largest football stadium) in March 2022, in front of thousands of carefully chosen religious families. It was a spectacle that Albert Speer and Leni Riefenstahl would have been proud of. I am planning to subject this song to a close comparative historical discourse analysis with songs produced by Nazi Germany such as the "Horst-Wessell-Lied" (Song of Horst Wessell), "Deutschland erwache!" (Germany Awake), and "Giovinezza" (Hymn of the Italian National Fascist Party).

For now, I will simply note that Salaam Farmandeh is, to use Situationist terminology, a prime example of recuperation. The regime's propagandists are keenly aware of the prevailing social discontent. The chief aim of the song is to compete with oppositional rap, pop, and classic Iranian music for the affections

46. Chehabi 1999, 150.

47. Neither the Pahlavi regime nor the Islamic Republic can be construed as fascistic in their entirety. Fascism of the twentieth-century European variety only constitutes part of their ideology. Neo-fascism, right-wing populism, neoliberalism, Stalinism, social democracy, and even classic liberal influences are also present. This is not the place to go into all that. The fascistic elements of both regimes, however, are openly on display in the official music produced for football.

48. Zia-Ebrahimi 2011, 445.

of Iranian youth. The rhythm is modern and the official video's production values are relatively high. It is also a further attempt toward the militarization of society and the early dreams of exporting Islamic culture to the far corners of the globe. The hymn has been translated into a number of languages.

The "Commander" addressed in the title is the Shia twelfth Imam, the so-called Hidden Imam. However, the signifier also doubles up for the incumbent spiritual leader of the nation, Ayatollah Khamenei. The Imam is worshipped explicitly; the Ayatollah gets in on the act, by implied default. The preteen generation of the 1390s (2010s CE), many of whom can be seen in cadet uniform in the video, are called upon to take up arms in defense of Islamic values, as the Hitler Youth were once compelled to sacrifice themselves for the Third Reich. The military salutes and the genuine tears of redemption are eerily reminiscent of similar pictures in black and white from Nazi Germany of the 1930–40s.[49]

The children and their politically immature parents are constantly reminded that life is meaningless without the Mahdi. Loyal support and solidarity are promised to the Hidden One, the moment he chooses to reveal himself. The children, in turn, pledge that despite their short stature they will fight valiantly, just like General Soleimani and Mirza Kuchik Khan. The former was blown up by the American military, and the latter was a leftist guerrilla fighter and the leader of the Forest Movement (1914–21). This recuperation of a leftist rebel should not surprise us since even Nazi songs routinely plagiarized leftist themes, melodies and style, in the same way the story of the anarchist Nestor Makhno is being rewritten by Ukrainian right-wing nationalists for internal consumption.[50]

While the emotional impact of the hymn on the remaining faithful is genuine, the mandatory singing of the song during the October 2022 protests created considerable resistance. When a group of female pupils in the northern city of Ardabil refused to participate in the hymn singing, security forces were called in. They were beaten, some arrested and one student allegedly died from her injuries.

To summarize this section: Both imperial Iran and Islamic Iran used music to boost their powerbase amongst football fans. They represent different branches of reactionary modernism. The people's music has emerged to counter this. What remains to be analyzed is the wealth of slogans and chants that have increasingly merged with a critical rap culture. I have begun gathering data for precisely this purpose.

49. The official video of Salam Farmandeh can be found at https://www.youtube.com/watch?v=Az7ZDIdSKkk

50. Darch 2020.

Concluding Remarks

An analysis purporting to put forward a feminist-proletarian model for Iranian football must display nodes of wealth generation as well as contours of power and alienation. Above all it must identify societal antagonisms and show whether they are being resolved or remain in a state of productive tension. I am fully cognizant that I have only partially succeeded in these aims. However, I hope I have managed to lay a firm foundation that can be verified, amended, and improved upon with future empirical research. This future forming approach (Kenneth Gergen) will support Iranian football in transitioning from what it has been in the past, to what it could be in a post-Islamic future.

I began this chapter by offering a new periodization of Iranian football, which locates it within specific capitalist social relations. As cities became the site of wealth generation, the state became responsible for ensuring capital accumulation, and football was chosen as one of the effective regulators of this process. My periodization employs a layered approach to football's timeline: one layer is socio-political and the other organizational. The socio-political factors acknowledge the influence of ruling-class policy making and the inevitable working-class resistance to it. They show how football became commercialized and then spectacularized (Guy Debord).[51]

The organizational factors I have employed remind us that Iranian football has been a site of experimentation, with traditionalists and modernists (and occasionally postmodernists) applying different prescriptions for the patient. On the whole football's history displays a tendency toward the spread of Fordist and Taylorist techniques for raising productivity. This paradigm was initially successful but eventually it reached an impasse, and in the 1970s the profitability crisis returned. When in power, the mullah-bourgeoisie first ignored football and then attempted to restore it to profitability. There have been moves to complete the modernization of the industry, and where possible post-modernize aspects of it.[52] But the transition from Fordism to post-Fordism has largely

---

51. In the 1970s imperial Iran turned football into an entertaining spectacle, and the working class mostly accepted this, as an alternative to the drudgery and tedium of wage-slavery.

52. I work on the assumption that modernism and postmodernism possess advantages as well as disadvantages for the people. Herf has shown what happens when modernism goes awry. It becomes "reactionary modernism." Perhaps the negative side of postmodernism (what we can term "reactionary postmodernism"), has been under-theorized. The Islamic Republic plagiarizes ideas from both reactionary modernism and reactionary postmodernism. From the former it has learned how to build missiles, suicide drones, and instruments of torture. From the latter it has learned how to manipulate technical language and this has led to a fetishization of jargons. This sophistry can also be used to idolize Islamic heroes and promote anti-Western sentiments. What Islam rejects in postmodernism ranges from self-reflexivity, to skepticism, absurdism, nihilism, and individuality. The Islamic Republic is, therefore, not against modernism and postmodernism per se. It merely rejects the potentially subversive aspects of these ideologies, so as to embrace the reactionary elements more fully.

failed to materialize, resulting in stagnation for Iranian football.[53] This matters because it is symptomatic of a wider economic fiasco.

The task I have set myself has been complex and the present work inevitably suffers from several shortcomings. I would like to briefly discuss one central shortcoming of the present study by reference to the (infamous and unfashionable) base-structure-superstructure metaphor. I do not have the time or space to convince the skeptic reader of its continued usefulness. When utilized sagaciously, these dimensions can be useful as building blocks for model-making. From my vantage point it is possible to characterize many of the features of the base and superstructure of Iranian football. In this text I have, for instance, discussed the means of production (tools, factories, and stadia) of the industry, as well as its relations of production (in terms of class antagonism and alliances, the transition between Fordism to post-Fordism). Regarding superstructure, I have analyzed footballing culture and politics, and shown the intransigence with which proletarians have opposed both imperial and Islamic musical edicts.

I have, however, said very little about the structures of football mediating between the base and superstructure. In order to assess these commercial football structures and the wheeler-dealing shenanigans that they hide, one has to be privy to insider information. Alas I fear no one will be able to shed much light on these matters until the overthrow of the Islamic Republic. Only then will we be able to go through the ledgers and develop a more precise understanding of the financial operations of clubs and affiliated industries. Once access to financial data is granted, I will be in a better position to evaluate the contribution of the likes of Peter Kennedy, who argues in relation to global football: "The industry cannot sustain surplus value extraction, but instead acts parasitically on outlying industries for external sources of revenues it cannot then control to develop a strategy towards surplus extraction within football. The industry is at best quasi-capitalist and a good example of the speculative nature of the current phase of capitalism."[54] Is this also true of Iranian football? I would like to reserve judgment until we are in possession of academically reliable figures.

Another avenue which may prove productive is Karak's Marxist analysis of the English Premiere League.[55] Karak argues that football accumulates by dispossession (David Harvey), and legitimizes capitalism by creating alienated consciousness. Many of Karak's insights can be eventually incorporated into the

53. The partial success of *legionnaires* in adapting to a post-Taylorist training and playing regiment in European clubs has only made the failures of Iranian post-Fordism more visible.

54. Kennedy 2012, 73.

55. I have benefited in this section from Ian McDonald's (2015) survey of Marxist and Neo-Marxist approaches to sport and Karak's (2017) application of the accumulation of dispossession thesis to the English Premier League. I do not, however, wish to become embroiled in the heated discussions between structural-Marxists, post-Structural-Marxists and post-Marxists.

model presented here. In fact, a great deal of what I have described can be classified as the battle between classes over "free time": the workers push for more free time and, in response, the bosses turning free time into yet another source of profit by commodifying leisure activities.

Finall,y let me end on this note: Iran is today in a state of pre-revolutionary flux. We cannot predict the future. The mullah-bourgeoise is resourceful, tenacious, and desperate. It may cling to power for some time yet. Alternatively, by the time this text sees the light of day, Iran may be an utterly transformed landscape. The mullah-bourgeoisie may have been overthrown; Islam may have been banished from popular culture; and the balance of class forces in Iran and the surrounding countries may have been altered in favor of the people. Should this latter scenario come to pass, football will rightly feel proud of the role it played in achieving freedom.

Works Cited

Afary, Janet. 2009. *Sexual Politics in Modern Iran.* Cambridge: Cambridge University Press.

Alabarces, Pablo. 1999. "Post-Modern Times: Identities and Violence in Argentine Football." In *Football Culture and Identities*, edited by G. Armstrong and R. Giulianotti, 77–85. London: Macmillan Press.

Anonymous. 2022. "Voria Ghafouri: A Captain Who Refuses to Stay Silent about Social Issues." *BBC Persian*, May 16. https://www.bbc.com /persian/sport-61407465.

Barrott, Jean. 2019. *Fascism/Anti-Fascism: With additional Aufheben review and Author J. Barrott's reply.* Active Distribution.

Brohm, Jean-Marie. 1978. *Sport: A Prison of Measured Time.* Translated by Ian Fraser. London: Ink Links Ltd.

Chehabi, Houchang. 1999. "From Revolutionary Tasnif to Patriotic Surud: Music and Nation-Building in Pre-World War II Iran." *Iran* 37:143–54.

———. 2002. "A Political History of Football in Iran." *Iranian Studies* 35:371–402.

———. 2014. "Mir Mehdi Varzandeh and the introduction of modern physical education in Iran." In *Culture and Cultural Politics Under Reza Shah: The Pahlavi State, New Bourgeoisie and the Creation of a Modern Society in Iran*, edited by B. Devos and C. Werner, 55–72. London and New York: Routledge.

———. 2019. "Gender Anxieties in the Iranian Zūrkhāneh," *International Journal of Middle East Studies* 51:395–421.

Darch, Colin. 2020. *Nestor Makhno and Rural Anarchism in Ukraine, 1917–1921*. London: Pluto Press.

Debord, Guy. 1967. *Society of the Spectacle*. Detroit, MI: Black & Red.

Deghan, Irak. 2018. "'Shoot some pepper gas at me!' Football Fans vs. Erdogan: Organized Politicization or Reactive Politics?" *Soccer & Society* 19:400–417.

Federici, Silvia. 2004. *Caliban and the Witch: Women, the Body and Primitive Accumulation*. Brooklyn: Autonomedia.

Floor, Willem. 2008. *A Social History of Sexual Relations in Iran*. Washington, DC: Mage Publishers.

Fozooni, Babak. 2004. "Religion, Politics and Class: Conflict and Contestation in the Development of Football in Iran." *Soccer & Society* 5:356–70.

———. 2006. "Towards a Critique of the Iranian Psy-Complex." *Annual Review of Critical Psychology* 5:69–88. https://studylib.net/doc/8483892/toward-a
-critique-of-the-iranian-psy-complex

———. 2007. "Iranian Women and Football." *Cultural Studies* 22:114- 33.

———. 2014. "Sexual Dysfunction(s) in Iran: Imaginary Encounters with Otto Gross and Wilhelm Reich." *Psychotherapy and Politics International* 12:80–98.

———. 2017. "World Cup 2014: Necromancy with Team Melli!" In *What is Critical Social Research? Volume II,* edited by B. Fozooni, 185–88. Peterborough: FastPrint Publishing.

Greene, Nile. 2016. "Fordist Connections: The Automotive Integration of the United States and Iran." *Comparative Studies in Society and History* 58:290–321.

Grodecki, Mateusz., and Radoslaw Kossakowski. 2021. "Class Wars Among Devoted Football Supporters. Hooligan Bourgeoisie and Non-Hooligan Proletariat." *Soccer & Society* 22:470–85.

Holloway, John. 2002. *Change the World Without Taking Power: The Meaning of Revolution Today*. London, Sterling/Virginia: Pluto Press.

Karak, Anirban. 2017. "Accumulation by Dispossession: A Marxist History of the Formation of the English Premier League." *Review of Radical Political Economics* 49:615–32.

Kennedy, Peter. 2012. "The Football Industry and the Capitalist Political Economy: A Square Peg in a Round Hole?" *Critique* 40:73–94.

Keshtidar, Mohammad., Talebpour, Mahdi., Abdi, Shahram., and Abadi, Mostafa Zangi. 2017. "A Prediction Model for Valuing Players in the Premier Football League of Iran." *International Sports Studies* 39:39–52.

McDonald, Ian. 2015. "Marxist and Neo-Marxist Approaches on Sport." In *Routledge Handbook of the Sociology of Sport*, edited by R. Giulianotti, 40–49. London: Routledge.

Pouryan, Ashkan Aavali. 2017. "History, Space, and Industrialization: An Industrial Archaeology of Labor at Tehran, Iran." *International Journal of Historical Archaeology* 21:708–24.

Rezai, Sahar. 2022. "Pay Scandal Leaves Iran's Female Football Referees Out of Pocket, in Hand-Me-Down Uniforms." *IranWire*, February 28. https://iranwire.com/en/sports/71380/.

Shah-Shuja, Mastaneh. 2008. *Zones of Proletarian Development*. London: OpenMute.

Sohn-Rethel, Alfred. 1987. *The Economy and Class Structure of German Fascism*. London: Free Association Books.

Viñas, Carles. 2022. *Football in the Land of the Soviets*. Translated by Luke Stobart. London and Las Vegas: Pluto Press.

Williams, Raymond. 1977. *Marxism and Literature*. Oxford: Oxford University Press.

Zia-Ebrahimi, Reza. 2011. "Self-Orientalization and Dislocation: The Uses and Abuses of the 'Aryan' Discourse in Iran." *Iranian Studies* 44:445–72.

Shahestān-e Pahlavi:
Envisioning a New Imperial Capital
Under Mohammad Reza Shah

Robert Steele

ON 1 SEPTEMBER 1975, the first anniversary of the beginning of the Seventh Asian Games, which had been held in Tehran, the secretary general of the Iranian National Olympic Committee (INOC), 'Ali Asghar Peyravi, officially announced Tehran's bid to host the 1984 Summer Olympic Games.[1] In accordance with official International Olympic Committee (IOC) guidelines, two letters were sent to its president, Lord Killanin. The first, by the head the INOC, Prince Gholāmrezā Pahlavi, confirmed that the INOC fully endorsed Tehran's bid. The second, by the mayor of Tehran, Gholāmrezā Nikpey, confirmed that the capital would be willing and able to host the event.[2] The selection would not be made until 1978, but from very early on, the INOC had been laying the necessary groundwork. At the IOC meeting in Rome in May 1975, for example, Peyravi had invited all IOC delegates to a luncheon, at which a color film of the 1974 Asian Games was screened.[3] Iran's hosting of the Asian Games had demonstrated its ability to hold major sporting events, but the Olympics was always the ultimate aspiration.[4] Given the reluctance of other cities to bid for the games, and the expectation that Iran would "have strong support among the African and Eastern European nations," it was thought that Iran would have a good chance of winning the bid.[5]

The Āryāmehr Sports Complex, built for the Asian Games, was referred to

---

1. "E'lāmiyeh-ye Komiteh-ye Melli-ye Olampik-e Irān," *Ettelā'āt*, 10 Shahrivar 1354/1 September 1975, 7.

2. In fact, these letters were signed on 14 and 12 August respectively and delivered to the IOC on 29 August. The INOC waited until 1 September (10 Shahrivar) to officially announce the candidature of Tehran. "Tehran's Bid for the 1984 Olympic Games," *Olympic Review*, September-October 1975, 425.

3. "Iran Will Bid for the 1984 Olympics," *Kayhan International*, 6 September 1975, 8.

4. One year before the Asian Games, Iran had even declared its readiness to bid for the 1980 Olympic Games. IOC chief Lord Killanin felt that Iran had the best chance to beat Moscow in the contest. "Iran to Bid for 1980 Olympics," *Kayhan International*, 29 September 1973, 2.

5. "1984 Olympics Delusion," *The New York Times*, 17 February 1977, 77. After Iran pulled out amidst revolutionary turmoil, Los Angeles remained the only candidate for the 1984 Games.

as Iran's Olympic Village, and its facilities met official Olympics requirements.[6] Japan's hosting of the 1964 Olympics had been important in cementing that country's international standing, and the shah felt that an Olympic Games in Tehran would similarly confirm Iran's status as a developed nation.[7] To demonstrate the development and modernity of Tehran, the city needed improvements to transport infrastructure, as well as the construction of hotels and recreational facilities to accommodate thousands of visitors. Central to the bid, and indeed the vision of modern Iran which the state sought to project, was the new satellite town planned to be constructed in the Abbas Abad district to the north-east of the city center, the Shahestān-e Pahlavi.

The Shahestān-e Pahlavi project was one of the most remarkable and ambitious projects of the late Pahlavi period. It was to be built on a site of ninety square kilometers and would serve as the cultural and political heart of the capital, with museums, parks, a large ceremonial square, a grand national library, long boulevards, housing, recreational facilities, commercial offices, ministry buildings, banks, municipal offices, and shopping areas. This chapter explores the performative and functional aspects of the Shahestān plan. Authoritarian regimes such as the Pahlavi monarchy, which are centered around the individual rule of a single person, frequently employ the political spectacle to win or maintain popular support.[8] Niccolò Machiavelli, writing in the sixteenth century, considered the spectacle as an exhibition of power and authority, through which the ruler, by showing himself "an example of courtesy and liberality; nevertheless, always maintaining the majesty of his rank," can gain the admiration and passivity of his citizens.[9] Performance was at the heart of the Shahestān. Its central square was designed as a place for major events and gatherings, and its very name, Shahestān, meaning "Place of the Shah," evoked the power and dominance of the monarch.

But the Shahestān was to be more than a performative space; it would be a functioning, modern city center, intended to "meet the needs of a big city on a global scale."[10] It was to have the most advanced transport infrastructure, with

6. "Aryamehr Sports Centre," *Iran Tribune*, October 1971, 42.

7. Chehabi 2002, 386. Comparisons were often drawn between Iran and Japan. In an interview Gholāmrezā Pahlavi said: "The Asian Games organized by the Japanese were, as you might expect perfect. The ancient Persian Empire could not do less well than the ancient Empire of the Rising Sun. And we succeeded." Cited in Huebner 2016, 230.

8. On sultanistic regimes, see Chehabi and Linz 1998, 3–25. On the political spectacle, see Edelman 1988.

9. Machiavelli 2008, 108.

10. "Porozheh-ye 'Azim-e Khāneh-ye Dāryush dar Qalb: Shahestān-e Pahlavi," cutout from *Talāsh* [undated], archives of Shojā'eddin Shafā, Bibliothèque universitaire des langues et civilisations (henceforth Shafā Archives).

a metro system running through and highways connecting the development to the rest of the city. Total private and public investment in the project was estimated to reach as much as $3.3 billion (equivalent to more than $14 billion in 2025).[11] The purpose of this urban center was "to prevent the scattered spread of the administrative and commercial facilities of the city" and to create an area where the administrative, commercial, social, and cultural activities of the capital could be concentrated.[12] In doing so, the project would essentially have transformed the hitherto desolate Abbas Abad region into the ceremonial, administrative and cultural heart of Tehran, and the seat of power of the Pahlavi state.

BACKGROUND TO THE SHAHESTĀN PROJECT

Although in the 1970s, the Shahestān was seen as a site in which the modernity of Iran could be projected and celebrated, Abbas Abad was to be developed initially to manage the expansion of the city. The population of Tehran expanded rapidly in the latter half of the twentieth century, rising from half a million in 1940 to 1.7 in 1956, 2.7 in 1966, and 4.6 million in 1976. This represented an annual growth rate of well over five percent between 1956 and 1976.[13] In 1976, the population of the capital represented twelve percent of the total population of Iran, as well as thirty-two percent of the total urban population.[14] This population growth was matched by the city's physical expansion, as its surface area grew by 300 percent between 1940 and 1956 alone. This extraordinary expansion, alongside a lack of comprehensive planning, led to problems such as traffic congestion, pollution and housing deficiency, while the divide between the affluent, educated and increasingly middle-class population in the north of the city, who were to some extent insulated from such issues, and the traditional working classes in the south became ever more perceptible.

In an attempt to alleviate these problems, the Tehran Comprehensive Plan, a city development strategy, was devised by the architectural firm Abdolaziz Farmanfarmaian and Associates, together with an American partner, Victor Gruen. To reduce the density of the city center, the plan proposed the establishment of several administrative centers, the intended result of which was to reorient growth and reorder social structures. The plan was approved in 1966 and its implementation began in 1968.[15] One of the ways that the Comprehen-

11. "Jāddeh-ye Sevvom Goshāyesh Yāft," *Ettelā'āt*, 29 Mordād 1354/20 August 1975, 4.
12. "Porozheh-ye 'Azim-e Khāneh-ye Dāriyush."
13. Costello 1981, 156.
14. Grigor 2016, 364.
15. Mashayekhi 2019, 863

sive Plan proposed to shift the high density of activities away from the historic center was to build a new district in the underdeveloped area of Abbas Abad. This was merely one of many new developments in the city under the Comprehensive Plan, and would serve as a commercial and residential area.[16] However, in 1971, the decision was taken to develop it into a governmental center and thus on 20 Khordād 1350 (10 June 1971) an imperial farmān was approved by the upper and lower houses, detailing the implementation of the "Abbas Abad modernization program" (barnāmeh-ye nowsāzi-ye ʿAbbās Ābād).[17] Article one of the law granted the Tehran municipality the right to purchase all the lands and properties in Abbas Abad. Compensation for the owners of houses, shops and other properties was to be agreed by a panel of ministers. Under the law, owners of properties would have three months from the date of acquisition to vacate the properties before they would be evicted.[18]

In 1973, Empress Farah's Special Office invited the American architect Louis Kahn and the Japanese architect Kenzo Tange to collaborate and together put forward a proposal for the design of the Abbas Abad development.[19] However, after the death of Kahn in March 1974, a rival proposal was submitted by the British firm Llewelyn-Davies International (LDI), a fifty-person team of professionals, led by Jaquelin Robertson. This proposal had the support of the mayor of Tehran, Gholāmrezā Nikpey. The proposal was presented to the shah, who also gave his unequivocal support. At the same time as LDI won the contract, the site was given a new name, Shahestān-e Pahlavi.[20]

The award of the contract to LDI coincided with the quadrupling of the price of oil, which meant that the budgets available for such grand projects increased drastically. To give a sense of the changing economic climate, the estimated oil revenue that would be allocated to the Fifth Development Plan, which was launched in 1973, was $25 billion. After the oil price hike, this was increased to nearly $100 billion.[21] The selection of LDI rather than Kahn and Tange was, it seems, less to do with different conceptions of modernity, as other scholars have suggested, than with upscaling the project and entrusting it to a multi-disciplinary international team with experience in such comprehensive urban transformations.[22] Moreover, while the shah was certainly concerned

16. Mozaffari and Westbrook 2020, 181.

17. Letter from the prime minister's office to the Ministry of the Interior, 29 Khordād 1350/19 June 1971, National Library and Archive of Iran, Tehran (Henceforth NLAI), 220/18134.

18. Article 11, ibid. Most of these buildings were relatively new, having been built during the construction boom of the 1960s. Bahrambeygui 1972.

19. Emami 2014, 76.

20. Mohajeri 2016, 154.

21. Daftary 1988.

22. Mozaffari and Westbrook 2020, 187.

with scale and grandiosity, he was also preoccupied with time. In speeches during the 1970s, he spoke not only about his desire for Iran to become a developed country, but also about how he wanted this to be achieved as quickly as possible. Since the LDI plan was set out in grids, it was "eminently implementable" as it allowed for certain areas to be constructed in stages according to need and budget.[23]

The LDI Master Plan, which was published in 1975 and authored by the director of the project, Jaquelin T. Robertson, stated the goals of the Shahestān-e Pahlavi as follows:

1. To serve as a transportation center capable of deflecting the city's traditional northward growth to the proposed development corridor stretching east and west of the city.

2. To be a model community built to meet North Tehran's need for a coherent center.

3. To be a national center befitting Iran's capital city.[24]

The last point was stated in the report as being the most important purpose. In this relatively small section of Tehran, many of the main government buildings would be located, including the Prime Minister's Office, fifteen ministries, the Plan and Budget Organization, the Imperial Organization for Social Services, five of the major banks and insurance companies, and Tehran City Hall. A comprehensive cultural center was also to be located adjacent to the main square, which would include museums, theaters, and the Pahlavi National Library.

CREATING A PAHLAVI CAPITAL

In many of the great imperial centers of the world, the ruling power is built into the fabric of the city. For example, the city center of Vienna feels like an open-air museum displaying the splendor and majesty of the Habsburgs, St Petersburg illuminates the culture and sophistication of the Romanovs, and Istanbul exhibits the magnificence and power of the Ottomans. In Iran, too, Isfahan is synonymous with the golden age of Safavid rule, and even in Shiraz, buildings associated with the Zand dynasty are part of the fabric of the city. However, Tehran was ostensibly a Qajar city. It had been made the capital city by Agha Mohammad Khan Qajar in 1786, so by the time Reza Pahlavi became shah in 1925, the city had been the capital of the Qajars for nearly 140 years. Although Reza Shah had tried to renovate the city and remove evidence of the Qajars, such as the

23. Mozaffari and Westbrook 2020, 187.
24. Robertson 1976, 31

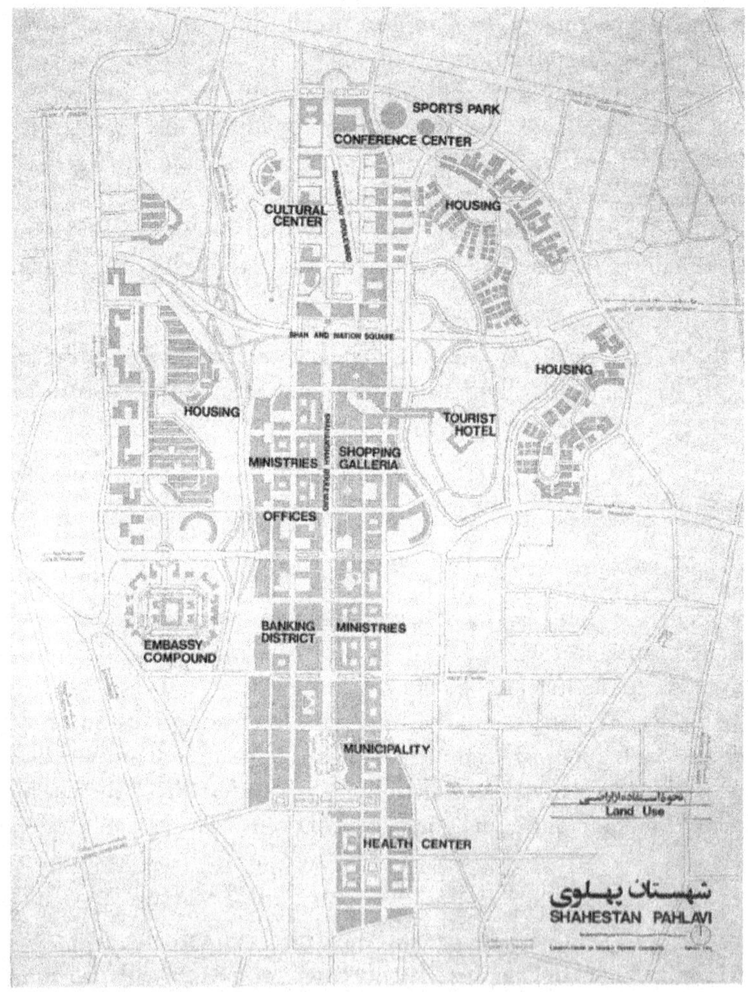

Figure 1. Layout of main building areas of the Shahestān, unpublished LDI report, NLAI 264/25073.

city walls, and build new structures in a modern style throughout the city, the remnants of the Qajar past remained. This was especially the case in the old city center, the beating heart of Tehran, which contained landmarks such as the Grand Bazaar, the Dār al-Fonun, Tupkhāneh Square, the Bahārestān, and, most importantly, the Golestān Palace; each reminders of the Qajar history of the city that had shaped modern Iran.

Throughout the city, there were reminders, too, of events that were uncomfortable for the Pahlavis, such as the Constitutional Revolution of 1906 and the

1953 coup, in the sense that both were associated with movements that sought to limit the power held by a shah. Considering this history, it could be argued that the shah never truly felt that Tehran was his capital. During preliminary plans for his coronation, for example, there were discussions about holding the ceremony in Persepolis rather than Tehran. A report from 1961 reads:

> It is the wish and request of the Central Council [for the Imperial Celebrations] from His Imperial Majesty that the coronation ceremony of the shah is held at Persepolis ... and that the coronation of all future generations of Iranian kings will also take place at Persepolis.[25]

Of course, the coronation was eventually held in 1967 at Golestān Palace, but it is remarkable that such a suggestion to hold the shah's coronation some 880 kilometers from his capital city was ever entertained.

Throughout the latter part of the 1960s and into the 70s, there was a concerted attempt by the Pahlavis to establish Tehran as a distinctly Pahlavi city and to shift the center of gravity of the city from the south to the north. In 1965, the shah left the Marble Palace, his residency in central Tehran, to move into Niyāvarān Palace in the far north of the city.[26] The Marble Palace was subsequently handed over to the municipality and was turned into a museum, the Pahlavi Museum, which opened in 1976.[27] After the coronation ceremony in 1967, the Golestān Palace, too, was opened as a museum, where visitors could see up close evidence of the antiquated style of the Qajars, and the places where both Pahlavi monarchs had been crowned. The shift to the north of the city represented an ideological as well as geographic shift. The north now represented the bright future of Iran, the march towards the Great Civilization, whereas the south represented the past, with glories to be commemorated, and tribulations to be forgotten.

The Shahestān-e Pahlavi was similar to other projects, such as the Shahyād Tower, in the sense that both were attempts to create landmarks that were instantly recognizable to Iranians as well as foreigners as Pahlavi. As Mozaffari and Westbrook argue:

> Both projects partake in, and are products of, the attempt by a newly ambitious developing nation to project itself onto the world stage through elaborate representations, through tourism and the media, and to its own population, through both internal tourism and local

---

25. Dovvomin gozāresh-e motāle'āt-e shurā-ye markazi-ye jashnhā-ye 2500 sāleh-ye shāhanshāhi-ye Irān, January 1961, *Bazm-e Ahriman* 1377/1998, 1:101.

26. Nikpey 1352/1973, 1–3.

27. See Bazyar and Steele 2023.

media. And both sites share a similar monumental language, of vast squares, gateways to an imagined future, interpretational museums, and grand urban ensembles of avenues, landscaping, and special sequences, through which the nation could be represented as a modern, progressive entity, occupying the global stage while retaining its own cultural character.[28]

In the 1970s, the Shahyād Tower became a symbol of modern Iran, appearing on banknotes, stamps, and in promotional literature for travel and tourism organizations. The Shahestān, too, had it been completed, would have become a major Pahlavi landmark, another symbol of Iranian modernity.

The focal point of the Shahestān was its central square, the so-called Shah and Nation Square (Meydān-e Shāh va Mellat). This square was designed to be one of the largest in the world, and was to have the same proportions, though a little larger, than the Meydān-e Naqsh-e Jahān in Isfahan. Indeed, Isfahan's grand square was the inspiration for the Shah and Nation Square. Of the Meydan-e Naqsh-e Jahān, Babak Rahimi has written that its construction "served as the ceremonial staging arena for the Safavid political order, wherein the promise of a future utopia was architecturally performed in an open field."[29] The Shah and Nation Square promised a similarly utopic vision for Iran under the Pahlavis. In the LDI masterplan, it was declared that "Such a centre would demonstrate to the world that Iran is rapidly moving towards HIM the Shahanshah Aryamehr's proclaimed 'Great Civilisation.'"[30] When deciding the order in which the construction would be carried out, the planners decided that the cheapest and most logical way would be to start from the outside and work inwards, but to do it this way would mean that the main square would be the last to be constructed. This, they argued, would negate the real purpose behind Shahestān-e Pahlavi, which was "to create a new ceremonial heart for Tehran."[31]

The square was to be not only a large public space for people to converge in everyday life, but it was also an area for events. The entire western part of the square, which was to be closed off from traffic (aside from limousines to ferry guests to special events), would "be sufficient size to accommodate all the necessary panoply of receptions."[32] This part of the square, which was also raised, would also be a space for outdoor exhibits. A special monument was to be erected in this part of the square, at which "visiting dignitaries and VIPs will be able to pay their respects to Iran's past." The LDI plan describes the monument as a

28. Mozaffari and Westbrook 2020, 176.
29. Rahimi 2012, 189.
30. Robertson 1976, 36.
31. Robertson 1976, 125.
32. Robertson 1976, 68.

"great portal, or *iwan*," which the planners might have envisaged as resembling the monuments and palaces of Isfahan. During the Safavid period, a Safavid shah would watch ceremonial and sporting events, in particular polo, from a viewing gallery in the upper level of ʿĀli Qāpu palace. Similarly, the Pahlavi monument would have contained a viewing platform from which a Pahlavi shah would be able to observe ceremonial events taking place on the square.[33]

According to LDI, "Shahestan's most important role is to serve as the national centre of Iran."[34] For this reason, many of the major political, commercial and economic headquarters would be located there. Notably absent in the design of the new political and administrative center was the symbol of constitutionalism, the parliament, which apparently would remain in the south of the city at the Bahārestān. Throughout the 1960s and 70s, the role of the majles had gradually weakened; the instigation of a one-party system in 1975 marked the ultimate diminishment of any democratic oversight of the shah's power. From this stage, as Ali Ansari has noted, "the Shah took to describing himself as the commander (*farmandeh*) who issued decrees (*farmans*), arguably liberating himself from whatever Constitutional limits remained."[35] Thus, as Emami has argued, "the physical form of the complex [Shahestān] was to achieve what the Resurgence Party attempted to create through political organization: to forge a direct relationship between the monarch and the people."[36]

Insofar as it was a projection of the shah's power and authority, Emami writes that the shah's "urban vision was not very different from that of the megalomaniac Nazi leader."[37] Of course, one could argue that the shah brought such comparisons with Hitler on himself by implementing a single-party system, having earlier written, in his first book, *Mission for my Country*, that, "If I were a dictator rather than a constitutional monarch, then I might be tempted to sponsor a single dominant party such as Hitler organized."[38] However, comparisons with Hitler are rarely helpful for all the connotations they bring, and the shah's

33. Robertson 1976, 68
34. Robertson 1976, 50.
35. Ansari 2012, 183.
36. Emami 2014, 94.
37. Emami 2014, 86.
38. Pahlavi 1960, 173. It is important to contextualize this text properly, too. It was originally written in English with the help of an American scholar, Donald Wilhelm Jr., and was subsequently translated in Persian, which indicates that its audience was not only, or perhaps not primarily, Iranian. Zonis 1991, fn. 10, 278. Indeed, at this time, the shah was under considerable pressure from the United States to liberalize the political system and allow greater popular participation in politics. At the same time as the publication of *Mission for my Country*, for instance, the shah had reluctantly appointed Ali Amini as prime minister due to his "reputed friendship with the Kennedys." Afkhami 2009, 213. Along with the launch of the shah's White Revolution reforms, *Mission for my Country* was part of the shah's strategy to "reinvent himself as a progressive monarch." Ansari 2019, 255. See also Shakibi 2020, 130–31.

understanding of imperial rule was rooted in a centuries-old tradition of Iranian monarchy, though it sometimes borrowed ideas and concepts from European enlightenment. The shah articulated these ideas in all of his published texts. For instance, quoting the Danish orientalist Arthur Christensen, the shah wrote in his *Enqelāb-e Sefid* (The White Revolution): "A real king in Iran is not only a political ruler, but is first and foremost a teacher and sage; one who does not only build roads, dams, bridges and canals, but also guides their [his people's] spirits, thoughts and hearts."[39] In this sense, the urban visions of the two autocratic rulers differed significantly. While Hitler's urban plan for Berlin, drawn up by his chief architect Albert Speer, was intended to overawe and intimidate, and reflect the Führerprinzip, Shahestān-e Pahlavi, in spite of its imperial grandeur, was supposed to create a modern, inviting center for Iranians and foreign visitors to use and enjoy, and enforce the idea of the shah as a progressive and modernizing leader.

The Cultural Heart of Tehran

In the late 1950s, a deputy court minister for culture was appointed at the Imperial Court for the first time. The court minister at the time, Hoseyn 'Alā, claimed that the reason for the creation of the position was the shah's desire to "to revive the Imperial Court's traditional role as patron of culture and literature."[40] The person appointed to this position was Shojā'eddin Shafā, who remained in the role until 1979, during which time he oversaw most of the main cultural initiatives launched by the court, served as the shah's primary speechwriter, and ghost-wrote two of his books. The Imperial Court's focus on cultural activity during the 1960s and 70s was designed in part to demonstrate that the shah was not a ruthless dictator, or some oriental despot, but a *despote éclairé*, who was a dedicated patron of culture.

As a result of these efforts, as well as Empress Farah's advocacy and sponsorship of the arts and culture, many museums, theaters, and other cultural institutes were built across the country, particularly in the capital. Museums included the Shahyād Museum (1971), the Pahlavi Museum (1976), the Reza Abbasi Museum (1977), the Museum of Contemporary Art (1977), the Carpet Museum (1977) and the Sixth Bahman Museum (1977), and theater and concert venues included Rudaki Hall (1967) and the City Theater (*Te'ātr-e Shahr*, 1972). These sites became important landmarks in the city center, and some, such as Rudaki Hall and the Pahlavi Museum, were printed on stamps

---

39. Pahlavi 1967, 2–3. The same passage was quoted in Pahlavi 2536/1977, 14. On the development of monarchical ideology in this period, see Ansari 2012, 166–179.

40. Shafā 2013, 65.

and banknotes, to infuse them into the national consciousness. Museums and cultural institutes would form a major part of the Shahestān, too.

According to the LDI plan, the Shahestān would serve as a "comprehensive cultural centre," which would "give Tehran a focal point for the nation's artistic and literary life.... There museum exhibitions, concerts, operas, plays and research... could take place in a creative atmosphere where each field cross-pollinates ideas into the others."[41] The north side of the Shah and Nation Square was to be the cultural heart of Iran and would include a National Carpet Museum, a Museum of Modern Art, a National Museum and the Pahlavi National Library. This area was allocated "the highest buildable elevation on the site" so that it could serve as "an Acropolis devoted to Iran's cultural pursuits."[42] It was connected to the south side of Shahbanu Park, to the east of which was a National Cultural Centre, which included the National Opera House and an outdoor amphitheater. The Ministry of Culture and Arts would also be situated on the west side of the Shahbanu Park "to strengthen the connection between cultural policies and the actual programmes carried out."[43]

Possibly the most important part of the cultural Acropolis was the Pahlavi National Library. This library, which was planned to "rank in size and facilities" with the great libraries of the world, such as the Library of Congress, the British Library, the Lenin Library and the Bibliothèque Nationale, would contain copies of all books, manuscripts and journals related to Iran published anywhere in the world.[44] The head of the Pahlavi National Library Project (Tarāhi-ye Ketābkhāneh-ye Melli-ye Pahlavi) was Shojā'eddin Shafā, who enlisted to help of a group of international consultants, who together with their Iranian counterparts, set the objectives and parameters of the project. Nasser Sharify, the dean of the Graduate School of Library and Information Science at the Pratt Institute, New York, was charged with preparing a comprehensive plan for the library.[45] The design of the building was chosen through an international competition, which resulted in over 3,000 submissions from eighty-seven different countries. Cultural relevance was one of the main criteria by which entries were judged.[46] To help prospective applicants, a supplementary booklet was printed, titled *Selected Principles of Traditional Iranian Architecture*, and a special exhibition was organized in which over 30,000 pictures and slides were displayed

41. Robertson 1976, 52.
42. Robertson 1976, 60.
43. Robertson 1976, 70.
44. Herman Liebaers in the preface to Clavel 1978, iv, Shafā Archives.
45. Steele 2019, 98.
46. Pahlavi National Library Project, International Architectural Competition 1977/1978: Public Exhibition of Projects (March 16—April 16 1978), 13, Shafā Archives.

showing examples of Iranian architecture. The Pompidou Centre in Paris was cited as an example of the type of modern structure they wanted to avoid.[47]

When announcing the winner of the competition, the German firm von Gerkan, Marg und Partner, on 16 March 1978, the shah expressed his wish that other buildings in the Shahestān would also be chosen through such competitions.[48] This emphasizes the problems in basing arguments about the shah's "zeal for gross signs of modernity"[49] on the LDI plan, because there is no evidence that any of the buildings or structures would resemble those depicted in its published report. Indeed, in December 1977, Kenzo Tange won the competition to design the Tehran City Hall, even beating LDI, which also submitted a design.[50] Not only did he beat LDI, but Tange even convinced the judges to allow him to alter the regulations, essentially re-asserting his influence over the Shahestān project.

The City Hall was located on the north front of the Shah and Nation Square; "the core" of the Shahestān Pahlavi project; or as Tange saw it, "the key building at the key point."[51] However, according to the parameters set by the LDI plan, to preserve the view of the Alborz mountains to the north of the square, the City Hall would have to be lower than other buildings on the square, and would not project into the square. Tange argued that according to this scheme, "The City Hall will [be] wrongly positioned." He continued: "The City Hall is not a mere governmental office, but acts as a national guest house as well.... In a word, the City Hall is the 'face' of the square. Therefore, it could come forth to the square." Although the competition specified that the height of the building was limited to a maximum of thirty-three meters, the major feature of the Tange proposal was a 100-meter gate structure connecting the different wings of the hall, through which the view of the mountains from the square would be preserved. Along with his winning design, Tange also proposed some modifications to the design of the square, including: the addition of car roads running around the formal square "so as to maintain the consistency of the square nature"; changing the position of the Ministry of Foreign Affairs building; and moving the royal box from the center of the square to the upper section of the City Hall.

It has been argued that the Kahn-Tange proposal for the Shahestān masterplan, favored before the LDI plan was selected, reflected the tastes of Empress

47. Clavel 1979, 120.
48. "Shahestan Cultural Center Among World's Best: Monarch," *Tehran Journal*, 18 March 1978.
49. Emami 2014, 90.
50. "Tange Proposal Takes First Place in Teheran City Hall Contest," *Japan Architect*, May 1978.
51. "Tehran City Hall: 'Modifying the Master Plan' How Kenzo Tange won the Competition," undated document, Shafā Archives.

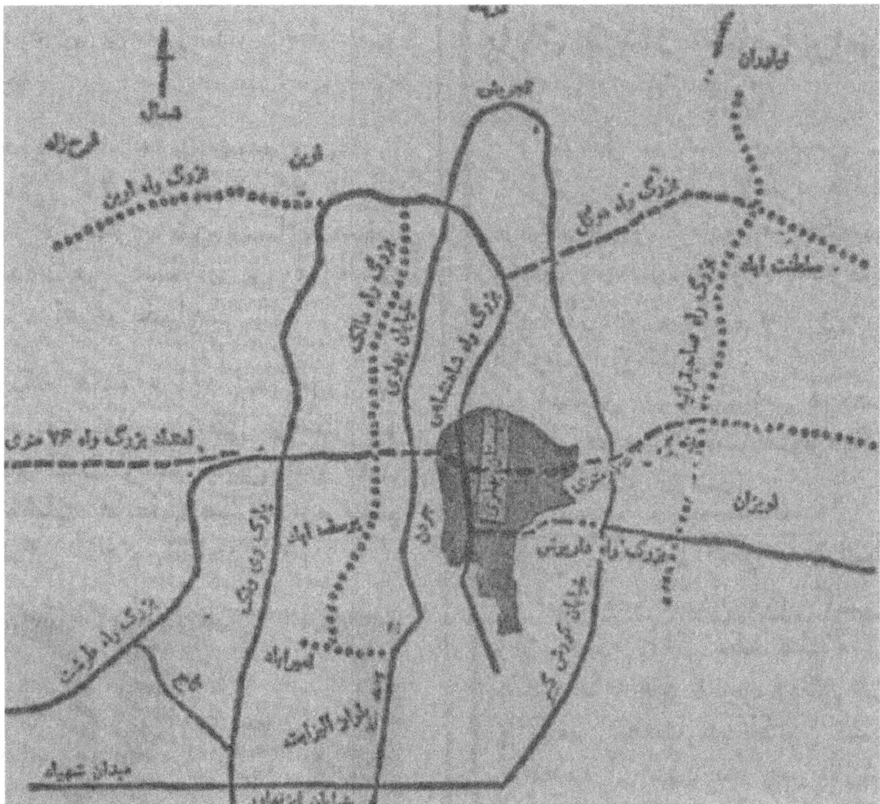

Figure 2. Map showing existing and planned roads in relation to the Shahestān-e Pahlavi. Ettelā'āt, 23 Khordād 1356/ 13 June 1977, 3.

Farah and her circle of advisors, who sought to introduce cultural elements into the design, while the LDI plan represented the "shah's despotic vision of unitary modernism, an ostentatious display of taste, style, and the architectural aesthetics of the White Revolution."[52] Emami argues that the LDI proposal "came at the expense of a more liberal and culturally sensitive modernism, proposed by the Queen and the architects attached to her court."[53] Such a characterization of the Kahn-Tange proposal as a "democratic counter-force to the authoritarian Pahlavi court" is, according to Mozaffari and Westbrook, problematic, not least since it largely ignores the motivations of the architects themselves.[54] In the case of Louis Kahn, the project would have allowed him to integrate the "ideas of ur-

52. Mohajeri 2016, 154.
53. Emami 2014, 71.
54. Mozaffari and Westbrook 2020, 184.

ban institutions" that he had explored in previous projects.[55] For Kenzo Tange, having lost out to LDI in 1974, just four years later, he felt confident that he would again have the opportunity to shape the heart of Shahestān-e Pahlavi. "At last, the master framework of the square will be my work," he said.[56]

TRAFFIC

One important aspect of the Tehran Comprehensive Plan was to address traffic congestion throughout the city, particularly in the center. Articles were printed in newspapers outlining the problems in the city. One read "Traffic in Tehran is not a laboratory animal!", meaning that city planners should seek not merely to try different untested methods in the hope of finding a positive solution, but should instead develop a comprehensive plan.[57] When the new mayor, Javād Shahrestāni, was appointed in 1977, he understood that traffic congestion was "the most pressing issue facing Tehran." The construction of major internal highways was one of the ways in which this issue would be addressed. It was hoped that after construction of east-west and north-south highways running through the capital, "commuting from one point to another point in Tehran will be easy."[58]

In addition to the construction of major roads cutting through the city, the construction of a metro system was considered an essential part of the plan to address traffic congestion. Traffic experts hired by the Tehran municipality expected that if commuters used the metro, this would reduce the current traffic load by up to seventy percent.[59] A journey that would normally take as much as an hour and a half by car, would take just half an hour by metro.[60] The Underground Railway of Tehran and the Suburbs Company (Sherkat-e Rāh Āhan-e Zir Zamini-ye Tehran va Humeh), established in Ābān 1354 (October/November 1975), was granted 120 million tomans for the first year ($16 million), and 7.8 billion tomans over the next seven years ($1.04 billion). By the summer of 1977, geological surveys had been completed, and workers were ready to start to dig the tunnels.[61]

55. Mozaffari and Westbrook 2020, 184.
56. Mozaffari and Westbrook 2020, 184.
57. "Terāfik-e Tehrān, Heyvān-e Āzmāyeshgāhi Nist!" *Ettelā'āt*, 17 Shahrivar 1356/8 September 1977, 5.
58. "Do Bozorgrāh-e Jadid az Shomāl beh Jonub-e Tehrān Sākhteh Mishavad," *Ettelā'āt*, 23 Khordād 1356/13 June 1977, 3.
59. "Hameh Chiz Darbāreh-ye Metro," *Ettelā'āt*, 25 Khordad 1356/15 June 1977, 5.
60. "Hameh Chiz Darbāreh-ye Metro," *Ettelā'āt*, 25 Khordad 1356/15 June 1977, 5.
61. "Istgāh-hā-ye Nokhostin Masir-e Metro Ta'yin Shod," *Ettelā'āt*, 24 Khordād 1356/14 June 1977, 32.

The first five subway stations were planned to be constructed in a north-south direction through the central spine of Shahestān-e Pahlavi, between 700 and 2,000 meters distance from one another, so that pedestrians would have to walk no more than five minutes to get to the closest station.[62] The idea was that after these first stations, the line would be extended to stretch from Tajrish in the north to the south of the city, better connecting the two parts of the city. With this strong focus on developing transport infrastructure, the city project aimed to address the problems of pollution and traffic congestion in Tehran as a whole, but also to connect the new center to other parts of the city. In fact, by the time of the revolution, this first section of the metro line was one of the only parts of the Shahestān on which construction had begun.[63]

Parks and Environmental Policy

On 5 March 1976 (15 Esfand 1354), the shah, along with senior members of the royal family, including Empress Farah, the crown prince, and Princesses Shahnāz, Farahnāz and Leilā, and government and military officials, planted saplings in the Shahestān as part of the commemorations marking the fiftieth anniversary of Pahlavi rule.[64] In this widely publicized event, the minister of agriculture, Mansur Ruhāni, gave a speech in which he commended the ancient Iranian tradition of respecting the environment, evoking examples from Zoroaster and the Achaemenids. Connecting the planting of trees at the Shahestān to broader environmental policy, Ruhāni spoke about the construction of large and small forest parks across the country, and the millions of hectares of desert lands that had been stabilized. Ruhāni declared that: "Fortunately, what the Achaemenians wished, Zoroaster preached, and our forefathers remembered, has been realized in this period of Iran's history."[65]

With the nationalization of forests, pastures, and water resources as part of the White Revolution, the conservation, protection and exploitation of natural resources came under direct government supervision.[66] The work of the Department of the Environment, headed by Eskandar Firuz, helped to convince the shah of the importance of rising to the growing environmental and ecological challenges of the twentieth century. In Ramsar in 1971, Iran had hosted the International Conference on the Conservation of Wildfowl and Wetlands,

---

62. Robertson 1976, 110.

63. The second was the head office of the National Iranian Petroleum Company, which was also unfinished.

64. *Gāhnāmeh-ye Panjāh Sāleh-ye Shāhanshāhi-ye Pahlavi.* 5:2404.

65. "29500 Hektār Derakhtkāri Shod," *Ettela'āt,* 16 Esfand 1354/6 March 1976, 29.

66. Pahlavi 2536/1977, 112.

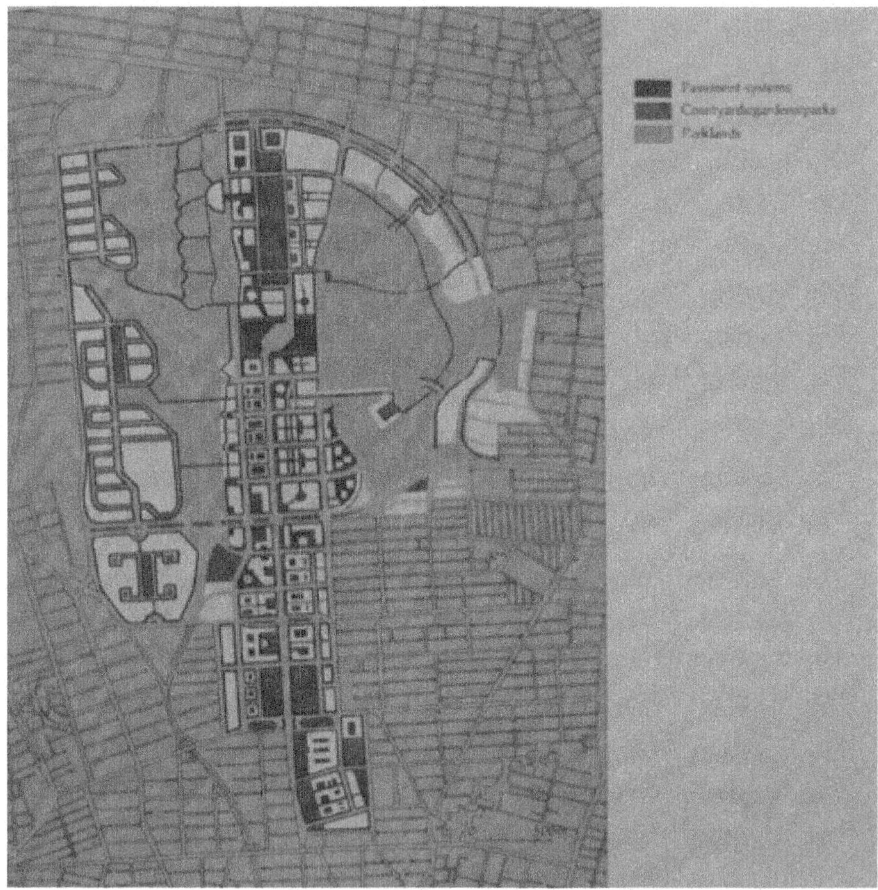

Figure 3.	Open spaces in the Shahestān. Robertson 1976, 59.

which resulted in the ratification of the Ramsar convention by eighteen countries. Opening the conference, the shah, in a speech read by his brother Prince ‘Abdolrezā, pledged to hand over one of its wetland ecosystems to a joint trust with an international agency such as the UN, "to conserve and administer for all of mankind."[67] Extensive plans for restoration, afforestation, and reafforestation were put into place, thousands of green belts were established around big cities, and inside cities themselves, parks were constructed. As well as the importance of this work from an environmental perspective, it also helped to strengthen the image of the shah internationally as an enlightened ruler, dedicated to solving the problems facing the world.

67.	Matthews 1993, 25.

Many parks were constructed in Tehran in the late 1960s and 1970s and they became a dominant feature of Tehran's urban landscape. They included Pārk-e Shāhanshāhi (1966), Farah (1967), Pahlavi (1967), Shafaq (1969), Niyā-varān (1969), and Jamshidiyeh (commissioned 1977). A particularly large park project in Tehran was the Pardisān, a 300-hectare site to the north-west of Tehran, designed to "describe and illuminate the constituent environment of Iran."[68] These green spaces were intended to demonstrate the respect of the Pahlavis toward the environment, but as Hooman Koliji has written, they were also "designed to expand public spaces" and "to convey a more modern image for the prosperous Pahlavi capital." Indeed, he adds, "one can see a distinct desire for showcasing a more contemporary interpretation of Tehran through modernist park design."[69] By the latter half of the 1970s, there were so many parks in the capital that the newspaper *Rastākhiz* proudly reported that it had "5 million square meters of parks."[70]

Parks were also an essential part of the development of Abbas Abad. According to the LDI Master Plan, forty percent of Shahestān-e Pahlavi would be dedicated to open spaces, as opposed to thirty-six percent to buildings. Twenty-two percent, over half of the open spaces, would be major parks.[71] These major parks were Shahestān-e Pahlavi National Park, Shahbanu Park and the Municipality Park. The space allocated to open spaces greatly exceeded that recommended by the Comprehensive Plan and was decided after recommendations by the Shahbanu.[72] According to the Master Plan, "This emphasis on open space will be a unique feature among city centres of the world."

The shah marked the beginning of the construction of Shahestān-e Pahlavi in a ceremony at the site of the Shah and Nation Square of 19 August 1975. Over one thousand guests gathered in Abbas Abad for the occasion, including members of the Imperial Court, cabinet ministers, members of the upper and lower houses, and municipality officials. Conducting the proceedings was the mayor of Tehran, Gholāmrezā Nikpey, who, donned in ceremonial dress, delivered a report and, on behalf of the city of Tehran, officially proclaimed the start of the project.[73] The shah was then invited to place a memorial plaque in the

68. The Mandala Collaborative/Wallace, McHarg, Roberts and Todd 1975, 43. On this project, see John-Alder 2019, 207–36.

69. Koliji 2016, 151.

70. "Tehrān 5 Milyun Metr Morbba' Pārk Dārad," *Rastākhiz*, 29 Farvardin 1355/18 April 1976, 16.

71. Robertson 1976, 77.

72. Robertson 1976, 74.

73. Press Release, Shahanshah breaks ground for new center for Tehran, 19 August 1975, NLAI 264/25073.

foundations of the square. This golden plaque, encased in a special blue cover, was engraved with the fourteen principles of the White Revolution.[74] After installing this memorial plaque, the shah broke ground with a silver headed pick to announce the official start of the project's construction.[75]

However, for all the publicity and fanfare, very little actual work was carried out on the project in the proceeding years; a consequence of budgetary restraints resulting from the downturn in oil revenues, and mismanagement. Bernard Hourcade has argued that, "the haste and indulgence, or even lack of seriousness, of the initial project of the Shahestan meant that it was fragile and lacked credibility. Instead of representing the crowning glory of a policy of development, the project of the Shahestan Pahlavi quickly became a caricature-like symbol of the abuses and controversial characters of the imperial regime."[76] It is true that like other grand projects of the late Pahlavi period, the Shahestān demonstrated the ubiquitous clash between the ambition and haste of the shah on the one hand, and the economic and organizational realities of the day on the other. But it should also be noted that the project was in its infancy when the revolution cut it short. In the weeks leading up to the Imperial Celebrations in 1971, Asadollāh 'Alam had been horrified to discover that construction on two of the hotels that were supposed to house guests had not yet been completed. However, by the time of the Celebrations they were ready.[77] If the goal was to have completed the central part of the Shahestān in time for the Olympic Games in 1984 – as was explicitly set out in the LDI report – then it is likely the project would have accelerated in the early 1980s.

Three and a half years after the shah had inaugurated the construction of the Shahestān project, he fled Iran to live out the rest of his life in exile, his dream of a Great Civilization dead, and his major urban project barely even begun. Writing in the early 1990s, Hourcade observed that "the concrete structures of the metro stations, isolated and out of place in the dry hills of Abbas Abad, bear a sad witness to one of the most visible failures of the imperial regime."[78] But two decades later, the picture is slightly different, and although the extensive development of the whole of Abbas Abad has not been carried out, several aspects of the LDI plan can be seen in the modern city. For example, the report mentioned the possible construction of a "communications tower" which would "give a graceful and exciting vertical accent to the carefully controlled

74. "Jādeh-ye Sevvom Goshāyesh Yāft," *Ettelā'āt*, 29 Mordad 1354/20 August 1975, 4.
75. Shahanshah breaks ground, NLAI 264/25073.
76. Hourcade 1992, 219.
77. Steele 2021, 38–39.
78. Hourcade 1992, 220.

height of the central spine; it would also serve as an easily visible identifying feature of the new city." With a viewing platform and revolving restaurant, the tower could become "a great attraction for visitors – judging from the success of similar examples in London, Liverpool, Toronto and Düsseldorf."[79] Such a tower was finally realized in the year 2000 with the construction of the Borj-e Milād, which was built not on the Abbas Abad site, but to the northwest, by the modern Pardisān Park. The height of the Milād tower is 435 meters, much higher than the 150 meters set out in the Shahestān plan, but the purpose was the same; to create an "identifying feature" for the city.

Several parks have also been built in Abbas Abad, roughly as set out in the LDI plan. For example, in the LDI plan, two parks would flank Shahanshahi (now Modares) highway as it passed through the area, bearing a striking resemblance to the current scheme, with Pārk-e Āb o Ātash on the west and Park-e Tāleghāni on the east of the highway. The modern Park-e Behesht-e Mādarān has been built on the site that would have been Shahestān-e Pahlavi National Park, on the east side of the Shahestān site. One of the main buildings of today's Abbas Abad district is the National Library of Iran, the ultimate manifestation of the Pahlavi National Library Project. Indeed, many former Pahlavi National Library staff members were involved in the later project and many of the ideas set out by the project's consultants were implemented. As one of the founders of the new National Library wrote in a letter to consultant Jean-Pierre Clavel, "everything we wanted to write about a 'should be' national library we referred to the previous reports made by you and other colleagues."[80]

Shahestān-e Pahlavi was intended to be an expression of Iran's development and modernity. It was to have modern transport infrastructure, with direct links to the new international airport, which was to be constructed outside of the city,[81] parks, cultural buildings, government headquarters, high-rise office buildings, and hotels. It was not just one grand project, it was multiple grand projects occurring at the same time. But Iran's new city center, though modern, would have its own character and those involved in the various building projects were committed to ensuring that building designs reflected Iran's rich cultural identity. With the expectation that the Olympic Games would be coming to Iran in 1984, the Shahestān would demonstrate to the world Iran's arrival as an advanced, affluent, and modern nation; the Japan of the Middle East.

79. Robertson 1976, 114.
80. Undated addressed to Jean-Pierre Clavel, in author's possession.
81. This was finally opened as Imam Khomeini International Airport in 2004. On the Pahlavi-era plan, see Prokosch 1977, 223–41; and Beny 1978, 345.

Works Cited

Afkhami, Gholam Reza. *The Life and Times of the Shah*. Berkeley: University of California Press.

Ansari, Ali. 2012. *The Politics of Nationalism in Modern Iran*. Cambridge: Cambridge University Press.

———. 2019. *Modern Iran since 1797: Reform and Revolution*. London: Routledge.

Bahrambeygui, H. 1972. "Tehran: An Urban Analysis." PhD thesis, Durham University. Available at Durham E-Theses Online: http://etheses.dur.ac.uk/10398/.

Bazm-e Ahriman: Jashnhā-ye 2500 Sāleh-ye Shāhanshāhi beh Revāyat-e Asnād-e Sāvāk va Darbār. 1377/1998. N.A. Tehran: Markaz-e Barresi-ye Asnād-e Tārikhi-ye Vezārat-e Ettelāʿāt.

Bazyar, Marziyeh and Robert Steele. 2023. "The Shah's House Became the People's House": Narrating Iran's Modern History at the Pahlavi Dynasty Museum." *Iranian Studies* 56:497–521.

Beny, Roloff. 1978. *Iran: Elements of Destiny*. Toronto: McClelland and Stewart Limited.

Chehabi, Houchang and Juan J. Linz. 1998. "A Theory of Sultanism 1: A Type of Nondemocratic Rule." In *Sultanistic Regimes*, edited by H. E. Chehabi and Juan J. Linz, 3–25. Baltimore: The John Hopkins University Press.

Chehabi, Houchang. 2002. "A Political History of Football in Iran." *Iranian Studies* 35:371–402.

Clavel, Jean-Pierre. 1979. "Pahlavi National Library." In *Vom Bauen Neuerer Bibliotheken: Erinnerungen, Erfahrungen, Planungen*, edited by Rolf Fuhlrott. Wiesbaden: Reichert Verlag.

Costello, V. F. 1981. "Tehran." In *Problems and Planning in Third World Cities*, edited by Michael Pacione, 156–86. London: Croom Helm.

Daftary, Farhad. 1988. "Barnamā-Rīzī." *EIr.* III, 809–14.

Emami, Farshid. 2014. "Urbanism of Grandiosity: Planning a New Urban Centre for Tehran (1973–76)." *International Journal of Islamic Architecture*, 3:69–102.

Gāhnāmeh-ye Panjāh Sāleh-ye Shāhanshāhi-ye Pahlavi. 1985. 5 Volumes. Paris: Soheil Publishers.

Grigor, Talinn. 2016. "Tehran: A Revolution in the Making." In *Political Landscapes of Capital Cities*, edited by Jessica Joyce Christie, Jelena Bogdanović and Eulogio Guzmán, 347–76. Boulder, CO: University Press of Colorado.

Hourcade, Bernard. 1992. "Urbanisme et Crise Urbaine Sous Mohammad-Reza Pahlav." In *Téhéran capitale bicentenaire*, edited by Chahryar Adle and Bernard Hourcade. Paris: Institut français de recherche en Iran.

Huebner, Stefan. 2016. *Pan-Asian Sports and the Emergence of Modern Asia, 1913–1974*. Singapore: NUS Press.

John-Alder, Kathleen. 2019. "Paradise by Design: Pardisan Park in Tehran." In *Architectural Dynamics in Pre-Revolutionary Iran: Dialogic Encounters between Tradition and Modernity*, edited by Mohammad Gharipour, 207–36. Bristol: Intellect.

Koliji, Hooman. 2016. "Aspiring Masonry: Designing Thinking and Experimental Vernacularism in Ferdowsi Garden." In *Contemporary Urban Landscapes of the Middle East*, ed. Mohammad Gharipour, 149–70. London: Routledge.

Machiavelli, Niccolò. 2008. *The Prince*. London: Arcturus Publishing Limited.

Mandala Collaborative/Wallace, McHarg, Roberts and Todd. 1975. *Pardisan: Plan for an Environmental Park in Tehran*. Philadelphia: Winchell Press.

Mashayekhi, Azadeh. "The 1968 Tehran Master Plan and the Politics of Planning Development in Iran (1945–1979)." *Planning Perspectives* 34:849–76.

Matthews, G. V. T. 1993. *The Ramsar Convention on Wetlands: Its History and Development*. Gland: Ramsar Convention Bureau.

Mohajeri, Shima. 2016. "The Shahestan Blueprint: The Vestigial Site of Modernity in Iran." In *The Historiography of Persian Architecture*, edited by Mohammad Gharipour, 147–172. Abingdon, Oxon: Routledge.

Mozaffari, Ali and Nigel Westbrook. 2020. *Development, Architecture, and the Formation of Heritage in Late Twentieth-Century Iran: A Vital* Past. Manchester: University of Manchester Press.

Nikpey, Gholām Rezā. 1352/1973. *Panjāh Sāl dar Kākh-e Marmar: Tajdid-e Hayāt-e Irān*. Tehran: Sherkat-e Ofset.

Pahlavi, Mohammad Reza. 1960. *Mission for My Country*. London: Hutchinson.

———. 1967. *Enqelāb-e Sefid*. Tehran: Ketābkhāneh-ye Pahlavi.

———. 2536/1977. *Beh Su-ye Tamaddon-e Bozorg*. Tehran: Ketābkhāneh-ye Pahlavi.

Prokosch, Walther. 1977. "Tehran International Airport." *Transportation Engineering Journal* 103:223–241.

Rahimi, Babak. 2012. *Theater State and the Formation of Early Modern Public Sphere in Iran: Studies on Safavid Muharram Rituals, 1590–1641 CE*. Leiden: Brill.

Robertson, Jaquelin T. 1976. *Shahestan Pahlavi: A New City Centre for Tehran, Book 1: The Master Plan*. London: Llewelyn-Davies International.

Shakibi, Zhand. 2020. *Pahlavi Iran and the Politics of Occidentalism: The Shah and the Rastakhiz Party*. London: I.B. Tauris.

Shafā, Shojāʿeddin. 2013. "Shojāʿeddin Shafā az Zabān-e Khodash." In *Yādnāmeh-ye Shojāʿeddin Shafā*, edited by Claudine Shafa. Paris.

Steele, Robert. 2019. "The Pahlavi National Library Project: Education and Modernization in Late Pahlavi Iran." *Iranian Studies* 52:85–110.

———. 2021. *The Shah's Imperial Celebrations of 1971: Nationalism, Culture and Politics in Late Pahlavi Iran*. London: I.B. Tauris.

Zonis, Marvin. 1991. *Majestic Failure: The Fall of the Shah*. Chicago: University of Chicago Press.

Reading Shariati in South Africa

Shamil Jeppie

"Today Iran, tomorrow Palestine. Today Iran, tomorrow South Africa"
chant by South African Muslim students

ONE OF THE BY-PRODUCTS of the Iranian revolution of 1978–79 was the importation into South Africa of a new body of religious and political ideas in the immediate aftermath of the revolution. South Africa, a country so distant from the Middle East, seems to be an unlikely candidate to which to export Islamic revolution. It had a small Muslim community, and not a Shi'ite one, and at the outbreak of the revolution apartheid South Africa and the shah's Iran were allies.[1] Indeed, for a while after the revolution the senior officials in the Iranian diplomatic mission in Pretoria remained at their posts as functionaries of the new regime. One assumes that they would not have been too keen to "export" revolution. However, the spirit, artefacts, and influence of Iran's revolution did make a mark in Africa's southernmost country – very soon after the revolution. The Middle Eastern revolution and the unfolding anti-apartheid struggle in southern Africa would intersect and intermingle in curious ways. But this encounter happened very much on the margins of the larger narrative of late twentieth-century South African political history.

The early- to mid-1980s would see the steady inflow of posters and postcards bearing images of Iranian revolutionary icons; video and audio cassettes of revolutionary songs and slogans, mostly in Farsi, landed in the country; large numbers of short tracts and some larger texts on aspects of the revolution and its progress were sent, and anti-American slogans, and the thought of leading intellectuals of the revolution all came into the country. Among the images and works and wisdom that arrived were those of Ayatollah Khomeini and Ali Shariati. Khomeini's speeches were available, partly through *Kayhan* – the Iranian national daily that at times somehow circulated informally in South Africa – and his work translated under the title "Islam and Revolution" was on sale. But Khomeini had less of an impact than Shariati among readers. Khomeini's stern bearded face and majestic wave to crowds were pinned-up on many walls. Fewer posters of the beardless Shariati were available. Khomeini's distinct image was

---

1. This is explored in detail in Chehabi 2016.

popular and his aphorisms may have been repeated but he was hardly read. Ayatollah Mutahhari's name and translated work was also known but also not digested, it would appear. Instead, it was the teacher from Mashhad, Ali Shariati, whose work appears to have been most widely known, and still manages to find a readership. In this paper I want to look briefly at the reception of Shariati's work in South Africa.

Contexts

If the unfolding dissent and opposition to the shah in Iran through the late 1960s and into the 1970s is necessary background to understanding Shariati[2] then looking at South Africa between the late 1970s and into the 1980s is necessary to understand why Shariati could have an enthusiastic audience there. During the countrywide uprisings that would be captured in the expression "Soweto 1976" a new breed of young people were prepared for the struggle against the apartheid state. It is from this generation of students and those involved in the new round of student protests in 1980 and 1981 that potential readers of Shariati came. In the latter round of school and university boycotts "Shariati" had just arrived in the country. From then on, through the early part of the 1980s there was an increasing flow of Iranian literature. The incipient political crisis in South Africa and the inflow of products of the revolution in Iran coincided.

Workers, civic associations, youth movements, and a whole host of other groups contributed to the struggle against apartheid. Numerous points of contention against the apartheid state moved "the struggle" forward. Student and youth uprisings over educational issues, and in support of other battles against the state, were of great significance in questioning the legitimacy of the government. It was through this layer of struggle, education, that the Iranian revolution connected with what was seen as the South African revolution-in-progress.

But the reception of Shariati was among a small minority in the South African student and youth population. The religious demography of the country has the Muslim population as between one and two percent of the entire population. Muslim students and youth were thus a minority group. They were also not, in most cases, identified as Muslim students, but by an ethnic term, as colored or Indian (there was a negligible number of Black Muslim students). But "Muslim" as a first or preferred marker of identification was becoming more and more prominent. It went together with the disavowal of what was interpreted as

---

2. Abrahamian 1982; Dabashi 1993.

apartheid labels such as "colored." It also came at the tail end of the Black Consciousness movement's rise and reassertion of black African identity as a radical statement of opposition against state policies and white racism.

But the minority position of Muslims is not evenly spread through the country, In certain places there is a greater concentration of Muslims than in other areas. The suburbs of Cape Town, the Indian Ocean port city of Durban, and parts of Johannesburg have denser concentrations of Muslims. Furthermore, Islam has a very long history in the western Cape, beginning with the birth of the colonial state in the mid-seventeenth century. Muslim youth and students in these urban areas were much more likely to see an image or hear a name from the Iranian revolution. They were also more likely to chant slogans (such as the one at the start of this paper) or attempt a song from the revolution (original in Persian but translated into English or Arabic).

With the expansion of the number of Indian and colored students (using apartheid racial classification in place at the time) at universities and colleges in the 1960s there was also a growing number of Muslim students from small towns in rural South Africa who studied in the bigger cities – Johannesburg, Durban, Cape Town (but also Rhodes University in Grahamstown in the rural eastern Cape). These were mainly children of Indian traders who had long settled in the small country towns. These students took back to their small towns the Islamic or secular radical rhetoric from the campuses. Those involved with, or even on the margin of, the Muslim student associations present at the larger campuses would be the most likely consumers of these new discourses.

Mobilizing for Islamic Change

The conduit for the proliferation of Iranian: revolutionary icons, images, and texts was the student and youth associations among Muslims that had grown increasingly activist from about the time of the Iranian revolution but not as a consequence of it.[3] The two most prominent were the Muslim Students' Association and the Muslim Youth Movement of South Africa. The former was by 1981 in the process of being "taken over" ideologically by the latter. It is also the Muslim Youth Movement (MYM) that had the resources, finances, and networks that could effectively transmit literature or videocassettes throughout much of the country. The MYM was, at the time, constituting itself very broadly in the mold of the Muslim Brotherhood of Egypt. Its leadership was in contact with former or ex-Brotherhood members who left their countries in

3. Tayob 1995.

the 1960s, as strongly anti-Brotherhood regimes were installed, and had settled in the West or a sympathetic Saudi Arabia. These men were, of course, all Arab Sunni Muslims.

But one or two South Africans also had some contact with Ibrahim Yazdi, the well-known Iranian liberal Muslim leader.[4] The events in Iran around 1979 were initially mediated to the MYM leadership through the interpretations of their "Brotherhood" contacts and people like Yazdi. But another grouping, which had then recently been established in Cape Town and known as *Qibla* (as in the direction of Mecca), promoted the Iranian revolution much more than the MYM. Qibla was founded in 1979 and rode on the wave of revolutionary zeal unleashed by the Iranian revolution. Yet, it remained at best a Cape movement devoted to revolutionary change in South Africa and addressing national issues and not simply repeating the language of the Iranian revolution. The MYM's enthusiasm for events in Iran was tempered by its Arab Sunni supporters and sources of information. The World Assembly of Muslim Youth (WAMY) based in Riyadh, Saudi Arabia, was one such source. So even while the revolution was promoted there was some skepticism because of what was seen as its radical Shiite character. The *'ulamā'* in the country were also almost universally suspicious of the revolution. They warned of its Shiite credentials and have persisted in warning against the "dangers" of Shiite propaganda amongst the youth. This attitude on the part of "establishment" Islam led by a clergy mostly suspicious of Shi'ism affected the way a group such as the MYM related to the revolution at a public level. But while there was some hesitation on the part of some of the leadership there was a different reception among the middle order membership and lower down. However, activities in support of the revolution were organized on a regional basis. In December 1979 a rally was held in Johannesburg in support of the revolution. Subsequently, there was a video and panel discussion road show through the country. The organization's monthly mouthpiece, *al-Qalam,* also covered the revolution and its aftermath.[5]

What Is To Be Read?

The MYM was committed to developing a literate membership. Reading was not a regular habit or zealous pursuit of even the educated section of the Muslim community. Even university students and graduates· were largely readers of only of their prescribed course material. And the idea of a body of "Islamic books" to collect and read was for the most part a novelty. Bookshops hardly

4. Chehabi 1990.
5. Tayob 1995, 148.

sold anything appealing and there a bookshop dedicated to "Islamic books" was hard to find. The MYM's purpose was not to produce voracious readers of just anything, even anything "Islamic." A generation of highly cultivated Muslim renaissance men was not their object. There was a very specific corpus of works that they hoped to have their members and, hopefully, the general public read. They focused on producing intensive readers of a limited number of prescribed texts. Members had to belong to study circles and read a range of preselected articles in addition to the study of sections of the Quran and the practice of the Prophet Muhammad, starting with a famous collection of "40 Hadith."

In addition to this, for the advanced or senior membership a training manual was published – *Islamic Training Programme Manual* – with an extensive set of articles on Islam as religion and ideology and its relation to other religions and ideologies, (a first edition of 300 copies was issued in 1978 and a completely revised edition was printed in 1981. This had a print run of 1000. The larger print run for the second edition reflects the actual expansion of the movement between 1978 and 1981.

"Ideology" was a term of some fascination at the time. Islam was said to be an "ideology" more than a mere religion. It was also said to be a "complete way of life" and "world view," not a "religion." The training manual therefore set out to show the way to "Islam as ideology." But it also had pieces on practical skills. These skills entailed advice on how to prepare a speech, how to manage one's time, even how to deliver the sermon for the Friday prayer and so on. Senior members were supposed to be skilled in numerous spheres of activity. And since the belief was that there is no clergy in Islam members should therefore also be prepared to deliver sermons to congregations on Fridays, an activity usually performed by trained Imams.

It is the intellectual content of the training manual that interests us. The orientation to the Muslim Brotherhood's strategy of Islamic reform is clear in this manual. Extracts from the writings of leading Brotherhood figures such as Sayyid Qutb, Hasan al-Banna, and Said Ramadan are well represented. Contemporary adherents of the Brotherhood are also given space. There is no Ali Shariati or any other Iranian Islamic intellectual in either the first or second editions of the manual. The second edition, however, does have an article on the Iranian revolution. It is the transcript of a talk delivered by a Muhammad Iqbal to the Imperial College of London Islamic society in January 1980. He mentions Shariati, in passing, alongside Ayatollahs Taleghani and Mutahhari, and Mehdi Bazargan.

Shariati therefore did not circulate through the most significant of MYM vehicles – its training program manual. His work was not part of the "official" or prescribed reading material for the study circles. However, the recently opened MYM bookstore and later its branches under the name International Book Service promoted his writings. The organization's press, Impress, printed at least one collection of his writings (*Thoughts of a Concerned Muslim*). The works, sold at MYM bookstalls, came from expatriate Iranian publishers and sympathizers of the revolution in places such as Houston, Texas, and Berkeley, California. With a rand-dollar exchange rate still very stable the cost of a Shariati paperback was within reach of every middle-class Muslim student.

The MYM and MSA's members were keener readers of Sayyid Qutb. His popular work, *Milestones,* and commentary on the Quran, *In the Shade of the Quran,* an English translation of the last section, were immensely popular (published in English in 1978 and 1981, respectively). The former came in copyright editions and distributed through MYM outlets and in cheaper pirated Pakistani versions sold at spice stores. Qutb's works were overall genuinely read "from cover to cover" and widely discussed, passages may even have been memorized. But it was hardly critically read. *Milestones* was consumed as a primer in Islamic personal and social transformation. Reading Qutb did not lead to further exploration, this was not the purpose of his work, it led to deeper devotion to Islam as "way of life" and as *the* "movement" of social transformation. But from about late 1986, there was a realization that more modest objectives should be set than what Qutb was advocating. But Qutb's mighty influence was the foundation on which the MYM rested intellectually in the late 1970s and into the mid-1980s.

The appearance of Shariati's writings never completely displaced Qutb's status or influence. Rather, Shariati offered something else. Those who were eager to see the South African situation more adequately addressed by the leadership of the "Islamic movement" in South Africa were particularly keen on Shariati, as were numerous Muslims in leadership positions in such populist organizations as the United Democratic Front (est. 1983).

Qutb articulates in his *Milestones* a highly Manichean view of the world. There is a battle between *jahiliyyah* and Islam. *Jahiliyyah* stands for ignorance and barbarism and in modern times this is expressed in both capitalist and socialist systems. A return to the "undiluted" Islam of the first generation of Muslims is the only solution to the crisis of Muslim societies and, indeed, of the world. He pays scant attention in *Milestones* to the dynamics of Western history or any redeeming features in its civilization. It is essentially all barbarism. Muslims must choose Islam or barbarism. This work has been called the "what is to be done?" of the Islamic movement.[6]

6. Kepel 1995.

This is a very brief summary of Qutb's most popular and influential work. It served to give a strong sense of "pure" Islamic identity to its readers, who were becoming committed members of the "Islamic movement." Shariati produced no equivalent charter for personal and collective transformation. None of Shariati's texts, at least those read in English translation in South Africa, could compare with Qutb's *Milestones.* Yet, Shariati had a huge impact among the same constituency that read Qutb.

ISLAM FOR THE TIMES

What in Shariati's oeuvre made his ideas so attractive to upwardly mobile young men and women in South Africa? It is perhaps not hard to see why university students, and a handful of high school students, would be attracted to Shariati's writings. After all, this was his constituency in Mashhad and Teheran. South African education was in turmoil and students were reading all sorts of pamphlets and tracts as a means to define their situation and how to push the movement against apartheid forward. They were not looking for coherence or consistency in a body of work; they were not looking for elegance in composition; they were not looking for learned treatises that would bore them. "The old is dying, the new is not yet born," a famous line of Antonio Gramsci, who was immensely popular among student and other activist theorists, gives expression to that interstitial moment of the 1980s. Fragments of full philosophies, strategic lessons from other struggles, ideas for action speaking to the crisis of the moment were what they wanted. There were many elements in Shariati's thought that could be used to define their situation. It is not necessary here to either give an overview of Shariati's role in the Iranian revolution or the content of his thought in that context.[7] How was Shariati seen by young South African Muslim readers?

It was clearly the case that Shariati's explicit attack on the ruling class in his work appealed to his South African readers. His analysis of power relations resonated with their experience in their own country. That he undertook such an analysis rooted in Islamic sources and imagery made him very attractive to Muslim students living through the dominance of the secular left on South African campuses where they found themselves. They could now more comfortably counter the hegemonic structuralist Marxism of white leftwing professors and their adepts, armed with a Shariatian view of Islam. Or they could adopt that Marxism but as conscious Muslims ready to defend a mixing of Marxism and Islam. It was not uncommon for the Islamic youth groups to have members who were both devout Muslims and very knowledgeable Marxist analysts of the

7. Dabashi 1993; Irfani 1981.

South African situation. Some of the pamphlets issued during the 1985 school boycotts reflect some of this blending of Marxism and Islam. Shariati's meandering through Western social theory and Islamic learning against Western materialism and materialist analysis was attractive. By adopting his work many of them felt less intimidated by materialist analytical tools that seemed to explain South African reality quite neatly.

The key concept in Shariati's work is the struggle between *Tawhid* or Islamic monotheism and *shirk* or polytheism. To Shariati the Oneness of God at a metaphysical level is the abstract model for the oneness of creation, of the world, and ultimately of society. Distinctions of class, status, race, and sex are therefore anathema to *tawhid* and therefore un- and anti-Islamic. The genuine Islamic struggle is to build a *tawhidi* society, which would be a classless society. Every other form of social organization is ultimately founded on *shirk,* in other words it compromises the values of God's oneness. Shariati takes a theological term and philosophical concept that had traditionally been taught, as he remarks, either to little children or debated in philosophico-theological circles.

He resuscitates this vital concept and turns it into the foundation of his sociology. *Tawhid* is a complete worldview (*jahān-bini*), for Shariati. It could be claimed that he turned a theological term into an "ideological weapon." When MYM members encountered his concept of *tawhid* they were also similarly engaged in reviving the notion of *tawhid* as more than a mere statement of Islamic monotheism. However, they did not push its implications as far as Shariati did. In him they found a completely radicalized interpretation, and one that was very relevant to the situation and struggle in South Africa.

From this radical *tawhid*ist foundation all the rest of human history, and Islamic history, can be explained. *Tawhid* is one part of a dialectical relation with *shirk* its other. All of history is a conflict between representatives – coming in the form of individuals or empires – of each of these "worldviews." Shariati digs deep into the founding images and issues in the Quran and early Islamic history for metaphors and supports for his argument. Even where there is very little documentation or "evidence" in the Quran or Islamic sources Shariati takes what little there is to make it work imaginatively for his project. Thus, the engine of history is epitomized in the struggle between Cain and Abel. They are not mentioned by name in the Quran but in later commentaries, yet Shariati employs this narrative to illustrate the workings of his historical sociology. They represent a clash of moralities, a conflict between two different modes of production and, ultimately for Shariati, the battle between the downtrodden (*mustazaffin*) and the bourgeoisie. The one stands for ownership and priesthood, the other for Allah and the people. Shariati's handling of this theme was particularly popular with the many politically active Muslim youth who read his work. The Quranic word for oppressed and downtrodden – *mustazaffin* – became widely used to describe the situation of the vast majority of South Africans. The South African situation was a local expression of that cosmic battle between Cain and Abel, the struggle of *tawhid* against *shirk*. The religions of the oppressed were irrelevant for they were the oppressed.

In Islamic history, the Prophet Muhammad is, of course, the model of good conduct and a revered figure and this is no different for Shariati. But while he always notes the important example of Muhammad he does not begin and end with him. His other heroes largely are those highly regarded in the Shi'ite tradition such as Ali, Muhammad's son-in-law and fourth caliph after the prophet's demise. Ali was married to Fatima, Muhammad's daughter. She is the subject of a work by Shariati in which he deals with her as the model of sacrifice and womanhood. Among women activists in the Muslim youth groups this was widely read. He also gives Abu Dharr, a companion of the Prophet, a major place in his pantheon, as a proto-socialist. Abu Dharr's name would become popular as a symbol of struggle against wealth and consumption; his name was invoked as a model of how Muslims should choose the side of the oppressed in the fight against capitalism in our own age and in South Africa.

Islamic rituals are also explained with reference to the *tawhid-shirk* binary opposition. In *Hajj*, also reissued in South Africa as *Hajj and Freedom*, he elaborates on the symbolism of Oneness and reinterprets the rituals of the pilgrimage in terms of the conflict between the powerful and the powerless. He says in the preface that *tawhid, jihād*, and *hajj* are the "most important pillars of the Islamic doctrine" making Muslims "conscious, free, honorable and socially responsible." As with the concept of *tawhid* here Shariati takes something out of its conventional context and completely revolutionizes it. In South Africa the pilgrimage to Mecca is an Islamic ritual obligation for which there is great enthusiasm with thousands undertaking the pilgrimage annually. It is undertaken for various reasons but certainly not explicitly political ones. (In 1982 there was an attempt by Iran to "politicize" the *hajj* by organizing demonstrations during the *hajj* season in Mecca. The MYM was invited to send "volunteers," with costs covered by the Iranian interest section in Pretoria, but they did not send anyone.) Shariati's book, however, has proven to be very popular among potential *hajjis*. It is still in use. While these potential *hajjis* go to classes to learn the rituals or read standard manuals to get the "meaning" of the event, Shariati's text remains a unique point of reference. This is indeed what he intended with this work: it was not a manual of ritual but an explication of the "meaning" of the event.

Conclusion

In the 1985 number of the *Journal for Islamic Studies,* then published by the Rand Afrikaans University (renamed the University of Johannesburg), there appeared an article by C. du P. Le Roux on Ali Shariati, which concluded with a section on "Shariati se denke en suid- Afrika" (Shariati's thought and South Africa). The author asks whether Shariati's "explosive mixture" of dialectics, Islam, and social justice can have a role in the fluid political situation in the country.

He adds that the younger generation of South African Muslims are well-versed in the writing of Shariati and see the status quo as a form of *shirk.* Collaboration with the status quo cannot be expected from them. He does not mention it but the piece was written around the time of the mobilization against the tri-camera system of government that was wholly rejected by the youth groups. It was also the time of a sustained Muslim presence in street battles against the police and in funeral marches of victims of police shootings on the Cape Flats.[8] While the Muslim youth reject collaboration, militant confrontation, based on a Shariati inspired reading of Islam – a replay of Iran in 1978–79, is not on the agenda, explains Le Roux. However, a handful of activist Muslims did leave the country to undertake military training, but none to Iran.

This article by an academic at an Afrikaans language university, who was far removed from where Shariati was read, is perhaps a reflection of the presence of Shariati in South Africa. It was not hard for Le Roux to pick up on a bold trend among local Muslim activists. Shariati's readers were more interested in material for their cause, against apartheid, and against the *'ulamā'.* The *'ulamā'* were more concerned about doctrinal purity than the evils of apartheid; more concerned with the spread of the "deviant" teachings of Shiism than the potential for revolution presented by some of its modern thinkers. Indeed, Shiism did find adherents in South Africa from this period onwards. But it was then, and remains, a negligible sect.

It is still unclear whether reading Shariati would have been a way into an acceptance of Shiism. Reading him in South Africa in the 1980s is hardly a conventional way into the details of the religious world of Shiism. His readers were not interested in the merits of Shiism over Sunnism or his thought for pursuing academic and theological discussions. Instead, various fragments were used for their own political purposes, which in any case was not at odds with Shariati's own purpose. As Hamid Dabashi writes, "Shariati wished to change, not interpret; lead, not argue; move, not convince; achieve, not rationalize."[9]

8. Jeppie 1990.
9. Dabashi 1993, 104.

Works Cited

Abrahamian, Ervand. 1983. *Iran Between Two Revolutions.* Princeton: Princeton University Press.

Chehabi, Houchang E. 1990. *Iranian Politics and Religious Modernism.* Ithaca NY: Cornell University Press.

———. 2016. "South Africa and Iran in the Apartheid Era." *Journal of Southern African Studies* 42:687–709.

Dabashi, Hamid. 1993. *Theology of Discontent.* New York: New York University Press.

Enayat, Hamid. 1982. *Modern Islamic Political Thought.* London: Macmillan.

Irfani, Shoroush. 1983. *Revolutionary Islam in Iran.* London: Zed Press.

Islamic Training Manual, revised edition. 1981. Durban: MYMSA.

Jeppie, Shamil. 1991. "Amandla and Allahu akbar: Muslims and Resistance in South Africa c. 1970 – 1987." *Journal for the Study of Religion* 4:3–19.

Kepel, Gilles. 1995. *The Revenge of God: The Resurgence of Islam, Christianity and Judaism in the Modern World.* University Park, PA: Pennsylvania State University Press.

Le Roux, C. du P. 1985. "Ali Shariati – teorie en praxis." *Journal for Islamic Studies* 5:77–86.

Meer, Fatima. 1985. *Towards Understanding Iran Today.* Durban: Institute of Black Research.

Shariati, Ali. 1978. *Hajj.* Second edition. Houston, TX: FILINC.

———. 1979. *On the Sociology of Islam.* Berkeley: Mizan Press.

———. 1980. *Culture and Ideology.* Houston, TX: FILINC.

———. 1980. *From Where Shall We Begin* and *The Machine in the Captivity of the Mechanism: Lectures by Ali Shariati.* Houston, TX: FILINC.

———. 1980. *Marxism and Other Western Fallacies: An Islamic Critique,* translated by Roy Campbell. Berkeley: Mizan Press 1980.

———. N.d. *Thoughts of a Concerned Muslim.* N.p.: Muslim Youth Movement of South Africa.

Tayob, Abdulkader. 1995. *Islamic Resurgence in South Africa: The Muslim Youth Movement.* Cape Town: University of Cape Town Press.

Democratic Confederalism and Iran's Undemocratic Nation-State

Afshin Matin-asgari

> "What shall we do to be saved? In politics, establish a constitutional cooperative system of world government."
>
> *World historian Arnold J. Toynbee*
> *in the aftermath of the Second World War[1]*

WHILE THE NATION-STATE CONTINUES TO BE the world's prevalent form of political organization, it is also the main site of global hierarchies of exploitation, discrimination, and war, conflicts threatening humanity's annihilation and the destruction of our planet's biosphere. Considering alternatives to the nation-state, this chapter will look into the historical trajectory and existing forms of federal/confederal governance, concluding with reflections on their applicability to the Middle East and particularly Iran. The chapter's premise is that our current global configuration of sovereign nation-states is in deep crisis, as we see increasing conflict among states and growing tension and repression within most. These trends have escalated with the rise of authoritarian nationalism in Europe, the United States, Russia, China, India, Brazil, Israel, Turkey, and Iran. The global immigration crisis also shows how nation-states fail to provide security and livelihood to their citizens or absorb economic and political refugees.

Considering alternatives to the nation-state, we must note that federal and confederal forms of governance have a long history and are already integral to the global order. Federalism divides political authority between central, provincial, and local governments, with the central, or federal government ultimately prevailing. Confederalism is a union of sovereign states, joined together as equal partners and having the right to leave the union. The most familiar example of federal government is the United States of America, while the European Union is the outstanding example of confederalism. In the case of the United States, member states cannot leave the union, an option that is possible in the Euro-

---

1. Arnold Toynbee, in a 1947 *New York Times* article, quoted in William H. McNeill 1989, 223.

pean Union, as in the recent case of the United Kingdom (Brexit). In practice, federalism and confederalism often overlap, due to the inevitable shifting balance of economic and political power within both. For example, due to its size and economic power, California has an exceptional place within the American federal government, as Germany and France do in the European Union.[2]

Modern federal and confederal governance has historical precursors in various kingdoms, empires, and tribal confederations of Eurasia, Africa, and the Americas. Ibn Khaldun's theory of sedentary empires originating in nomadic tribal confederations shows the recurrence of such patterns of governance in world history. More concretely, we find the *moluk al-tawā'if* (pattern of fragmented and overlapping sovereignties) among Eurasian kingdoms/fiefdoms from medieval Spain to nineteenth-century Iran.[3] In early modern Europe, fragmented sovereignties gradually gave rise to centralized Ottoman, French, and Spanish monarchies. British, French, Spanish, and Portuguese monarchies then became core regions of overseas empires imposing multi-level governance, as did the Aztec, Maya, and Mughal empires they incorporated.[4] However, modern confederate governance, uniting autonomous cantons and regions, emerged only in small European kingdoms and republics, such as Switzerland and the Netherlands. The United States initially was a loose union of thirteen former British colonies, joined together according to the Articles of Confederation, a document that mentioned the term "nation" only when referring to a "nation of Indians."[5] Nor was an American "nation" mentioned in the US Constitution, which introduced a federal form of government whose specific powers, vis-à-vis its thirteen constituent parts, was the subject of an intense debate in the famous *Federalist Papers*. Federalism made the United States stronger vis-à-vis its British and Spanish imperial rivals, allowing it to extend its own "Empire of Liberty" across the continent by conquering the land of indigenous peoples. Built on African slave labor and Native American land expropriation, the US federal government was imperialist by design.[6] Less noted is how American federalism protected social hierarchy and class privilege among its citizens. In a famous passage foreshadowing *The Communist Manifesto*, James Madison, the leading advocate of American federalism, defined the purpose of government as regulating social conflict, particularly those related to class differences and property ownership:

2. Toohey 2022.
3. Burbank and Copper 2010; Wasserstein 1985; Khazeni 2009.
4. Greene 2004.
5. Lepore 2019, 29.
6. Dunbar-Ortiz 2014.

> Those who hold and those who are without property have ever
> formed distinct interests in society. Those who are creditors, and
> those who are debtors, fall under a like discrimination. A landed
> interest, a manufacturing interest, a mercantile interest, a moneyed
> interest, with many lesser interests, grow up of necessity in civilized
> nations, and divide them into different classes, actuated by different
> sentiments and views. The regulation of these various and interfering
> interests forms the principal task of modern legislation, and involves
> the spirit of party and faction in the necessary and ordinary opera-
> tions of the government....[7]

Madison then went on to explain how a large federal republic could contain "democracy" because its growing population inevitably would fragment into political factions, effectively preventing majority consensus against minority privilege, primarily the concentration of wealth in private hands:

> A rage for paper money, for an abolition of debts, for an equal divi-
> sion of property, or for any other improper or wicked project, will
> be less apt to pervade the whole body of the Union than a particular
> member of it; in the same proportion as such a malady is more likely
> to taint a particular county or district, than an entire State.[8]

Thus, the undemocratic design of the US Constitution has preserved and perpetuated class hierarchy precisely as Madison brilliantly predicted more than two centuries ago. Though conservative in comparison to its contemporary Haitian Revolution, the American Revolution and the federal republic it created became inspirational political models throughout the world. The Atlantic Revolutions, in North and South America, seemed to confirm Europe's utopian tropes linking social and political egalitarianism to the Americas. Influential tracts like Thomas Moore's *Utopia*, John Eliot's *The Christian Commonwealth*, Voltaire's *Candide*, and Etienne Cabet's *The Voyage to Icaria* located their ideal society in the New World. Moreover, numerous religious and political sects tried to set up model utopian communities in Colonial America and later in the Unites States. Often, these were Christian "socialist" ventures, each aspiring to be "a community of perfect equality, absolute toleration, and mutual sharing in all things – a communistic welfare society where people would contribute what

---

7. James Madison quoted in Federalist No. 10. https://billofrightsinstitute.org/primary-sources/federalist-no-10. Accessed 1/17.2023. In *An Economic Interpretation of the Constitution of the Unites States* (1913) highly influential historian Charles A. Beard cited Federalist No.10 as prime evidence to argue the US Constitution was designed to protect the interests of a property-owning ruling class.

8. Madison.

they could and take what they needed."[9] Somewhat in the tradition of these "utopian socialists," the cofounder of "scientific socialism," Frederick Engels, too tied his theory of state formation, patriarchy, and private property to North America, particularly the Iroquois confederacy. Engels, however, was mainly interested in Iroquois communal property holding and matrilineal family lineage, rather than their system of confederate governance.[10] In the late twentieth century, a debate in American history focused on the purported impact of the Iroquois confederation on the US Constitution. However, historians agreed that although some "Founding Founders" admired the Iroquois Confederacy, it had no direct impact on the US Constitution.[11] Nevertheless, the New World's dazzling array of indigenous polities, especially decentralized confederal forms of governance, influenced modern Latin America's independence and revolutionary movements. The Inca Empire's legacy inspired the eighteenth-century Tupac Amaru revolution and the twentieth-century Tupamaro leftist guerrilla movement; while Peruvian Marxist, Carlos Mariategui, considered the Inca "welfare state" as an indigenous American form of socialism.[12] In Mexico, the modern nation-state emerged after the bloody suppression of a rival, indigenous-based nation-state-building project during the Yucatan Wars.[13]

In the twentieth century, federalism and confederalism built on two broad trajectories, one liberal-democratic and the other socialist-anarchist. The liberal-democratic track is that of the United States, the British Commonwealth, and the European Union. The leftist tradition goes back to anarchist and socialist internationalism, proposals for a socialist federation of Europe and the original idea of the Soviet Union. The project of a European confederation received a major boost after the experience of two World Wars. Following WWI, the idea of a world government, encompassing the voluntary federation of member states, gained currency as the remedy to the destructive madness of European nationalism and imperialism. Both Marxists and liberals called for a "United States of Europe" to prepare the grounds for a future "United States of the World." The Italian diplomat and future president, Luigi Einaudi, saw the anarchic international order based on each individual state's claim to absolute sovereignty as the ultimate cause of war, proposing a European federation of states as the remedy. He wrote:

9. Bailyn 2005, 76–81. Quoted on 79. In mid-nineteenth century, Cabet and his followers set up their socialist community of Icaria in the American state of Illinois, an experiment that, like several other attempts at building self-contained ideal communities, quickly failed. Wilson 1953, 104–7.

10. Engels 1972; and Engels 1903.

11. La Croix 2010, 229.

12. Liss 1984, 134–35.

13. Gabbert 2019.

> The truth lies in the ties between, not the sovereignty of, the states. The truth is the interdependence of free people, not their absolute independence. A thousand signs manifest the truth that people are dependent on one another, that they are not absolute sovereigns and judges, with no limits, of their own fates, that they cannot make their will prevail regardless of those of others. To the truth of the national idea that "We belong to ourselves," we must add the truth of the community of nations: "We also belong to others."[14]

Similarly, Russian revolutionary leader, Leon Trotsky, called for a "United States of Europe," achieved via revolutionary, socialist internationalism.[15] Lofty proposals for a United Europe and/or world government came to nothing as the Anglo-British dominated League of Nations prepared the ground for another world war by crushing Germany under the burden of war guilt and debt, expanded European colonialism and shut the USSR out of the international order. Meanwhile, the United States withdrew into its isolationism and the Russian Revolution's original promise of national self-determination degenerated into Russian imperialism under Stalin.[16] In the 1920s, the communist-backed League Against Imperialism and Colonial Oppression brought together representatives of future Third World nations, then struggling against European colonialism.[17] Neither the League of Nations nor the League Against Imperialism could prevent the clash of nation-states lined up against each other in the Second World War, in which genocidal acts included the American burning of German and Japanese cities and nuclear bombing of civilians. Following Germany's surrender, the possibility of a new world order based on wartime US-Soviet alliance was derailed when President Truman cut off Lend-Lease support of the USSR while rattling America's nuclear saber in Stalin's face.[18] Those who, like world historian Arnold Toynbee, called for world government and disarmament were dismissed as naïve utopians and Truman triggered the global nuclear arms race by refusing to halt making atomic weapons or to place them under UN control. Relying on preponderant military might, the Truman Doctrine declared the United States would defend the "Free World" against communist aggression. In reality, Cold War anti-communism justified the expansion of American imperial power across the globe. Already the domineer-

14. Quoted in D'Auria 2012, 294.

15. Trotsky, Leon. "Is the Time Ripe For the Slogan: 'The United States of Europe?'" *Pravda*, June 30, 1923. https://www.revolutionary-history.co.uk/.

16. Lewin 1978.

17. Prashad 2007, 16–30.

18. Anderson 2013, 24.

ing "dangerous nation" of the American continent, the United States became the global hegemon after the Second World War.[19] Following the example set by the United States, first the USSR and then France and the United Kingdom became nuclear powers. The United Nations proved incapable of keeping world peace and the Cold War raged on, spreading to the newly independent nation-states of Asia and Africa. The United States set new standards of wanton military destructiveness in Vietnam as the world watched the staggering cost of victory in wars of national liberation. Meanwhile, the new bloc of newly independent Third World countries quickly abandoned their purported path of peace and cooperation as China, India, and Pakistan fought each other and developed nuclear arsenals.[20] Nor did the fall of the Soviet bloc make the world safer or more peaceful, proving "the communist threat" was not the cause of global militarism and nuclear arms race. By the early twenty-first century, the United States had escalated its military hegemony, expanding NATO right to the borders of the Russian Federation.[21] The international system of rival sovereign states became more dangerously unstable as China's growing economic and military clout tipped the global balance of power away from the United States[22] Meanwhile, the nuclear arms race raged on, diverting enormous resources to destructive ends and bringing humanity ever closer to the verge of total annihilation.[23] The division of our world into sovereign nation-states, and their lining up into contending alliances, has not served humanity well.

As recent cases, such as the US invasion and occupation of Iraq and Russia's invasion of Ukraine show, the United Nations is incapable of preventing war and military aggression, effectively delegating the job of policing the world to the US-led military alliance of NATO. Nor do we have adequate liberal democratic responses to the challenge of conceiving a peaceful world order. Tracing back to Kant's cosmopolitan reflections on "Perpetual Peace," contemporary

19. On Toynbee and world government see McNeill 2006. On the US responsibility for starting the Cold War and the global arms race see Brands 1993. On American militarism and wars see Vine 2020.

20. Prashad 2007; Westad 2011.

21. Nugent 2008.

22. Mearsheimer 2001. See also Mearsheimer 2018.

23. The Bulletin of the Atomic Scientists, an organization founded in 1945 by scientists who built the first atomic bombs, has developed a Doomsday Clock, counting down humanity's edging closer to a catastrophic "midnight" of nuclear holocaust. The Bulletin's March 2022 statement (see Mecklin 2022), released in the wake of Russia's invasion of Ukraine, stated: "[T]he Clock remains the closest it has ever been to civilization-ending apocalypse because the world remains stuck in an extremely dangerous moment.... Last year, despite laudable efforts by some leaders and the public, negative trends in nuclear and biological weapons, climate change, and a variety of disruptive technologies – all exacerbated by a corrupted information ecosphere that undermines rational decision making – kept the world within a stone's throw of apocalypse."

proposals like John Rawls's "Law of Peoples" or Jürgen Habermas's upholding of "postnational" human rights and European Union principles cannot address a chaotic international system eschewing liberal democratic values, norms increasingly under siege even in Europe and the United States[24]

A Middle Eastern Alternative to the Nation-State?

As noted above, there have been countless critical reflections on, and alternatives proposed, to the nation-state. A recent influential example has been the work of anthropologist and political scientist James C. Scott, who argues for countering the nation-state by the empowerment of rural and nomadic communities and their "local knowledge." According to Scott, historically states have depended on urban-literary "knowledge grids" allowing them to contain and devour rural-nomadic communities. The modern state takes this form of knowledge to a new pitch, producing massive regulatory projects, which ultimately are failures as far as the quality of human life is concerned. In *Seeing Like a State*, Scott focused on Soviet and Third Wordlist industrialization, adding that capitalism and the market could be the most powerful force of global homogenization alongside modern state power. Scott acknowledges affinity for anarchism, particularly its valorization of grassroots, local, and "mutual" knowledge production.[25] Applying Scott's perspective to the Middle East, historian Cyrus Schayegh has shown how Pahlavi Iran's elite "saw like a state," implementing top-down modernization, while modern Iranian historical consciousness has suffered from "methodological statism."[26] Outside the academe, and barely noted by scholars, radically critical perspectives on the nation-state, as well as concrete experimental alternatives to it, recently have emerged in the Middle East. Below, we will look at one of the most prominent and promising of such examples, namely democratic confederalism.

Though its intellectual genealogy is eclectically global, the theoretical formulation and practical application of democratic confederalism are indigenous to the Middle East. The theory's articulation is credited to Abdullah Öcalan, former leader of the Kurdistan Workers' Party (PKK), a Marxist-Leninist organization that fought for Kurdish independence in Turkey from the 1980s through the 1990s. While on the run and in exile, Öcalan was captured and brought back to Turkey in 1999. He was condemned to death, but the sen-

---

24. Smith and Fine 2004, 5–22. For a stronger criticism of Rawls and Habermas see Anderson 2007, chapter 7. See also Rawls 2001; Habermas 2001.

25. Scott 1998; Scott 2009.

26. Schayegh 2010, 38.

tence was commuted to life imprisonment when Turkey abolished the death penalty. During his long solitary confinement, Öcalan read and wrote a lot, revised his stance on armed struggle and helped negotiate ceasefires between the PKK and the Turkish government. In 2005, he issued the "Declaration of Democratic Confederalism in Kurdistan," calling for the establishment of a confederate union of autonomous Kurdish regions in Turkey, Syria, Iraq, and Iran. Though not fully independent, each of these regions would function under local Kurdish and European Union jurisdiction, as well as the constitution of the state within whose borders the region was confined. Thus, while partially accepting the nation-state frame, democratic confederalism in practice defies the nation-state's claim to undivided sovereignty. Following this model, the Peoples' Democratic Party in Turkey, known by its Turkish initials as HDP, advocates the voluntary coexistence, within a confederate state, of both Turkish and Kurdish nations.[27] As international relations scholar Kamran Matin has observed, emocratic confederalism ultimately is a transnational project that cannot be fully implemented within an individual nation-state.[28]

Still in prison, Öcalan elaborated on the theory of democratic confederalism in a number of writings, making it universal in scope, radically gender-egalitarian, and based on a political economy of producers' cooperation and informed by deep ecological concerns. Drawing on a number of thinkers, Öcalan essentially built on Engels's classic hypothesis, linking private property, patriarchal family, and the state, supplemented by the ideas of American anarchist thinker and activist Murray Bookchin.[29] During the 1960s, Bookchin had developed the theory of "Social Ecology" in response to what he saw as the shortcomings of both socialism and anarchism. He argued that ecological crises arise from social pathologies, particularly the "colonization" of political life by the structural hierarchies of capitalism, patriarchy, and the nation-state. As an alternative, he proposed that feminist, ecological, and grassroots, democratic movements join to establish decentralized communities, closely adapting to the natural ecosystems. Starting locally, these "communal" movements would first radically democratize municipal governments, gradually confederating them to create an alternate power structure alongside national states. Bookchin therefore did not reject parliamentary politics, but proposed ways of pushing it closer to direct popular sovereignty. Like Noam Chomsky,

---

27. Matin 2021. See Öcalan 1999; Öcalan 2007; Öcalan 2013; Öcalan 2020.
28. Matin 2001.
29. Öcalan 2013; Knapp et. al 2016.

he argued that anarchists should participate in elections and personally worked with American and German Green parties.[30]

Following the conceptual track laid down by Öcalan, a new organization, called the Peoples' Democratic Party (HDP), was formed and quickly made its mark on Turkish politics. Officially founded in 2012, the Peoples' Democratic Party participated in peace negotiations between the government and armed Kurdish insurgents, while prompting its radically gender-egalitarian, environmentalist and pro-labor agenda. The HDP is a member of the Socialist International and aligned with Europe's democratic left parties like Greece's SYRIZA and Spain's Podemos. Co-chaired by a man and a woman, it participated in Turkey's 2015 general election and received over thirteen percent of the national vote, coming third after the two parties that traditionally have ruled the country. Though most of its candidates were secular, leftist Kurds, they also included devout Muslims, Armenians, Alevis, Romanis, and LGBT activists. Almost half of the party's 550 candidates were women and one was openly gay, a first in Turkish politics.[31] Moreover, the HDP is Turkey's only major party that does not deny the Armenian Genocide and asks for its open and public investigation by a truth commission. In 2016 the government launched a wave of repression, jailing the HDP's co-chairs, parliamentary deputies and thousands of members on trumped up charges of supporting terrorism. Successfully resisting repression, the party eventually regained its legal status and was able to receive around twelve percent of the national vote again and elect sixty-seven members to the parliament. It is running in Turkey's 2023 general and presidential elections, whose outcome it could decisively influence by aligning with one of the larger parties.[32]

The exceptional success of the Peoples' Democratic Party could relate to the fact that Turkey is the Middle Eastern country with the longest experience of meaningful parliamentary politics, albeit punctured by periods of authoritarian and/or military rule. However, in addition to this evolutionary parliamentary route, democratic confederalism has opened up a trailblazing revolutionary political path, once again unique in the Middle East. Also taking inspiration from Öcalan's ideas, this is the "Rojava Revolution," an experiment in radical social organization taking place in the midst of Syria's civil war. Between 2014 and 2016, and responding to state collapse and the rise of the Islamic State (ISIS) in Syria, three autonomous Kurdish "cantons" in the northeastern part of the country joined together to form the Democratic Federation of Rojava. Ac-

30. Biehl 2015.
31. Anonymous 2015; Anonymous 2022.
32. Anonymous 2023.

cording to its constitution, the Rojava confederation is governed by grass-roots councils, presiding over a cooperative economy, implementing radical gender egalitarianism and allowing non-Kurds equal political and cultural representation. Given the chaotic and violent conditions of Syria's civil war, Rojava formed "peoples' protection units," consisting of armed women and men, to defend its community against attacks by the Islamic State, the Syrian government and the Turkish military. The most internationally noted and admired feature of Rojava has been the effective participation of its female militias (women's protection units) in fighting the arch-misogynist ISIS.[33] The Rojava revolution fits the pattern of late twentieth-century alter-globalization, social justice and indigenous rights movements like the World Social Forum and Mexico's Zapatistas. Historically, Rojava's precursors are the anarchist councils and communes formed in the Spanish civil war of the 1930s, in Ukraine during Russia's revolutionary upheavals of 1918–1921, or during the Paris Commune. Like its historical precursors, Rojava occurred in conditions of civil war and state collapse and was not allowed to continue when "normal" state power came back to assert itself. This, however, does not diminish Rojava's revolutionary significance as an inspirational model of radical gender, socio-economic, and ethnic-national egalitarianism. It is not coincidental, for example, that the most inspirational slogan of Iran's 2022 protest movement, "Woman, Life, Freedom," originated in Kurdish circles in Turkey and echoed internationally during the Rojava revolution.[34]

Beyond Iran's Undemocratic Nation-state?

"The legitimacy of cession and the necessity of autonomy and federalism," these are dangerous refrains circulating in Iran and abroad these days. Despite their alluring appearance, many analysts believe these dreams cover up nightmarish threats to Iranian history, civilization and territorial integrity.[35]

The above phrase, quoted from a leading reformist newspaper in 2023, sums up the assumptions that Iranian nationalists of various stripes, including some on the left, share with the Islamic Republic, the Pahlavi monarchy, and the bulk of Iran's political opposition in diaspora. Belief in Iran as a historically indivisible polity is rooted in the assumption of continuity in Iranian "national" history, directly linking the existing nation-state to medieval or even ancient empires.

33. Yasin Sunca 2022.
34. Lazarus 2019.
35. Beykoghli 2023.

The fallacy here is the conflation of pre-modern notions of Iran, as an empire, with contemporary Iran as a nation-state.[36] Removing the conceptual blinders that make the Iranian public, as well as the intellectual and scholarly elite, "see like a state" requires a critical reexamination of the undemocratic path of nation-state formation in modern Iran. The following sections of this chapter are preliminary steps toward constructing that critical perspective.

Despite the claims of nationalist historiography, prior to the twentieth century, Iran was neither a nation nor a state in the modern sense of these terms. Politically, pre-modern notions of Iran were imperial, their latest iteration being the Safavid Empire, which the Qajar Dynasty tried to emulate and revive. Like all empire-builders, the Qajar dynasty's founder, Aqa Mohammad Khan, cobbled together "the Protected Domains of Iran" (*mamalek-e mahruse-ye Iran*), and not an Iranian nation-state, by forcibly subjugating ethno-linguistically diverse urban and rural populations. Persian continued to function as the language of government and literary high culture, but Qajar Iran had no national language. The shahs and the Qajar elite spoke Turkish and the majority of their subjects were not Persian speakers. "Persian" was neither an ethnicity nor a proto-nationality, though European Orientalists were using it as both.[37] With no standing army, uniform jurisdiction, or taxation system, the Qajar kingdom had no monopoly of legitimate violence over its subjects, hence not measuring up to Max Weber's famous definition of the state.[38] The shahs precariously presided over a traditional *moluk al-tawiā'f* network where autonomous tribes functioned as "states-within-the state."[39] Thus, according to a leading historian of tribal Iran, the Qajar domain had a "confederate" structure:

> [T]he Qajar dynasty exhibited a flexibility that allowed for tribal autonomy and a plurality of power on the margins of empire. The state possessed a decentralized structure and the tribes remained effectively beyond its reach. … Such a system in turn allowed tribal subjects to retain political and cultural autonomy while providing nominal allegiance and services to the state, most often by paying light taxes and offering retinues to the royal cavalry. *This confederate and decentralized state structure was the hallmark of the early modern state in Iran.*[40]

At the level of social structure, clan-based kinship networks, called *tai'feh*,

---

36. Matin-asgari 2012; Di Cosmo 2018.
37. Matin-asgari 2012. See also Āshuri 2005, 175–94.
38. Martin 2005, 13–14 and Marashi 2014.
39. Tapper 1997, 101–112.
40. Khazeni 2009, 193, emphasis added.

were prevalent in Iran's rural and urban areas, persisting well into the twentieth century.[41] Another important pre-national marker of collective identity was
qowmiat, designating larger ethno-linguistic populations, such as Kurds, Lurs,
Bakhtiāris, Arabs, Turkmens, or Baluchis.[42]

Historians generally see the Constitutional Revolution of 1906–1911
as the turning point in the rise of an Iranian nation-state. As Afshin Marashi
has argued, the emergence of Iranian nationhood was a project initiated by
the modern state implementing a uniform national culture and historical consciousness. Focusing on state-sponsored nationalist public education, archaeo-
logical iconography, monuments and museums, Marashi notes the pivotal role
of "the pedagogic state" in nation building.[43]

From a similar cultural history perspective, Houchang Chehabi has analyzed twentieth-century nation-state formation in terms of "culture wars" causing a deep chasm between "cosmopolitan" elites and "local segments," the latter
being peripheral, in both physical and cultural distance, to the modern state and
the "authoritarian Europeanization" it promoted as nationally normative. "The
culture wars that erupted in the 1920s under the Westernizing rule of Reza Shah
(r.1925–1941)," writes Chehabi, "have continued to plague Iranian society, forty years of Islamic rule notwithstanding."[44] In addition to these cogent cultural
accounts, we need probing attention to the systematic violence, both political
and cultural, endemic to nation-state formation in Iran. To take full measure
of the latter, we must take a critical look at its birth moment, roughly from
the Constitutional Revolution to the consolidation of Reza Shah's dictatorship.
Going back to the Constitutional era, we can trace the origin of nationalist narratives that project Iranian nationhood back into history. This nationalist master narrative originated with British Orientalist Edward Granville Browne, who
wrote *The Persian Revolution* in the midst of Iran's revolutionary civil war,
claiming the constitutionalists were "nationalists" fighting to revive "Persia" as a
great "nation" that had existed since antiquity.[45] Contrary to such claims, even
a decade after the Constitutional Revolution, the most ardent Iranian nationalists readily admitted that neither a nation nor a functioning state existed in
Iran. For instance, in 1919 future prime minister, Mohammad-'Ali Foroughi,
lamented: "There is no Iranian nation, and Iranians do not want to become hu-

41. On the significance and persistence of *ta'ifeh* see Hegland 2014. Garthwaite 1983.
42. Vahabzadeh 2023.
43. Marashi 2008, 86–109.
44. Chehabi 2018, 27, 39–40, quoted on 17. For Chehabi's view of class and center-periphery
hierarchies in modern Iran see Chehabi 1997, 235–53 and Chehabi 2019, 43–63.
45. Browne 2006, preface, xiii.

man beings."[46] Leading nationalist historian of interwar Iran, Ahmad Kasravi, also bemoaned the vast linguistic, cultural and religious differences that divided Iran's inhabitants, advocating the imposition of a unitary national culture, exclusively using Persian.[47] By the mid-1920s, belief in creating "national unity" via a uniform language and culture was the common creed of official and unofficial nationalism:

> Perfecting national unity means the spread of Persian language throughout the country, getting rid of "fractured sovereignties" (*muluk al-tawā'efi*) and regional differences in behavior, appearance, etc; and making Kurds, Lurs, Qashqāis, Arabs, Turks and Turkomans speak the same language and dress the same.... Unless we can make uniform all of Iran's various regions and different ethnicities, in other words, making all of them truly Iranian, we face a dark future.[48]

In the aftermath of WWI, advocates of authoritarian nationalism insisted that without uniformity in national culture Iran's very survival was in danger. In 1921, the first coherent political program of Iranian nationalism, appearing in the Berlin-based publication *Kāveh*, called for unconditionally accepting "the principles of European civilization" and maintaining "Iran's national unity" by promoting European-style education via Persian as "national language."[49] Starting with mildly social democratic constitutionalism during the war, *Kāveh* became an advocate of nation building via "Enlightened Despotism" in the war's immediate aftermath. A more blatant advocate of dictatorial nation building was another Berlin-publication, *Nāmeh-e Farangestān*, whose first issue recommended a fascist regime:

> The current Italian Prime Minister, Mussolini, is a dictator. He is indifferent to monarchism or republicanism, as long as fascists are in power.... He pretends to believe in the parliament, but when necessary, uses threats to produce his own parliamentary majority.... Iran too needs such a dictator.[50]

---

46. Foroughi, quoted in Iraj Parsinejad, "*Yāddāshthā-ye yek Irāni-ye motemadden-e bā-ma'rafat*," *Bokhara* 108 (October – November): 463–93, 471.

47. Kasravi n.d., 44, 47, 56–57, 118–19.

48. Mahmud Afshār in *Āyandeh*, no. 1, quoted in Nader Entekhabi, *Nasionālism va tajaddod dar Iran va Torkieh* (Tehran, 2011), 42.

49. Matin-asgari 2018, 59.

50. *Nāmeh-e Farangestān*, no. 1, quoted in Entekhabi 2011, 179.

Advocates of dictatorial nation-state building repeated the assumption that the constitutional experiment had failed and post-WWI Iran faced chaos and disintegration caused by foreign occupation. As one scholar has put it:

> ... [t]he practical failure of the Constitutional movement, the inability to achieve a working consensus in the new parliament and the havoc of the Great War, persuaded the country's intellectuals that Iran's salvation lay with a "strong man."[51]

However, as Stephanie Cronin has argued, this "catastrophic perspective" on post-war conditions was not an accurate description of actual historical conditions, but the justification of the dictatorial regime that emerged after the British-instigated 1921 coup.[52] In fact, by 1921 Iran was farther from chaos and foreign domination than any time during the previous decade. On 16 April 1921, soon after becoming prime minister, Seyyed Zi'auddin Tabātabā'i, leader of the 1921 coup, officially declared that Britain and Soviet Russia no longer threatened Iran's independence. "I am confident that our northern neighbor has joined the rank of our friends, sending its representative to our capital and posing no threat to Iran," declared the prime minister's first statement, while his second said: "The British army's movement [out of Iran] proves our great neighbor has no intention of violating Iranian rights...."[53]

Nor did the Qajar regime's post-war domestic challengers threaten Iran with "cession" or "disintegration." The early 1920s autonomous regimes in Gilan, Azerbaijan, and Khorasan were nationalist and more committed to constitutionalism than Tehran's British-backed government. In an important sense, these provincial challenges were the continuation of center-periphery struggles of the previous decade, when popular militias from the provinces, particularly Azerbaijan and Gilan, had fought to save Tehran's fledgling constitutional regime. Revolutionary popular militias were tied to the regional and provincial councils (*anjomanhā-ye ayālati va velāyti*) set up by the new constitution for the oversight of local affairs. These regional councils quickly took the lead in defending and broadening the democratic content of constitutional government, serving as a counterweight to undemocratic centralizing trends in Tehran.[54] The newly formed popular councils helped establish a new "public sphere" that expanded the grassroots democratic content of constitutionalism:

51. Ansari 2013, 132.
52. Cronin 2010, 4–5.
53. Quoted in Āqeli 1990, 1:106.
54. Afary 1996, 73–81.

> The new circulation of newspapers, the proliferation of a novel
> print-culture made possible by emerging print technologies, and the
> energetic quality of the literary-polemical discourse of the years sur-
> rounding the constitutional revolution, all testify to the formation of
> an *Iranian public sphere* that was capable of giving form to a *general-
> ized opinion* to speak for the national community.[55]

Significantly, the post-war democratic public sphere was multi-lingual, particularly when aligned with movements of provincial autonomy. Azerbaijan's
1920 autonomous government, for example, pioneered in bilingual modernist
cultural production, as its flagship publication *Tajaddod* (modernity) radically
challenged the hegemony of Persian literary canons. However, whether bilingual or Persian-centric, the constitutional public sphere was destroyed as independent newspapers were shut down and journalists jailed or murdered by
Reza Khan's creeping nationalist dictatorship between 1921 and 1925. Far from
acting single-handedly, Reza Khan in fact was a perfect fit for the dictatorial role
assigned to him by nationalist elites who had abandoned constitutionalism to
embrace authoritarian nation building.[56] On the other hand, the Pahlavi state's
top-down nation building was resisted by segments of the urban and rural poor,
the new working class in the oil fields, and particularly by tribal people. Recent studies of the rise of the Turkish Republic show a similar process of "resistance and dissent" to the modern nation formation form below.[57] Here, another
comparison between Iranian and Turkish nation building could be instructive.
Mustafa Kemal and his followers forged a new nation-state in the ruins of the
Ottoman Empire by fighting foreign occupation armies. But the Iranian nation-state consolidated its "territorial integrity" (*tamamiyat-e arzi*) in wars not
against foreign enemies but against non-Persian-speaking tribal populations at
borderlands with Anatolia, Central Asia, and India, as well as in traditionally
autonomous "internal" tribal spaces.[58] After Reza Shah's fall, a Majles deputy
gave the following description of his regime's recruitment of Iran's nomadic
people into nationhood:

---

55. Marashi 2014, 14–15, emphasis in the original. On the formation of a public sphere
during the Constitutional Revolution see also Nabavi 2005, 307–21.

56. Reza Khan used his position as prime minister and minister of war to end press freedom and si-
lence critics of his personal dictatorship through exemplary displays of violence, such as murdering the
modernist poet and journalist Mirzādeh ʿEshqi and the attempted murder of politician and nationalist
poet Mohammad-Taqi Bahār. Matin-asgari 2002, 92–98.

57. For popular resistance to nation-state building in Iran see Cronin, *Soldiers, Shahs and Subalterns in Iran*. For Turkey, see Metinsoy 2021.

58. Khazeni 2009, 193.

> The Qashqāi, Bakhtiyāri, Kuhgiluya and other nomads ... not only has
> their tribal property been looted, but group after group of these tribes
> have been executed without trial.... The way they settled the tribes
> was the way of execution and annihilation, not education and reform.
> And it is precisely this approach that has sapped the strength of the
> Iranian society and weakened the hope of national unity.[59]

The forced settlement of tribal populations, inevitably causing the destruction of their culture, is a common feature of nation-building projects globally and across the Middle East. Mexican sociologist Pablo Gonzales Casanova and dependency theorist Andre Gunder Frank have called such nation-building strategies "internal colonialism," while Palestinian scholar Joseph Massad refers to them as "the colonial effect."[60] Political theorist Hannah Arendt too had noted the modern nation-state's drive toward the forcible assimilation, elimination, or genocide of "minorities." According to Arendt, the Anglo-French victors of the First World War imposed the nation-state structure on central and Eastern Europe, knowing it was incompatible with the ethnic and linguistic diversity of almost every new country. "The representatives of the great nations," she wrote, "knew only to too well that minorities within nation-states must sooner or later be either assimilated or liquidated." In passing, Arendt notes how modern nation-states treat ethnic minorities as if they were under colonial rule: "So far, nobody has bothered to find out the characteristic similarities between colonialism and minority exploitation."[61] In the Iranian case, Marashi notes "the colonial effect" when drawing parallels between the British Raj's colonial modernization of India and modern nation-building in Iran. According to him, "the Pahlavi state thus came to play the role of a *surrogate colonial state*, and in turn came to take on the political character of an external presence against which discursive and political forces came to position themselves."[62] The "colonial effect," including its racist features, is blatantly present in major works by the intellectual architects of Pahlavi era nation building. An example is *Ancient Iran (Iran-e bastan)*, the outstanding work of Reza Shah era historiography, penned by Hasan Pirniā, several times prime minister and among Reza Khan's intellectual tutors during the 1920s. Quite unselfconsciously, Pirniā writes:

> Coming to the Iranian Plateau, the Aryans found there people who
> were ugly and inferior in race, habits, morals and religion.... The

59. Quoted in Katouzian 2003, 15–36, 28.
60. Soleimani and Mohammadpour 2019, 1–23, 3. Massad 2001, 56–59.
61. Ardent 1979, 270–73; quoted on 273.
62. Marashi 2014, 18–19.

Aryans called these native people *tur* or *div* [demon].... Considering them inferior, the Aryans treated these people as victors treat the vanquished. Therefore, at first [the Aryans] accorded them no rights whatsoever, fighting and killing them wherever they were found. But later, when natives no longer posed any threat, the Aryans assigned to them difficult tasks, such as farming, animal husbandry, and domestic services. Thus, being needed, the natives received certain rights, such as those accorded slaves and concubines living under their masters' protection ... The Aryans came to Iran not to conquer and plunder, but to settle in this country; therefore, they had to take the natives' lands.[63]

The extreme racist and colonialist perspective of this passage could apply to the emergence of India's caste system, the dispossession and genocide of the American indigenous people by US colonial expansion, or the Pahlavi state's treatment of Iran's non-Persian speaking subjects, particularly the "uncivilized" tribal people.

Conclusion: Is a Democratic Iranian Nation-State Possible?

The question facing us today is how, given this half-baked [Iranian] nation-state, the product of a century of political and ideological developments, we might build a nation-state free of national uniformity and allowing cultural and linguistic diversity in a society of citizen subjects.

Essayist and translator Dariush Āshuri, 2005. [64]

Taking the above question seriously, this chapter concludes by suggesting a future democratic Iran needs a confederal political structure. The leading role of Kurdistan and Sistan-Baluchistan provinces in Iran's 2022 protest movement once again showed the explosion of historically accumulated grievances in non-Persian speaking regions.[65] Significantly, these regions are also the main targets of the state's repression since half of the casualties inflicted by state violence come from Kurdistan and Sistan-Baluchistan. The position of non-Persian-speaking regions as nodal points of resistance to the state became visible in 2022 under extraordinary conditions of national crisis and state dysfunction, as it had been in the past when the Iranian state had collapsed due to revolution or foreign occupation. The most familiar of such past cases are the 1945–1946 formation of

---

63. Pirniā 1932, 157–58.
64. Āshuri 2005, 194.
65. On Turning Iran's non-Persian-speaking populations into "minorities" see Elling 2013.

autonomous regimes in Azerbaijan and Kurdistan and the effective autonomy of Kurdistan during the 1978–1979 revolution. Exposing deep fractures in the fabric of the Iranian nation-state, these crises were "solved" through the massive deployment of violence by Tehran's central government, which blamed them on foreign intrigue and intervention.[66] According to contemporary Iranian and foreign observers, however, the autonomous governments of Azerbaijan and Kurdistan enjoyed significant popular support because they addressed real local grievances. In 1946, for example, the British council in Tabriz agreed with the view of the Azerbaijan crisis expressed by Tehran's independent press:

> I cannot help observing that there is among the workers and peasants
> of this province what has always seemed to me genuine exasperation
> with the incompetence and corruption of the Iranian government,
> and that there exists real miseries and injustices which in any other
> country would be enough to produce a spontaneous revolt. I do not
> believe that the Russians have fabricated the whole movement: it
> seems to me rather that they are exploiting a genuine revolutionary
> situation....[67]

At about the same time, an American consular team visiting the Kurdish autonomous region recorded similar views. Among the four-member team was Archie Roosevelt Jr., a US military attaché in Iran and later CIA agent, who published a sympathetic firsthand account of the Kurdish republic. According to him, the proper response to the crisis was granting Kurdistan autonomy in a federalist state structure:

> If the states the Kurds inhabit allow their Kurdish population a
> degree of local autonomy and give up the attempt to force an alien na-
> tionalism upon them, they may succeed in obtaining a loyalty similar
> to that found in Switzerland with its multi-national population.[68]

Admitting the existence of national oppression is a highly sensitive topic among Iranians, openly voiced only by members of oppressed ethnic or national minorities or by radical leftist intellectuals and organizations. The ex-communist

---

66. In fall 1946, the Iranian military invaded Azerbaijan and Kurdistan, crushing their autonomous governments. The Army command announced about 2,500 executions alone, while various sources estimated close to 20,000 civilians were killed by the military and rightwing vigilantes in Azerbaijan alone. JAMA n.d., 2:422, 429.

67. Abrahamian 1982, 218. On popular support of Azerbaijan government see JAMA, 1: 292–95, 306–8.

68. Wilford 2013, 53. See chapter four on Archie Roosevelt's intelligence career, including his brief stint in Iran. On the 1946 Kurdish republic see Vali 2019.

writer Jalāl Āl-Ahmad, for instance, was the rare Persian-speaking intellectual who in the 1960s could acknowledge that "Iranian intellectuals include Turkish speakers from Azerbaijan, Kurdish-speakers from Kurdistan, and Arabic speakers from Khuzistan," and that "Iran is a multi-lingual nation."[69] Focusing on Azeris, Iran's largest non-Persian-speaking group, he argued:

> At least six to seven of Iran's twenty-five million inhabitants are born and live in a Turkish language zone. But they do not have the right to use their mother-tongue in the cultural and artistic realms or in the print and other communication media or the social services. Instead, they are forced to use Persian, a language imposed on them from outside their native language zone.... We have deprived six to seven million people from the most basic of human rights, which is the freedom to use any language they want.[70]

Āl-Ahmad's solution was the cultural and linguistic autonomy of Iran's non-Persian-speaking regions. Moreover, he went as far as condemning the forced imposition of Persian as "colonial" practice, amounting to cultural genocide:

> If Azerbaijan were allowed to administer its own cultural affairs, using its own language in education, print and other media, there should be no fear of any gravitational pull from across the border. Moreover, we would enrich our country's intellectual production.... More explicitly, I would say that from the birth of the nation concept in the constitutional era to the present, Tehran governments have considered Azerbaijan a colony, if not politically and economically, but certainly in a cultural sense. *The first detrimental result of this cultural colonialism is the killing of Turkish culture in Azerbaijan.*

Leaving no doubt about his literal use of the term "colonialism," Āl-Ahmad followed the above passage by quoting the French-Martinique poet, Aimé Césaire on the imposition of French language on France's African colonies.[71] Apart from a few public intellectuals like Āl-Ahmad, only pre-revolutionary Iran's radical leftist circles debated questions such as national oppression or whether Iran was a multi-national country. However, the left mainly repeated Marxist-Leninist formulas, having little clarity or consensus on such topics. The Organization of the Iranian People's Fadā'i Guerrillas, for example, had declared Iran a multi-national country, despite the fact the organization's name referred to "the Iranian

69. Āl-Ahmad 1977, 278, 280.
70. Āl-Ahmad 1977, 304–5.
71. Āl-Ahmad 1977, 417. Emphasis added.

people" in the singular. In *Azerbaijan and the National Question*, the Fadā'i organization had said: "Iran's nations and nationalities have formed a country within state borders imposed by a chauvinistic Persian bourgeoisie." At the same time, the pamphlet attacked "petty bourgeois nationalists" who sought separate solutions to the national question in places such as Azerbaijan and Kurdistan. This was so because "the peoples of Iran can win democratic freedoms, including the liberation of oppressed nations, only through a common struggle against their common enemy."[72] The most familiar usage of the term "confederation," in pre-revolutionary Iran's political culture, refers to the Confederation of Iranian Students/National Union (CISNU). As its official title indicates, the CISNU was Iran's "national union of students," transformed into an international "confederation" during the 1960s-1970s when student political activity was banned inside the country. The CISNU's confederate structure tied together individual country federations in an elaborate international structure, reflecting membership tallies in different countries. The organization had member federations or affiliate chapters in the United Kingdom, Belgium, Switzerland, France, Canada, Italy, Austria, West Germany, the United States, India, Turkey, Bulgaria, Poland, and the Soviet Union. The CISNU also stands out for systematically practicing pluralistic politics, starting out as a coalition of socialist, nationalist, and Islamic groups and eventually aligning with the international New Left, though never becoming politically monolithic. A distinct characteristic of the CISNU political experience was attention to national oppression and to whether Iran might be a multi-national country.[73]

When the monarchy collapsed during the 1978–1979 revolution, national oppression and federalism suddenly became urgent questions since parts of the country, most notably Kurdistan, had become virtually autonomous. With significant popular backing, Kurdish political parties asked for autonomy within a presumably federal Iran, a demand unacceptable to the fledgling Islamic Republic. In the ensuing civil war, small leftist organizations fought alongside Kurdish parties defending the region's autonomy, but most of the left had no coherent position, some effectively siding with a newly forming repressive state.[74] Soon, the Iran-Iraq war overshadowed all other issues, allowing the Islamic Republic to impose an "anti-imperialist" national security regime, treating all dissident as treason. The Islamic Republic's security state posture continues to the present, justifying dictatorial rule as necessary to Iran's defense against foreign enemies. In the meantime, and particularly in response to recent mass protests, the na-

72. Organization of the Iranian Peoples' Fadā'i Guerrillas 1977, 5, 8.
73. Matin-asgari 2002. Moradian 2022.
74. Vali, *Kurds* 2014. Mojab, ed. 2001. Mojab and Hassanpour 2021.

tionalist diaspora opposition and reformist factions inside Iran have converged on demanding the restoration of basic democratic rights and freedoms. As a rule, however, even the most liberal opposition groups abroad, as well as reformists in Iran, agree with the regime in denying national oppression and rejecting any talk of regional autonomy or federalism in Iran. As before the revolution, only the radical left and those speaking for ethnic and/or national minorities address such issues, including proposals for a democratic, confederalist Iran.[75] Although that prospect may seem remote or utopian, as this chapter has argued, critical historical consciousness and the obvious oppression of ordinary people because of where they live in Iran tell us to take it seriously.

75. For an example of supposedly scholarly but mostly ideological defense of Iranian nationalism published in Iran see the collection of articles in Ahmadi 2006. For debates on national oppression and federalism, including the views of Kurdish and other non-Persian speaking intellectuals and academics, see the leftist sites https://www.akhbar-rooz.com and https://pecritique .com . See also https://iran-federal.net for a coalition of Kurdish, Turkmen, Arab, Luri, Baluchi, Azerbaijani, and Bakhtiāri organizations advocating for a democratic federal republic in Iran.

Works Cited

Abrahamian, Ervand. 1982. *Iran Between Two Revolutions*. Princeton: Princeton University Press.

Afary, Janet. 1996. *The Iranian Constitutional Revolution, 1906–1911: Grassroots Democracy, Social Democracy and the Origins of Feminism*. New York, Columbia University Press.

Ahmadi, Hamid. 2006. *Iran: Howiyat, Melliyat, Qowmiyat*. Tehran: n.p.

Āl-Ahmad, Jalāl. 1977. *Dar Khedmat va Khiānat-e Roshanfekrān*. Tehran: n.p.

Anonymous. 2015. "Inclusive HDP candidate list aspires to pass 10 pct election threshold." *Hurriyet,* April 8. https://www.hurriyetdailynews.com /inclusive-hdp-candidate-list-aspires-to-pass-10-pct-election -threshold-80731.

Anonymous. 2022. "First-ever openly gay parliamentary candidate stands for election in Turkey." *Independent,* January 30. https://www .independent.co.uk/news/uk/firstever-openly-gay-parliamentar y-candidate-stands-for-election-in-turkey-10274746.html.

Anonymous. 2023. "Peoples' Democratic Party (HDP) and the upcoming Turkish elections 2023." *Medyanews,* January 30. https://medyanews.net/peoples -democratic-party-hdp-and-the-upcoming-turkish-elections-2023.

Āqeli, Bāqer. 1990. *Ruzshomār-e tārikh-e Iran: Az mashruteh tā enqelāb-e eslāmi*. Tehran: Guftār.

Ardent, Hannah. 1979. *The Origins of Totalitarianism.* New York: Harvest/ HBJ.

Āshuri, Daruish. 2005. "*Iran: az Emperaturi beh Dowlat-Mellat.*" In *Ma va Moderniyat*, edited by Daruish Āshuri, 175–94. Tehran: n.p.

Anderson, Perry. 2013. "Imperium." *New Left Review* 83:5–111.

Ansari, Ali M. 2013. "Nationalism, Myth and History in modern Iran." In *Iran and the Challenges of the Twenty-first Century*, edited by H. E. Chehabi, Farhad Khosrokhavar, and Clement Therme. Costa Mesa, CA: Mazda Publishers.

Bailyn, Bernard. 2005. *Atlantic History: Concepts and Contours.* Cambridge MA: Harvard University Press.

Beykoghli, Mehdi. 2023. "Demokrasi va tose'eh sad-e rah-e tajziehtalabist." *Ettemad*, January 2. https://www.etemadnewspaper.ir/fa/main /detail/195708/1/2/2023/.

Brands, H. W. 1993. *The Devil We Know: Americans and the Cold War.* New York: Oxford University Press.

Biehl, Janet. 2015. *Ecology or Catastrophe: The Life of Murray Bookchin.* Oxford: Oxford University Press.

Browne, Edward Granville. 2006. *The Persian Revolution of 1906–1909.* Washington DC: Mage.

Burbank, Jane and Frederik Copper. 2010. *Empires in World History: Power and the Politics of Difference.* Princeton: Princeton University Press.

Cağlayan, Handan. 2020. *Women in the Kurdish Movement: Mothers, Comrades, Goddesses.* New York: Palgrave Macmillan.

Chehabi, Houchang. 1997. "Ardebil Becomes a Province: Center-Periphery Relations in Iran." *International Journal of Middle East Studies* 29:235– 53.

———. 2018. *Culture Wars and Dual Society in Iran.* Amsterdam: Farman-Farmaian Institute of Social History.

———. 2019. "The Rise of the Middle Class in Iran before the Second World War." In *The Global Bourgeoisie: The Rise of the Middle Classes in the Age of Empire*, edited by Christof Dejung, David Motadel, and Jurgen Osterhammel, 43–63. Princeton: Princeton University Press.

Cronin, Stephanie. 2010. *Soldiers, Shahs and Subalterns in Iran: Opposition, Protest and Revolt, 1921–1941.* New York: Palgrave Macmillan.

D'Auria, Matthew. 2012. "Junius and the 'President Professor': Luigi Einaudi's European Federalism." In *Europe in Crisis : Intellectuals and the European Idea, 1917–1957*, edited by Mark Hewitson and Matthew D'Auria, 289–304. New York and Oxford: Berghahn Books.

Di Cosmo, Nicola, ed. 2018. *Empires and Exchanges in Eurasian Late Antiquity : Rome, China, Iran, and the Steppe, ca. 250–750*. New York and Cambridge: Cambridge University Press.

Dunbar-Ortiz, Roxanne. 2014. *An Indigenous Peoples' History of the United States*. Boston MA: Beacon Press.

Elling, Rasmus. 2013. *Minorities in Iran: Nationalism and Ethnicity after Khomeini*. New York: Palgrave Macmillan.

Engels, Frederick. 1972. *The Origin of the Family, Private Property and the State*. New York: International Publishers.

———. 1903. *Socialism: Utopian and Scientific*. Chicago: Charles H. Kerr.

Entekhabi, Nader. 2011. *Nasionālism va tajaddod dar Iran va Torkieh*. Tehran, n.p.

Gabbert, Wolfgang. 2019. *Violence and the Caste War of Yucatan*. Cambridge: Cambridge University Press.

Garthwaite, Gene R. 1983. *Khans and Shahs: A Documentary Analysis of the Bakhtiyari in Iran*. New York: Cambridge University Press.

Greene, Jack P. 2004. "State Formation, Resistance, and the Creation of Revolutionary Traditions in the Early Modern Era." In *Revolutionary Currents: Nation Building in the Transatlantic World*, edited by Michael A. Morrison and Melinda Zook. New York: Rowman and Littlefield.

Habermas, Jürgen. 2001. *The Postnational Constellation: Political Essays*. Translated by Max Pensky. Cambridge, MA: MIT Press.

Hegland, Mary Elaine. 2014. *Days of Revolution: Political Unrest in an Iranian Village*. Stanford: Stanford University Press.

Iranian Peoples' Fadā'i Guerrillas. 1977. *Azerbaijan va Masala-ye Melli*. N.p.

JAMA. n.d. *Gozashteh Cherāgh-e Rāh-e Āyandeh Āst*. Tehran.

James, C. L. R. 1963. *The Black Jacobins*. New York: Vintage.

Kasravi, Ahmad. N.d. *Varjāvand-e Bonyād*. N.p.

Katouzian, Homa. 2003. "Riza Shah's Political Legitimacy and Social Base." In *The Making of Modern Iran: State and Society under Riza Shah, 1921–1941*, edited by Stephanie Cronin, 15–36. London and New York: Routledge.

Khazeni, Arash. 2009. *Tribes and Empire on the Margins of Nineteenth-century Iran*. Seattle: University of Washington Press.

Knapp, Michael, Ercan Ayboğa, and Anja Flach. 2016. *Revolution in Rojava: Democratic Autonomy and Women's Liberation in Syrian Kurdistan*. London: Pluto Press.

La Croix, Allison L. 2010. *The Ideological Origins of American Federalism.* Cambridge, MA: Harvard University Press.

Lazarus, Sarah. 2019. "Women. Life. Freedom. Female fighters of Kurdistan." *CNN,* January 28. https://www.cnn.com/2019/01/27/homepage2/kurdish-female-fighters/index.html.

Lepore, Jill. 2019. *This America: The Case for the Nation.* New York and London: Norton.

Lewin, Moshe. 1978. *Lenin's Last Struggle.* New York: Monthly Review Press.

Liss, Sheldon B. 1984. *Marxist Thought in Latin America.* Berkeley and Los Angeles: University of California Press.

Marashi, Afshin. 2008. *Nationalizing Iran: Culture, Power, and the State, 1870–1940.* Seattle: University of Washington Press.

———. 2014. "Paradigms of Iranian Nationalism: History, Theory and Historiography." In *Rethinking Iranian Nationalism and Modernity,* edited by Kamran Scot Aghaie and Afshin Marashi, 3–24. Austin: University of Texas Press.

Martin, Vanessa. 2005. *The Qajar Pact: Bargaining, Protest and the State in Nineteenth-century Persia.* New York: I.B. Tauris.

Massad, Joseph. 2001. *Colonial Effects: The Making of National Identity in Jordan.* New York: Columbia University Press.

Matin, Kamran. 2021. "Democratic Confederalism and Societal Multiplicity: A Sympathetic Critique of Adullah Öcalan's State Theory." *Geopolitics* 26:1075–94.

Matin-asgari, Afshin. 2002. *Iranian Student Opposition to the Shah: 1960s–1970s.* Costa Mesa, CA: Mazda Publishers.

———. 2012. "The Academic Debate on Iranian Identity," In *Facing Others: Iranian Identity Boundaries and Modern Political Cultures,* edited by Abbas Amanat and Farzin Vejdani, 171–90. London and New York: Routledge.

———. 2018. *Both Eastern and Western: An Intellectual History of Iranian Modernity.* Cambridge: Cambridge University Press.

McNeill, William H. 1989. *Arnold J. Toynbee: A life.* New York and Oxford: Oxford University Press.

Mearsheimer, John J. 2001. *The Tragedy of Great Power Politics.* New York: Norton.

———. *The Great Delusion: Liberal Dreams and International Realities.* New Haven: Yale University Press.

Mecklin, John. 2022. "At doom's doorstep: It is 100 seconds to midnight." *Bulletin of the Atomic Scientists*. https://thebulletin.org/doomsday-clock /current-time/.

Metinsoy, Murat. 2021. *The Power of the People: Everyday Resistance and Dissent in the Making of Modern Turkey, 1923–38*. Cambridge: Cambridge University Press.

Mojab, Shahrzad, ed. 2001. *Women of a Non-State Nation: The Kurds*. Costa Mesa, CA: Mazda Publishers.

Mojab, Shahrzad and Amir Hassanpour. 2021. *Women of Kurdistan: A Historical and Bibliographic Study*. London: Transnational Press.

Moradian, Manijeh. 2022. *This Flame Within: Iranian Revolutionaries in the United States*. Durham: Duke University Press.

Nabavi, Negin. 2005. "Spreading the Word: Iran's First Constitutional Press and the Shaping of a 'New Era.'" *Critique: Critical Middle Eastern Studies* 14:307–21.

Nugent, Walter. 2008. *Habits of Empire: A History of American Expansion*. New York: Vintage Books.

Öcalan, Adullah. 1999. *Declaration on the Democratic Solution of the Kurdish Question*. London: Mesopotamian Publishers.

———. 2007. *Prison Writing: The Roots of Civilisation*. London: Pluto Press.

———. 2013. *Democratic Confederalism*. Cologne: International Initiative.

———. 2020. *The Sociology of Freedom: Manifesto of the Democratic Civilization*, Volume III. Oakland, CA.: PM Press, 2020.

Organization of the Iranian Peoples' Fadā'i Guerrillas. 1977. *Azerbaijan va Masala-ye Melli*. n.p.

Pirniā, Hasan. 1932. *Irān-e Bāstān*. Tehrān, n.p.

Prashad, Vijay. 2007. *The Darker Nations: A People's History of the Third World*. New York and London: The New Press.

Rawls, John and Jürgen Habermas. 2007. "Arms and Rights: The Adjustable Centre." In *Spectrum*, edited by Perry Anderson, 140–74. London and New York: Verso.

Rawls, John. 2001. *The Law of Peoples*. Cambridge, MA: Harvard University Press.

Schayegh, Cyrus. 2010. "'Seeing Like a State': An Essay on the Historiography of Modern Iran." *International Journal of Middle East Studies* 42:37–61.

Scott, James C. 1998. *Seeing Like a State: How Certain Schemes to Improve the Human Condition Have Failed*. New Haven and London: Yale University Press.

———. 2009. *The Art of Not Being Governed: An Anarchist History of Upland Southeast Asia*. New Haven: Yale University Press.

Smith, William and Robert Fine. 2004. "Kantian Cosmopolitanism Today: John Rawls and Jürgen Habermas on Immanuel Kant's *Foedus Pacificum*." *King's Law Journal* 15:5–22.

Soleimani, Kamal and Ahmad Mohammadpour. 2019. "Can non-Persians Speak? The Sovereign's Narration of "Iranian identity"." *Ethnicities* 19:715–39.

Tapper, Richard. 1997. *Frontier Nomads of Iran: A Political and Social History of the Shahsevan*. New York: Cambridge University Press.

Toohey, G. 2022. "Despite all the critics, California could soon rise to the world's 4th-largest economy." *Los Angeles Times*, November 2. https:// www.latimes.com/california/story/2022–11–02/what-does-it-mean-if -california-becomes-worlds-4th-largest-economy.

Vahabzadeh, Peyman. 2023. "*Iran etnic nadrād.*" *Akhbār Ruz*, January 10. https://akhbar-rooz.com/178128.

Vali, Abbas. 2014. *Kurds and the State in Iran: The Making of Kurdish Identity*. London: I.B. Tauris.

———. 2019. *The Forgotten Years of Kurdish Nationalism in Iran*. New York: Palgrave Macmillan.

Vine, David. 2020. *The United States of War: A Global History of America's Endless Conflicts, From Columbia to the Islamic State*. Oakland, CA: University of California Press.

Wasserstein, David. 1985. *The Rise and Fall of the Party-kings: Politics and Society in Islamic Spain 1002–1086*. Princeton, NJ: Princeton University Press.

Westad, Odd Arne. 2011. *Global Cold War: Third World Interventions and the Making of Our Times*. Cambridge: Cambridge University Press.

Wilford, Hugh. 2013. *America's Great Game: The CIA's Secret Arabists and the Shaping of the Modern Middle East*. New York: Basic Books.

Wilson, Edmund. 1953. *To the Finland Station*. New York: Anchor Books.

Yasin Sunca, Jan. 2022. "Growing Utopian Crack: Ten Years of the Rojava Revolution." *Jadaliyya*, November 14. https://www.jadaliyya.com /Details/44581.

The Politics of Performing Joy in Public

Nahid Siamdoust

IN A SHORT VIDEO CLIP that circulated on social media in 2018, we see a young couple dancing amorously in an urban street corner to a live band's rendition of the song "Nemiyād" (He Ain't Coming) by Googoosh.[1] The clip bears similarities to others like it, which were also circulated on platforms like Facebook, Telegram, and Instagram. In most other political and social contexts, including Middle Eastern ones, this video would not be viral-worthy. But in Iran, these videos that captured public and usually spontaneous instances of joyful music and dance began to constitute a genre of videos that were circulated widely before the 2022 revolutionary uprising, engaging national as well as transnational diasporic audiences. Videos exhibiting this genre of what one might call "performative counterpublicity"[2] appeared in the online sphere around 2016/7 and over the years of their constitution as a recognizable "genre" accrued certain politically rooted, affective meanings. As I will discuss in the following pages, both in their production as well as their wide circulation, these videos have come to serve a poetic worldmaking in which creations of joyful spaces and affects are posited as counter to an Islamic Republic that promulgates an "ethos of grief," rendering them politically salient. Furthermore, I will argue that the state's disciplinary biopolitics, which is concerned with regulating the vices that might arise from the bodies of women in particular, is taken to task in these videos by a preponderance of women enacting the untethering of their bodies from state control. An overarching concern of my work here is to articulate an idea of affective and performative joy as revolutionary in the specific Iranian context, conditioned as it is by a unique form of Islamist governance. Although in recent years the idea of joy as transformative or even radical has percolated in writings about black lives[3] – especially in the wake of the Black Lives Matter movement,

---

1. Anonymous 2018, https://www.instagram.com/p/Bj5FG1Xnj3L/?utm_medium=copy_link. Based on some of the comments, this scene most likely took place in Tehran.

2. I am drawing on three concepts here, namely "utopian performatives" by Jill Dolan, "publics and counterpublics" by Michael Warner, and "visceral performativity" by Stephanie Larson, as I will discuss.

3. See, for example, Lewis-Giggetts 2020 and Perry 2020.

whereby joy is often formulated as an act of resistance – joy as an important political force is "all but ignored by the social sciences."[4]

Over the course of the Islamic Republic, Iranians have utilized various media technologies in order to perform independent publics. I draw here on Charles Tripp who argues that it is "through performance that identities, social formations, and relations, as well as dispositions, are constituted [...]," adding that "it is this that makes an understanding of the performative so central to an understanding of power."[5] However, the particular development that I will be examining here is how the salience of these viral dance videos is conditioned by two interweaving processes, and how the outcome serves as a mediated public space for audiences to engage in mostly anti-Islam and anti-Islamic Republic discourses. The first process I will examine is the affectively constructed nature of these videos, rooted as they are in performances of joy in contradistinction to an official culture that censures and punishes certain kinds of joyful conduct. The second process is the way in which the state's repression and securitization of Iran's underground cultural scene, which flourished in the 2000s, eventually resulted in a mediated form that has in some ways reverted to the pre-Internet era, face-to-face kinds of interactions and street events (such as the dance videos) that are then mass-mediated on social media. The circulation of these videos, and the space for commentary below them, serve as spaces for people to express both their counterpublicness and counterpublicity. These terms are distinct in that the first, formulated by Nancy Fraser and in my use here, Michael Warner, expresses a relation among strangers, as constituted through mere attention, and as poetic worldmaking. Warner further argues that a counterpublic, unlike a public, "maintains an awareness of its subordinate status" and the political and cultural horizon against which it marks itself off is a dominant one.[6] The latter term, counterpublicity, is partly formulated by Stephanie Larson to point to the dissemination of a certain positionality, in this context via the use of social media, and the "vital role bodies play in shaping how subjects connect to public life."[7] In this framing of "visceral counterpublicity," embodied performances become central to advancing a certain rhetorical stance. Together, these ideas help us formulate an understanding of these dance videos as a means through which people create and disseminate a counterpublic centered on the freeing of the joyful body.

4. Quote from the project description for Theology of Joy and the Good Life at the Yale Center for Faith and Culture and the Yale Divinity School; https://faith.yale.edu/legacy-projects/theology -of-joy.

5. Tripp 2014.

6. Warner 2002, 86.

7. Larson 2028, 123–44.

What's All the Crying About?

For anyone who knows post-revolutionary Iran, establishing that the Islamic Republic has since its inception promulgated an "ethos of mourning," as stated above, would be superfluous. However, although this particular politics has colored every aspect of Iran's social and political life over the last forty-some years, there is no serious academic treatment of the subject in English or Persian. Most writings on the topic of joy are either within works of self-help or psychology, or examinations of the parameters of joyful conduct – such as music and dance – within Islam. As the author of one of the few pieces on the subject comments, although "lack of communal joy is one of the important social deprivations of contemporary Iranians," it "appears there is a research lacuna" and "this subject has not been treated seriously in Iranian sociology."[8] Perhaps researchers have regarded the subject matter as "too light" for academic work. In the Iranian academy, researchers may have found the topic too sensitive politically. Although the distinguished theorist Hannah Arendt wrote about the subject of happiness in her book "On Revolution" already in 1963, commenting on the difference between the French and American revolutions in that the outcome of the latter afforded for happiness, it appears that most other writings on the subject, especially in the last few decades, have viewed topics such as "joy" and "hope" within culturalist and consumerist entrapments that purvey a particular mode of living informed by "false-consciousness" neoliberal economies.[9] Given these entanglements, it is necessary to articulate a concept of joy that gives serious consideration to the affective and embodied politics at play in the circulation of the dance video genre at the center of my discussion here.

When the 1979 Iranian revolution happened, one of the revolutionaries' main charges was that the Pahlavi monarchy had ruled Iranian society with westernizing policies, alienating it from any sense of authenticity. As is well known, this was best encapsuled in the writer Jalal Ale-Ahmad's term "occidentosis" in the 1960s, where he elaborates, "I speak of 'occidentosis' as of tuberculosis," a disease that strikes a social body from within. Entailed in this critique of "occidentosis," often translated as "westoxification," was the notion of a society removed from its own roots and culture, one that imitated the consumerism and entertainment culture of the West, and – in brief – lacked dignity and gravitas. As far as the eventual leader of the revolution Ayatollah Ruhollah Khomeini and his followers were concerned, the social ills that manifested themselves

---

8. Gilvayi and Savji 2013, 97.

9. See, for example, Sukarieh 2012, where she discusses PR campaigns of "hope" and "optimism" across three Arab countries post-Arab Spring, which she argues simultaneously "facilitate and legitimate a set of neoliberal economic, political, and legal reform" (115).

across society, but especially in the mingling of the sexes and the consumption of lewd entertainment and alcohol in cabarets, needed to be uprooted with a turn to Islam. In their interpretations of the cultural contingencies that culminated in the revolution, the revolutionaries and especially the Islamists among them, had created an ontological link between joyous entertainment or community and Pahlavi era social "westoxicated" depravity.

When the revolution succeeded, entertainment centers like cinemas, concert halls and cabarets were some of the first establishments to be vandalized and burnt to the ground. Legions of entertainers left the country for exile. The new revolutionary state was firmly established on Islamic principles. In one of his early speeches, Khomeini compared pre-revolutionary society to addicts, stating:

> All the time he's just wondering when it'll be summer and when he can go to the beach, when it'll finally be evening so he can go to the cinema, when certain programs will be on television so he can sit and watch. He just can't. Just like the opium addict who can't leave the pipe and go seek, let's say, construction jihad, while at the pipe he can't think about what is happening to his country, its culture, its economy, he can't think. And that's exactly what they want, those who want to rob us, they want to rob us without being bothered, they say let's create this path of fun and pleasure for them, they entertain themselves while we rob them.[10]

Elsewhere, Khomeini had declared various versions of the theme above, in one speech saying, "they wanted to empty our brains, replace the brain of a serious person with a 'lahw wa la'abi' brain,"[11] using the Qoranic term "lahw wa la'ab," which translates to "idle talk" or "fun and games" and has been used by jurists for centuries to interpret scriptural injunctions against music and entertainment.[12]

As is common knowledge, a large segment of the Iranian population was religious and engaged in Shia rites even before the revolution. Many of these communal traditions are commemorations of the deaths or martyrdoms of imams and other sanctities and involve *nohe* (eulogy) recitations and collective crying. But with the revolution, Khomeini highlighted the political potential of crying in his speeches and elevated the nature of these religious commemorations above and beyond religion and reframed them as anti-Imperialist communal

10. Khomeini 1991, 9:74.

11. Khomeini 1991, 9:154–55. All translations mine unless otherwise indicated.

12. See Chehabi 2025. For a discussion of the Islamic debate on music in the Persianate world, see the chapter on music in Beeman 2011.

experiences that were central to the survival of the newly born Islamic nation. In one speech, the charismatic leader told the worshipping crowd:

> It is not so that you should imagine crying is crying. No, it's not crying. It's a political, psychological, social issue [...] it saves the essence of our religion [...] it is these chest-beating processions, these eulogy recitations, it is these that are the secret to our victory. All over the country there should be mourning gatherings, all should be mourning, and all should be crying.[13]

Elsewhere Khomeini said, "we are a nation of political crying, we are a nation that will cause floods with our tears and tear down the dams that stand against Islam."[14]

Once the new regime was firmly established, it gradually imposed a culture of mourning that had both religious and political exigencies in many spheres of life. State-affiliated foundations and organizations heavily funded mourning commemorations, the morality committees policed bodies and considered dark colors – especially in women's clothing – as the only acceptable "revolutionary" attire, state media broadcast a preponderance of sad eulogies and music, and religious and political authorities expressed dismay at the celebration of joyous Persian holidays, some of which constitute the most important holidays for nearly all Iranians to this day, regardless of their ethnicity, religion, or religiosity. This atmosphere of grief was substantiated in the real lives of Iranians by the bloody war with Iraq, which had devastating effects on the lives of most Iranians, whether through loss of loved ones, physical and emotional injury, destruction of homes in urban air bombings, or emigration and the separation of families.

These developments in society were mirrored in some of the works of art at the time, perhaps none more evocative than Ahmad Shamloo's famous poem "Dar In Bonbast" (In This Blind Alley), which encapsulates the dark and repressive mood of that first post-revolutionary decade. These were times in which roadblocks and house raids were carried out to enforce a piety that left little room for song and joy, as the following two stanzas best illustrate:

> In this crooked blind alley, at the turn of the chill
> > they feed the fire
> > with logs of songs and poetry.
> > Hazard not a thought.
> > > Strange times, my dear!

13. Khomeini 1991, 10:217.
14. Khomeini 1991, 13:156.

> He who knocks at your door in the noon of the night
> has come to kill the light.
> > We should hide light in the larder.
>
> There, butchers
> posted in passageways
> with bloody chopping blocks and cleavers.
> > Strange times, my dear!
> And they chop smiles off lips
> songs off the mouth.
> > We should hide joy in the larder.[15]

In their rare article on religion and joy in post-revolutionary Iran mentioned above, Gilvayi and Savji examine the positions of religious conservatives, moderates, and reformists, and conclude that all but some reformist clerics oppose activities generally associated with joy, such as most music, dancing, clapping, and even the celebration of pre-Islamic holidays. Furthermore, they maintain that the most conservative views have prevailed in influencing official state policy while reformist views have been sidelined. They quote the theoretician Abdolkareem Soroush, who has stated that there is a national tendency toward sadness and grief supported by the state in Iran. They also quote other occasional newspaper articles commenting on the lack of communal joy, with one writer commenting: "Many of our preachers and eulogists spread false ideas in society about joy in Islam. In their view, joy is an issue that is abominable at best and haram at worst. With this perspective, Islam has become a religion of depression, grief, mourning and weeping."[16]

ANXIETIES OVER DANCE

Because of the particular injunctions that jurists have used to interpret an Islamic ban on most kinds of joyful music and dance, these two art forms have been construed as the most problematic within the religio-political realm of the Islamic Republic. However, for various political and pragmatic reasons that I have examined in my book *Soundtrack of the Revolution*,[17] strict views toward music, even Khomeini's own, gave way to flexible policies on the subject so that gradually over the course of about a decade starting in the late 1990s, state policies evolved to allow for rhythmically fast and joyful music.[18] Still, the issue

15. Shamloo 2009.
16. Gilvayi and Savji 2013, 110.
17. Siamdoust 2017.
18. However, as one of the concert attendees in my book notes, due to state restrictions on artists and audiences, the purveyed affect is "an empty joy" (*shadi-ye puch*) rather than agentive, free joy.

of dance has been more problematic, as Ida Meftahi demonstrates in her book *Gender and Dance in Modern Iran*.[19] Women's dance, conventionally referred to as *raqs* in Persian, was instantly prohibited with the advent of the revolution as it was deemed to purvey "prostitution" (*fahshā*), "eroticism" (*shahvat*), and "degeneration" (*ibtizāl*).[20] When dance finally reappeared on the theater stage, it was defamiliarized and renamed *harekāt-e mawzun* (rhythmic movements), and inspection committees placed all kinds of restrictions on theater performances to stamp out movements that could resemble "lightness, carefreeness, or spontaneity."[21] Female bodies and their movements needed to be portrayed as purposeful "rather than merely exhibitionist and entertaining for the gaze of the spectators to differentiate them from the pre-revolutionary cabaret dancers who were associated with 'degeneration.'"[22]

These governmental anxieties over the issue of dance were manifested in three highly publicized instances in recent years. In 2019, a famous, recently expatriated, musician called Sasy released a track called "Gentleman," which went viral and led to dozens of copycat videos of school children dancing to the song, sometimes orchestrated and filmed by their own teachers.[23] Conservatives rose in furor, and the second deputy speaker of parliament, Ali Motahhari, demanded of the minister of education that the directors "of such schools [...] be replaced."[24] This became a national news story as the song was now ubiquitous in Iranian soundscapes both inside the country and in the global diaspora, and Iran's Islamic leaders fumbled to counter it. The minister soon declared that the "videos are fabricated" and that "there are political intentions behind them," and called Iran's Internet police, FATA, to help authorities apprehend the culprits.[25] The absurdity of this extreme political reaction was on display in the stark contrast between school children dancing and grown men in parliament calling for their censure. Sasy weighed in by posting a challenge to Motahhari on his Instagram account, in effect reflecting the general mood on this on social media:

> Mr. Motahhari, I invite you to a challenge. Listen to "Gentleman" and turn up the volume, if it doesn't move you to dance, you win. That's

19. Meftahi 2016.
20. Meftahi 2016, 150.
21. Meftahi 2016, 163.
22. Meftahi 2016, 163.
23. See *Peykelran*, 8 May 2019, https://www.youtube.com/watch?v=OzN6u4atDX0, or *Aparat*, 2019, https://www.aparat.com/v/zaMSV
24. See "Sāsy Mānkan dar Majles," *RadioFarda*, 7 May 2019; https://www.radiofarda.com/a/29925900.html.
25. See *Eqtesādnews*, 7 May 2019; https://www.eghtesadnews.com/fa/tiny/news-281975.

> when you're going to DM me (Sasy, get up bro and make everyone
> dance!). Seriously, seriously, you've forgotten about the exchange
> rate hike, the price of meat, inflation, etc. etc. and today are making
> decisions about "Gentleman"???????[26]

In another episode, on 21 December 2020, a guest by the name of Dr. Fahimi on a state television health program advised people that when they gather for Shab-e Yalda (the Persian Winter Solstice holiday), they should "dance, I implore them to dance." The program host, Rozita Qobadi let out a nervous laugh to which the guest made a perplexed comment, "Your laugh was strange," before continuing to lecture on the value of dance: "Why do I say this? Because physical movement allows people to sleep better at night."[27] By highlighting Ms. Qobadi's awkward response, the guest revealed the absurdity of the "public transcript," James C. Scott's term for the critique of power spoken behind its back.[28] Once on break, the guest was asked to apologize for suggesting that people dance, which he refused, and the host was asked to apologize as well, which she did. As she revealed in an Instagram live later, she was given the exact script for the apology and told she needed to apologize three times.[29] However, she was subsequently fired anyway for not having reacted disapprovingly right away.[30]

In a third instance, a video was posted to social media in late December 2020 that showed the communications director of the Hormozgan Province Central Post Office, Gholamreza Tayebi, dancing around the room in what looks like an office meeting.[31] User comments on social media highlight the sensitive nature of this incident. One user writes, "He'll be fired tomorrow. In this land they don't apologize for killing people but they apologize for even mentioning the word 'dance,'" and another writes, "God willing he won't be fired. What did the poor thing do except for being happy? Why is joyfulness haram for us?"[32] This video went viral, and soon thereafter, there was news that Tayebi had indeed been fired from his post. The director general of the Hormozgan Post Office issued a statement that read in part, "The mentioned person was removed from

---

26. See Zeitoon; https://www.zeitoons.com/63077.

27. See www.khabaronline.ir/xgvx2.

28. Scott's main argument is that against the public transcript "every subordinate group creates, out of its ordeal, a 'hidden transcript' that represents a critique of power spoken behind the back of the dominant," see. Scott 1990.

29. See faradeed.ir/000NYl.

30. See https://www.shomanews.com/fa/tiny/news-974233

31. For the video, see *RadioFarda*, 23 Dec 2020; https://twitter.com/RadioFarda_/status/1341701587694194688.

32. See comments by @BornInDey and @tania.ceramic.studio under the *RadioFarda* clip in fn 30.

his post due to actions and behavior that are opposed to professional and bureaucratic dignity and has been referred to the unit for office violations."[33]

These three prominent "media events," as one might call them, demonstrate the degree of official disapproval and disavowal that the issue of dance – in one instance here even just the word "dance" – garners. This is in stark contrast to the role that music and dance play not just in young, but also cross-generational private social occasions in Iran. The imposition of a "public transcript" that is so at odds with private life creates an absurd effect that leaves much space for humorous engagement, as is evident from comments under most of these posts. The heightened reaction of state organs and officials to such instances, even when they involve children dancing, demarcates the issue as highly political. It is within this context that we can understand the viral circulation of dance videos, such as the one presented at the beginning of this article, as staging performative counterpublicness vis-à-vis the dominant political ideology. The centrality of the body and emotions at the center of these public spectacles are key factors that contribute to the making of these joyous counterpublics as both embodied and affective. Grounded both in the body and feeling, "these are articulations of counterpublic activity oriented toward the state and constitute a discursive space of opposition grounded in the body and feeling."[34]

The state imposition of a particular mode of Islamic living is something we now take for granted, but in understanding the private and later more public maintenance of joyful spaces in post-revolutionary Iran, we must consider the drastic nature of these changes in society. Most forms of entertainment were suddenly curtailed by the new regime, and Iranians more so than before, sought relief in their private spaces. And in these spaces, various media technologies have played a central role in allowing for alternative worldmakings, the rhetorical and performative means that Iranian publics have employed to shape worlds that they have aspired to inhabit. Even with the state's external impositions, Iranians have engaged in the day-to-day formation of their lives creatively, infusing their spaces with joyful sounds and affects. Public broadcasting was strictly controlled to purvey mostly religious programming or content related to the war with Iraq and the many brave souls who gave their lives or their children, brothers, and husbands to the war. During the dire 1980s, it was cassette tapes and later in the decade, VHS tapes that afforded this space. As one of my interviewees on the subject, forty-five-year old Parisa, who now lives in Los Angeles, told me,

33. See *PeykeIran*; https://www.peykeiran.com/Content.aspx?ID=220325
34. Larson 2018, 125.

> There were only two channels in Iran and it was all 'gham o ghosse'
> (sadness and grief) … but then my cousin would come, especially
> during Eid (Persian New Year), and say "the videos are here!" This was
> war time, missiles and bunkers, outside your life was gray, these videos
> brought in a world of color. It was like going to Luna Park (a Tehran
> amusement park).

Or as the musician Mohsen Namjoo has said, "there was no room for joyfulness,
but then Los Angeles was like a paradise from where these sounds would come
in." Namjoo has also spoken about the immense importance of the song "Pariya"
by Shahram Shabpareh, which as he has said, "all Iranians danced to under the
most depressing circumstances."[35]

With the end of the war and the slight opening of public spaces in the
1990s, Iranians maintained these spaces, now powered by programming content streaming in through satellite television technology. As I've learned from
my interviews with some of the very first producers of the "LA programs" that
Iranians would access first on VHS tapes and then later on satellite TV, for several years and even past the mid-1980s, the diasporic community was producing
many of these videos for their own survival away from the homeland. They barely had viewers back in Iran in mind. As Manouchehr Bibiyan, a pioneer of pop
music in the Pahlavi era and then the founder of Jaam-e Jam TV in LA told me,

> You have to imagine those years. People had lost everything. They
> didn't know the language. And then the hostage crisis happened.
> People would say they're Afghans or Italians, anything but Iranians.
> The men would die of heart attacks. The women would run the
> households, often doing menial jobs when in Iran they had been
> professionals. We produced our Nowruz videos to give hope and joy
> to people here.

And Alireza Amirghassemi, a prolific producer of music videos and later founder of Tapesh TV, professed to me that his aim was to create shiny videos to
match those seen in the West and that his first realization that his videos were
being watched in Iran didn't happen until the late 1980s when someone used
the phone number that was often superimposed on the videos to call in the middle of the night from Iran to ask if he could speak with the famous singer Sattar,
whom he had just seen on the tape.[36]

---

35. Namjoo 2014.
36. Both interviews conducted by author in person, Los Angeles, May 5, 2018.

It was only then that the diaspora increasingly started creating content with Iranian viewers in mind, especially once satellite TV technology became widely used starting in the mid-1990s. Back in Iran, these videos afforded the possibility for a community and conviviality that crossed walls and houses, when there were no other means for free publicness. And here the materiality of the video cassette came into play, as it contributed to the formation of an alternative communality or counterpublic early on. In the many copies and recopies in the circulation of these videos, they would lose quality so that the most sought-after parts of the tapes were *khat-khati* (static lines) and the most replayed parts of those were totally *barfaki* (snowy or cloud-like imagery). It was on these VHS tape clouds and the imaginaries that they afforded that Iranians during some of the most draconian post-revolutionary years connected with each other, in the recognition that out there were thousands of others who had equally enjoyed this particular tape and especially that one particular section of it "where Susan Roshan was doing a 'gher' (gyration) in her leather clothes," as one interviewee told me. Within these counterpublics, the mediation of joy via these tapes was as important as the possibilities for both trans-local and transnational publicness and collectivity that they afforded.

I won't be able to go into a detailed progression of alternative media use spanning forty-four years of post-revolutionary Iran, as my aim here is to offer a necessarily broad and somewhat short overview of these alternative world-makings toward the central subject matter of this piece, namely the emergence and salience of the kind of viral dance videos discussed earlier. Suffice it to say that starting in the 2000s, the Internet greatly expanded the possibilities for alternative community-building and publicness. This was best expressed in the formation of Iran's vibrant cultural underground, mediated online, throughout the first decade of the new millennium. This underground cultural space was dynamic and allowed for more open social and political debates as well as artistic expression.[37] It also contributed to the kind of organizing and campaigning that brought out millions of people in support of reformist candidate Mir-Hossein Moussavi leading up to the 2009 Presidential Election.

The 2009 Green Uprising was a real shock to the Islamic Republic system. It was the biggest protest movement since the 1979 revolution and the authorities took note that this other entirely independent cultural and political sphere enabled in its mediation and circulation by the Internet posed a threat to their narrative, if not the state's survival. This leads me to discuss the second process contributing to the salience of the micro dance videos, as mentioned in the beginning. By 2011, the Police Force had formed the Cyberpolice commonly

---

37. See, for example, Akhavan 2013; Sreberny and Khiabany 2010.

referred to as FATA (acronym of the Persian name of the unit), which in conjunction with other state institutions, began to systematically eradicate the cultural underground. They used different methods to do this. They arrested and jailed politically critical writers, raided recording studios, interrogated cultural producers and forced them to stop their productions. Soon they went beyond cultural producers to include individuals promoting what the authorities denounced as culturally Western, depraved content; any youths who were deemed to be conduits for the infiltration of Western cultural invasion (*tahajom-e farhangi*), a term Iran's Supreme Leader has deployed since the 1990s,[38] were arrested and interrogated, though often let go within days.

Perhaps the most highly publicized and reported such arrest early on was the apprehension of Tehran's "Happy Kids," a group of six young adults who followed the global meme of staging their own dance to Pharrell Williams' "Happy" song, and posted it on YouTube, titled "Happy: Tehran Pharrell William's [sic] Fans."[39] It is by all accounts an innocent video of three young men and three young women dancing, goofing around, and having fun, with the closing caption, "We have made this video as Pharell William's [sic] fans in 8hrs, with iPhone 5S. 'Happy' was an excuse to be happy. We enjoyed every second of making it. Hope it puts a smile on your face."[40] The Happy Kids were soon apprehended by the cyberpolice and paraded on state television for confessions. A few years later, in 2018, the same pattern of treatment happened to then teenage Instagram dance sensation, Maedeh Hojabri. The eighteen-year-old had posted videos of herself dancing in her small Tehran bedroom on Instagram, and she too, was brought on state television to atone for her sins. In a sign of the generative quality of these "events," and the popularity of the product and personas that the Happy Kids and Hojabri had traded, both became after their arrests and in subsequent years celebrities who were sought after to attend restaurant and gallery openings, advertise for products, or appear with famous entertainers.

I bring up these specific examples to highlight the trajectory through which counterpublic performances online (in most cases not political presentations per se) – whether the work of underground musicians or dance videos that attracted a lot of attention – were systematically targeted and shut down. The repression of these online spaces and these acts had two prominent consequences, as mentioned at the beginning. On the one hand, "raqs" (dance), which – as discussed earlier – the Islamic state had already marked as problematic and imposed various regulations on, accrued more of a mantle of resistance vis-à-vis

38. Siamdoust 2017, 7, 98.
39. Anonymous 2014.
40. Anonymous 2014.

the state. On the other hand, this persecution of online "celebrities" caused a performative and technological transformation in these presentations. The construction of popular personas or accounts online that veered far off state ideology and regulations had become too costly. Increasingly, starting around 2018/19, it was spontaneous moments captured at home, in the streets, or on public transport, such as Tehran's metro and buses, that played an important role in the staging of these repertoires of contention. These spontaneous, in-person, "analog" texts and events, were much harder to trace to individuals, and as long as they were not explicitly political, but rather, political meaning could be read into them in the act of mediation and consumption, or "secondary production,"[41] their makers were mostly safe from apprehension.

Indeed, not unlike the impact of print journalism on the Mashruti protest verse from the constitutional era, or the impact of small media such as cassette tapes on the production and circulation of protest sermons at the time of the 1979 revolution, social media have fundamentally reshaped the expression of protest in contemporary Iran, and the references and sensory faculties that are employed for its expression. If leading up to and during the 1905–1911 Revolution, constitutionalists used the spaces afforded by newspapers and pamphlets to present modernist verses on republican ideals and pride in a somewhat new notion of the nation-state of Iran, and Islamists used the cassette tape to create an aural soundscape that reverberated Khomeini's revolutionary anger, those opposed to the ethos of the governing state today are using the visual capacities of the social media video format to signal a joyous liberation of the body, or bodily autonomy, as a key component of their alternative worldmaking. Among these hundreds of short videoclips that are in circulation on social media, many present a nostalgic, corporeal embodiment of a pre-revolutionary imaginary set to 1970s Iranian pop music, or very contemporary exhibitions of a youthful joyfulness tied into global music trends or memes. Together, these micro-clips purvey soundscapes that create spaces and condition, discipline, and move bodies, in function perhaps not so different from what Charles Hirschkind describes as the ethical soundscapes of Cairo, though in the Egyptian context cassette tapes of Islamic sermons serve as vehicles for ethical self-improvement and pious living, whereas these joyous Iranian soundscapes work to rupture the state's "Islamic" disciplining of bodies.

And in these hundreds of independent "micro-clips" circulated on social media, the majority are of women staging the kinds of street-level, face-to-face repertories of spontaneity and joy invoked earlier, where women flout officially

41. de Certeau 1984.

sanctioned frameworks for public comportment and use their bodies to stage what Marwan Kraidy has called "creative insurgencies."[42] The necessity for these in-person "creative insurgencies" was caused by the securitization of online spaces. In most of these videos we see women spontaneously breaking into dance in response to street music. In one such video, for example, a young woman starts dancing in front of two street musicians. This video clip, like most others, is less than a minute long but has accrued more than one million views. Having read the comments below on a couple of such videos, one can anticipate the comments for most. Below this one, nail.tattoo.arezoo writes, "They've taken away our joy. A sad people always mourning and eulogizing." Another commenter says, "In the end they will even arrest God for the crime of (woman) creation." Another user, called zahramahdiyani2, says, "The foundations of Islam are shaking with this dance. So let's dance until this Islamic state is destroyed. Dance so we dance." What makes people take note of these instances of public dancing, record them, and post them on social media is that the mounting of such joyous counterpublics in the public space have by now accumulated affective value, a sort of "stickiness," to use Sara Ahmed's term,[43] a repetition that signals this very simple act as a significant – perhaps political – repertoire, within the given context, or visceral counterpublicity.

Stripped of possibilities in the cultural underground, public spaces became theaters of performance. Indeed, one might take the term "theater" literally, because not unlike theater, these live performatives are ephemeral, and in their brief staging, allow for a "processual, momentary feeling of affinity, in which spectators experience themselves as a congenial public constituted by the performance's address."[44] These vistas that are mounted onto public spaces in these micro acts, and then mass mediated on social media as micro-clips, point us toward a narrative that diverges from official productions. On these representational sites,[45] we see alternative representations of the kinds of sites that Islamic Republic institutions have enforced on public spaces. These alternative sites perform a poetic worldmaking, imagining a more open and permissive public square, the kind that the people enacting them would like to inhabit. And for a few hours or days, they manage to mount these imaginaries onto public spaces, whether on the streets or in the metro, or in their virtual circulation in the parallel public sphere exercised on social media. As Dolan states, "Utopian per-

42. Kraidy 2016.
43. Ahmed 2010.
44. Dolan 2016, 246.
45. Lefebvre 1992.

formatives, in their doings, make palpable an affective vision of how the world might be better."[46]

Importantly, these mediated dance videos create collective experiences that mirror the embodied communal mourning publics whose importance Khomeini highlighted in his speeches in the early years of the revolution. While those publics were affectively rooted in Shia traditions that were revived in the country's anti-imperialist revolution, these dance videos and the discursive sites that accompany them often draw on nostalgic pre-revolutionary music and joyous affects that have been devalued by the country's religious authorities. As is evident in the commentaries below these videos on social media sites, those engaging the circulation and consumption of these videos have constructed a by now well-established discursive link between Islam and mourning and sadness, countered by another that articulates a joyous life as rooted in Iran's non- and pre-Islamic culture. On these sites, Khomeini's "political crying" is countered by an organically forming politics of joy. This politics of joy erupted in spectacular manner during the 2022 Woman, Life, Freedom protests, but had been in the making for years.

46. Dolan 2016, 240.

Works Cited

Ahmed, Sara. 2010. "Happy Objects." In *The Affect Theory Reader,* edited by Melissa Gregg and Gregory J. Seigworth, 29–51. Durham: Duke University Press.

Akhavan, Niki. 2013. *Electronic Iran : The Cultural Politics of an Online Evolution.* New Brunswick: Rutgers University Press.

Anonymous. 2014. "Happy We Are from Tehran." Posted by Ah T, May 19. https://www.youtube.com/watch?v=RYnLRf-SNxY

Anonymous 2018. https://www.instagram.com/p/Bj5FG1Xnj3L/?utm _medium=copy_link

Anonymous. 2019a. "Sāsy Mānkan dar Majles." *RadioFarda,* May https:// www.radiofarda.com/a/29925900.html

Anonymous. 2019b. *Eqtesādnews,* May 7. https://www.eghtesadnews.com/fa /tiny/news-281975

Anonymous. 2020. *RadioFarda,* December 23. https://twitter.com/Radio Farda_/status/1341701587694194688

Beeman. William. 2011. *Iranian Performance Traditions.* Costa Mesa, Calif.: Mazda Publishers.

Certeau, Michel de.1984. *The Practice of Everyday Life.* Berkeley: University of California Press.

Chehabi, Houchang. 2025. "Music, Religion, and Charismatic Authority in the Revolutionary Decade." In *Iran Amplified: One Hundred Years of Music and Society,* edited by Nahid Siamdoust and Houchang Chehabi. Boston: Mizan Project.

Dolan, Jill. 2016. "Utopian Performatives." In *Performance Studies Reader,* edited by Henry Bial and Sara Brady. London: Routledge.

Gilvayi, Hassan Mohadessi and Elham Qorbani Savji. 2013. "Shādi va Gerāyeshhā-ye Dini dar Irān pas az Enqelāb" (Joy and Religious Tendencies in Post-Revolutionary Iran). *Faslnāmeh Motāle'āt-e Jāme'shenākhti-ye Iran,* 8:97.

Khomeini, Ruhollah. 1991. *Sahifeh-ye Nur.* Tehrān: Sāzmān-e Chāp va Enteshārāt-e Vezārat-e Farhang va Ershād-e Islāmī.

Kraidy, Marwan M. 2016. *The Naked Blogger of Cairo : Creative Insurgency in the Arab World.* Cambridge, MA: Harvard University Press.

Larson, Stephanie R. 2018. "'Everything Inside Me Was Silenced': (Re)defining Rape through Visceral Counterpublicity." *The Quarterly Journal of Speech* 104:123–44.

Lefebvre, Henri. 1992. *The Production of Space.* London: Wiley-Blackwell.

Lewis-Giggetts, Tracey Michael. 2020. "My Daughter Reminded Me That Black Joy Is a Form of Resistance." *The Washington Post,* June 19.

Meftahi, Ida. 2016. *Gender and Dance in Modern Iran: Biopolitics on Stage.* London: Routledge.

Namjoo, Mohsen. 2014. "Musical Talk: Shahram Shabpareh, Honesty and Minor Scale." Brown University, May 19. https://www.youtube.com /watch?v=tKbimDu3-Ug

Perry, Imani. 2020. "Racism Is Terrible. Blackness Is Not." *The Atlantic,* June 15.

Scott, James C. 1990. *Domination and the Arts of Resistance: Hidden Transcripts.* New Haven, CT: Yale University Press.

Shamloo, Ahmad. 2009. "In This Blind Alley." Translated by Ahmad Karimi Hakkak. In *Strange Times in Persia: An Anthology of Contemporary Iranian Literature,* edited by Nahid Mozaffari & Ahmad Karimi Hakkak, 372. London: I.B.Tauris, 2009.

Siamdoust, Nahid. 2017. *Soundtrack of the Revolution: The Politics of Music in Iran.* Stanford, Calif.: Stanford University Press.

Sreberny, Annabelle and Gholam Khiabany. 2010. *Blogistan: The Internet and Politics in Iran.* London: I.B.Tauris.

Sukarieh. Mayssoun. 2012. "The Hope Crusades: Culturalism and Reform in the Arab World." *Political and Legal Anthropology Review* 35:115–34.
Tripp, Charles. 2014. "The Politics of Resistance and the Arab uprisings." In *The New Middle East: Protest and Revolution in the Arab World*, edited by Fawaz A. Gerges, 135–54. New York: Cambridge University Press.
Warner, Michael. 2002. "Publics and Counterpublics." *Public Culture* 14:86.

"You were born in a shit hole; I was born in imperial Iran": Ethnic Reality TV and Inventing Persianness in *Shahs of Sunset*

Lior Sternfeld and Babak Rahimi

THIS CHAPTER ATTENDS TO THE QUESTION of diasporic identity in *Shahs of Sunset*, an American reality TV show aired on Bravo between 2012 and 2021.[1] *Shahs of Sunset* signals a specific example in the subgenre of reality TV programming that makes visible characters *as* performers with the potential not only for celebrity status but also identity construction. Our focus on five of the six Iranian-American cast members, portraying a diasporic life of luxury in "Tehrangeles," is meant to analyze the significance of the dramatization of personality interaction and hence complex practices of identity, which the American reality TV depicts.[2] *Shahs of Sunset* invites us to experience being "Persian" in a Southern Californian context wherein reality and performance run parallel and overlap in complexities of class, ethnicity, gender, class, sexuality, race, and status.

Since space precludes us from examining all the characters in nine seasons, we will concentrate on the five cast members in season three, which aired from November 5, 2013, to February 25, 2014, although references to other seasons will also be made. With its sixteen episodes, including "Reunion," when all reality television characters meet for a face-off, season three is unique in how its episodic narrative brings the diasporic identity of the Iranian-Americans into conversation. Five key cast members, – "Asa" (Asa Soltani Rahmati), "GG" (Golnesa Gharachedaghi), "Reza" (Reza Farahan), and "Mike" (Mike Shouhed), and "MJ" (Mercedes Javid) – participate in an apparent unscripted reality television program that stages confessional selves, comprised of interview segments that offer gossip-like insights to their inter-personal stories as immigrants to the United States.[3] However, crucial to the identity of cast members' immigrant story is the ostensible glamorization of status and wealth that

---

1. Bravo is a division of NBC Universal, a leading US media and entertainment company with a global audience.

2. For a study of the cultural life of "Tehrangeles" Iranians, see Hemmasi 2020.

3. We leave out several characters from our discussion, though we will turn to Lilly Ghalichi, who played a more visible role in season three, toward the end of the present paper.

remains conflicted in the experience of immigration. What ultimately defines the identity of *Shahs of Sunset* is a narrative divided between the two homelands, Iran and America, where claims to Persianness play an ambiguous role in dramatizing self and reality.

What is Persianness? We argue that the diasporic identity of Los Angeles-based Iranian Americans, as depicted in *Shahs of Sunset*, revolves around a conception of "Persianness" as citational performances of ethnicity that reify the cast members as frivolous and superficial on the screen. However, such reification is intimately tied to the 1979 revolution as a temporal marker—an event of rupture and discontinuity that shattered and reshaped the exilic lives of Iranians. Importantly, this discontinuity provides the opportunity for subjective opening to self-reconstruct in American consumerist culture. *Shahs of Sunset* expresses such culture through its key cast members in two crucial ways.

First, despite individualized personalities, a common theme among the characters of *Shahs of Sunset* under study is the self-branding practice through which "Persian" becomes an exotic ethnicity of superficial character for (reality) television consumption. Second, *Shahs of Sunset*'s personas depict a yearning in a felt distance for a lost homeland imagined as something crossed over without the possibility of a return. Yet such distance is marketized in branding terms of a new identity to underscore the narrative of progress made in the experience of immigration from Iran to America, where the new homeland, in contrast to the static old one, promises a dynamic identity for self-expression.

In many ways, the presentation of "Persianness" in *Shahs of Sunset* traverses consumerist themes such as celebrity fame, fashion, lifestyle, luxury, gossip culture, drama, intimate confessional diary, and tabloid, all of which have been a staple of American reality television shows since the 1990s. But, in this particular program, the theme of dislocation appears at center stage. *Shahs of Sunset* emphasizes a distinct exilic habitus where physical or imagined encounters with transnational belonging offer the promise of self-development in the experience of immigration – to America. While dislocation is about longing for a departed homeland, in *Shahs of Sunset*, it becomes an opening for re-invention. The opportunity to reconstruct becomes closely connected with the narrative of an encounter with the past left behind (Iran) and the present now (America) for re-invention. Such re-invention becomes possible in the American media industry, where "Persianness" takes the signified forms of fluffy cats, comfortable carpets, professional laborers such as attorneys, entrepreneurs, medical doctors, real estate agents, and, in the case of *Shahs of Sunset*, new celebrities. All in all, what *Shahs of Sunset* characters reveal is a kind of celebrity culture, in which

"Persian" signifies a distinct branding of ethnic identity as glamorous, rich but equally part of the broader multicultural life of Southern California.

This show allows us to examine the social, sociological, and generational composition of the Iranian community in Los Angeles. While most participants came to the United States soon after the 1979 revolution and most were born in Iran, some of the characters that joined later are of different backgrounds, which helps to emphasized the unique dynamic of the Los Angeles community, or as they proudly call it: "Tehrangeles."[4] Additionally, while in Iran Iranian Jewish community accounts, and historically accounted for less than half of a percent of the population, it is estimated that in Los Angeles they make up at least ten percent of the Iranian diaspora.[5] In a way, this show gives space to that too (perhaps unintentionally). Mike is Jewish, Sammy who was core member in the first season and made cameos appearances in later seasons is Jewish too. Reza is half-Jewish on his father's side, which becomes an important theme in season one when Reza reunites with his estranged father.

This chapter divides into three sections. The first offers an account of reality TV as a distinct programming genre, while typologizing *Shahs of Sunset* as a distinct form of ethnic reality TV show. The second section offers a brief interpretation of five personas in the *Shahs of Sunset*, all of which are identified in sharing the common practice of self-branding that projects success and wealth as Persian identity. The third section looks at two cast members, Asa Soltan Rahmati and Reza Farahan, who travel to the Iranian-Turkish border in nostalgia for a lost homeland. The invisible border they encounter is discussed to reflect a subjective void in the ambiguity of belonging, but ultimately helping them recognize their Persian identity in diaspora as an expression of an imagined multicultural America.

Ethnic Reality TV

If we follow Raymond Williams' diagnoses of television as a development of earlier media forms, in particular, advertisement and theater, with an emphasis on dramatized visualization, then reality TV is a genre of dramatic form of a documentary program in which in a controlled environment characters display their personal lives in a distinct public stage.[6] This public stage is inherently about the audience who participate in watching a genre of narrative that docu-

---

4. The sole exception is "GG," who was born in Los Angeles in 1981.

5. See more regarding the ethnic and religious composition of the Iranian diaspora in the United States: Bozorgmehr 2002, 1169.

6. Williams 2003, 39–76.

ments individual realities who undergo subjective change through encounters, trials, and conflict. For the most part, conflicts in reality TV are about individuals who express themselves and their relations in terms of class, gender, race, and sexuality and work through ostensibly unscripted plots that remain contingent on the unfolding storyline on the screen. Often the drama's protagonists reinforce conflict in their daily lives through overlapping but conflict-ridden relations in the form of enmity, family, friendship, and marriage. Yet characters in reality TV are mainly archetypes, representing a range of villains and heroes who embody complex emotions with ethical implications. Meanwhile, dramatic stories of reality TV are based on characters who perform their selves in relation to others in experiences of love, hate, vengeance, redemption, loss, and death.

The coming of reality TV programs in the 1990s, facilitated by the growing global media industry, changed the genre of TV drama into documentary-like life dramas (day-in-the-life), in which everyday events in a person's life, entangled with familial and friendship relations, come under surveillance with the potential for dramatic outbreak.[7] Following William, we can speak here of a structure of feeling in the emergence of reality TV, reproducing a representation of a reality upon which individual stories are framed as the central theme on the screen. Yet televised identities are primarily mediated through the space of choreographed television, where "reality" is staged into a self-performing platform. For more than three decades, reality TV has evolved into multiple subgenres, particularly as its distinct programming has increasingly overlapped with online fandom and consumption practices. The digitized dimension has not only expanded the audience size, but also changed the experience of viewing television, when first the mass technology became popularized in the 1960s, with the online component incorporated into the show's produced TV content.

The oldest subgenre of reality TV includes game shows that take place in a choreographic environment, a set designed for clash between individuals as contenders competing in isolation for a prize. While shows such as *The Bachelor* (2002–) and *Top Chef* (2006–) revolve around competition over skills or romance, the subgenre of reality TV games are fundamentally about the cast members as contestants who display themselves through stages of trial through which the gaming nature of the show is naturalized into individual or group contestation based on values of personal skill, talent, perseverance or wealth. Connected with gaming shows, makeover programs such as *Queer Eye* (2018–) and *Extreme Makeover: Home Edition* (2014–) emphasize self-improvement through an internal competition as an individual is self-challenged with the help of an expert, usually a celebrity professional, to undergo self-transforma-

---

7. Sender 2011, 4.

tion. Shows such as *America's Next Top Model* combine gaming and the make-over subgenre in staging the cast members into both competitors and persons who undergo self-transformation. In both subgenres the individual experiences a hyperbolic version of themselves in the performance of gaming or self-improvement.

Gaming and makeover shows, however, identify a visual counterpoint to popular celebrity reality TV programs. In celebrity TV, best exemplified by *Keeping Up with the Kardashians* (2007–2021), it is the famed *persona*, embodying wealth, fame, racial identity, gender, lifestyle, and conspicuous consumption, that takes center stage. The spectacle of celebrity reality TV is a reminder that fame and wealth maintain representational value because of their association with products which the celebrity persona embodies as (symbolic) capital. Unlike gaming shows, celebrity personas do not engage in competition with others but remain, as Sean Redmond observes, self-reflexive of their performing bodies made famous under the camera's gaze.[8] Unlike the themes of self-improvement, celebrity reality TV rejects self-identity as self- upgrading since the celebrity life is already an upgrade for others to aspire to. However, conflict still remains a dominant theme in celebrity reality TV's ideal of "famous for being famous," since celebrities' desires and needs, at times malicious in nature, are thwarted, endangered by others' desires, longings, betrayals, or jealousies. The source of tension in celebrity reality TV lies in preserving fame, weaving between self-absorption and endangerment of notability.

Aspiration is an important theme since narratives of reality TV celebrities revolve around the display of self-presentation of consumption practices that viewers desire to attain. Seen in this way, it is not merely the celebrities who display fame that are participants in the programming plots but also those around them and, of course, the audience who aspire to a life of fame revered or mocked but still watched for its viewership appeal. The "democratizing" effect of aspiration has become part of a broader cultural yearning for fame and visibility, which has led to a distinct modality of celebrity reality TV programming, which can be described as "ordinary" celebrity. The term "ordinary" is meant to underscore the growth of reality TV shows with relatively unknown cast members, whose very appearance in the programs make thme famous for, well, wanting to become famous. But it is important to note that the distinction between celebrity and "ordinary celebrity" is hard to define in the age of reality TV programming, as figures such as Kim Kardashian became famous for performing famousness.

For our discussion, the notion of "ordinary" mainly implies a distinct por-

8. Redmond 2008, 149–61.

trayal of middle-class life that reinforces stereotypes of heteronormative practices of gender, family, and race. The franchise of *Real Housewives*, launched
in 2006 across Australia, Canada, the United Kingdom and the United States,
best depicts this appeal to the "ordinary." The franchise portrays women of
influence, mainly of an entrepreneurial type, based on their appeal to sexual
powers, youth, vitality, and at times a cut-throat competitive nature for success.
Though mostly unknown prior to the filming, with the show the cast members gain fame in performing themselves, producing a unique form of celebrity
that is self-performed. In this sense, self-performance serves as a self-branding
practice in a show that frames the cast members as self-promoters who actively
participate in a series of advertisement environments that include restaurants
at which they have dined and hotels in which they have stayed, where often
personal conflicts of gendered and racialized nature unfold. In an example of
the centrality of race, the famed MTV show, *Laguna Beach: The Real Orange
County* (2004–2006), portrays friends in an upper-middle class community in
Orange County where whiteness, friendship, and success are in tension with
jealousy, competition, and betrayal. All in all, in celebrity reality TV, gender and
race play the most important roles in character-narrative structure.

Within the subgenre of ordinary reality TV grew the dramatization of
friendships or families based on ethnic identity. In the North American context, ethnicity is perceived in a racialized categorization of a group of people
understood to share an essentialized cultural trait linked through a distinct
racial makeup. The racial features can be implicit in the narrative but they appear intimately connected with expressions of ethnic culture segmented into a
geographical community mainly in a (sub) urban context. *Jersey Shore* (2009–
2012) is a good example of ethnic reality TV as it depicts reified notions of
Italian-American identity as aggressive, mischievous, and uncouth. Racialized
cast members reveal their character in highly staged personal conflicts that bol-
ster stereotypes while simultaneously enhancing the visibility of the characters
as either aspiring to up-and-coming careers, or successful artists, entrepreneurs
or professionals.

Shahs of Sunset is modeled after *Jersey Shore*, fusing dramas of persona conflict with the ethnic/racial culture of the cast members portrayed on screen. In
many ways, the personas in ethnic reality TV are encouraged to express their
ethnicity, often referencing their heritage in art, fashion, marriage, or daily conversations, as they participate in multicultural expressions of diversity and appearing as postracial chic, beyond cultural material stereotypes. But the element
of being foreign is reinforced by depicting the cast members as people who are
different, racially unique, though still familiar in their Americanized entertainment value for a largely white audience.

In *Shahs of Sunset*, the ethnicity of the cast members as "Persians" config-ures as racialized identity, appearing between foreignness and whiteness.[9] *Shahs of Sunset* follows the celebrity-like persona of the cast members but does so by emphasizing distinct racial markers expressed in cultural behaviors perceived as distinctively "Persian." From branding of the show as "Shahs" to depictions of physical smoothness, dandiness, boastfulness, crassness, violence, and, most importantly, deceptiveness, perpetuates tropes of Persianness commonly found in Western literary and visual traditions since the early modern travel accounts. The diasporic aspect also stresses the element of foreignness, which the show zooms on its characters who are balancing their American lives in Beverly Hills and Iranian traditions that involve expectations of sexual or gender identity and material or marital success. However, there is a key difference between *Shahs of Sunset* and diaspora reality TV programs such as UK-based Manoto's *befar-mayid sham* ("Dinner Is Served"), which is funded and managed by Iranians in diaspora. *Shahs of Sunset,* in contrast, is produced by the Bravo network and the American Entertainment production company, Ryan Seacrest Production, which has overseen the production of numerous reality TV programs since the mid-2000s. The production aspect of *Shahs of Sunset* reflects a broader cultur-al industry of reality TV shows that continue to produce programs of diverse themes for a targeted audience demographic, focusing on the personal lives of cast members perceived to display distinct racial identities.

Ethnic-Diasporic Personas

The gleaming, flashy and, of course, fashionable traits of *Shahs of Sunset,* best depicted in the show's title sequence, serve visual markers that accentuate the glamorous and celebrity-like status of the cast members. The lyrics of the up-beat opening song, "Cut a lot of girls, cut a lot of checks, that's the life here on sunset, rich and famous, I am success," matches the celebrity rhythm of affluence and glamor that characterizes the show. Central in the emphasis on superficial-ity and materialistic lifestyle are the personas who are the driving force of the show. It is in "Asa," "GG," "Reza," "Mike," and "MJ" that *Shahs of Sunset* displays the complicated relationship between wealth and Persianness in the show's narrative trajectory. When it comes to self-presentation, celebrity culture that the cast members depict conflate Iranianness with "Persian," which the show portrays in terms of a racial marker beyond Iran's diverse ethnic and linguistic makeup.

There is also the appeal to the ancient tradition of monarchy. The title,

9. The reference to this whiteness ambiguity is best explained by Maghbouleh when she shows how Iranians in America are perceived not as white enough to avoid racial discrimination. See especial-ly, Maghbouleh 2017, 14–48.

Shahs of Sunset, embodies the persona-driven charactesr of the reality show, especially Reza, who claim Iranian identity in reference to an imagined imperial past defined by the monarchy, the feudal political institution overthrown by the 1979 revolution. It is ironic that the plural title of "Shahs," meaning kings, representing a failed political institution, takes center stage for a show that displays a glitzy life of Iranian success in Southern California. For the most part, though, in the diasporic imagination of many Southern-Californian Iranians who left after the revolution and their children, the shah stands as a tale of triumphant nationalism. For the diaspora, Farzaneh Hemmasi explains, Iran under the Pahlavi "represents the last version of Iran they truly knew or, in the case of the second generation (who often have had limited exposure to pre-postrevolutionary Iran), the only Iran they understand in positive terms.[10]

Yet in the irony lies a hint of tragedy. In the personas who claim success, there is a struggle to come to terms with a revolution that forced the cast members to migrate to America, and also a reckoning with a monarchy that upon its collapse the characters claim identity. But the form of identity the "shahs" adopt is a branding tactic to promote the show for an audience seeking to watch (pseudo) royalty fused with personality drama marked by ethnic stereotypes.[11] The branding of *Shahs of Sunset* concerns itself with the depicted personas who self-promote in the idiom and symbolics of celebrity fame and status. In many ways, the major cast members of the show are performing celebrity branding in fetishizing their immigrant stories into a reified Persian identity.

The following short descriptions of the five cast members are meant to draw out differences in each of the show's personalities while stressing similarities of celebrity branding practices.

Reza

Reza is the larger-than-life character in the show. He is what is culturally and colloquially called half Jewish. His father is Jewish, and his mother is Muslim, so he is not Halakhically Jewish. The Jewish identity, however, is something that he wears proudly, and it grows with the progression of the show. In the first episodes, before the viewers get to learn of his family background, one can see subtle Jewish décor in his office. But what we see is something that is as Iranian

---

10. Hemmasi 2020, 129.

11. This study does not discuss the reality TV show's audience. However, based on research on the size of the audience for the first season, which was 1.5 million, the primary demographic for *Shahs of Sunset* is aged between 18 and 49. http://www.thefutoncritic.com/ratings/2012/03/27/bravo -medias-shahs-of-sunset-earned-series-highs-among-all-key-demos-with-15-million-total-viewers-up- 56-percent-among-adults-18–49–709010/20120327bravo01/. Last accessed March 23, 2023.

and Middle Eastern as much as it is Jewish. We see *Hamsa* (or in the non-Jewish culture: *Fatimah's hand*) with the blessing of the business [Birkat Ha'esek] inscribed.

When Reza takes the crew to meet his Jewish family in Great Neck, NY (including his father and grandmother, with whom he had lost touch) his connection to his Jewish identity becoming increasingly dominant. As they were driving around, he said: "Great Neck is a mini version of Beverly Hills, except there's zero Muslims." Then, he goes on to tell MJ that "they're all Jewish, and when I say Jewish, they're, like, super Jewish." The Great Neck community, comprised of Mashhadi Jews and those who came after the revolution, are considered to be more religious than the Los Angeles community, and perhaps even more socially tight than them. "I feel more Jewish than I do Muslim," Reza told MJ. "I've been to a thousand Bar Mitzvahs and Bat Mitzvahs, like, I've worn more yarmulkes than I have turbans." When they arrive at Reza's Jewish family, Asa presents the family with *Esther's Children*, which is a diasporic celebration of Iranian Jewish culture edited by Houman Sarshar and featuring images and essays on a wide plethora of themes.

Then, we witness the reunion of Reza and his estranged father, Manoochehr. We get a glimpse into a story of over four decades starting in Tehran and continuing in Los Angeles and New York. Reza confronts his father about his leaving the family and moving to NY and not showing any interest in their lives. Manoochehr then tells Reza that his mother, Reza's grandmother, never approved of Manoochehr's marriage with Reza's mom, because of her Muslim religion, and she always strove to create a chasm between Manoochehr and his family. "They are *goyim*," Reza's grandmother would tell his father about his own family. It appeared that towards the end of the season, Reza's relations with his father, but also grandmother, ipmroved significantly, which allowed him to connect even more to his Jewish identity.

Reza's Muslimness is revealed in connection with his (non-practicing) Muslim mother, whose marriage to his Jewish father caused considerable controversy since he had converted to Islam. Since Reza's mother is not accepted in his father's Jewish family, as half Muslim, Reza suffers from a deep sense of rejection. It is perhaps because of this inner conflict, with his mother as the source of stigma, that Reza not only downplays but at times even violently denies his background as a Muslim, however secular it may be. But we can also frame it as a diasporic reaction of the generation of 1979 to the revolution. The rationale of this articulation can be summarized as follows: if the revolution is Islamic, and we wish to distance ourselves from it – let's say we're not Muslim, if the revolution is Iranian – then we will call ourselves Persian.

Reza adheres to an expression of his Persian identity that glorifies an ancient imperial past. As a monarchist, Reza wears his Persianness with gold watches, flashy chains with pre-Islamic symbols of Faravahar (while Reza also espouses, anti-Islamic sentiments throughout the show, the symbols themselves convey a wide array of sentiments. Consider, for example, GG's wearing them alongside very Muslim symbols, like *Allah*), and a large commemorative gold mold with the bust of Pahlavi kings pinned on his designer clothes. As a staunch monarchist, Reza's style of self-branding combines his public expression of sexuality with elegance and conspicuous wealth. There is connection between fashion and wealth, as Reza expresses his class through venture entrepreneurship, self-promoting his various businesses from home, intending to own a line of luxury haircare products.

Asa

As the least bombastic character in the show, Asa Soltan Rahmati is an artist from Venice, California, whose artistic works have appeared in public. Educated and smart, Asa, who appeared in six seasons of the show, is a more recent immigrant, a "political refugee" since the age of eight, and hence more of an outsider in a group of cast members. Born in the southern-city of Ahwaz, Asa's provincial background distinguishes her Iranian identity from the other characters, whose families originate from Tehran. Equally important is Asa's place of familial residence, as she calls it the "ghetto" of Beverly Hills, which implies a marginal identification as a racial enclave of urban geography.

Asa is also a businesswoman, actively marketing herself in what Kira Ganga Kieffer calls "spiritual entrepreneurship," an extensive set of business practices that revolve around spiritual themes and values coded as "feminine."[12] "Welcome to the World of Diamond Water." Asa welcomes her parents to the facility where her new branded water, "Diamond Water," is bottled. "The priestess is working all the time," observes her mom, visibly disapproving her career choices like a typical migrant parent. Asa articulates her spiritual entrepreneurship when promoting her brand of spiritual merchandise, a luxury high-pH alkaline water to rejuvenate body, mind, and soul. The name "Diamond Water" foregrounds a spirituality primarily tied to wealth, marketed as organic and nourishing, while "priestess" evokes images of healing and guidance: as a businesswoman, Asa represents a gendered capitalism that involves self-branding in product advertisement. Meanwhile, as she seeks support for self-promotion from diasporic women leaders such as Jewish-Iranian media personality Homa Sarshar, Asa's

---

12. Kieffer 2020, 80–104.

character bolsters a modern image of entrepreneurial success while maintaining a traditional notion of spiritual femininity.

As she promotes herself and her product in season two, we see Asa speak strategically about her ethnicity and cultural background, even if a hyped form of new age spiritualism, to enhance her brand as organic and marketable to a health-minded white audience. In a symbolic way, identity embodies Diamond Water. There is a moment, as Asa gives a tour of the water facility to her parents, when her mother suggests shipping a bottle of Diamond Water to Iran. "It is a big deal," she explains, "if they can drink Diamond Water in Iran, too." Asa's response is a sigh of enthusiasm: "Oh, I wish. Inshallah, one day." While fulfilment can be described as an unconscious desire manifested in past and present dreams, Asa's wish is one of conscious futurity, her "one day" aspiration for her branded alkaline water to be consumed by her fellow Iranians. What also gets to be consumed is the modernity of a luxury cultur,e which Asa now embodies as her personalized brand. Asa's diasporic identity, spiritual and material, fuses American entrepreneurship with a displaced yearning for home. Diamond water provides an allegorized self-portrait of a future in glamorous commodity.

Meanwhile, the expression "inshallah" (God willing), a trans-cultural practice also shared by Jewish-Iranians, may signify Asa's Muslimness without stating it explicitly. While her character has its subversive moments, especially when she shows awareness of her recent immigration to the United States or class position, Asa exemplifies a form of self-branding Persian that combines art, luxury, business spirituality, and politics. Asa advertises her politics like an advertisement for a product. Among the cast members, Asa is also the most expressive of her Iranian identity as a source of spirituality. But her spirituality is of a new-age kind with a mixture of priestess magic and Muslim mysticism, including observing the fasting month of Ramadan. Her defense of wearing a veil (*hijab*) based on a person's free choice while arguing with Reza over public display of Islam during their trip to Turkey reflects a deeper multi-cultural attitude towards Islam, a kind of cultural secularism that GG also echoes somewhat.

Mike

Mike is the Iranian Jewish member of the crew. He epitomizes being Jewish and Iranian in the Southern California culture. The Iranian Jewish community is very much an active part of creating the diasporic identity in Los Angeles. Hamid Naficy argues that

> Self-employment [that is, independent contracting and employment
> by other Iranians] allows Iranians to create not only an exilic and

ethnic economy but also what might be called an interethnic or sub-
ethnic one. The repercussions of this situation for T.V. become clear
when we consider that with two exceptions all Iranian exile television
programs are commercially driven and must rely for their livelihood
on Iranian businesses. The high percentage of self-employment among
Jews and Armenians that means they have a disproportionate role in
sustaining exile television and an extraordinary power to influence
Iranian exile discourses. In addition, if we take into account the high
representation of Jews, Armenians, and Baha'is in the production and
distribution of music and entertainment recordings, the extent of
their influence becomes more evident.[13]

This also contributed to their distinct identity internally among Iranian Jews
and vis-à-vis non-Jewish Iranians, and also non-Iranian Jews. All these dynamics
translated into a very protective behavior of the community and guidelines that
aim at self-preservation.

In one of the earlier episodes, when Mike's dating habits were being discussed, Mike and the crew made it clear that Mike may date women of many
backgrounds, but he would marry only an Iranian Jewish woman. "Being a Persian Jew, it's been embedded in our minds from childhood, we stick within our
race, we stick within our religion." When he started dating Jessica, an Italian
Christian, he said: "so this is, like, a [beep] double whammy. My poor grandfa-
ther's gonna turn over in his grave.[...] She's not Persian, and she's not Jewish."
Jessica later went on to convert to Judaism and picked up some Persian, and
Persian cooking, to please Mike's parents.

In a very emotional encounter Mike tells his parents about Julia. Mike's
father is saddened that his soon-to-be daughter-in-law would not speak Persian.
He said that he always hoped that his daughter-in-law would be like a daughter
to him, but his inability to communicate in Persian and his limited abilities in
English will pose a challenge. Throughout the seasons, we see how the family
got closer together with an equal place for Persianness and Jewish identity.

GG or Golnesa Gharachedaghi

Golnesa is the hot-tempered character among the shahs. She also personifies a
kind of superficiality that combines wealth and good looks. When describing
herself in season one, Golnesa states, "Two things I don't like: I don't like ants
and I don't like ugly people."[14] While she possesses some of the stereotypical

13. Naficy 1993, 27.
14. Season one, episode one.

attributes that are often associated with the Iranian community of Los Angeles, she does not perform anything that is inherently Persian. She speaks Persian, of course, and is part of the crew, her role in the show is to disrupt. She does not hide her Muslim identity; she has tattoos and jewelry that express that much. However, nothing new is revealed to us about the community or the diaspora culture through her. Passively, she was accused by Reza of making hateful comments about his half Jewish-half Muslim background, when he said that "the girl calls me the piece of you-know-what that comes out when a Muslim and a Jew have a kid."

Throughout the seasons she moves between attempts to do right by her friends, and fierce confrontations, which sometimes suggest that she was on the side that was right. While she has many personal and family problems, her ethnicity shows up only when she discusses some social ostracizing she experienced as a brown kid in white Los Angeles. We are led to believe that her behavior as an adult somehow compensate for the social hardships she had had before.

As for self-branding, Golnesa too actively engages in reality TV entrepreneurship. In the second season (episode six), Golnesa introducers her business venture. While having lunch with her wealthy architect father, Mahmoud Gharachedaghi, Golnesa describes the new company, which she launched with her sister. "It's called 'GG's Extensions.' So I decided that I'm taking complete control of the launch party. And I'm gonna do it all on my own. I don't need anyone else's help." At this crucial point in her self-development as a reality TV star, GG's Extensions reinvents Golnesa based on the myth of the entrepreneurial subject: individualistic, self-reliant, and ready for venture toward prosperity. Throughout the nine seasons of the show, Golnesa goes back-and-forth between a self-assured business venturer and an unruly, privileged woman, followed by motherhood in season nine.

MJ or Mercedes Javid

MJ represents a Persian of superficial wealth and the least expressive of her diasporic Iranian identity among the cast members. A realtor of self-promotional and, at times, mean spirit, MJ is also a villain in the storyline. While she struggles with her weight and alcohol, MJ typifies a back-stabbing persona whose role in the story is mainly in-between Asa, GG, Reza, and Mike, initiating rumors or promoting conflict for her advantage. Calculated in her intentions, including her marriage to Tommy Feight, MJ personifies a deceiving figure, but one who still receives sympathy for her challenges as a woman balancing her success with her Iranian tradition.

In season three, during her trip to Turkey, MJ experiences the stress of an expected heterosexual marriage. While Asa visits her family in Istanbul, MJ confronts her deepest anxiety: becoming a mother as her mother, Vida, keeps a critical eye on her troubled love life. But without the prospect of a marriage, MJ is emotionally troubled because of an uncertain future, as the "biological tick" threatens her fertility and hence her status as a potential maternal figure in the community. The branding of MJ's Persianness appears as a mixture of deceiver, debauchee, and established entrepreneur. She is both crass and business-smart, portraying a kind of Persian who is unruly and still fashionably wealthy.

MJ's remote relations with her identity, culture, heritage, and tradition, and her visiting a Muslim country like Turkey, also enable the closer examination of the experience of a young Iranian Muslim professional in Southern California.

> When you're a Muslim kid in America and you look like this, you
> hide it. When I'm asked if I'm Muslim, I respond, "yes, but ..." I
> always said, "yes, but I'm not practicing"; yes, because I'm afraid that
> I'm gonna be labeled as a terrorist, and for the first time in my life
> there was no shame attached to being Muslim."

Being in Turkey allowed her to shed the identity conflict between being an American businesswoman, Iranian-American, and Muslim.

"Spiritual Pilgrimage" to the Homeland

In two episodes (12 and 13), titled "Return to the Homeland," season three shows Asa, GG, Mike, MJ, and Reza embark on a vacation trip to Turkey. While Asa's aim for the trip is to partake in a family reunion, the other cast members explore Istanbul. Each experiences a foreign country in a unique way. But Turkey also offers racial familiarity, as, before their departure, Asa says to Reza, "Do you realize we're gonna be in a place where we're gonna look like everybody else? Everyone's gonna look like us." Except, she continues, "we're gonna be better-looking, of course." Meanwhile, Reza sees the journey as a way of self-discovery of his Persian "heritage." Turkey, he explains, is "the closest thing that I have to Iran." MJ describes her intentions for traveling as bringing the crew "closer to our culture." While Islam is referenced several times throughout the trip, all the characters focus on Iran, where they claim a cultural heritage.

But tensions over identity simmer on the trip. While Reza wrestles with his gay identity in a Muslim nation, MJ, GG, and Asa emotionally respond to hearing the call for prayer outside of the Blue Mosque. It is as though they have arrived home through the call for prayer without visiting Iran itself.

Mike, however, has a different emotional realization or reaction upon hearing the *azaan* (call for prayer). He confessed that ,

> no disrespect to Muslims, but it scared the hell out of me. People are just rushing into the mosque. I got this overwhelming feeling inside of me that I just couldn't help. I felt like a little kid that had lost his mom and dad, and I was looking for them. It was really weird. My poor mom was pregnant with me and they'd be on the loudspeakers like this. My mom was afraid she's like "[beep], what's gonna happen?" [...] all I could think of is "oh my god, this is what my parents were submerged in when they were fleeing for our lives. It's a pro-Muslim, very fanatical, very crazy country that kicked us out, that said, "You cannot be a part of this country anymore, you must hand over what you have, and if you don't like it, we're gonna throw you in jail."

Mike's interpretation of the situation and his feelings calls for an analysis of the community memory that became, inevitably, very personal. Mike's family had been in Iran, presumably, for generations. Iran has been Muslim since the seventh century. We can conclude that many generations of the Shouhed family heard the *azaan* as part of their daily routine. And more often than not, it did not signal a sense of emergency as Mike felt that day outside the Blue Mosque in Istanbul. The circumstances under which the family left can cause trauma, but it may also unify the narrative of exile among the community members.

Mike concluded that day outside the mosque saying, "It was scary to be a Jewish man surrounded by thousands and thousands of Muslims at this very given moment I'm feeling more Jewish than I am feeling Iranian. Because of my religion, I could have left Iran and went to Israel if I chose to because they would take me in. My country didn't want me, but my religion does." Again, we see a narrative that perhaps came out of the collective memory that was created in the context of the Iranian Jewish community in Los Angeles, that accumulated experience of Jews in Iran over two-and-a-half millennia. It is interesting to compare it to the personal account of the scholar Leah Mirakhor, who wrote about diasporic identity, in which she recounts that:

> When my family moved to Flushing, Queens, from Tehran, I knew without ever having to be told that we were *both* Iranian and Jewish. At six years old, that wasn't a confusing phenomenon, aberration, or strange set of affinities. It just was. I couldn't be Iranian without being Jewish or Jewish without being Iranian.[15]

15. Mirakhor 2016, 52–76.

The climactic scene of this episode is when Asa and Reza travel to the Iran-Turkey border. While wearing a black veil, Asa takes the lead in what she describes as a "spiritual pilgrimage" to the homeland which lies beyond an invisible border, generating emotions of longing for an Iran left behind. "We are going to a spot where everything our eye sees is Iran," Asa tells her mother, Zinat, who also accompanies them. Asa then elatedly describes her emotions as she walks toward the spot where she could see Iran: "I feel different," she says. "I feel almost euphoric. Suddenly, it is all coming together. There it is. All of this is Iran." Uplifting music plays over the scene where Iran appears as green rolling hills shadowed by moving clouds. "This is so magical to me," Asa describes. "It is lit up by the sun. It's like a painting. And I was born there." Following Asa, Reza exclaims: "Wow. There is Iran. That is the place I was born. My parents were born, and their parents were born. And it's also the country that drove us away." In tears, Zinat talks about her longing for a lost Iran, her deceased parents and their graves, which she cannot visit. The following scene shows Zinat shouting to the distance, "I'm happy with the memories. I'm happy with the memories!" Home is the dwelling of memory.

Intense emotions unfold in relation to a displaced ancestral space. With the prospect of never being able to visit Iran, the scene shows how Asa and Reza emotionally meld with the landscape. Yet there is something almost biblical in this scene; to see their connection to the land, the soil, the place that shaped so much of their personalities, yet their inability to touch it, feel it, and breath its air. Distance lies in an affective geography that expands into a horizon. The Iran of Asa, her mother, and Reza lies in their memories projected into a distant land, the place of their birth, where dreams and hopes for home evoke an uncanny sense of "looking back" while, ironically, gazing toward the horizon.

CONCLUSION

This study has presented an analysis of the relationship between identity and reality TV programming in the diaspora Iranian community of Southern California. The above discussion explored the way *Shahs of Sunset* presents and popularizes ideas regarding the Iranian community, and shared bits of relevant history on the making of this community. "Image," MJ boasts, "is everything," and it is so because it is believed to be real. "To outsiders, it probably looks like we live a very glamorous life. And, in fact, we do," MJ boasts about her friends.[16] To be an image is to perform being an image.

But beyond the image lies the life of diasporic subjects, those who have

16. Season one, episode one.

left their country of origin for a better life. "We talk shit about each other, we fight with one another, but at the end of the day what really matters is they have my back and I have theirs," Reza explains. "Hello, we're Persians," he humorously utters. Yet such Persianness takes place outside of Iran in aesthetically marketized spaces of diaspora sociability; reconstructed in art galleries, musical performances, and businesses Persian identity becomes imbricated by exotic wealth. The experience of exile remains integral to identity. As depicted in the trip to Turkey in season three, longing for the homeland haunts the characters, though in different ways.

Beyond these five characters, we get to meet others that help us develop a well-rounded understanding of this community as a phenomenon, and compared to other Iranian communities. For example, One of the characters in season two is Lilly Ghalichi. She joined the crew from Texas, where the Iranian community is sociologically different.[17] She seems to share similar habits and standards regarding wealth, beauty, aesthetics, and visibility. Still, despite her best efforts (and some of the others'), she remains an outsider. In one conversation with Reza, she says, "If this is how the Persian community in L.A. behaves and acts, I don't want to have any part of it." In the interview segment later, she adds: "Persians in Houston are very different from Persians in L.A., because Persians in Houston definitely do not party as hard as Persians in L.A." Then, referring to an incident earlier where she had been mistreated by some of the shahs, she added: "if any of my own friend were behaving that way the rest of us would ask them to leave." We can read here an observation and critique of the group dynamic that is stereotypical of the Iranian community in Los Angeles.

There is also a good amount of exceptionalism in the Tehrangeles self-perception. Adam, who was Reza's boyfriend in that season (later they got married) was originally from Oklahoma. Reza commented, "I don't know what Oklahoma is like. We don't like to get all up in the bowels of the United States. We tend to stay on, you know, L.A., New York, Miami. Like you know, the pretty parts." Ironically, Oklahoma was one of the earlier places Iranians settled in upon arrival to the United States.[18]

Another example attests to the generational differences. The title of this chapter is taken from a conversation Reza had with Sasha, a younger gay Iranian man who wanted to hang out with the crew. He had recently arrived to the United States, having been harassed by the Islamic Republic for his sexual orientation. Sasha suggested that the differences between them should not be so big. In response, Reza said: "Me and you were born in the same geographical

17. Mobasher 2012.
18. Honey 1978, 21–23.

spot," to which Sasha replied, "Then you're Iranian for the rest of your life." Reza's answer to that was pretty revealing for the entire identity of the Iranian community in Los Angeles: "No, you were born in a shit hole. I was born in the Imperial Kingdom of Iran. The country that I was born in stopped existing in 1979."

WORKS CITED

Bozorgmehr, Mehdi. 2001. "Iran." In *Encyclopedia of American Immigration*, edited by James Ciment, 1169. Armonk, NY: Sharpe Reference.

Hemmasi, Farzaneh. 2020. *Tehrangeles Dreaming: Intimacy and Imaginiation in Southern California's Iranian Pop Music*. Durham, NC: Duke University Press.

Honey, Charles. 1978. "Iranians in Oklahoma: Learning the Hard Way." *Change: The Magazine of Higher Learning* 10:21–23.

Kieffer, Kira Ganga. 2020. "Manifesting Millions: How Women's Spiritual Entrepreneurship Genders Capitalism." *Nova Religion: The Journal of Alternative and Emergent Religions* 24:80–104.

Maghbouleh, Neda. 2017. *The Limits of Whiteness: Iranian Americans and the Everyday Politics of Race*. Stanford, CA: Stanford University Press.

Mirakhor, Leah. 2016. "After the Revolution to the War on Terror: Iranian Jewish American Literature in the United States." *Studies in American Jewish Literature* 35:52–76.

Mobasher, Mohsen M. 2012. *Iranians in Texas: Migration, Politics, and Ethnic Identity*. Austin, TX: University of Texas Press.

Naficy, Hamid. 1993. *The Making of Exile Cultures: Iranian Television in Los Angeles*. Minneapolis: University of Minnesota Press.

Williams, Raymond. 2003. *Television: Technology and Cultural Form*. London and New York: Routledge.

Redmond, Sean. 2008. "Pieces of Me: Celebrity Confessional Carnality." *Social Semiotics* 18:149–61.

Sender, Katherine. "Real Worlds." In *The Politics of Reality Television: Global Perspectives*, edited by Marwan M. Kraidy and Katherine Sender. London: Routledge.

Publications of H. E. Chehabi

1971

1. "Die Emirate am Persischen Golf." *Deutsche Zeitung für Briefmarkenkunde*, no. 20 (1971): 15–16.

1975

2. "Triest: Hall-e ākharin mas'aleh-ye marzi dar Orupā." *Ettelāāt* 11 Āzar 1354 (1 December 1975): 6.

1976

3. "Oqdeh-e Māyot va tahavollāt-e jadid-e Oqyānus-e Hend." *Ettelāāt* 17 Esfand 1354 (8 March 1976): 6.

4. "Sosiālizm-e Orupā va mas'aleh-ye e'telāf bā komunisthā." *Ettelāāt* 15 Farvardin 2535 (4 April 1976): 6 and 8.

1980

5. "The Absence of Consociationalism in Sri Lanka." *Plural Societies* 11, no. 4 (1980): 55–65.

1982

6. "Die Falkland-Affäre: Ein Einzelfall?" *Aus Politik und Zeitgeschichte* B46/82 (20 November 1982): 33–36.

7. "Insularité et particularisme." *Esprit*, no. 62 (February 1982): 215–17.

1985

8. "Self-Determination, Territorial Integrity, and the Falkland Islands." *Political Science Quarterly* 100, no. 2 (1985): 215–25. Augmented English version of 6.

9. "Society and State in Islamic Liberalism." *State, Culture, and Society* 1, no. 3 (1985): 85–101.

1986

10. Review article of two translated works of Mahmud Taleqani. *Iranian Studies* 19, no. 1 (1986): 97–104.

1989

11. Review of *The Vanished Imam: Musa Sadr and the Shia of Lebanon*, by Fouad Ajami. *Iranian Studies* 22, nos. 2–3 (1989): 143–45.

1990

12. *Iranian Politics and Religious Modernism: The Liberation Movement of Iran under the Shah and Khomeini*. Ithaca, NY: Cornell University Press, and London: I.B. Tauris, 1990.

1991

13. "Religion and Politics in Iran: How Theocratic is the Islamic Republic?" *Daedalus* 120, no. 3 (1991): 69–91.

1993

14. "Klerus und Staat in der Islamischen Republik Iran." *Aus Politik und Zeitgeschichte* B33/93 (13 August 1993): 17–23.

15. "Staging the Emperor's New Clothes: Dress Codes and Nation-Building under Reza Shah." *Iranian Studies* 26, nos. 3–4 (1993): 209–29.

16. Review of *Der Khan aus Tirol: Albert Joseph Gasteiger Freiherr von Ravenstein und Kobach; Diplomat, Ingenieur und Forschungsreisender am persischen Hof (1823–1890)*, by Reinhard Pohanka and Ingrid Thurner. *Iranian Studies* 26, nos. 1–2 (1993): 175–76.

17. Review of *Iran nach dem Sturz des Schahs: Die provisorische Revolutionsregierung Bazargans*, by Ahmad Mahrad. *Iranian Studies* 26, nos. 3–4 (1993): 431–32.

18. Map: "Geographic Distribution of Sample Firms." In *Business and Democracy in Spain*, by Robert E. Martínez, 13.

1994

19. Review of *Die Wiedersprüche in der Verfassung der Islamischen Republik vor dem Hintergrund der politischen Auseinandersetzungen im nachrevolutionären Iran*, by Asghar Schirazi. *Iranian Studies* 27, nos. 1–4 (1994): 183–84.

1995

20. Editor, with Alfred Stepan. *Politics, Society, and Democracy: Comparative Studies*. Boulder, CO: Westview, 1995.

21. "Sport and Politics in Iran: The Legend of Gholamreza Takhti." *International Journal of the History of Sport* 12, no. 3 (1995): 48–60.

22. "The provisional government and the transition from monarchy to Islamic Republic in Iran." In *Between States: Interim Governments and Democratic Transitions*, edited by Yossi Shain and Juan J. Linz, 127–43 and 278–81. Cambridge: Cambridge University Press, 1995.

23. "Liberation Movement of Iran." *The Oxford Encyclopedia of the Modern Islamic World*, 3:1–2. New York, NY: Oxford University Press, 1995.

24. "Taleqani, Mahmud." *The Oxford Encyclopedia of the Modern Islamic World*, 4:181–82. New York, NY: Oxford University Press, 1995.

1996

25. "The Impossible Republic: Contradictions of the Islamic State in Iran." *Contention* 5, no. 3 (1996): 135–54.

26. "The Imam as Dandy: The Case of Musa Sadr." *Harvard Middle Eastern and Islamic Review* 3, nos. 1–2 (1996): 20–42.

27. "Das wahre Reich der Mitte." *du*, no. 3 (March 1996): 33–34, 51–52.

28. "Small Island States." *The Encyclopedia of Democracy*, 4: 1134–37. Washington, DC: Congressional Quarterly Inc., 1996.

1997

29. "Ardabil Becomes a Province: Center-Periphery Relations in the Islamic Republic of Iran." *International Journal of Middle East Studies* 29, no. 2 (1997): 235–53.

30. "Das politische Regime der Islamischen Republik Iran." *WeltTrends* 5, no. 15 (1997): 124–41.

31. "Eighteen Years Later: Assessing the Islamic Republic of Iran." *Harvard International Review* 19, no. 2 (1997): 28–31.

32. Review of *Khomeini's Forgotten Sons: The Story of Iran's Boy Soldiers*, by Ian Brown. *Iranian Studies* 30, nos. 1–2 (1997): 148–50.

1998

33. Edited with Juan J. Linz. *Sultanistic Regimes*. Baltimore: The Johns Hopkins University Press, 1998.

34. "Az tasnif-e enqelābi tā sorud-e vatani: musiqi va nāsionālizm dar Irān." *Iran Nameh* 16, no. 1 (1998): 69–96. Persian translation of **43**.

35. "Ostān shodan-e Ardabil: negāhi beh ravābet-e hāshieh-markaz dar Irān." *Goft-o-Gu*, no. 20 (1377/1998): 59–85. Persian translation of **29**.

36. "Das politische System der islamischen Republik Iran." In *Naher Osten: Politik und Gesellschaft*, edited by Renate Schmidt, 180–99. Berlin: Berliner Debatte Wissenschaftsverlag, 1998. Completely rewritten version of **30**.

37. With Juan J. Linz. "A Theory of Sultanism 1: A Type of Non-Democratic Rule." In *Sultanistic Regimes*, edited by H. E. Chehabi and Juan J. Linz, 1–25. Baltimore: The Johns Hopkins University Press, 1998. Chapter 1 of **33**.

38. With Juan J. Linz. "A Theory of Sultanism 2: Genesis and Demise of Sultanistic Regimes." In *Sultanistic Regimes*, edited by H. E. Chehabi and Juan J. Linz, 26–48. Baltimore: The Johns Hopkins University Press, 1998. Chapter 2 of **33**.

39. "Reformism v. Extremism: The Case of Iran." In *The Future of Islam-West Relations: A CSIS Islamic Studies Conference Report*, edited by Shireen T. Hunter, 43–46. Washington, DC: Center for Strategic and International Studies, 1998.

40. "The Pahlavi Period." *Iranian Studies* 31, nos. 3–4 (1998): 495–502.

41. Review of *Presse und Öffentlichkeit im Nahen Osten*, edited by Christoph Herzog, Raoul Motika, and Anja Pistor-Hatam. *Iranian Studies* 31, no. 2 (1998): 276–78.

1999

42. "Moruri bar tārikh-e ejtemāʿi va siyāsi-ye futbāl dar Irān." *Iran Nameh* 17 (1378/1999): 89–113. Persian translation of **59**.

43. "From Revolutionary *Tasnif* to Patriotic *Surūd*: Music and Nation-Building in Early Twentieth-Century Iran." *Iran* 37, no. 1 (1999): 143–54.

44. "Football." *Encyclopaedia Iranica*, 10: 79–80. New York, NY: Bibliotheca Persica Press, 1999.

45. "Goethe Institute." *Encyclopaedia Iranica*, 11:43–44. New York, NY: Bibliotheca Persica Press, 1999.

46. Review of *Die iranische Schia und die islamische Einheit 1979–1996*, by Wilfried Buchta. *Middle East Bulletin* 33, no. 1 (1999): 78–79.

47. Review of *Shi'a Islam: From Religion to Revolution*, by Heinz Halm. *al-Abhath* 47 (1999): 103–5.

48. Review of *La Belle rivale de Farah et les jeux du destin*, by Anna-Lisa Vafa. *Iranian Studies* 32, no. 4 (1999): 592–93.

2000

49. "Voices Unveiled: Women Singers in Modern Iran." In *Iran and Beyond: Essays in Middle Eastern History in Honor of Nikki R. Keddie*, edited by Rudi Matthee and Beth Baron, 151–66. Costa Mesa, CA: Mazda, 2000.

50. "Democratization: The Balance Sheet." In *Iran Before and After the Elections*, 58–61. Washington, DC: Woodrow Wilson International Center for Scholars, 2000.

2001

51. Edited with Juan J. Linz. *Nezāmhā-ye soltāni*. Tehran: Nashr-e Shirāzeh, 1380/2001. Persian translation of **33**.

52. "The Political Regime of the Islamic Republic in Comparative Perspective." *Government and Opposition* 36, no. 1 (2001): 48–70.

53. "US-Iranian Sports Diplomacy." *Diplomacy and Statecraft* 12, no. 1 (2001): 89–106.

54. "Jews and Sport in Modern Iran." In *The History of Contemporary Iranian Jews*, edited by Homa Sarshar and Houman Sarshar, 4:3–24. Beverly Hills, CA: Center for Iranian Jewish Oral History, 2001.

55. "Yahudiyān dar arsehhā-ye varzeshi-ye Irān." *Iran Nameh* 19, nos. 1–2 (1379–80/2001): 125–50. Persian translation of **54**.

56. "Foreword." In *A Diplomatic History of the Caspian Sea: Treaties, Diaries, and Other Stories*, by Guive Mirfendereski, viii-ix. New York, NY: St. Martin's, 2001.

57. "Iran." *The International Encyclopedia of Women and Sport*, 586–87. New York, NY: Macmillan, 2001.

2002

58. Guest Editor, Special Issue on Sports and Games. *Iranian Studies* 35, no. 4 (2002).

59. "A Political History of Football in Iran." *Iranian Studies* 35, no. 4 (2002): 371–402.

60. "The Juggernaut of Globalization: Sport and Modernization in Iran." *International Journal of the History of Sport* 19, nos. 2–3 (2002): 275–94.

61. With Allen Guttmann. "From Iran to All of Asia: The Origin and Diffusion of Polo." *International Journal of the History of Sport* 19, nos. 2–3 (2002): 384–400.

62. "Sport." In *Esther's Children: A Portrait of Iranian Jews*, edited by Houman Sarshar, 373–78. Beverly Hills, CA: The Center for Iranian Jewish Oral History, 2002.

63. "Zūrkhāna." *Encyclopaedia of Islam*, 11: 572–74. Leiden: E.J. Brill, 2002.

64. "An Annotated Bibliography of Sports and Games in the Iranian World." *Iranian Studies* 35, no. 4 (2002): 403–19.

2003

65. "The Westernization of Iranian Culinary Culture." *Iranian Studies* 36, no. 1 (2003): 43–61.

66. "The Banning of the Veil and its Consequences." In *The Making of Modern Iran: State and Society under Riza Shah, 1921–1941*, edited by Stephanie Cronin, 193–210. London: Curzon, 2003.

67. "The Juggernaut of Globalization: Sport and Modernization in Iran." In *Sport in Asian Society: Past and Present*, edited by J.A. Mangan and Fan Hong, 225–39. London: Frank Cass, 2003. Same as **60**.

68. With Allen Guttmann. "From Iran to all of Asia: The Origin and Diffusion of Polo." In *Sport in Asian Society: Past and Present*, edited by J.A. Mangan and Fan Hong, 309–21. London: Frank Cass, 2003. Same as **61**.

69. Review of *The Persian Sphinx: Amir Abbas Hoveyda and the Riddle of the Iranian Revolution*, by Abbas Milani. *Iranian Studies* 36, no. 2 (2003): 302–7.

2004

70. "Dress Codes for Men in Turkey and Iran." In *Men of Order: Authoritarian Modernization under Atatürk and Reza Shah*, edited by Touraj Atabaki and Erik Zürcher, 209–37. London: I.B. Tauris, 2004.

71. "The Need to Spread the Perimeter of One's Curiosity Beyond One's Own Borders." In *Playing with Modernity*, edited by Ramin Jahanbegloo, 285–92. Tehran: Cultural Research Bureau, 2004.

2005

72. "Diplomāsi-ye varzesh beyn-e Ayālāt-e Mottahedeh va Irān." *Goft-o-Gu*, no. 42 (1383/2005): 7–25. Persian translation of **53**.

73. "İran'da Yeme İçme Kültürünün Batılılaşması." *Yemek ve Kültür*, no. 3 (2005): 84–103. Turkish translation of a rewritten version of **65**.

74. "Iran." *Berkshire Encyclopedia of World Sport*, 2: 836–39. Great Barrington, MA: Berkshire Publishing Group, 2005.

75. "Zūrkhāna." *Encyclopédie de l'Islam*, 11:618–20. Leiden: E.J. Brill, 2005. French translation of **63**.

2006

76. With others. *Distant Relations: Iran and Lebanon in the last 500 Years*. Oxford: Centre for Lebanese Studies; London: I.B. Tauris, 2006.

77. Editor. *Robert Michels, Political Sociology, and the Future of Democracy*, by Juan J. Linz. New Brunswick, NJ: Transaction Books, 2006.

78. "The Politics of Football in Iran." *Soccer and Society* 7: nos. 2–3 (2006): 233–61. Updated version of **59**.

79. "Moqarrarāt-e lebās pushidan barā-ye mardān dar Torkieh va Irān." In *Tajaddod-e āmerāneh*, edited by Turaj Atābaki, 183–222. Tehran: Qoqnus, 1385/2006. Persian translation of **70**.

80. "A Bibliography of Juan J. Linz." In *Robert Michels, Political Sociology, and the Future of Democracy* by Juan Linz, edited by H. E. Chehabi, 205–24. New Brunswick, NJ: Transaction Books, 2006.

81. "Une bibliographie de Juan J. Linz." *Revue Internationale de Politique Comparée* 13, no. 1 (2006): 27–56. French translation of **80**.

82. "Una bibliografía de Juan J. Linz." *Revista Española de Investigaciones Sociológicas*, no. 114 (2006): 175–210. Spanish translation of **80**.

83. Review of *Anglo-Iranian Relations since 1800*, edited by Vanessa Martin. *Middle Eastern Studies* 42, no. 6 (2006): 1044–46.

84. Review of *Greater Iran: A 20th-Century Odyssey*, by Richard Frye. *Harvard Middle Eastern and Islamic Review* 7 (2006): 230–32.

2007

85. *Bibliographia Iranica*. Tehran: Amir Kabir, 2007.

86. "How Caviar Turned Out to Be *Halal*." *Gastronomica* 7, no. 2 (2007): 17–23.

87. "Anatomy of Prejudice: Reflections on Secular Anti-Baha'ism in Iran." In *The Baha'is of Iran: Socio-Historical Studies*, edited by Dominic Parviz Brookshaw and Seena B. Fazel, 184–99. London: Routledge, 2007.

88. With Arang Keshavarzian. "Politics in Iran." In *Comparative Politics Today: A World View*, edited by Gabriel A. Almond, G. Bingham Powell, Jr., Kaare Strøm, and Russell J. Dalton, 457–501. New York, NY: Pearson, 2007.

89. Review of *La République islamique d'Iran: De la maison du Guide à la raison d'État*, by Azadeh Kian-Thiébaut. *Iranian Studies* 40, no. 3 (2007): 439–40.

90. Review of *Die Briefmarken Irans als Mittel der Politischen Bildpropaganda*, by Roman Siebertz. *International Journal of Middle East Studies* 39, no. 3 (2007): 499–501.

2008

91. With Arang Keshavarzian. "Politics in Iran." In *Comparative Politics Today: A World View*, edited by Gabriel A. Almond, G. Bingham Powell, Jr., Kaare Strøm, and Russell J. Dalton, 9th edition, 562–607. New York, NY: Pearson, 2008. Updated version of **88**.

92. "*Es darf auch manchmal Kaviar sein*: How Caviar Turned Out To Be *Halal*." In *Iran und iranisch geprägte Kulturen: Studien zum 65. Geburtstag von Bert G. Fragner*, edited by Markus Ritter, Ralph Kauz, and Birgitt Hoffmann, 401–9. Wiesbaden: Dr. Ludwig Reichert Verlag, 2008. Almost the same as **86**.

93. "The Politics of Football in Iran." In *Fringe Nations in World Soccer*, edited by Kausik Bandyopadhyay and Sabyasachi Mallick, 77–105. London: Routledge, 2008. Same as **78**.

94. "Ruyāru'i-ye sonnat va moderniteh dar tarbiyat-e badani-ye Irān." *Iran Nameh* 24, no 1 (1387/2008): 81–103.

95. With Fotini Christia. "The Art of State Persuasion: Iran's Post-Revolutionary Murals." *Persica* 22 (2008): 1–13.

96. "Ja'fari, Ša'bān." *Encyclopædia Iranica*, 14:366–67. New York, NY: Encyclopædia Iranica Foundation, 2008.

97. "Kar, Mehrangiz." *Biographical Encyclopedia of the Modern Middle East and North Africa*, 1:401–3. Detroit, MI: Gale Group, 2008.

98. "Rezazadeh, Hossein." *Biographical Encyclopedia of the Modern Middle East and North Africa*, 2:657–58. Detroit, MI: Gale Group, 2008.

99. "Shajarian, Mohamed Reza." *Biographical Encyclopedia of the Modern Middle East and North Africa*, 2:736–38. Detroit, MI: Gale Group, 2008.

100. "Sports." *Iran Today: An Encyclopedia of Life in the Islamic Republic*, 2:463–69. Westport, CT: Greenwood Press, 2008.

101. "Una bibliografía de Juan J. Linz." In *Juan J. Linz, Obras Escogidas*, vol. 1, *Fascismo: perspectivas históricas y comparadas*, edited by José Ramón Montero and Thomas Jeffrey Miley, lxxv-ciii. Madrid: Centro de Estudios Políticos y Constitucionales, 2008. Updated version of **82**.

2009

102. "The Paranoid Style in Iranian Historiography." In *Iran in the 20ᵗʰ Century: Historiography and Political Culture*, edited by Touraj Atabaki, 155–76 and 294–303. London: I.B. Tauris, 2009.

103. With Juan J. Linz. "Una teoría del sultanismo (1): un tipo de régimen no democrático." In *Juan J. Linz, Obras escogidas*, vol. 3, *Sistemas totalitarios y regímenes autoritarios*, edited by José Ramón Montero and Thomas Jeffrey Miley, 525–551. Madrid: Centro de Estudios Políticos y Constitucionales, 2009. Spanish translation of **37**.

104. With Juan J. Linz. "Una teoría del sultanismo (2): génesis y caída de los regímenes sultanísticos." In *Juan J. Linz, Obras escogidas*, vol. 3, *Sistemas totalitarios y regímenes autoritarios*, edited by José Ramón Montero and Thomas Jeffrey Miley, 553–77. Madrid: Centro de Estudios Políticos y Constitucionales, 2009. Spanish translation of **38**.

105. "Nezām-e jadid-e pushāk va ensejām-e mellat dar dowreh-ye Rezā Shāh." *RahAvard*, no. 85 (2009): 127–47. Persian translation of **15**.

106. "Religious Apartheid in Iran." *Viewpoints, Special Edition: The Iranian Revolution at 30* (2009): 119–21.

107. "Bazargan, Mahdi." *Oxford Encyclopedia of the Islamic World*, 1:328–30. New York, NY: Oxford University Press, 2009.

108. "Freedom Movement of Iran." *Oxford Encyclopedia of the Islamic World*, 2:266–68. New York, NY: Oxford University Press, 2009. Updated version of **23**.

109. Review of *The Impact of Religious Factors on Educational Change in Iran: Islam in Policy and Islam in Practice*, by Hossein Godazgar. *Insight Turkey* 11, no. 1 (2009): 153–55.

110. Review of *Kleidungspolitik in Iran: Die Durchsetzung der Kleidungsvorschriften für Männer unter Riżā Šāh*, by Bianca Devos. *Iranian Studies* 42, no. 1 (2009): 148–49.

111. Review of *Nauru, île dévastée: Comment la civilization capitaliste a anéanti le pays le plus riche du monde*, by Luc Folliet. *Island Studies Journal* 4, no. 2 (2009): 243–45.

2010

112. Editor, with Vanessa Martin. *Iran's Constitutional Revolution: Popular Politics, Cultural Transformations and Transnational Connections*. London: I.B. Tauris, 2010.

113. Editor. *Persian Literature and Judeo-Persian Culture: Collected Writings* by Sorour S. Soroudi. Boston: Ilex Foundation, 2010.

114. "*Li Kulli Fir'awn Musa*: The Myth of Moses and Pharaoh in the Iranian

Revolution in Comparative Perspective." Brandeis University, Crown Center for Middle Eastern Studies Crown Papers, no. 4 (November 2010).

115. With Arang Keshavarzian. "Politics in Iran." In *Comparative Politics Today: A World View*, edited by Gabriel A. Almond, G. Bingham Powell, Jr., Russell J. Dalton, and Kaare Strøm, updated 9th edition, 556–601. New York, NY: Pearson, 2010. Updated version of **91**.

116. "How Caviar Turned Out to Be Halal." In *The Gastronomica Reader*, edited by Darra Goldstein, 129–38. Berkeley, CA: University of California Press, 2010. Same as **86**.

117. "Souverän im Chaos." *Spiegel Geschichte*, no. 2 (2010): 82–88.

118. "General Comments on Language, Dialect and Nationhood." In *Languages and Memories: The Multi-Layered Human Experiences and the Varieties of Interpretations: Papers from the 3rd LiCCOSEC International Symposium (October 31 – November 1, 2009)*, edited by Y. Takashina and others, 49–54. Osaka: Research Institute for World Languages, Osaka University, 2010.

119. "The Introduction of Family Names under Reza Shah Pahlavi." In *Languages and Memories: The Multi-Layered Human Experiences and the Varieties of Interpretations: Papers from the 3rd LiCCOSEC International Symposium (October 31 – November 1, 2009)*, edited by Y. Takashina and others, 286–91. Osaka: Research Institute for World Languages, Osaka University, 2010.

120. Review of *The Crypto-Jewish Mashhadis: The Shaping of Religious and Communal Identity in Their Journey from Iran to New York*, by Hilda Nissimi. *Comparative Studies of South Asia, Africa and the Middle East* 30, no. 1 (2010): 147–48.

121. Review of *Besoin d'îles*, by Louis Brigand. *Island Studies Journal* 5, no. 1 (2010): 121–23.

122. Review of *Poets & Pahlevans: A Journey into the Heart of Iran*, by Marcello Di Cintio. *The International Journal of the History of Sport* 27, no. 11 (2010): 1996–98.

2011

123. "Diversity at Alborz." *Iranian Studies* 44, no. 5 (2011): 715–29.

124. "Sākhtār-e yek ta'assob: Ta'ammolāti dar Bahā'i-setizi-ye sekulār dar Irān." In *Bahā'iyān-e Irān: Pazhuheshhā-ye tārikhi-jāme'ehshenākhti*, edited by Dominik Parviz Brukshā and Sinā Fāzel, 310–33. Stockholm: Bārān, 2011. Persian translation of **87**.

125. "Das politische System der Islamischen Republik Iran: Eine vergleichende Studie." In *Das politische System Irans*, edited by Azadeh Zamirirad, 33–52. Potsdam: WeltTrends, 2011. Reprint of **36**.

126. Review of *Schiitischer Messianismus und Mahdi-Glaube in der Neuzeit*, by Mariella Ourghi. *Iranian Studies* 44, no. 3 (2011): 442–43.

127. Review of *Power, Islam, and Political Elite in Iran: A Study of the Iranian Political Elite from Khomeini to Ahmadinejad*, by Eva Patricia Rakel. *Insight Turkey* 13, no. 4 (2011): 218–19.

2012

128. Guest editor of Thematic Issue on "Islam and Constitutionalism in the Persianate World." *Journal of Persianate Studies* 5, no. 2 (2012).

129. With Ali Schirazi. "The Islamic Republic of Iran." *Journal of Persianate Studies* 5, no. 2 (2012): 175–204. In **128**.

130. "Iran and Iraq: Intersocietal Linkages and Secular Nationalisms." In *Iran Facing Others: Identity Boundaries in a Historical Perspective*, edited by Abbas Amanat and Farzin Vejdani, 191–216. New York: Palgrave Macmillan, 2012.

131. "The Reform of Iranian Nomenclature and Titulature in the Fifth Majles." In *Convergent Zones: Persian Literary Tradition and the Writing of History: Studies in Honor of Amin Banani*, edited by Wali Ahmadi, 84–116. Costa Mesa, CA: Mazda, 2012.

132. With Arang Keshavarzian. "Politics in Iran." In *Comparative Politics Today: A World View: AP Edition*, edited by Gabriel A. Almond, G. Bingham Powell, Jr., Russell J. Dalton, and Kaare Strøm, 10th edition, 332–79. New York, NY: Pearson, 2012. Updated and substantially revised version of **113**.

133. With Arang Keshavarzian. "Politics in Iran." In *Comparative Politics Today: A World View*, edited by Gabriel A. Almond, G. Bingham Powell, Jr., Russell J. Dalton, and Kaare Strøm, 10th edition, 520–67. New York: Pearson, 2012. Same as **132**.

134. "Eslāh talabān va tarbiyat-e badan." *Andisheh-ye Puyā* 1, no. 2 (Tir-Mordād 1391/ Summer 2012): 46–53. Persian translation of **148**.

135. "Türkiye ve İran'da Erkekler İçin Kıyafet Kanunları." In *Türkiye ve İran'da Otoriter Modernleşme: Atatürk ve Riza Şah Dönemleri*, edited by Touraj Atabaki and Erik J. Zürcher, 189–214. Istanbul: İstanbul Bilgi Üniversitesi Yayınları, 2012. Turkish translation of **70**.

136. "The International Society for Iranian Studies: A Short History." *Catalogue of the Ninth Biennial of the Iranian Studies Conference*, 11–15. Istanbul, 2012.

2013

137. Edited with Farhad Khosrokhavar and Clément Therme. *Iran and the Challenges of the 21ˢᵗ Century: Essays in Honour of Mohammad-Reza Djalili*. Costa Mesa, CA: Mazda, 2013.

138. Editor, with Vanessa Martin. *Enqelāb-e mashruteh-ye Irān*. Tehran: Pārseh, 2013. Persian translation of **112**.

139. "The Shah's Two Liberalizations: Re-Equilibration and Breakdown." In *Iran and the Challenges of the 21ˢᵗ Century: Essays in Honour of Mohammad-Reza Djalili*, edited by H. E. Chehabi, Farhad Khosrokhavar, and Clément Therme, 24–49. Costa Mesa, CA: Mazda, 2013. Chapter 2 of **137**.

140. "Iranian History 1945–79." In *Iran Modern*, edited by Fereshteh Daftary and Layla S. Diba, 13–16. New York, NY: Asia Society Museum in Association with Yale University Press, 2013.

141. "The Islamic Republic of Iran and the Muslim World." In *Iranian Influences in Oecumenic Cultural Exchanges, 77–84*. Seoul: Korean Association for Central Asian Studies, 2013.

142. "Iran Isŭllam konghwaguk kwa musŭllim segye." In *Tongsŏ munhwa kyoryu esŏ Iran ŭi yŏnghyang*, 85–92. Seoul: Korean Association for Central Asian Studies, 2013. Korean translation of **141**.

143. "Islands Beyond: Ouessant's Scottish Connection Discovered." *Scottish Islands Explorer* 14, no. 2 (March-April 2013): 15.

144. "Obituary, Reza Alavi, 1935–2012." *Iranian Studies* 46, no. 6 (2013): 995–97.

2014

145. Editor. *Juan J. Linz: Scholar, Teacher, Friend*. Cambridge, MA: Tŷ Aur Press, 2014.

146. "Iran Isŭllam konghwaguk kwa musŭllim segye." *Chung'ang Asia Yŏn'gu / Central Asian Studies* 19, no. 1 (2014): 133–44. Expanded version of **142**.

147. "Beyond the 'Case of Spain.'" In *Juan J. Linz: Scholar, Teacher, Friend*, edited by H. E. Chehabi, 28–34. Cambridge, MA: Tŷ Aur Press, 2014. In **145**.

148. "Mir Mehdi Varzandeh and the Introduction of Modern Physical Education in Iran." In *Culture and Cultural Politics Under Reza Shah: The Pahlavi State, New*

Bourgeoisie and the Creation of a Modern Society in Iran, edited by Bianca Devos and Christoph Werner, 55–72. London: Routledge, 2014.

149. "Eslāh va enqelāb." *Andisheh-ye Puyā* 2, no. 13 (Bahman-Esfand 1392/Winter 2013–14): 55–62. Persian translation of **139**.

150. "Farangi shodan-e zā'eqeh-ye irāni." *Andisheh-ye Puyā* 3, no. 15 (Ordibehesht 1393/April 2014): 96–102. Persian translation of **65**.

151. "Dowlat mellat sāzi va enqelāb-e alqāb." *Andisheh-ye Puyā* 3, no. 17 (Tir 1393/ June 2014): 70–77. Partial Persian translation of **131**.

152. "Gholām-Rezā Takhti." *Andisheh-ye Puyā* 3, no. 18 (Mordād 1393/July 2014): Persian translation of **21**.

153. "Pāshneh āshilhā: seh mas'aleh va mo'zaleh-ye dowlat-e movaqqat." *Andisheh-ye Puyā* 3, no. 21 (Ābān 1393/October 2014): 68–69. Persian translation of excerpts of chapter 7 of **12**.

154. "Mokhālefān-e irāni-ye zedd-e Shāh va Lobnān." *Andisheh-ye Puyā* 3, no. 22 (Āzar 1393/November 2014): 87–91. Persian translation of chapter 8 of **76**.

155. With Arang Keshavarzian. "Politics in Iran." In *Comparative Politics Today: A World View*, edited by Gabriel A. Almond, G. Bingham Powell, Jr., Russell J. Dalton, and Kaare Strøm, 11th edition, 532–81. New York: Pearson, 2014. Updated and substantially revised version of **132**.

156. "A Bibliography of Juan Linz." In *Juan J. Linz: Scholar, Teacher, Friend*, edited by H. E. Chehabi, 415–449. Cambridge, MA: Tŷ Aur Press, 2014. Updated and corrected version of **80**.

157. "The International Society for Iranian Studies: A Short History." *Catalogue of the Tenth Biennial Iranian Studies Conference*, 10–12. Montreal, August 2014. Updated version of **136**.

2015

158. Editor, with Peyman Jafari and Maral Jafroudi. *Iran in the Middle East: Transnational Encounters and Social History*. London: I.B. Tauris, 2015.

159. Editor, with Grace Neville. *Erin and Iran: Cultural Encounters between the Irish and the Iranians*. Boston: Ilex Foundation, 2015.

160. "'The Paris of the Middle East': Iranians in Cosmopolitan Beirut." In *Iran in the Middle East: Transnational Encounters and Social History*, edited by H. E. Chehabi, Peyman Jafari, and Maral Jafroudi, 120–34. London: I.B. Tauris, 2015. Chapter 5 of **158**.

161. "Emām-e dandi: Musā Sadr." *Andisheh-ye Puyā* 4, no. 29 (Mehr 1394/September 2015): 94–98. Persian translation of **26**.

162. "An Indo-Persian in Ireland, anno 1799: Mirzā Abu Tāleb Khān." In *Erin and Iran: Cultural Encounters between the Irish and the Iranians*, edited by H. E. Chehabi and Grace Neville, 129–55. Boston: Ilex Foundation, 2015. Chapter 8 of **159**.

163. "Une bibliographie de Juan J. Linz." *Pôle Sud* 41, no. 2 (2014): 151–78. French translation of **156**.

2016

164. "Recovering Asia's Lost West: Iran's Asian Connections in the Realm of Sport." *Annals of the Japan Society of Middle Eastern Studies* 31, no. 2 (2015): 303–29.

165. "South Africa and Iran in the Apartheid Era." *Journal of Southern African Studies* 42, no. 4 (2016): 687–709.

166. Review of *Law, State, and Society in Modern Iran: Constitutionalism, Autocracy, and Legal Reform, 1906–1941*, by Hadi Enayat. *Insight Turkey* 18, no. 1 (2016): 251–52.

167. Review of *Un autre Iran*, by Christian Bromberger. *Iranian Studies* 49, no. 5 (2016): 920–22.

2018

168. *Culture Wars and Dual Society in Iran*. Amsterdam: International Institute of Social History, 2018.

169. "Wrestling in the *Shahnameh* and Later Persian Epics." In *The Layered Heart: Essays on Persian Poetry*, edited by Asghar Seyed-Ghorab, 237–82. Washington, DC: Mage, 2018.

170. "A Cosmopolitan Dandy: Amir Abbas Hoveyda." In *The Age of Aryamehr: Late Pahlavi Iran and its Global Entanglements*, edited by Roham Alvandi, 147–67. London: Gingko, 2018.

171. "The Shiraz Festival and its Place in Iran's Revolutionary Mythology." In *The Age of Aryamehr: Late Pahlavi Iran and its Global Entanglements*, 168–201. London: Gingko Library, 2018.

172. "Pāris-e Khāvar-e Miyāneh: Irāniyān dar jahānshahr-e Beyrut." *Andisheh-ye Puyā* 7, no. 51 (Tir 1397 / June-July 2018): 56–59. Persian translation of **160**.

173. With Arang Keshavarzian. "Politics in Iran." In *Comparative Politics Today: A*

World View, edited by G. Bingham Powell, Jr., Kaare Strøm, and Melanie Manion, 12ᵗʰ edition, 466–508. New York: Pearson, 2018. Updated version of **155**.

174. "The Association for Iranian Studies: A Short History." *Catalogue of the Twelfth Biennial Iranian Studies Conference*, 21–26. University of California, Irvine, August 14–17, 2018. Updated version of **157**.

175. "Notes on Maltese." In *Hollyfest.org: A Digital Festschrift*. http://www.thehollyfest.org/index.php/h-e-chehabi/

176. Review of *Gender and Dance in Modern Iran: Biopolitics on Stage*, by Ida Meftahi. *Iranian Studies* 51, no. 4 (2018): 645–46.

177. Review of *Corse et Sardaigne, îles autonomes?*, by Jean-François Ferrandi. *Small States & Territories* 1, no. 2 (2018): 207–8.

2019

178. "Gender Anxieties in the Iranian *Zūrkhānah*." *International Journal of Middle East Studies* 51, no. 3 (2019): 395–421.

179. "The Rise of the Middle Class in Iran before the Second World War." In *The Global Bourgeoisie: The Rise of the Middle Classes in the Age of Empire*, edited by Christof Dejung, David Motadel, and Jürgen Osterhammel, 43–63. Princeton: Princeton University Press, 2019.

180. "Jensiyat va zurkhāneh-ye irāni." *Andisheh-ye Puyā* no. 62 (Ābān 1398 / November 2019): 78–81. Abbreviated Persian translation of **178**.

2020

181. *Onomastic Reforms: Family Names and State Building in Iran*. Boston: Ilex Foundation, 2020.

182. "Approche comparée du constitutionalisme en Iran." *Confluences Méditerranées*, no. 113 (2020): 41–52.

183. "Janghā-ye farhang va jāmeh'eh-ye dogāneh dar Irān." *Andisheh-ye Puya* No. 89 (Tir 1999 / June 2020): 88–92. Abbreviated Persian translation of **168**.

184. "Havyar nasıl helâl oldu." *Yemek ve Kültür*, no. 61 (Autumn 2020): 40–49. Turkish translation of **86**.

185. "Préface." *Confluences Méditerranée*, no. 113 (2020): 9–11.

186. Review of *Diplomatie nippo-iranienne: Enjeu énergétique et interférences américaines: Concilier l'inconciliable*, by Morgane Humbert. *Iranian Studies* 53, nos. 5–6 (2020): 1020–21.

187. "The Cats That Did Not Meow: An Historian of Iran Discovers Thailand."
https://mizanproject.org/the-cats-that-did-not-meow/

2021

188. Review of *The Jewish Athletes of Iran: The Sports Activities and Achievements of the Jews of Iran*, by Arsalan Geula. *Iranian Studies* 54, no. 1–2 (2021): 325.

189. Review of *A Power in the World: The Hawaiian Kingdom in Oceania*, by Lorenz Gonschor. *Island Studies Journal* 15, no. 1 (2021): 389–91.

190. "Vom Reiz der Inseln." *Mare*, no. 147 (August-September 2021): 38–39.

2022

191. *An International Bibliography of Islands.* Cambridge, MA: Tỷ Aur Press 2022.

192. "Enttäuschte Hoffnungen: Die wechselvolle Geschichte von Fußball und Politik in Iran." In *Das rebellische Spiel: Die Macht des Fußballs im Nahen Osten und die Katar-WM*, edited by Jan Busse and René Wildangel, 167–78. Bielefeld: Verlag die Werkstatt, 2022.

193. Review of *Iranian Music and Popular Entertainment: From Motrebi to Losanjelesi and Beyond*, edited by G. J. Breyley and Sasan Fatemi. *Iranian Studies* 52, no. 2 (2022): 580–82.

194. "Ham motedayyen bud, ham motemadden." *Tajrobeh* 10 (Mordād 1401 / July 2022): 28–31.

2024

195. Editor, with David Motadel. *Unconquered States: Non-European Powers in the Imperial Age.* Oxford: Oxford University Press, 2024.

196. With David Motadel. "Struggles for Sovereignty in the Age of Empire." In *Unconquered States: Non-European Powers in the Imperial Age*, edited by H. E. Chehabi and David Motadel, 1–70. Oxford: Oxford University Press, 2024. Introductory chapter of **195**.

197. "Qajar Iran's Global Diplomacy." In *Unconquered States: Non-European Powers in the Imperial Age*, edited by H. E. Chehabi and David Motadel, 263–80. Oxford: Oxford University Press, 2024. Chapter 11 of **195**.

198. With Ali Gheisari. "Extraterritoriality and Capitulations in Qajar Iran." In *Unconquered States: Non-European Powers in the Imperial Age*, edited by H. E. Chehabi and David Motadel, 190–204. Oxford: Oxford University Press, 2024. Chapter 7 of **195**.

199. "'Dandi-ye' jahān vatan." *Andisheh-ye Puyā*, no. 92 (Mehr 1403 / September 2024): 67–69. Abridged Persian translation of **170**.

200. "Zoroastrian life in Iran and beyond." *Indiran: The newsletter of the Ancient India & Iran Trust*, no. 18 (Winter 2024/25): 9.

2025

201. Editor. *Political, Social and Cultural History of Modern Iran: Essays in Honour of Ervand Abrahamian*. Edinburgh: Edinburgh University Press, 2025.

202. "Mohammad Mosaddeq and the 'Standard of Civilisation.'" In *Political, Social and Cultural History of Modern Iran: Essays in Honour of Ervand Abrahamian*, edited by H. E. Chehabi, 43–68. Edinburgh: Edinburgh University Press, 2025. Chapter 2 of **201**.

203. "A Bibliography of Ervand Abrahamian." In *Political, Social and Cultural History of Modern Iran: Essays in Honour of Ervand Abrahamian*, edited by H. E. Chehabi, 18–27. Edinburgh: Edinburgh University Press, 2025. In **201**.

204. "Royal exile in the Indian Ocean: Reza Shah's sojourn in Mauritius." In *Iran and Persianate Culture in the Indian Ocean World*, edited by A.C.S. Peacock, 323–45. London: I.B. Tauris, 2025.

205. With Ali Qeysari. "Hoquq-e farāsarzamini va kāpitulāsion dar Irān-e dowrān-e Qājār." *Bokhārā* 30, no. 168 (2025): 101–27. Persian translation of **198**.

206. "Sabk-e pārāno'id dar tārikhnegāri-ye irāni." In *Dasiseh pendāri*, edited by Hāmun Neyshāburi, 75–117. Los Angeles: Nashr-e Āsu, 2025. Persian translation of **102**.

TRANSLATIONS

1. From German: Leonhard, Wolfgang. *The Kremlin and the West*. New York: W.W. Norton, 1986.

2. From Persian: Parvizi, Rasul. "Patched Pants." *Iranian Studies* 26, nos. 3–4 (1993): 230–33.

3. From German: Gholamasad Dawud. Review of *Klerus, Basar und die iranische Revolution*, by Mahdi Naficy. *Iranian Studies* 32, no. 1 (1999): 120–23.

4. From French: Rochard, Philippe. "The Identities of the *Zūrkhānah*." *Iranian Studies* 35, no. 4 (2002): 313–40.

5. From Spanish: Linz, Juan J. "Freedom and Autonomy of Intellectuals and Artists." In *Robert Michels, Political Sociology, and the Future of Democracy*, edited by H. E. Chehabi, 185–204. New Brunswick, NJ: Transaction Books, 2006.

6. From Persian: Miransari, Ali. "The Constitutional Revolution and Persian Dramatic Works: An Observation on Social Relations Criticism in the Plays of the Constitutional Era." In *Iran's Constitutional Revolution: Politics, Cultural Transformations, and Transnational Connections*, edited by H. E. Chehabi and Vanessa Martin, 239–48. London: I.B. Tauris, 2010.

7. From Portuguese: Cardoso, Fernando Enrique. "The Significance of Juan Linz." In *Juan J. Linz: Scholar, Teacher, Friend*, edited by H. E. Chehabi, 18–20. Cambridge: MA: Tŷ Aur Press, 2014.

8. From German: Schirazi, Asghar. "In Memoriam: Khosrow Shakeri (1938–2015), Historian of Modern Iran." *Iranian Studies* 51, no. 2 (2018): 337–40.

9. From Persian: Boochani, Behrouz. "Foreword: Slippers and a Broken Guitar." In *My Body Was Left on the Street: Music Education and Displacement*, edited by Kính T. Vũ and André de Quadros, ix-x. Leiden: Brill, 2020.

10. From French: Hourcade, Bernard. "Obituary [Christophe Balaÿ]." *Iranian Studies* 57, no. 1 (2024): 191–92.

Contributors

Roham Alvandi is Associate Professor of International History at the London School of Economics and Political Science.

Ali M. Ansari is Professor of History at the University of St. Andrews in Scotland.

Olga M. Davidson is a Research Fellow in the Institute for the Study of Muslim Societies and Civilizations at Boston University.

Bianca Devos is Professor of Iranian Studies at Marburg University.

Babak Fozooni is Associate Lecturer at The Open University in London.

Roxane Haag-Higuchi is Associate Professor of Iranian Studies at the University of Bamberg.

Shamil Jeppie is Associate Professor of History at the University of Cape Town.

Mikiya Koyagi is Associate Professor in the Department of Middle Eastern Studies at the University of Texas at Austin.

David Motadel is Associate Professor of International History at the London School of Economics and Political Science.

Afshin Marashi is Professor of Modern Iranian History at the University of Oklahoma.

Afshin Matin-Asgari is Professor of History at California State University, Los Angeles.

Babak Rahimi is Associate Professor of Literature at the University of California, San Diego.

Monica Ringer is Professor of History and Asian Languages and Civilizations at Amherst College.

Sunil Sharma is Professor of Persianate and Comparative Literature at Boston University.

Nahid Siamdoust is Assistant Professor in the Department of Middle Eastern Studies at the University of Texas at Austin.

Robert Steele is a Postdoctoral Fellow in the Institute of Iranian Studies at the Austrian Academy of Sciences.

Lior Sternfeld is Associate Professor of History and Jewish Studies at Penn State University.

Farzin Vejdani is Associate Professor of Middle Eastern History at Toronto Metropolitan University.

Christoph U. Werner holds the Chair in Iranian Studies at the University of Bamberg.